BUSINESS AND
GENERAL
REFERENCE
BOOK SERIES
FROM IDG

Home Improvement For Dummies®

Quick Reference Card

P9-DHF-528

Wallpaper Calculator

Determine how much wallpaper to purchase by calculating the area you plan to paper and dividing that number by the usable yield per roll of paper.

Wall Area:
[Total Length of All Walls] × [Wall Height] = Wall Area

Unpapered Areas:
[Window Height] × [Window Width] × [Number of Windows] = Window Area

[Door Height] × [Door Width] × [Number of Doors] = Door Area

Wallpapering Area:
[Wall Area] – [Unpapered Areas] = Wallpapering Area

Wallpaper to Order:
[Wallpapering Area] ÷ [Usable Yield] = Number of Single Rolls Needed

Usable Yield Charts:

Pattern Repeat (Drop)	Usable Yield (American Rolls)	Usable Yield (European Rolls)
0 to 6 in.	32 sq. ft.	25 sq. ft.
7 to 12 in.	30 sq. ft.	22 sq. ft.
13 to 18 in.	27 sq. ft.	20 sq. ft.
19 to 23 in.	25 sq. ft.	18 sq. ft.

Wall Paint Calculator

To determine how much paint to buy, find the square footage of the area you plan to paint, and divide by the number of square feet covered by a gallon of paint.

Total Wall Area:
[Total Length of All Walls] × [Wall Height] = Total Wall Area

Unpainted Areas:
[Window Height] × [Window Width] × [Number of Windows] = Window Area

[Door Height] × [Door Width] × [Number of Doors] = Door Area

Paintable Wall Area:
[Total Wall Area] – [Window Area] – [Door Area] = Paintable Area

Paint to Order:
[Paintable Area] ÷ 350 = Number of Gallons Needed for Smooth Walls

[Paintable Area] ÷ 300 = Number of Gallons Needed for Rough, Textured Walls or Unpainted Wallboard

IDG BOOKS WORLDWIDE™

...For Dummies: Bestselling Book Series for Beginners

Home Improvement For Dummies®

Quick Reference Card

Ceramic Tile Calculator

Determine how many ceramic tiles you need by calculating the area you plan to cover and dividing that number by the size of one tile.

Total Area (Floor, Wall, Countertop):
Length (ft.) × Width (ft.) = Total Area (sq. ft.)

Tile to Order:
For 4" Tiles:
Total Area ÷ 0.1089 = Number of 4" Tiles Needed

For 6" Tiles:
Total Area ÷ 0.25 = Number of 6" Tiles Needed

For 9" Tiles:
Total Area ÷ 0.5625 = Number of 9" Tiles Needed

For 12" Tiles:
Total Area = Number of 12" Tiles Needed

For 18" Tiles:
Total Area ÷ 2.25 = Number of 18" Tiles Needed

Sheet Vinyl Flooring Calculator

Determine how much vinyl flooring to purchase by calculating the square footage of floor you plan to cover and dividing that number by 9 to get the number of square yards of flooring you need.

Floor Area:
[Length of Floor (ft.)] × [Width of Floor (ft.)] = Floor Area (sq. ft.)

Sheet Vinyl to Order:
[Floor Area] ÷ 9 = Number of Sq. Yards of Floor Covering Needed

Vinyl Floor Tile Calculator

Determine how many vinyl tiles to purchase by calculating the area of floor you plan to cover and dividing that number by the size of one tile.

Floor Area:
[Length of Floor] × [Width of Floor] = Floor Area

Tiles to Order:
For 9" Tiles:
Floor Area ÷ 0.5625 = Number of 9" Tiles Needed

For 12" Tiles:
Floor Area = Number of 12" Tiles Needed

Carpeting Calculator

To determine how much carpeting to buy, calculate the square footage of floor you plan to cover and divide that number by 9 to get the number of square yards of carpeting you need.

Floor Area:
[Length of Floor (ft.)] × [Width of Floor (ft.)] = Floor Area (sq. ft.)

Carpeting to Order:
[Floor Area] ÷ 9 = Number of Sq. Yards of Carpeting Needed

...For Dummies: Bestselling Book Series for Beginners

Praise for Gene and Katie Hamilton

"*Home Improvement For Dummies* is the most comprehensive guide available for those of us who are 'home improvement challenged.' . . . If you're thinking of starting a home improvement project, don't start until you've read Katie and Gene Hamilton's *Home Improvement For Dummies.*"

— Susan Powell, Host of Discovery Channel's *Home Matters*

"Think of HouseNet as your home improvement toolbox, and caretakers Gene and Katie Hamilton as your helpful neighbors. Within these (online) pages, you'll find remodeling tips, home repair tutorials, money-saving ideas, and a do-it-yourself message board."

— *Chicago Tribune*

"For home renovators looking for tips, building specs, or simply someone to commiserate with at any time of the day or night, HouseNet is the place to go."

— Katie Hafner, *Newsweek*

"Voted the best place on the Web for fixing up your home."

— Editors of Kipler's *Personal Finance Magazine*

"The latest in home improvement information and services is just a few mouse clicks away with the relaunch of HouseNet on the World Wide Web."

— Bill Cunniff, *Chicago Sun-Times*

"Throughout the renovation of my home, HouseNet gave me ideas, guided me through the process, and let me know what steps to take next."

— Elyse Gerard, New Jersey

"Before you embark on a home improvement project, check our HouseNet's cost guides to determine whether it's really worth doing yourself. The how-to section is particularly rich in detail and covers a broad range of topics, from how to install an air conditioner to instructions for the first-time wallpaper hanger."

— Yahoo! *Internet Life,* New York

"Whether you're looking for tips on rejuvenating wood floors or culling creative ideas for holiday decorating, pay a visit to Katie and Gene Hamilton. Their HouseNet Web site offers lots of do-it-yourself know-how."

— *USA Today*

"HouseNet, with its magazine-style look, is a very inviting and easy-to-use home-related site. It will guide your repairs down to the smallest detail, including a calculator to help accurately figure measurements."

— *Today's Homeowner*

HOME IMPROVEMENT FOR DUMMIES®

by Gene Hamilton and Katie Hamilton
of HouseNet Inc.

IDG Books Worldwide, Inc.
An International Data Group Company

Foster City, CA ♦ Chicago, IL ♦ Indianapolis, IN ♦ New York, NY ♦ Southlake, TX

Home Improvement For Dummies®

Published by
IDG Books Worldwide, Inc.
An International Data Group Company
919 E. Hillsdale Blvd.
Suite 400
Foster City, CA 94404
www.idgbooks.com (IDG Books Worldwide Web site)
www.dummies.com (Dummies Press Web site)

Library of Congress Catalog Card No.: 98-84303

ISBN: 0-7645-5005-5

Printed in the United States of America

10 9 8 7 6 5 4 3 2 1

1B/ST/QT/ZY/IN

Distributed in the United States by IDG Books Worldwide, Inc.

Distributed by Macmillan Canada for Canada; by Transworld Publishers Limited in the United Kingdom; by IDG Norge Books for Norway; by IDG Sweden Books for Sweden; by Woodslane Pty. Ltd. for Australia; by Woodslane Enterprises Ltd. for New Zealand; by Longman Singapore Publishers Ltd. for Singapore, Malaysia, Thailand, and Indonesia; by Simron Pty. Ltd. for South Africa; by Toppan Company Ltd. for Japan; by Distribuidora Cuspide for Argentina; by Livraria Cultura for Brazil; by Ediciencia S.A. for Ecuador; by Addison-Wesley Publishing Company for Korea; by Ediciones ZETA S.C.R. Ltda. for Peru; by WS Computer Publishing Corporation, Inc., for the Philippines; by Unalis Corporation for Taiwan; by Contemporanea de Ediciones for Venezuela; by Computer Book & Magazine Store for Puerto Rico; by Express Computer Distributors for the Caribbean and West Indies. Authorized Sales Agent: Anthony Rudkin Associates for the Middle East and North Africa.

For general information on IDG Books Worldwide's books in the U.S., please call our Consumer Customer Service department at 800-762-2974. For reseller information, including discounts and premium sales, please call our Reseller Customer Service department at 800-434-3422.

For information on where to purchase IDG Books Worldwide's books outside the U.S., please contact our International Sales department at 650-655-3200 or fax 650-655-3295.

For information on foreign language translations, please contact our Foreign & Subsidiary Rights department at 650-655-3021 or fax 650-655-3281.

For sales inquiries and special prices for bulk quantities, please contact our Sales department at 650-655-3200 or write to the address above.

For information on using IDG Books Worldwide's books in the classroom or for ordering examination copies, please contact our Educational Sales department at 800-434-2086 or fax 817-251-8174.

For press review copies, author interviews, or other publicity information, please contact our Public Relations department at 650-655-3000 or fax 650-655-3299.

For authorization to photocopy items for corporate, personal, or educational use, please contact Copyright Clearance Center, 222 Rosewood Drive, Danvers, MA 01923, or fax 978-750-4470.

 is a trademark under exclusive license to IDG Books Worldwide, Inc., from International Data Group, Inc.

About the Authors

Gene and Katie Hamilton are the husband-and-wife author team of the popular and witty syndicated newspaper column "Do It Yourself . . . or Not?" and of over a dozen bestselling books on home improvement. They are also the creators of HouseNet, a comprehensive online resource for homeowners, building professionals, and do-it-yourselfers. They have been featured in numerous publications and television shows, including: *Newsweek, Family Circle, CNN Today,* and *Dateline.* In their 15 years as home-repair experts, the Hamiltons have successfully renovated 14 homes.

ABOUT IDG BOOKS WORLDWIDE

Welcome to the world of IDG Books Worldwide.

IDG Books Worldwide, Inc., is a subsidiary of International Data Group, the world's largest publisher of computer-related information and the leading global provider of information services on information technology. IDG was founded more than 25 years ago and now employs more than 8,500 people worldwide. IDG publishes more than 275 computer publications in over 75 countries (see listing below). More than 60 million people read one or more IDG publications each month.

Launched in 1990, IDG Books Worldwide is today the #1 publisher of best-selling computer books in the United States. We are proud to have received eight awards from the Computer Press Association in recognition of editorial excellence and three from *Computer Currents'* First Annual Readers' Choice Awards. Our best-selling *...For Dummies*® series has more than 30 million copies in print with translations in 30 languages. IDG Books Worldwide, through a joint venture with IDG's Hi-Tech Beijing, became the first U.S. publisher to publish a computer book in the People's Republic of China. In record time, IDG Books Worldwide has become the first choice for millions of readers around the world who want to learn how to better manage their businesses.

Our mission is simple: Every one of our books is designed to bring extra value and skill-building instructions to the reader. Our books are written by experts who understand and care about our readers. The knowledge base of our editorial staff comes from years of experience in publishing, education, and journalism — experience we use to produce books for the '90s. In short, we care about books, so we attract the best people. We devote special attention to details such as audience, interior design, use of icons, and illustrations. And because we use an efficient process of authoring, editing, and desktop publishing our books electronically, we can spend more time ensuring superior content and spend less time on the technicalities of making books.

You can count on our commitment to deliver high-quality books at competitive prices on topics you want to read about. At IDG Books Worldwide, we continue in the IDG tradition of delivering quality for more than 25 years. You'll find no better book on a subject than one from IDG Books Worldwide.

John Kilcullen
CEO
IDG Books Worldwide, Inc.

Steven Berkowitz
President and Publisher
IDG Books Worldwide, Inc.

Eighth Annual Computer Press Awards ≥1992

Ninth Annual Computer Press Awards ≥1993

Tenth Annual Computer Press Awards ≥1994

Eleventh Annual Computer Press Awards ≥1995

Dedication

We dedicate this book to our online community, the visitors to HouseNet, whom we first met way back in 1991 when we started HouseNet BBS, a computer bulletin board system. When we hooked up an old laptop to a 2,400 baud modem, added all the articles we had written, and joined the online world, we had no idea where it would lead us. We've met thousands of you in our chat room and through message folders, and we're convinced you are the brightest, most innovative and resourceful do-it-yourselfers on the planet Earth. We hope that you enjoy this book, because you're the inspiration for writing it.

Authors' Acknowledgments

Where do we start? From the very beginning, we've enjoyed working with the team at IDG Books Worldwide. Trust us, they are no Dummies! From the first time we sat down with Publisher Kathy Welton and Acquisitions and Product Development Director Mary Bednarek, we knew that we had found the ultimate publishers for what we wanted to write — the mother of all home improvement books. Our editors, Colleen Rainsberger and Shannon Ross, have kept us on track, and copy editors Linda Stark and Tammy Castleman have made sense of our words.

We're more than grateful to our contributing editors — Gary Branson, Phil McCafferty, and John Kosmer — all pros in the field and seasoned home and workshop writers. We have the one and only Joe Truini to thank for adding his wit and wisdom. Joe's offbeat, quirky sense of humor makes even the most challenging of jobs laughable. Roy Barnhart had the final word as the technical editor, making sure that we got all the details right.

Bringing the words to life are the fine drawings by illustrators George Retseck and Tony Davis, and assistant illustrators Wendy Pagano, Ron Carboni, and Arlo Faber. We hope their detailed illustrations help you visualize what to expect as you tackle a project.

Our agent, Jane Jordan Browne, has shepherded us along this long process and, as always, she's been a guiding light and good friend for many years.

Finally, we'd be remiss if we didn't include everyone at www.housenet.com and HouseNet on America Online who left us alone so we could work on this book. That includes a lot of pretty special people. In our Annapolis, Maryland office, there's Bernie, Anna, Connie, Sandra, Jenn, Barbara, and Joel. In Downers Grove, Illinois, the team includes Kim, Donna, Kendra, Peggy, Maura, Mike, John, Basu, Rebecca, Andrew, Jon, Brian, Kathryn, Jim, Aleathea, and Mary Lee. We're particularly grateful to our remote staff of volunteer contractors and professionals who host our Ask the Experts chats and answer the thousands of questions posted by our online visitors. HouseNet just wouldn't be HouseNet without all these terrific people.

Publisher's Acknowledgments

We're proud of this book; please register your comments through our IDG Books Worldwide Online Registration Form located at http://my2cents.dummies.com.

Some of the people who helped bring this book to market include the following:

Acquisitions, Development, and Editorial

Project Editors: Colleen Rainsberger, Shannon Ross

Acquisitions Editor: Holly McGuire

Copy Editor: Linda S. Stark

Technical Editor: Roy Barnhart

Editorial Managers: Leah Cameron, Mary Corder

Editorial Assistants: Michael D. Sullivan, Donna Love

Production

Project Coordinator: Valery Bourke

Layout and Graphics: Steve Arany, Cameron Booker, Lou Boudreau, Linda M. Boyer, J. Tyler Connor, Angela F. Hunckler, Drew R. Moore, Brent Savage, M. Anne Sipahimalani

Special Art: George Retseck and Tony Davis

Proofreaders: Kelli Botta, Rachel Garvey, Nancy L. Reinhardt, Rebecca Senninger, Janet M. Withers

Indexer: Ann Norcross

Special Help

Suzanne Thomas, Tamara Castleman, Elizabeth Netedu Kuball, Jennifer Ehrlich, Constance Carlisle

General and Administrative

IDG Books Worldwide, Inc.: John Kilcullen, CEO; Steven Berkowitz, President and Publisher

IDG Books Technology Publishing: Brenda McLaughlin, Senior Vice President and Group Publisher

Dummies Technology Press and Dummies Editorial: Diane Graves Steele, Vice President and Associate Publisher; Mary Bednarek, Acquisitions and Product Development Director; Kristin A. Cocks, Editorial Director

Dummies Trade Press: Kathleen A. Welton, Vice President and Publisher; Kevin Thornton, Acquisitions Manager; Maureen F. Kelly, Editorial Coordinator

IDG Books Production for Dummies Press: Beth Jenkins Roberts, Production Director; Cindy L. Phipps, Manager of Project Coordination, Production Proofreading, and Indexing; Kathie S. Schutte, Supervisor of Page Layout; Shelley Lea, Supervisor of Graphics and Design; Debbie J. Gates, Production Systems Specialist; Robert Springer, Supervisor of Proofreading; Debbie Stailey, Special Projects Coordinator; Tony Augsburger, Supervisor of Reprints and Bluelines; Leslie Popplewell, Media Archive Coordinator

Dummies Packaging and Book Design: Patti Crane, Packaging Specialist; Kavish + Kavish, Cover Design

◆

The publisher would like to give special thanks to Patrick J. McGovern, without whom this book would not have been possible.

◆

Contents at a Glance

Cartoons at a Glance

By Rich Tennant

"Douglas, I don't recall beer taps being a part of our bathroom remodeling plan."

page 5

"Oh Dave is very handy around the house. He manually entered the phone numbers for the electrician, the carpenter, and the plumber on our speed dial."

page 131

"I swear, Frank, it's not a pyramid scam. You help a few guys with their home improvements and then, after you bring in ten friends, you'll be enjoying each and every Saturday as much as I do."

page 25

"You'd be surprised how much a fresh coat of polish and some new laces increase the resale value."

page 319

All I said was it'd be nice to have a deck and a privacy fence. But you know Stuart, since his retirement he's been so restless for things to do...

page 377

"It's a thank-you note from the plumber's kid. He says our bathroom repair paid for his next two years of college."

page 211

Fax: 978-546-7747 • **E-mail:** the5wave@tiac.net

Table of Contents

Introduction

Welcome to *Home Improvement For Dummies,* a whole-house repair manual. One glance through this book and you quickly see that it's not overloaded with technical details and obscure advice that you'll never want or need to know. Our goal was to write a book that explains, in a fun and easy-to-understand style, how to complete a wide range of projects. This anybody-can-do-it approach appeals to fledging do-it-yourselfers and seasoned handymen and -women. We want to encourage you to dust off your toolbox and tackle simple repairs and improvements using our goof-proof instructions.

This book contains a combination of need-to-know techniques and nice-to-know information. Basic steps and illustrations throughout the book walk you through the key points of maintaining and improving your home. We've pulled together the best and the brightest ideas and tips from the experts and callers of HouseNet Inc., a home improvement resource on America Online and the World Wide Web. These are tried-and-true solutions to everyday home decorating, repair, and improvement questions.

Home Improvement For Dummies is the only home repair and maintenance reference with a lighthearted, but not lightweight, approach.

How to Use This Book

You can use this book in two ways:

- ✔ If you want information about a specific topic, such as plugging up cold drafts with weather-stripping or cleaning out gutters, you can flip to that section and get your answer pronto. (We promise to have you back on the couch in no time.)
- ✔ If you want to be a home improvement guru, read the whole book cover to cover, and a wealth of knowledge will spill forth from your lips whenever the word "house" comes up in a conversation. You'll know so much, Bob Vila will be calling you for advice.

The book is organized in six parts, and the chapters within each part cover specific topics in detail. You can read each chapter or part without reading what came before, so you don't have to waste time reading what doesn't apply to your specific situation. Occasionally, we refer you to another area in the book where you can find more details on a particular subject.

Part I: Getting Down to Business

Sure, home improvement takes time, money, and effort. But oftentimes, the biggest barrier preventing you from making the improvements you long for is in your own mind. Not knowing how to begin repairs keeps many people living in uncomfortable or unsafe environments. The first few chapters of this book get you off to a good start with ideas for easy first-time projects, advice on which projects to tackle yourself and which ones to leave to the pros, tips for getting quality help with your projects and cutting your repair bills, and even a shopping list of tools and gadgets that any homeowner should have on hand.

Part II: Painting and Decorating

"All it needs is a fresh coat of paint."

You hear this phrase uttered about everything from a rundown house to a garage-sale boudoir to a garishly wallpapered sitting room. Trouble is, "just a fresh coat of paint" is often easier said that done.

What about removing the old paint, wallpaper, or stain? What kind of new paint should you use? What if you want to add a stencil, border, or other accents? Where do you start when it comes to big wallpapering projects? Questions like these often keep ugly-duckling projects from ever becoming the swans you thought you could make them. Lucky for you, the chapters in this part provide quick answers and step-by-step instructions for giving your house a facelift, inside and out.

Part III: The Nuts and Bolts of Carpentry

Creaky floors, jammed doors, and broken windows are the bane of any homeowner's existence. But you don't have to live with these nuisances. Fixing the problem can be as easy as a $10 Saturday-afternoon project.

Check out the chapters in this part for a helping hand with maintaining garage doors, changing locks, installing flooring, fixing creaky floors and steps, replacing broken window panes, installing window blinds, and much, much more.

Part IV: Plumbing and Electricity

Homeowners spend untold fortunes on plumbing and electrical repair bills. The sad part is that many of these repairs are things they could do themselves, if they only knew how. With the information in these chapters, you can become the master of your own pipes and wiring.

But these chapters tell more than how to fix problems in your sinks, toilets, lighting, outlets, and appliances — they also explain how to maintain these systems so that they're less likely to break down in the first place.

Part V: Improvements Inside and Out

This is the catch-all part for general improvement and repair projects for your home, inside and out. Some of the interior projects covered in this part include repairing damaged walls, adding molding and trim, building shelves, installing and repairing ceramic tile, adding backsplashes in the tub and sink areas, and insulating your home. For the outside of your home, discover how to repair siding and stucco, clean and fix gutters, seal out leaks and moisture, and power-wash decks and siding.

Part VI: The Part of Tens

No ...*For Dummies* book would be complete without the Part of Tens. And we think you'll find the chapters in this part especially useful and meaty. Read up on ways to protect your home from intruders, cut your energy bills, hire quality contractors, make your home safer and more accessible, and more. These chapters are a great inspiration to get you thinking about ways to turn your house into a home . . . or your home into a palace.

Those Funny Little Icons

We use the familiar ...*For Dummies* icons to help guide you through the material in this book:

Get on target with these great time-saving, money-saving, and sanity-saving tips!

Always remember and never forget these key tidbits of information that come into play in many aspects of your home improvement adventures.

We don't want to scare you off, but some of the projects discussed in this book can be dangerous, even deadly, if not approached properly. This icon alerts you to potential hazards and signals information about how to steer clear of them. We also use this symbol to mark safety advice for making your home safer for everyone, including young kids.

Some fixer-upper mistakes are so common that you can see them coming a mile away. Let this icon serve as a warning that you are treading in trouble-prone waters. Why should you have to learn from your own mistakes, when you can learn just as well from other people's?

Some products on the market do such a darn good job that we can't resist sharing them with you. This icon points you to great products and techniques that we recommend to help you do the job better or faster.

Some people are in home improvement for the fun of it, some for the increased resale value, some for aesthetics . . . and some for the tools. Tools that buzz, click, clank, thump, churn, and spin — it's a tinkerer's dream come true. If you have an obsession with gadgets and gizmos that can make your repair job easier (and your neighbors jealous), keep an eye out for this icon.

Most people want their toilets to flush, but some folks aren't happy until they know how the toilet flushes. This book doesn't bombard you with a bunch of technical trivia, but some background tidbits are too good to leave out. If you're an engineer-type who craves obscure details that most normal people don't care about, seek out these icons. If you'd rather live in ignorant bliss, by all means, skip these little diversions.

Give two people some tools and a repair job, and your bound to get some great stories. Heck, you might even be able to make a prime-time sitcom out of it. (Oops, too late.) This icon marks true-life stories; we couldn't make this stuff up!

Well, What Are You Waiting For?

We don't care whether you start with the Table of Contents, the Index, Chapter 12, or even Chapter 1 (what a novel idea!), the important thing is that you get going. A better home is just around the corner. . . .

Part I
Getting Down to Business

The 5th Wave   By Rich Tennant

©RICHTENNANT

"Douglas, I don't recall beer taps being a part of our bathroom remodeling plan."

In this part . . .

Where do you start? What materials, tools, and knowledge do you need? Can you do it yourself? Dig into these chapters for a solid foundation that can frame answers to these knotty questions.

Collecting basic household tools and the right stuff for specific jobs doesn't have to be a struggle. Venturing into the local hardware store need not signal safari-time — although with the size of home repair centers these days, you may need to pack a lunch.

Whether you want to estimate the time and cost involved in a job or check out the possibility of adding more hands-on adventures to your "to do" list, you can build comfort and confidence with a cruise through this part.

Chapter 1

The Biggest Room in Your House

In This Chapter

▶ What you have to gain by improving your home

▶ Words of encouragement for the skeptical do-it-yourselfer

▶ Advice on taking the first steps

*T*hink about it for a moment: What's the biggest room in your house? The living room? The master bedroom? If you're like most people, the biggest room in your house is the *room for improvement.*

There's no such thing as a perfect house. Even if your home is free of squeaky floors, sticking doors, dripping faucets, and clogged drains, wouldn't a fresh coat of paint look great in the living room? Or what about updating that kitchen wallpaper with something a bit more your style?

Improving Your Home — Why Bother?

We can list a whole slew of reasons to consider improving your home. You can increase the resale value of your house, save on energy costs, make your home safer and more accessible, improve your quality of life, and fix small problems before they become costly disasters.

A real estate speculator who invests in a house for its resale value only makes the essential improvements — cosmetic changes with paint or new carpeting, system upgrades like a new furnace or appliance, and repair of structural defects like a hole in a roof. Homeowners make those same necessary improvements, but they also tend to make quality-of-life improvements, because they don't just want to increase the value of the house, they want to make it their home. Home improvement is an economic investment to be sure, but because your home is your family's place to live, play, and work, home improvement is also a personal commitment.

Depending on where you live, the improvements you make to your house can increase its value. Just call a local Realtor to give you a free appraisal, and ask about the value of different improvements within your neighborhood. You can use this information to help you decide whether you can expect a payback on installing a new kitchen floor or paneling in the basement. But don't let this information be the ultimate deciding factor. Recouping the cost of the what you spend on a project is great, but the real value is in creating a home that's just right for your family and lifestyle.

You can't think about an improvement that pays for itself without zeroing in on energy-saving projects. Simple measures like caulking around doors and windows to plug up air leaks (see Chapter 5) pay you back for years to come with lower energy bills. Another must-do energy-conscious improvement is installing a setback thermostat (see Chapter 14); you're sure to recoup your cost on this item within the first heating season. And although no one will come into your home and say, "Wow, where did you get that good-looking weather stripping?", *you* certainly appreciate it when you pay your utility bill.

An ounce of preventive maintenance goes a long way toward keeping a house working smoothly. As you find out how to change the filter on the furnace and clean out gutters, these tasks become a routine that helps prevent damage to the house in the future. As you take on repair and maintenance tasks, you develop your own unique style of managing your home and all its systems. We've always thought that this skill set is worth including on a job resume.

Becoming your own repair person carries another valuable benefit: For a homeowner with little or no fix-it experience, learning to do simple home improvement tasks provides a feeling of accomplishment and self-sufficiency. Completing simple repairs that make a house safer and better puts you in control of your own home. And with every job you successfully complete, your sense of confidence grows. After you learn how to repair one broken windowpane from an overkicked soccer ball, you're ready the next time it happens (and it will).

Yes, You Can

Intimidation — it may work on the playing fields, but don't fall for it around the house. Sure, some home improvement projects can be daunting, but we encourage you to avoid those biggies and start with the easy stuff. You don't want to hang a room with wallboard as a first project; much better to tackle repairing little nail holes in the wallboard first. Don't make your first refinishing project a dining-room set; instead, learn the process by refinishing a small end table. You get the idea. Biting off more than you can chew can be very tempting — sometimes, it's almost impossible to stifle yourself when your enthusiasm is high — but before you jump in the deep end, splash around a bit in the shallow water. After getting your feet wet, there's no limit to what you can accomplish as a do-it-yourselfer.

In days gone by, many projects required brute strength just to lift the tool or transport the materials, but times have changed. Today's tools are lightweight and compact, so energy and enthusiasm replace size and muscle power as the key requirements. Building products are now available in component parts, so they're easy to transport. You can load a new closet shelving system in your car and then assemble and install it right out of the box. And having materials delivered to your door has never been easier!

What's more, modern products are being designed and marketed specifically for homeowners bent on "doing it themselves." Manufacturers are now marketing tools they designed for professionals to do-it-yourselfers. Gadgets for removing wallpaper, ceiling fans designed for easy installation, and specialty tools once distributed solely to the pros are all now available in home centers and hardware stores across the country.

Many hardware stores and home centers now offer classes and demonstrations to show you how to do a variety of projects. Attending these demos is a great way to watch the steps of a job, see what tools are involved, and ask questions. Look for store flyers or call and ask for a schedule; then plan your shopping around a demonstration that interests you.

Getting Off to a Good Start

This book covers a wide range of improvements. If you look at the Table of Contents, you see that the main categories are painting and decorating, carpentry, plumbing, electricity, and interior and exterior improvements. That's a whole lot of stuff. We suggest a conservative approach if you're new to the handy-homeowner role. Start small: Focus on a simple repair like unclogging the faucet aerator, or an energy-saver like replacing a door threshold, and you're off to a good beginning.

Whatever you do, at first *don't work on more than one project at a time.* After you gain some experience working with tools, estimating your time, and working on various projects, you can have a few different jobs in the works. But when you're starting out, begin and end a project before you start another one. Countless houses across the country are full of unfinished projects — a new kitchen floor minus the baseboard molding, nicely patched walls with no paint on them, a smoke detector installed with no batteries. We know, because we speak from experience.

Sometimes, the weather and changing seasons help you decide when to schedule a project. If you have a long list of repairs and improvements, consider the best time of year to schedule them. Plan your work so that the conditions are helpful, not harmful. During the winter, while you're cooped up inside the house, is a good time to decorate. Come spring, add insulation in the attic before it gets too beastly hot up there. Repairing and painting the siding is ideal for summer months when rainfall is low. In the autumn, schedule time to tune up the furnace and button up the house for the winter.

Chapter 2

Do It Yourself or Hire a Pro?

● ●

In This Chapter

▶ Sizing up costs, time, and skill level

▶ Choosing the right person for the job

▶ Getting down to business

● ●

*Y*ou can expect to save at least 20 percent, and sometimes 100 percent, of the cost of any job by doing the work yourself. What's more, you can enjoy the sense of pride and accomplishment that comes with a job well done. That said, you must remember that most of us are hard-pressed for time and energy, and some projects require special skills and tools that the average Joe may not possess.

We're not suggesting that you tackle these really advanced jobs. But countless other projects, like removing wallpaper or sanding wood, require little in the way of tools and talent. By beginning with unglamorous repairs such as fixing a broken window screen or tightening a loose hinge, you can quickly build your do-it-yourself skills and confidence. The bonus is that doing these projects makes your house a better and more comfortable place — a convenience that won't go unnoticed by you or anyone else in the house. Install a ceiling fan, and everyone will notice the balmy breezes; paint the garage, and your neighbors will rave. The idea is to choose projects that make a difference in the livability of your house and, at the same time, build your skills and confidence.

And just how do you know your limitations? Now that's the $64 question. We know that there's nothing a handy homeowner can't do, but that's not the issue. When it comes to massive projects like replacing all the walls in a house or building a large addition, you have other factors to consider. As you build skills and gain experience, you'll develop a sixth sense that enables you to evaluate your limits and your situation. That's what this chapter is all about.

Taking Everything into Account

Three factors go into the decisions of whether and how to do a job yourself: time, money, and skills. If you have plenty of time, you can tackle almost any project, using only some basic tools and gaining the skills you need as you go. If you have lots of dough, you can purchase plenty of time-saving tools and gear, or even hire someone else to do the job for you. And if you already have a treasure-trove of home improvement skills, you can do the job yourself quickly and for a moderate cost (maybe even without using this book!).

But for most of us mere mortals, the question of to do or not to do the work all by yourself involves finding a balance of all three factors, and then doing some soul-searching for a reasonable response.

Calculating the cost

First up, consider the cost of materials. Don't become another statistic of the Do-It-Yourself Damage Factor. If the materials are expensive, you're taking a big risk by doing the job yourself. If, for example, you're laying $30-a-yard wool carpeting, you're gambling with expensive dice. Make one miscut, and you suddenly find yourself in the carpet-remnant business. You have to replace the damaged material, and you'll probably end up calling in a carpet installer to finish the job, after all. Not much savings there; plus, you wasted a lot of time in the process.

If you're considering a project and want to get a ballpark figure of the labor costs involved, go to a home center and ask whether an installation service is available. Many retailers feature this one-stop-shopping service, farming the work out to contractors. These stores often display materials such as doors, windows, and ceiling fans with two costs: a *do-it-yourself* price and an *installed* price. The difference between the two figures is the cost of the labor.

This figure gives you a starting point for looking objectively at the cost of doing a project. But don't forget the other part of the equation — the cost of tools that you may need. Look at tools as a long-term investment: If you're a budding do-it-yourselfer, you want to add to your stash so that you have a complete workbench that will last a lifetime. However, if a project requires an expensive tool that you may only need once in your life, consider other options such as renting or borrowing.

Although perfectly affordable rental tools are available for many jobs, some people love any excuse to buy their own new tools. And that's okay. In fact, you might even say that it's your civic duty to nurture the home improvement market and keep it a healthy contributor to our growing national economy. We list our top tool and gadget picks in Chapter 3.

Tallying the time

Large home centers provide a convenient and simple source for estimating the cost of materials. Calculating the time investment, however, is not quite as easy.

Time is a real consideration when you're deciding whether to tackle home repairs and improvements yourself. Whether you're skilled or not, working around the house takes time, sometimes an amazing amount of it. For all handypersons — and wannabes — estimating time to complete a job is not an exact science. If you're new to the do-it-yourself realm, heed these words about estimating how long a job is likely to take: Bone up on what's involved, write down the process in step-by-step fashion (as you perceive it), include the shopping time, working time, and cleanup time. Translate the work into numbers of hours . . . and then *triple it*. The result you get is liable to be pretty close. The more projects you complete, the more you realize the value of estimating accurately.

Many novice do-it-yourselfers make the tragic mistake of underestimating time and then box themselves into an unrealistic deadline like painting the living room before Christmas, or building a deck for the Fourth of July family reunion — both noble ideas, but they warrant considerably more time than you initially imagine. The first time you do any job, the work takes much longer than you anticipated. Setting an inflexible deadline only adds more pressure to the project.

Scrutinizing your skills

Now for a touchy subject: recognizing your talent or Do-It-Yourself Skill Level. This topic is sensitive because some of us are born naturally handy — a fluke of nature like having blue eyes or red hair. Some people are innately gifted with an artistic or mechanical sense; the ability to hang wallpaper or repair a loose hinge seems to come naturally to them. Others are less gifted. For the mechanically challenged, these seemingly simple tasks are tantamount to building the Taj Mahal over a long weekend.

Remember when your gym teacher shared this wisdom: "You may be good at sports, but it takes a lot more than that to be a professional athlete"? Well, here's where the tide of fate flows in your favor. You may not have been born with a hammer in your hand, but you can develop the skills of a confident do-it-yourselfer and go on to accomplish amazing feats. You can gain and hone the skills of a handy homeowner — without the drudgery of running laps or lifting weights to stay in shape! It's true; as you get older, you get better! Figuring out how to install a dimmer switch is like riding a bicycle; you never forget. (And if you do, you can always refer to Chapter 13.)

Starting small

Even if you're not a do-it-yourselfer, and you have no desire to become one, you can participate in projects and save money by doing the grunt work. We're talking about simple jobs like removing wallpaper, tearing up old floors, scraping paint, and many other tasks that require more time and enthusiasm than talent.

The bottom line: If you're a first-timer, choose projects that are within your range of skills and don't require expensive materials and tools. Avoid boxing yourself in with unrealistic deadlines, and by all means invest your time as sweat equity and do the grunt work yourself.

Hiring Help the Smart Way

You can find entire books devoted to hiring a contractor, but here are the basics that we think you need to know. If the job is a simple project, like replacing a closet door or repairing a faulty dishwasher, the plan is pretty straightforward. Get a couple of estimates and compare them, making sure that you specify the full scope of the job and the quality of materials. Remember: You want estimates that compare apples to apples.

This advice becomes dicey when the project is more complex — say, bathroom remodeling that involves opening a wall, replacing the fixtures, and upgrading the flooring — all subject to surprises, hidden costs, and unexpected complications. Professionals have difficulty bidding on a job without knowing what they may find when the wall comes down, or the old floor comes up. An accurate bid is based on complete and accurate information and the cost of fixtures, which can range from low-end to luxury. As a consumer, you have to spell out exact styles, models, and colors for a precise estimate.

Finding a good contractor

Shop 'til you drop . . . for the right contractor, that is. Spend as much time reviewing contractors as you do choosing a doctor. Start in your neighborhood and branch out to a network of friends and acquaintances who can provide referrals. Most contractors are listed in the Yellow Pages, but contractors rely on their reputations, not the phone company, for new customers.

Check out the service trucks you see working in your neighborhood; the most familiar one probably has a good repeat business there. Stop by or call the neighbor (yes, be that bold!) and explain that you're looking for a contractor. Ask about your neighbor's experience with getting the job done. Is the homeowner pleased with the contractor's work? Most often, people are quick to share their thoughts, positive or otherwise.

This seat-of-the-pants screening process is the best way that we know to find competent contractors — it's direct, immediate, and tells you what you want to know from a reliable source, another homeowner just like you.

Whether you live in a suburban subdivision or a historic urban neighborhood, look for contractors who work on homes similar to yours. Kitchens and bathrooms in tract ranch houses are repeat subjects of remodeling, and the contractor who works in the neighborhood knows what to expect. Along the same lines, a carpenter who specializes in historic houses is more likely to know the intricacies of older homes, so he or she is your best choice for restoration.

For the same reasons that you don't usually go to a proctologist for an ear ache, don't hire a rough carpenter to do fine woodworking. Sure, the carpenter can do the work, but you get the biggest bang for your buck by hiring someone with skills and experience for the specific job. Take advantage of individual expertise — that's what you're paying for!

Know what you want before talking to a contractor. No, you don't have to know the serial number of the new faucet, but you do need an idea of the type, style, and features that you want. First of all, a contractor can't bid on a job without knowing what you expect to have installed, repaired, or built. Secondly, the only accurate way to compare bids from different contractors is to be sure that the work is based on the same specifications.

Some people may tell you to get three bids from different contractors and choose the middle one — easier said than done. If you do your homework and are satisfied with the references and professional manner of a contractor, you may be hard-pressed or time-restricted to scour up two more. The bottom line is use your best judgment and common sense and don't let a time schedule force you into making a decision. If you interview a contractor and are thrilled with what you find, don't balk at having to wait until he's available. Never rush a job and settle for someone you're not completely satisfied with. After all, you only build an addition or remodel your kitchen once in your lifetime — that is, if you get the job done right the first time.

When you meet with a contractor, ask for customer referrals of work similar to your project, and then check out those references. This task takes time, but you can benefit greatly by listening to someone with firsthand experience. Many people use the Better Business Bureau as a resource, or contact a local Chamber of Commerce for a list of referrals. Even if you find a contractor through one of these sources, you should still ask the contractor for a list of satisfied customers in your area that you can call for a recommendation.

Covering all your bases

After narrowing down your search for the perfect contractor, you're ready to get down to business. At this point, it's critical to get everything in writing:

✔ **Liability:** Ask for a certificate of insurance and make sure that the contractor is licensed and bonded to cover any injuries that may occur on the job. Reputable contractors carry workers' compensation insurance and insurance that covers them in the event of personal liability or property damage. Checking out a contractor's liability is very important because you may be held liable if the contractor or one of his workers is injured while working on your job. You may also be held liable if the contractor or one of his employees injures someone else. Check with your insurance agent about getting some additional umbrella liability coverage for the duration of a major building or remodeling project.

✔ **Contract:** A complete contract includes a detailed description of the project with a listing of specific materials and products to be used. For a job that involves various stages of completion, a payment schedule itemizes when money is to be paid. A procedure for handling any disputes between you and the contractor is also important, along with an explanation of how changes for additional work or different materials will be handled.

If the project involves removing debris, or if it's intrinsically messy (hanging drywall, for example), make sure that the contract has a clean-up clause that clearly defines the contractor's responsibility to leave the work site "broom clean" and orderly. Also make sure that the contract spells out who's expected to apply and pay for the building permit and what's necessary to meet those requirements.

Most states require a recision clause allowing you to cancel the agreement within three days of signing it. This arrangement gives you some time to think things over and helps prevent you from being pressured into signing the contract.

✔ **Warranty:** If the contractor offers a warranty, be sure that the provisions include the name and address of the person or institution offering the warranty and the duration of the coverage. Read the document closely to be sure that it's written clearly and that you understand all the terms and conditions. A *full warranty* covers the repair or replacement of the product, or a refund of your money within a certain time period. If the warranty is *limited,* find out what those limitations are.

✔ **Building Permit:** Most towns or counties require a permit to build on or change the property. The fee is based on the scope of the improvements and is either paid by the homeowner or included in the contractor's bid (which the homeowner pays eventually). If you're doing work that requires a building permit, you must fill out an application and pay a fee. If you hire contractors, you're better off having them apply for the permit, because their license is on the line. During different stages of the job, and at its completion, the work is inspected to ensure that it meets the building codes. These inspections are your best assurance that the work is done correctly, or at least that it meets minimum government standards.

Chapter 3

Gearing Up for Your Home Improvement Adventures

In This Chapter

▶ Stocking up your toolbox

▶ Investing in great gadgets and gear

*H*ow can you expect to create miracles without a magic wand? Well, of course you can't. And by the same token, you can't expect to do projects around the house without reliable tools.

People take different approaches to owning tools. Tool-obsessed individuals look for any excuse to add to their collection — these folks simply can't own too many tools. The more practical do-it-yourselfers want to own only what's required to do the job. Both approaches have their place, but whichever your persuasion, you need a stockpile of core tools — the essentials that you never want to be caught without.

If you think of every tool you buy as a long-term investment, you'll gradually acquire a reliable stash that can get you through most home repairs and improvements. In this chapter, we walk you through the basic tools essential to any toolbox, but we can't resist also tempting you with some of our favorite gadgets and gizmos designed to delight any do-it-yourselfer.

Sure, everyone dreams of a workshop like Norm's. But in the real world, most of us are hard-pressed for the space. At the bare minimum, find room for a workbench somewhere in your house, garage, basement, or shed. Designate this space as a work area, where you can take a door lock apart or stir a can of paint, lay out a window frame that needs new screening or stow your tool tote and rechargeable power tools. Your workspace doesn't have to be fancy, anywhere with good lighting and electrical power will do. Lay a flat work surface across two sawhorses or, if space is at a premium, get a portable bench that you can fold up and store out of the way.

The Top Tools for Any Homebody

Shop for the tools you need in home centers, hardware stores, or any large mart. Don't try to buy all the tools you'll ever need at one time; instead, buy tools as you need them. Focus on quality rather than quantity, and buy the best quality tool you can afford.

The tool-buying experience can be daunting for a first-time handy homeowner. As you roam the aisles of mega-stores, don't let the overwhelming selection intimidate you. Ask a salesperson for help and explain that you're new to the do-it-yourself scene. A knowledgeable salesperson can help you make your decision by explaining how the wide range of prices reflects the quality, features, and materials of various tools.

So here it is, our list of the basic tools you need to get on the road to home improvement adventures:

- ✓ **³/₈-inch variable speed reversible drill:** This tool, available as plug-in or cordless, uses steel blades called *bits* to drive in or remove screws, drill holes, sand wood, mix piña coladas, and do other important home improvement tasks. See Figure 3-1.

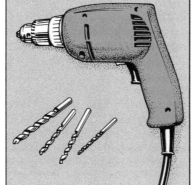

Figure 3-1:
An electric drill with a variety of bits.

- ✓ **Claw hammer:** We recommend a 16-ounce hammer with a fiberglass handle to cushion the blow to your hand. Watch out for *carpal tunnel syndrome,* an injury that can occur from repetitive motions, like constantly hitting your thumb and then hopping around the room.

- ✓ **Pliers:** Slip-joint pliers have toothed jaws that enable you to grip various sized objects, like a water pipe, the top of a gallon of mineral spirits, or the tape measure you accidentally dropped into the toilet. Because its jaws are adjustable, pliers give you leverage to open and firmly grip the object.

✔ **Toolbox saw:** A small, easy-to-use handsaw is useful for cutting such materials as paneling or shelving.

✔ **Assorted pack of screwdrivers:** Be sure that you have both slotted (flat-head) and Phillips screwdrivers in a variety of sizes. The slotted type has a straight, flat blade; the Phillips blade has a cross or plus-sign that fits into the grooves of Phillips-head screws.

✔ **Utility knife:** Choose a compact knife with replaceable blades that's strong enough to open heavy cardboard boxes and precise enough for trimming wallpaper.

Buy the type with a retractable blade; you'll appreciate it the first time you squat down with the knife you your pocket. (Ouch!)

✔ **Staple gun:** You can use this tool for a variety of jobs, like securing insulation, ceiling tile, plastic sheeting, and fabrics. We don't recommend using it to keep your hat from blowing off during windy days.

✔ **Carpenter's level:** A straight-edge tool that has a series of glass tubes containing liquid with a bubble of air. When the bubble in a single tube is framed between marks on the glass, it shows that the surface is *level* (horizontal) or *plumb* (vertical). See Figure 3-2.

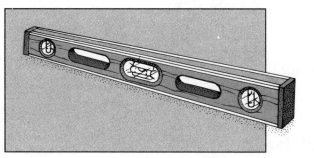

Figure 3-2:
A standard carpenter's level for finding level and plumb lines.

✔ **Metal file:** Filing tools like those shown in Figure 3-3 are flat metal bars with shallow grooves that form teeth. Metal files are useful for sharpening the edges of scrapers, putty knives, and even shovels and garden trowels. These durable little guys have proven to be unaffected by exposure to flour, milk, and eggs, even when baked at 350 degrees for two hours and then festively decorated.

✔ **Allen wrench:** These L-shaped metal bars, often sold in sets like the one in Figure 3-4, are designed for turning screws or bolts that have hexagonal sockets in their heads. This tool also goes by the name *hex-key* or *set-screw wrench*. Used to assemble everything from knock-down furniture to bicycles to gas grills, this tool was invented by a man named, umm, let's see, his name was . . . we'll have to get back to you on that one.

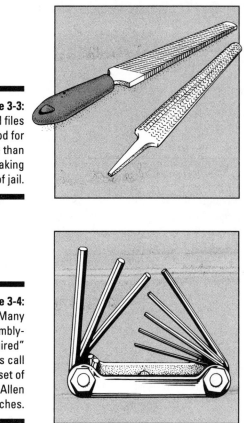

Figure 3-3: Metal files are good for more than breaking out of jail.

Figure 3-4: Many "assembly-required" items call for a set of Allen wrenches.

Gizmos and Gear

Tools alone don't lead to a life of joyful home improvements. You gotta have gadgets, too. Some really great gadgets are available to keep you organized, efficient, safe, and comfortable:

- ✔ **Itty-bitty notebook:** Keep a reference of your home improvement needs in your car or purse, and use it when shopping. Instead of jotting down notes on scraps of paper that you're more likely to lose than use, keep all this stuff in one place. Buying a new lampshade? Jot down the dimensions of the old one. Replacing the tray to your ice-cube maker? Make a note of the model number. Keep a record of paint colors and wallpaper patterns and a zillion other details (like your wedding anniversary) in this little notebook.

✔ **Tool tote:** Keep a stash of the tools you use most often in some kind of portable toolbox or crate. Be sure to include a stock of string, a pair of scissors, and other accessories you commonly use. Many repairs must be done onsite, so having a tool bag that you can take with you to the project can be invaluable.

✔ **Kneepads:** Cushioned rubber pads, held in place with elastic strips, protect your knee joints from the impact of kneeling on hard surfaces. (Pretend that you're rollerblading, and you won't feel so silly.) Kneepads are especially important to wear when you're crawling around on hard, debris-strewn surfaces. See Figure 3-5.

Figure 3-5: Kneepads make long repair jobs easier on your joints.

✔ **Eye goggles:** Remember how your mom always made you wear a hat when it was cold outside? Well, if she saw you with a hammer or chipping away at something with a chisel, she'd say "Put on your safety goggles!" A tiny chip of wood or a speck of metal or hardened paint can seriously damage your eyes, so protect them at all costs. Mother knows best.

Goggles used to be clunky contraptions that only kids wanted to wear, but now they're available in designer styles (well, sort of). Goggles are an inexpensive investment that may save your eyesight. Just remember to put them on!

✔ **Gray duct tape:** Sure, this product was designed for taping heating ducts, but it's a national icon for do-it-yourselfers. Use it to seal window screens, patch old sneakers . . . heck, we've seen it patching dents in cars!

✔ **Neon circuit tester:** This two-buck item, pictured in Figure 3-6, can be a lifesaver whenever you have to work on an electrical switch, receptacle, or power source. before you begin tinkering with a device, use this circuit tester to make sure that power isn't flowing to it.

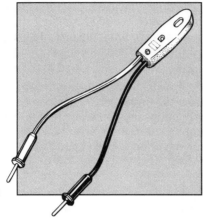

Figure 3-6: Electricity can be deadly. Use a circuit tester to make sure that wires are safe to handle.

✔ **Wire brush:** This item, shown in Figure 3-7, looks like a lethal toothbrush. It's useful for scraping blistered paint, removing rust from metal, and taking corrosion off spark plugs.

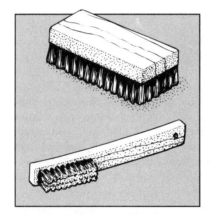

Figure 3-7: This is one brush you don't want to take into the shower with you.

✔ **Stud finder:** No, this tool isn't for finding hunky guys (unless they're trapped in your walls). A *wall stud* is the vertical wood framing to which wallboard is fastened. A stud finder, shown in Figure 3-8, is an electronic device that locates the metal fasteners behind finished walls, so you can find a sturdy place to hang pictures, mirrors, and shelving.

Figure 3-8:
Use a stud finder to avoid hanging heavy items over hollow wallboard.

✔ **Ladders:** Get a stepladder for household chores like changing light bulbs and painting rooms; get a taller self-supporting or extension-type ladder for outdoor maintenance like cleaning gutters and trimming trees. In general, aluminum ladders are lightweight and strong; wood ladders are solid, heavy, and economical; and fiberglass ladders are strong, electrically nonconductive, and expensive. If you can afford it, fiberglass is the best choice.

Ladders come in four basic types:

- Type IA, for extra heavy-duty industrial use, carries a 300-pound duty rating.

- Type I, for heavy duty industrial use, has a 250-pound duty rating.

- Type II, for commercial light-maintenance work, has a 225-pound duty rating.

- Type III, for general light-duty household use, carries a 200-pound duty rating

A *duty rating* is the maximum safe-load capacity of the ladder. This weight includes the person plus the weight of any tools and materials being carried onto the ladder. Translated, it's your weight plus all the stuff you wear and haul up the ladder with you.

Part II
Painting and Decorating

The 5th Wave   By Rich Tennant

"I swear, Frank, it's not a pyramid scam. You help a few guys with their home improvements and then, after you bring in ten friends, you'll be enjoying each and every Saturday as much as I do."

In this part . . .

Are you tired of the way the rooms in your house look? Don't move yet, the walls may only need a coat of paint. This part gives you the nitty-most-needed-gritty on tools, supplies, and tips to spruce up that dull interior landscape.

Get ready to roll with wallpaper, paint, and woodwork stains. Refreshing the appearance of your home — inside or out — can work wonders on your spirits. And, after all, what's a facelift worth if it doesn't come complete with a smile or two?

Chapter 4

Interior Painting: A Quick Facelift for Your Rooms

● ●

In This Chapter

▶ Choosing the right paint and equipment for the job

▶ Stripping away old paint

▶ Brush and roller painting tips and techniques

▶ Using an electric spray painter

● ●

Applying a fresh coat of paint is the easiest and most economical way to transform a room. If you're a first-time painter, you're in luck; painting is an ideal project for novice do-it-yourselfers. You can acquire the necessary skills on the job, and the cost of paint and equipment is minor considering the payback. Plus, painting's relatively safe work that you can perform at a leisurely pace.

Don't be intimidated by the process of painting; just dig in. Admittedly, if you're new to the sport, painting appears to be a daunting task. But after reading this chapter, you'll feel confident enough to tackle even the trickiest painting problems. Once you get started and see the dramatic results of freshly painted walls, you'll find more reasons (and rooms) to paint.

Setting Your Goals

Michaelangelo didn't begin his painting career with the Sistine Chapel, and you should follow his lead. If you're a first-time painter, start with an easy project, one you can complete quickly and without much preparation work. Here are three approaches to consider, taking into account your skills and time constraints:

✔ **Goof-proof easiest approach:** You can't make too many mistakes if you paint the walls and ceiling the same color. This all-for-one method eliminates much of the tedious *cutting in* (painting a straight line at the edge of a painted area) that's required when you use two colors. The one-color-fits-all method is the easiest, quickest way to get a room looking new and feeling clean.

✔ **More challenging endeavor:** If the monochromatic look doesn't sound very appealing, you can apply different colors on the ceiling and walls. Even using two shades of white requires time to cut in around the perimeter of the room where the walls meet the ceiling. Cutting in requires a steady hand because you have to paint right into the corner without letting any different-colored paint get on the adjoining surface. The more distinct the contrast between the colors, the more noticeable any paint goofs are. Even a small drop of a dark-colored paint on a light surface will be visible. Paint the ceiling first and take your time to get a nice, clean line between the ceiling and walls.

✔ **For gifted painters only:** Okay, you Michaelangelos (and Michaelangel-ettes), if you really want to create a masterpiece, use different colors or shades of a color on the ceiling, walls, *and* woodwork. Variation may not be the best plan for a first-time painter, but you can master the skills with some patience and perseverance. (Using masking tape, described later in this chapter under "Those little extras," helps you pull off this work of art.)

Picking the Paint

The greatest painting hurdle you're likely to face isn't on your walls or ceilings; it's in the aisles of your home center. The warehouse approach to selling home improvement products is supposed to impress you with the vast array of available merchandise and materials. In fact, the unknowing are often terrified, especially in the paint department where mile-long shelves are loaded to the ceiling with mountains of paint cans and accessories. You stand there musing, "How the heck do I know what kind of paint to buy?"

The experience can be dizzying, leaving the most intrepid person trembling with uncertainty. Fear of the unknown is natural, so take heart. You may not be genetically gifted with the knowledge, but you can learn rather easily.

Deciding what type of paint you need

You can choose from two major types of paint: oil-based *(alkyd)* and water-based *(latex)*. Alkyd paint creates more durable and washable surfaces, but it's harder to work with and requires you to clean your rollers and brushes with paint thinner (also known as *mineral spirits*).

Latex paint is much easier to work with because it cleans up with soap and water. Latex is the best choice for a first-time painter. Although many professionals prefer the durability of alkyd paints, you can still achieve professional-looking results with latex. Latex paints also dry much more quickly and smell less offensive than alkyd.

A good strategy is to use latex paint on the walls and alkyd paint on window and door trim, where you need a hard finish that stands up to frequent washings.

Paints come in different gloss ranges, or *sheens,* that determine the shine and brightness on your walls and ceilings:

- ✔ *Flat paint* is at the low end of the brightness spectrum. It's often used on walls and ceilings because it's easy on the eye. Flat paints reflect a minimum of light off walls, reducing glare and helping hide small surface imperfections.

- ✔ *Eggshell, lo-lustre,* and *satin* paints have a slight sheen and hold up a bit better and are easier to wash than flat paints. These types of finishes are a good choice for hallways and high-traffic areas that require frequent washing.

- ✔ *Semigloss paint* has a slightly greater sheen that makes it more washable than satin paint. The kitchen, bathroom, hallways, and especially the kids' rooms are likely candidates for this type of paint.

- ✔ *Gloss* and *high-gloss paint,* also called *enamel,* dries to a very hard, very shiny finish with an almost mirrorlike sheen. Enamel is used on woodwork, furniture, and cabinets because the surface can withstand heavy use and scrubbing. The problem with high-gloss paint is that it reflects every little surface imperfection.

Another important consideration focuses on paint brands. Which is the better choice: a well-known name brand or a generic, store brand? Name-brand paint comes in different grades. The low-end product from a brand-name paint company usually doesn't perform as well as the top-of-the-line paint from a house brand.

Factoring in special promotions and paint sales, your best clue to the quality of any paint is its price. In most cases, better quality costs more money. The price difference can be substantial, however, especially when you compare a regularly priced, high-end brand name with a chain store's top-of-the-line house label on sale. Our advice is to buy the best paint you can afford. Hey, your labor puts it on the wall, so why skimp on quality?

Paint is made of the following: *pigment,* which provides color and hiding power; a *vehicle,* which is the resins that bind the pigments and provide the backbone for the dried paint film; and a *carrier* (water for latex paints and petroleum distillates for oil paints). In a top-quality latex flat paint, the pigment accounts for about 40 percent of the total.

Estimating how much paint to buy

To estimate the amount of paint you need in order to cover the walls of a room, you have to dust off a math formula you probably picked up in fourth grade. Add together the length of all the walls and then multiply the number by the height of the room, from floor to ceiling. The number you get is the room's square footage. Is that math class coming back to you now?

Now you have to determine how much of that square footage is paintable surface area. Because you use a different paint on the doors and windows, subtract those areas from the room total. No sweat, just subtract 20 square feet for each door and 15 square feet for each average-sized window in the room. You end up with a number that is close to the actual wall area you have to cover with paint.

In general, you can expect 1 gallon of paint to cover about 350 square feet. You need slightly more than a gallon if the walls are unpainted drywall, which absorbs more of the paint. You also need to consider whether to paint more than one coat. If you're painting walls that are unfinished, heavily patched, or dark in color, plan on applying two coats of paint.

Instead of two coats of regular expensive paint, most professionals use a primer for the first coat over hard-to-cover surfaces. Primer paint is designed to cover well, but because it is an undercoat, it doesn't need to be washable like standard paint, making it less expensive. When painting a dark color, pros often add a color tint to the white primer. Tints for both latex or alkyd paints are available at most paint stores. For best results, choose a tint shade that's closest to the top coat color.

Now for the clincher of the math problem. Divide the paintable wall area by 350 (the square-foot coverage in each gallon can) to find the number of gallons of paint you need for the walls. You can round uneven numbers; if the remainder is less than .5, order a couple of quarts of wall paint to go with the gallons; if the remainder is more than .5, order an extra gallon. Of course, buying in bulk is usually more economical, so you may discover that 3 quarts of paint cost as much as a gallon.

When you're buying paint, ask for extra paint sticks and an opener. The store usually gives these items away for free. The stick is for stirring the paint and for cleaning out the roller. The opener is handy for opening the paint can and other tightly sealed metal containers.

Paint estimators

The following examples walk you through the calculations for determining how much paint you need for a 14-x-20-foot room that's 8 feet tall and has two doors and two windows.

Ceiling paint estimator

Use the following formula to estimate the amount of ceiling paint you need. Double the result if the ceiling requires two coats.

1. **Multiply the length of the ceiling times its width to find its area.**

   $14 \times 20 = 280$ square feet

2. **Divide that number by 350 (the estimated square feet covered per gallon) to figure out how many gallons of paint you need.**

   $280 \div 350 = .8$

For this example, you want to buy 1 gallon of ceiling paint for a single coat.

Wall paint estimator

Use the following formula to estimate the amount of wall paint you need. Double the result if the walls require two coats.

1. **Add together the length of each wall.**

   $14 + 20 + 14 + 20 = 68$ feet

2. **Multiply the sum by the wall height, to find the total wall area.**

   $68 \times 8 = 544$ square feet

3. **Subtract 20 square feet for each door ($20 \times 2 = 40$) and 15 square feet for each window ($15 \times 2 = 30$) to find the actual amount of wall area you're painting.**

   $544 - 70 = 474$ square feet

4. **Divide this figure by the paint coverage (350 square feet per gallon), and the result is the number of gallons to purchase.**

   $474 \div 350 = 1.4$

For this example, you want to buy 1 gallon and 2 quarts of paint for a single coat.

Woodwork paint estimator

Measure the length of the trim in feet, and multiply that number by $\frac{1}{2}$ foot, (.5) as a rough size for the width of the trim. Include all the trim around doors and windows, at baseboards, along the ceiling, and for any built-in furniture.

As an example, imagine that you have ceiling molding running around a room that is 14 feet wide and 20 feet long.

1. **Determine the total length of molding around the room by adding together the length of all the walls that the molding covers.**

   Round the numbers off to the nearest foot.

   $14 + 20 + 14 + 20 = 68$ feet

2. **Multiply the sum by .5 for an estimated width of the molding.**

   $68 \times .5 = 34$ square feet

3. **Divide this number by 350 to estimate the gallons of paint required to cover the molding.**

   $34 \div 350 = .09$

The result in this example is much less than a quart, but you may paint other woodwork in the room the same color, so buying a full quart may not be terribly wasteful.

Door and window estimator

Use the same figure for estimating door coverage as you use in your wall-area calculations — 20 square feet = one door. Multiply the number of doors by 20, doubling the answer if you plan to paint both sides. Wall paint estimates allow for 15 square feet for each window. Use about half that window area to figure trim and inside sash — the glass isn't important to the calculation.

For the room in this example:

1. **Multiply the number of doors by 20.**

   $2 \times 20 = 40$ square feet

2. **Multiply the number of windows by 7.5.**

   2 Windows $\times 7.5 = 15$ square feet

3. **Add these numbers together.**

   $40 + 15 = 55$

4. **Divide the result by 350 (the estimated square feet covered per gallon).**

   $54 \div 350 = .16$

Often, you end up needing to buy only a quart of paint, which goes a long way on doors and window trim.

Arming Yourself with the Right Equipment

This section includes a rundown of all the equipment you need for interior painting and an explanation of what each one can do for you. When buying any painting equipment, invest in the best quality that you can afford and keep everything in good working order through proper cleaning.

If you're a tool-fanatic you'll want to check out power-paint systems. Cordless and electric rollers and brush painters, as well as airless spray equipment are available for purchase or rent. The advantage of power-painting gear is that, after you adjust it, you can paint like crazy, putting a lot of paint out in record speed. On the downside, using these systems requires a lot of setup and cleanup time. But if you're the Tim Taylor-type person, you just *gotta* try 'em.

Consider renting airless spray equipment if you have a basement or large open area to paint. Spraying makes sense when you're painting everything one color. Refer to "Spray Painting," later in this chapter.

Paint rollers — sleeves and handles

To apply paint to broad, flat surfaces like walls and ceilings, use a 9-inch roller and a shallow roller pan.

Choose a roller with a heavy wire frame and a comfortable handle that has a threaded end to accept an extension pole. (The pole is a must-have item if you're painting a ceiling or high walls.) Don't be cheap; avoid economy-grade handles that tend to flex as you apply pressure, or you may wind up with an uneven coat of paint. Choose a heavy, stiff roller that lets you work the roller with a constant pressure and into corners without bending.

The soft painting surface of the roller (called a *sleeve* or *cover*) slides on and off the roller cage for cleaning and storing. Buy a sleeve with a core made of plastic rather than cardboard, which tends to fall apart over time. If you clean the roller out thoroughly after every job, you can use it for years.

Use $^1/_4$-inch nap roller for applying paint on smooth surfaces; use a $^3/_8$-inch nap for slightly irregular surfaces; and a $^3/_4$-inch or longer nap for painting over heavy textures or stucco.

The cheaper, disposable covers are okay for one-time use. Try them with alkyd (oil-based) paints to save time with cleanup. However, cheap rollers shed nap that ends up in the paint, and they may come apart at the core if you attempt several uses.

To use a roller, first wet the sleeve with water (for latex) or paint thinner (for alkyd), and spin or wring out the excess. Dip, but don't submerge, the sleeve in the paint you poured in the roller pan. Then roll it lightly up and down the ramp of the pan to distribute the paint evenly.

Brushes

To paint a room, you need a couple of good brushes to *cut in* (paint a clean edge along) the corners, ceiling, windows, and doorways. For painting walls and ceilings with either latex or alkyd paint, invest in a good-quality brush.

Don't use natural-bristle brushes for applying latex paints. The water in the paint softens the bristles, and the brush becomes limp. Instead, look for a brush with nylon or polyester bristles.

For alkyd paints, purchase a natural bristle or polyester brush. Don't purchase an inexpensive brush, because its bristles will come loose and end up on whatever you're painting and mess up the finish. A professional-quality natural-bristle brush is very expensive, so unless you're planning to apply a lot of alkyd paint to doors, trim, or kitchen cabinets, the investment may not pay off. The best compromise for general indoor painting is a good-quality polyester brush.

How a brush is put together is as important as what it's made of. A good-quality brush has bristle tips that are *flagged,* or split. You may not want split ends in your hair, but you really do want them in your paint brush. Flagged bristles look a bit fuzzy at the tip and allow each individual bristle to spread the paint evenly over the surface. In a nylon or polyester brush, each bristle may have a slightly lighter color at the tip where it is flagged.

Pass up brushes with a flattop cut. The end of a good-quality brush is contoured or chiseled to an oval or rounded edge. This chiseled or tapered end permits you to cut a fine line along trim and at corners where the wall meets the ceiling.

Look for a brush that has a sturdy *ferrule* — the metal band that secures the bristles to the handle. Cheap ferrules rust when exposed to latex paint or solvents, and the rust may stain and contaminate the paint. Quality brushes have sturdy, reinforced ferrules made of noncorrosive metal and nailed to the handle.

For painting narrow areas of windows, doors, and molding, use a *sash brush*. This type brush has a long, thin handle that you can grip like a pencil. Sash brushes are made with either straight or angled bristles. Some painters prefer the angle cut, others use the straight cut. The best approach is probably to use a combination of these two types: The angled sash brush is great for painting into areas like window *muntins* (the narrow horizontal and vertical dividers in the window sash), and the straight brush is just right for narrow, flat surfaces like the window jamb.

Having combination of a 1-inch angled sash brush, a $2^1/_2$-inch angled sash brush, and a $2^1/_2$-inch straight brush (all shown in Figure 4-1), enables you to paint narrow and wide areas with ease.

Figure 4-1: A 1-inch and a $2^1/_2$-inch tapered sash brush, and a $2^1/_2$-inch standard sash brush will cover most painting situations.

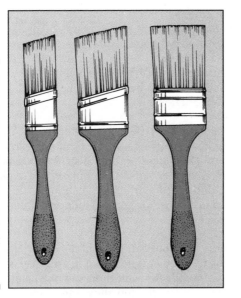

Those little extras

The familiar paintbrush and roller are still the most popular tools for spreading paint on woodwork and walls, but some additional painting aids are available to help you do the job better and faster.

Even if you're not a gadget guru, you can appreciate these inexpensive gizmos — they empower you. Lend this painting gear to friends — not necessarily a recommended practice unless you like buying replacements — and they assume that you have untold paint-it-yourselfer wisdom and experience:

✔ **Paint pan:** If you decide to use a paint pan, buy a sturdy one that's made of heavy plastic with legs or corner brackets that hook over the top of a ladder. Don't buy a flimsy cheap pan because, when you fill it with paint and pick it up, one corner flexes and spills the paint. Figure 4-2 shows a typical paint pan in action.

Disposable plastic liners for paint pans make short work of cleaning out the pan; you just throw out the liner.

✔ **5-gallon bucket:** As a substitute for a standard paint pan, try using a 5-gallon bucket with a roller screen, which is a metal meshlike grate designed to fit in the bucket. (See Figure 4-2.) Painting pros often choose buckets for obvious reasons: The 5-gallon containers hold more paint than the pan, are easier to move around, and most importantly, they reduce the chances that your big foot lands squarely in the soup. We're not saying that accidents can't still happen, but the likelihood of your foot hitting the high sides of the bucket is greater than the prospects of your planting your whole sole right in the unused paint. The wide low paint pan is an open invitation for a visit from your clodhoppers.

The bonus of this bucket-and-screen rig is that you don't have to stop frequently to reload it with paint. Start by pouring in 2 to 3 gallons, and then you can paint like crazy before you have to stop to reload. The painting screen is designed to hook over the top edge of the bucket and hang into the container. Dip the roller into the paint, and work it up and down the screen to wring out excess paint.

When you're ready to take a break, just drop the screen into the bucket, snap on the lid, and wrap the roller in aluminum foil or plastic wrap; all your equipment stays fresh for hours. Pop the roller into the refrigerator, and it'll keep overnight. Don't put it in the freezer.

✔ **Extension handle:** Get an inexpensive wood extension handle that screws into the end of the roller handle, and you can avoid countless trips up and down the ladder. This inexpensive item does double-duty because you can use it with a sanding pole attachment to make it a sanding stick, a useful tool for sanding ceiling and walls. Telescopic fiberglass extension handles are also available, but they do cost quite a bit more than the wooden ones.

✔ **Trim guard:** A trim guard, also called an *edger,* is a must-have for painting trim around windows and floor moldings. Holding onto the handle, you press the metal blade of the guard against the surface you want to shield from the fresh paint, as shown in Figure 4-2. When painting a window, you can prevent paint from getting on the glass by holding the edger against vertical and horizontal dividers *(muntins)* of a window sash. On flooring, press the guard against the carpeting or floor surface while painting the shoe molding that hides the gap between the wall and the floor. The trick to using this tool effectively is to frequently wipe both its edges clean of paint. Otherwise, you leave telltale paint smears as you go.

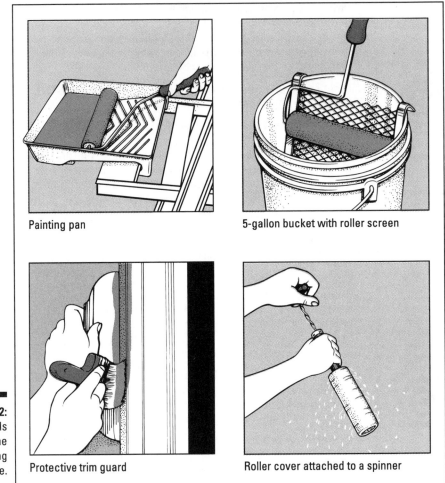

Painting pan

5-gallon bucket with roller screen

Protective trim guard

Roller cover attached to a spinner

Figure 4-2:
Some tools
of the
painting
trade.

✔ **Mini-roller:** Get a mini-roller with a wire handle and a 4- or 6-inch-long cover. Some small roller covers come with a nap (the fuzzy cover) that extends over one end. This feature allows the roller to paint into corners. These little rollers are great for painting the inside bookcase shelves or behind a radiator. For touch-up jobs, use a mini-roller with a mini-screen that fits inside a 1-gallon can; you can paint right out of the can, just as with the 5-gallon bucket and paint screen described earlier.

✔ **Dropcloths:** Pick up disposable plastic dropcloths to protect furnishings and flooring. You can find the best selection in home centers and paint stores. To protect items permanently fixed in the room (ceiling fan, fireplace mantle, built-in furniture, and so on) you have to seal them completely from the spatter of a paint roller. For that task, use pretaped plastic dropcloths. The tape, sold in various widths and sizes, eliminates seepage and gives you a clean, straight edge to lay down. These pretaped dropcloths don't damage the surface you apply them to, and when you're finished, you simply remove and dispose of them. By applying the tape to the top of a baseboard, you can protect floor or carpeting and baseboards at the same time.

Dropcloths come in a range of their protection: 6 mil extra heavy use, 4 mil heavy-duty use, 2 mil heavy use, 1 mil medium use, and .7 mil light use. In general, the heavier (higher mil number), the better.

If you plan to do a lot of painting, invest in some room-size canvas (or canvaslike) dropcloths. Long, narrow dropcloths, called *runners,* are ideal for hallways. Runners are heavy enough to withstand foot traffic and can save your carpeting or flooring from wandering paint-splattered feet.

✔ **Masking tape:** Use rolls of 1-inch or wider paper tape that is sticky on one edge only. Apply the sticky edge to window glass and any other surfaces that you want to protect from paint spatters. Press the edge firmly in place so that paint can't seep behind it.

✔ **Ladder:** Don't depend on a rickety old ladder to be a safe work platform for painting or any other project. Nothing slows down the job like falling off a ladder and breaking your arm. Invest in a good ladder that's level and steady and has a fold-down shelf to hold a paint can. For most indoors painting projects, a small three-rung step ladder and a taller 5- to 6-foot step ladder are sufficient. For painting tall ceilings and stairways, you need longer ladders or scaffolding.

✔ **Paint spinner:** For cleanup, buy a paint spinner — a favorite tool of pros because it cleans brushes and rollers to perfection. The spinner looks like a bicycle pump and works like an old-fashioned spinning-top toy. After you clean the brush or roller in water or mineral spirits, use the spinner to complete the job. The centrifugal force of the spinning brush or roller cover forces out the excess water or mineral spirits as shown in Figure 4-2. Picture a shaggy dog shaking himself dry after a swim.

You can use this handy tool to clean either a brush or roller, because the spinner has a clamp on its end to hold a brush handle and a roller cover will also slide over this clamp. Be sure to put the spinner in an empty bucket to catch the excess paint, and then work the handle up and down to start the spinning action.

Preparation, Preparation, Preparation

Think defensively when you dress for your painting adventure; dig up some old shoes that could only benefit from a paint job. Old shirts and pants with oversized pockets are best because you can keep rags in them. And listen to your mother's advice, "Put on your hat!" White hair creeps up on us soon enough without adding an early streak of silver (or whatever color you're painting).

Clearing the room

Before you begin a painting project, pretend that you're moving. Now's the time to throw out or recycle all the old magazines piled in the corner, and get rid of the ugly chair you never liked. The idea is to empty the room as much as possible so that you have free and easy access to move around. You need room to move a ladder and enough floor space for your paint rig so the more furniture you can drag out, the better. Stash it in the hall and other rooms, or wherever it's out of the way. What you can't easily move, protect with dropcloths and old sheets and blankets. (Don't sprain your back moving an overstuffed sofa. Save your strength for pushing that paint roller around!)

Go through the following checklist to get your room ready for the big makeover. When you're done, the room should look something like Figure 4-3.

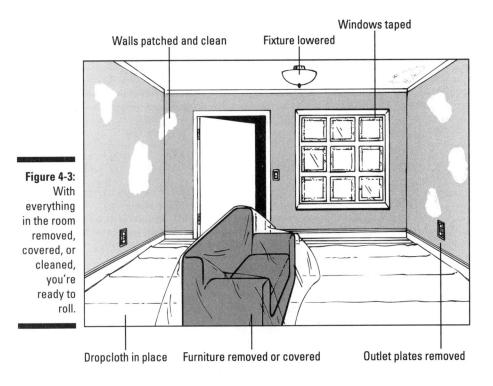

Walls patched and clean   Fixture lowered   Windows taped

Figure 4-3:
With everything in the room removed, covered, or cleaned, you're ready to roll.

Dropcloth in place   Furniture removed or covered   Outlet plates removed

✔ If it's a very large room, stack the covered furniture in two areas with space between them. In a smaller room pile everything in the center at least three feet away from the walls.

✔ Remove any area rugs and cover the flooring with dropcloths.

✔ Take down pictures from the wall, remove the nails or fasteners, and loosen the light fixture so the cover plate drops down slightly.

✔ Use a screwdriver to remove all the electrical switch plates and receptacle covers. Do this job in the daytime, with the electricity turned off. If you're working at night, bring in a work light that's plugged into a receptacle outside the room. To protect the switches and receptacles, cover them with wide masking tape. If you're feeling flush, you can replace them with new ones when the painting is over. You'll be amazed at what a difference new hardware makes.

✔ Unscrew the metal or plastic cold-air return covers and any other covers or hardware on the walls and ceiling.

Getting rid of the old paint to make way for the new

You can paint right over just about any surface, but there are times when the underlying paint is in such poor condition that is must be removed first. The woodwork in many old houses, and some not-so-old houses, requires more than a good cleaning before it's ready to be painted. If your woodwork has layers of chipped or peeling paint, you have some work to do before you can begin painting. (You may also want to remove the existing paint so that you can refinish the wood with a stain and varnish.)

Removing lead paint

If your house was painted before the late 1970s (when leaded house paints were banned), chances are good that lead paint was used. The toxic metal is a poison, especially dangerous to children and pregnant women, so take special steps when removing it from walls and woodwork. The last thing you want to do is sand or scrape off the paint, scattering tiny lead particles throughout your house.

For information about lead poisoning and suggestions about removing lead paint, call the National Safety Council's Lead Information Center at 800/LEADFYI.

Stripping off the old coat paint isn't difficult, but it is time-consuming and it does take a lot of elbow grease. We don't have a secret formula for getting this job done effortlessly, but paint-stripping techniques have improved. Chemical paint strippers are more user friendly than they used to be, and the advent of heat guns has made removing paint a bit easier, in some cases.

Scraping off old paint

You may be able to get away with simply scraping off the chipping paint and smoothing damaged areas. To bypass chemical and heat-based paint removers, try these old-fashioned steps:

1. **Use a paint scraper to remove loose and flaking paint.**

   A hook-type scraper, which has a curved blade that you drag over the area to be scraped, works better than a putty knife. Remove all loose paint, right down to bare wood if necessary.

2. **Sand the surface with a medium-grit (No. 80) sandpaper to smooth and even it, feathering the edges between scraped and unscraped areas.**

3. **Fill in any holes and indentations with spackling compound.**

   If the areas are deep or the wood is gouged, use a two-part polyester-based wood putty to fill the depressions. After the filler hardens, sand the areas smooth.

4. **If you sand down to bare wood, apply a paint primer before painting.**

Shine a bright light at an angle to the surface to highlight rough spots or areas that need smoothing or repair.

Removing paint with a heat gun

A heat gun is an electric appliance that looks like a heavy-duty hair dryer (don't even think about it, unless you like the nickname Old Blisterhead). Its best application is for removing paint from flat surfaces like a door or tabletop.

Hardware stores and home centers sell heat guns in the power-tools section. Like most tools, heat guns come in a range of prices — from $30 to $40 for the consumer grade guns, to over $100 for heavy-duty professional units. If you don't have a lot of area to strip, consider renting a heat gun from a rental center. A large project requiring several weeks of work usually justifies purchasing your own heat gun.

Heat guns vary in features, but most come with shaped nozzles that fit on the tip of the tool to direct the heat in different directions. The gun directs a dangerously hot air stream concentrated in a small area, so be careful when operating one.

Wear heavy leather gloves to protect your hands and be very careful where you point and set down the heat gun — it removes paint, but it can also melt plastic, cause severe burns, and do a lot of other damage if not used cautiously.

Direct the gun at the painted surface and move the gun slowly around the area until bubbles of paint lift off the surface, as shown in Figure 4-4. Don't leave the heat on one spot or you'll burn the paint, rather than melt it. Remove the softened paint with a paint scraper or putty knife. Hold the gun in one hand and a scraper in the other; when the gun gets heavy, switch hands. You may discover more than one layer of paint as the layers melt away, which means more than one application of heat.

Figure 4-4:
When used with care, a heat gun can make paint-removal problems melt away.

A. Move the heat gun 6 inches from the surface.

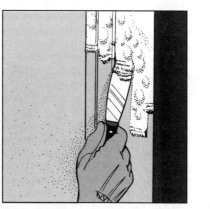

B. Scrape off the softened paint as you go.

Removing paint with stripper solvents

Using a chemical stripper is another approach to removing paint, and it works particularly well on finely shaped items like woodwork, molding, or furniture. For the environment's sake, choose water-based strippers; they're biodegradable and remove layers of paint without toxic chemicals. You can purchase these gel-like strippers at paint stores and home centers. Because they're thicker than a liquid, they work well on installed pieces, such as woodwork and ceiling molding. Read the instructions carefully, because the steps for using different strippers vary depending on the product.

In general, you apply these solvents to a painted surface with an old paint brush. Setting up time varies, but you see the action as the paint bubbles up off the surface. Even if the instructions say that gloves aren't required, wear them. The old paint gets under your fingernails and is very difficult to remove. Then again, if you're often called a slacker, dirty fingernails will be proof that you've been working.

To scrape off the globs of old paint, assemble an assortment of tools:

- ✔ An old-fashioned church-key can opener works well for getting paint out of crevices.

- ✔ Putty knives with flexible blades of varying sizes are useful for removing paint from flat surfaces. Because the flexible blades are thinner than the stiff type, they get under the paint more easily and are less likely to gouge the wood.

- ✔ A set of contoured woodworker's scraping tools make easy work of carved moldings and surfaces, as shown in Figure 4-5.

To contain the messy residue that you scrape off the wood, use a sturdy cardboard box with its flaps cut off at the top. As you work, wipe globs of paint off of the putty knife onto the sides of the box. When the gunk hardens into a glob of dried paint, just scrape it off to reuse the box.

Figure 4-5: Have a variety of tools on hand to reach into grooves and remove the softened paint.

Old wallpaper — don't paint it, remove it

Unless you never, ever plan to take that old wallpaper off the wall, don't paint it. You may be tempted to just paint over old wallpaper, but resist the urge. After you apply paint to wallpaper, removing the paper is just about impossible. Not only that, but paint just looks better when applied to bare walls.

Chapter 7 explains how to strip off old wallpaper. If the room you plan to paint is papered, visit Chapter 7 before you pick up the paintbrush!

Dull that shine

Paint does not adhere well to shiny surfaces. If the old paint is shiny, use a paint deglosser to knock down the sheen. Deglossers, available at most home centers and paint stores, contain strong solvents that melt the top surface of oil-based (alkyd) paints. But unlike paint strippers, deglossers stop working after a short time. They only etch the surface of the paint and, at the same time, are very effective at removing grease and other dirt from the painted surface.

Follow the specific manufacturers directions, but in general, all you have to do is wipe on the deglosser with a clean rag and then wipe away the dirt and gloss. It's strong stuff, so wear a pair of rubber gloves and open the windows for good cross-ventilation.

Woodwork that's been stained is usually protected by several coats of clear varnish. Before painting over varnished woodwork, prepare it just as you would a shiny enameled surface: Either sand the surface to break down the sheen or use a deglosser. Unvarnished woodwork tends to look dull and flat, and to be a bit rough to the touch. You can paint over unvarnished wood without any special preparation.

Priming: The painter's problem solver

New wood, scraped bare wood, and new wallboard all require a prime coat before painting. Paint primers are specially formulated paints that adhere well to bare surfaces and provide the best possible base for other paint to stick to. Primers are designed to be painted over, so they don't require high washability and other characteristics of top-coat paint. For this reason, primers are usually less expensive than regular paint.

  ✔ For bare wood, use an interior latex primer and apply it with a brush or roller, depending on how large the surface is. Choose a primer that's quick drying to speed up the job.

  ✔ For sealing the surface of new wallboard, use a special wall primer specifically designed for wallboard. Primer prevents the wallboard from absorbing the new paint, and gives you a smooth, even topcoat.

  ✔ If you have kids, you probably have stains on walls from felt-tip markers. You could get new kids, but that won't stop the stains from bleeding through a new coat of paint. To prevent the bleed-through, first apply a stain blocker or white pigmented shellac. These primers are available in spray cans for small spots (see Figure 4-6) and in quart and gallon containers for large stained areas.

Figure 4-6:
Several coats of stain blocker may be necessary to cover pen marks on walls.

Cleaning walls and woodwork

If the surface you're about to paint is not damaged, a quick cleanup is all that's needed before you can start painting. Make your mama proud; dust away the cobwebs in ceiling corners and vacuum up the dirt along the baseboards. When you're cleaning windows, open them and remove any leaves or dirt inside the sill. And don't forget to clean inside the closet!

Wash the walls and woodwork free of all stubborn dirt, grease, or mildew. Wash the area with a sponge and phosphate-free household cleaner, following the manufacturer's instructions. Then rinse the surfaces with clear water and let them dry. Use a rag wrapped around a broom, a damp mop, or a vacuum crevice tool to make the room as dust-free as possible.

You may have to wash really dirty areas more than once to get them thoroughly clean. With mildew, you can wash it away, but sometimes stains remain. Try removing them with a 50/50 bleach and water solution, sanding them out, or priming them with a stain blocker which is a pigmented shellac that prevents the stain from bleeding through paint.

Mildewcide is an important ingredient in paint used in rooms with a high moisture content such as the bathroom or kitchen. Paint manufacturers specially formulate paint for moist areas where mildew tends to grow, such as bathroom ceilings. These paints include chemicals that deter mildew growth. In addition, you can also buy additives that you can pour directly into the paint to make it more mildew resistant.

Taking the paint-can plunge

Prepare an area for the paint can by laying down a heavy section of newspaper, giving yourself plenty of room for mixing. Use a paint can opener (available where the paint is sold) to remove the lid from the can. Working your way around the can, pry up the lid in three or four places until the seal is broken and the lid lifts up.

Of course, you'll read the directions on the side of the can and follow them explicitly, stirring the paint as directed. Most paint requires about five minutes of stirring; be sure to ask for a stirring stick when you purchase the paint. To stir, plunge the stick down to the bottom of the can and pull it up to the top in a smooth motion until the paint is thoroughly mixed.

Prevent MPC (Messy Paint Can) syndrome by using a hammer and nail to drive a ring of holes in the lip of the paint can, as shown in Figure 4-7. As you wipe the loaded brush on the top of the can, the excess paint drips through the holes and back into the can. You can also place the can in a pie pan or box to catch any drips that may escape down the side, and to create a resting place for the brush.

Figure 4-7: To make cleanup easy, punch small holes in the rim of the paint can and line the paint pan with aluminum foil.

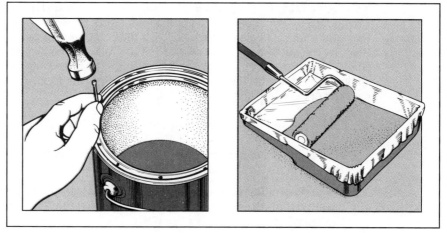

To eliminate having to clean out a roller pan, line it with a double layer of wide, heavy-duty aluminum foil (see Figure 4-7). When you're finished painting, just throw away the liner.

Painting the Room from Top to Bottom

When painting a room, start at the top and work your way down. Paint the ceiling first, and then the walls, the door trim, the door, and wrap it up with the baseboard trim. That sequence may seem obvious, but you'd be surprised how many people get it all mixed up and end up dripping paint onto previously painted areas.

You can't spread paint evenly if you're leaning or reaching at an awkward angle. Move yourself and the ladder often to position yourself close to the painting task at hand.

Walls and ceilings

Painting is a project that's best divided into two job descriptions: outliner and roller. The outliner uses a brush to *cut in,* or outline, all the areas a paint roller can't reach. The roller spreads paint on the ceiling and walls. When you have a painting partner, you each have a specific assignment; if you're painting solo, you get to change hats by switching tools and performing both tasks.

If you're painting with a partner, give the outliner a head start to begin spreading a two-inch band of paint along the joint between the ceiling and wall. You want this paint to blend in with the paint applied by the roller. Don't let the outliner get too far ahead of the roller, or you'll lose the wet edge. Lap marks result when you allow the cut-in paint to dry before you apply the roller paint, because the rolled-on paint acts like a second coat over the dry cut-in paint.

The outliner observers the top-down rule, painting in the following sequence:

1. **First paint the ceiling molding, if there is any, and then outline a band of paint on the ceiling and wall.**

2. **When the ceiling outline around the room is complete, outline the corners of all the walls, laying on a two-inch-wide flow of paint from the top of the corner down the walls.**

3. **Next, cut in a band of paint around all windows and doors.**

4. **Cut in a band of paint around any areas where the roller can't reach, such as light fixtures or radiators. Also paint around the light switches and electrical receptacles.**

5. **Finish up the outlining at the baseboards around the floor.**

   For outlining these straight areas, use the trim guard to keep paint off of the baseboard and surrounding flooring or carpeting.

After the outliner cuts in around the edges, the roller can begin on the ceiling, working from the corner outward into the room parallel with the longest wall. Work your way across the ceiling in 3- or 4-foot square patches and, when you reach the opposite wall, go back to the first wall. This approach, illustrated in Figure 4-8, lets you spread paint into new areas without creating lap marks.

To paint the walls, begin at the upper third of the wall and work the roller down the wall. Step back and observe your work frequently, checking for lap marks or missed spots.

For a perfect paint job with no drips, no runs, and no errors, follow the brush and roller techniques in the next sections.

Figure 4-8:
Roll paint on small sections of ceiling at a time, without giving the paint a chance to dry before you start the next area.

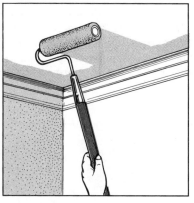

Brush techniques

Don't overload the brush bristles with paint. Dip them only about a third of the way into the paint and tap, don't wipe, them on the side of the can to shake off excess paint.

When you're cutting in around the edges, use the narrow tip of the brush, pressing slightly to flex the bristles. Work slowly and paint from dry areas into wet, to prevent leaving lap marks. When applying paint in corners, use the wide edge of the brush and spread the paint evenly with a slight flex of the bristles.

Roller techniques

To make sure that the paint coverage is uniform, adjust your stroke to apply equal pressure on the roller. Spread the paint evenly, but don't press the roller too hard. As you roll along, lift the roller at the end of each sweep. Keep a damp rag handy to wipe up any paint drips and spatters.

Dip the roller in the paint frequently, but don't completely submerge it, or paint will get inside the roller, which causes runs, drips, and uneven coverage as the paint leaks out. Lay on the paint with W or N shapes, spreading it from left to right. Finish with light vertical strokes.

When you're working on a ladder, keep yourself centered on the area you're painting, with the ladder in front of what you're working on. Center your weight on the ladder, as well; instead of leaning or stretching, move the ladder. A good safety tip to remember is to always keep your hips between the ladder's rails.

Window trim

Paint from the inside out — sounds simple enough, but sometimes painting a window gets confusing. If you're working on a double-hung window, begin painting the thin vertical and horizontal dividers *(muntins)* between the panes of glass. Some new double-hung windows have removable dividers, called *grilles,* that you can take out and paint separately. To paint a modern window, begin on the inside frame. Figure 4-9 shows proper window-painting techniques.

Figure 4-9:
Paint the inside gridwork of the window first; paint the wide, flat areas of the window trim last.

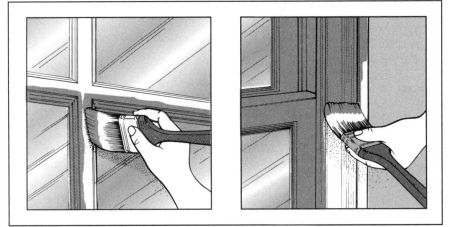

To paint muntins or grilles, use a $1^1/_2$-inch sash brush and always paint toward an edge. Don't drag your brush back across the edge because the corner will scrape off some paint and cause a drip or run.

If you're painting a double-hung window and the upper, outer sash is movable, reverse the positions of the lower, inner sash and upper sash. Paint the lower half of the outer sash first, and then paint the inner sash. Don't paint the top edge where the lock is just yet; save it for last. Return the sashes to their normal positions, but don't close the window completely. Now paint the top of the outer sash and the top edge of the inner sash.

If the upper sash is painted shut (as it is in many old houses) and you can't move it, just paint it from the inside, and then open the lower sash and paint it. Leave the window slightly open until the paint dries, or you'll end up with two stuck sashes.

Switch to a wider $2^1/_2$-inch brush to paint the window frames. Work from the inside out toward the casing trim. The last things to paint are the window sill (called the *stool*) and the apron nailed to the wall beneath the sill.

Doors

Leave doors hanging on their hinges while you paint them so that you can paint both sides at the same time. However, remove the door lock mechanism or use masking tape to shield it from paint. Also mask the hinges and any other hardware.

If the bottom edge of the door isn't already painted, paint it now. True, no one will see it — but the paint seals out moisture that could warp or damage the door. For basic, flat doors, use a sash brush to cut in around the hinges, and then paint the door with a roller, applying an even coat to one side at a time. When painting a panel door, use the same inside-out approach used for a window (illustrated in Figure 4-10):

1. **First, paint all four panels.**

   Begin with the decorative molding surrounding a panel; then paint the panel itself.

2. **Paint the horizontal rail between the panels.**

3. **Paint the vertical muntins between the panels.**

4. **Paint the door edges.**

5. **Paint the horizontal rails at the top and bottom of the door.**

6. **Finally, paint the vertical outside stiles.**

After painting the door itself, paint the door jamb, beginning at the inside or door stop, and working out. Make the final cut along the outside edge and wall and then finish painting the face of the molding.

A. Paint the inside panels of the door first, starting with the trim around each panel.

B. Next, paint the vertical surfaces.

C. Paint the horizontal surfaces of the door last.

Figure 4-10:
Paint a
paneled
door from
the inside
out.

When painting molding or door panels, don't work too far ahead of yourself or the paint will set up and get tacky as your brush drags over or sticks to an area you've painted. Our best advice when this occurs is to leave it alone. Don't try to smooth over the area with a wet brush; wait until it dries and then sand it lightly and repaint.

Baseboards and molding

Choose a sash brush that matches the size of the woodwork you're painting. One that's comfortable to hold at various angles works best, because painting baseboard trim or a fireplace mantle can sometimes require the flexibility of a contortionist. This job is especially challenging — and not particularly comfortable — when you're crawling along the floor on your hands and knees.

As you paint, hold the brush at an angle so that you can coat all the surfaces with paint evenly.

When painting woodwork, use a paint box with the sides folded down to hold the can of paint and a rag. This rig keeps everything close at hand and provides a convenient place to plop down a wet brush.

The floor

One of the quickest and least expensive facelifts for an old wooden floor is a coat of paint. A fresh coat of paint is cheaper and easier than carpeting, and it works just as well at unifying the floor space and making the room appear larger. The downside is that you have to remove all the furnishings from the room, often a more arduous and time-consuming chore than the actual painting.

Wear knee pads when you're down on your hands and knees working on any flooring projects. Most hardware stores and home centers sell rubber cushioned pads that strap to your legs and protect your knees. Of course, if you have a pair of sports knee pads, you can use them, instead.

Whatever the floor's finish (painted, sealed, or varnished), you must rough up the surface. You want to apply the new paint to a clean floor that's free of any gloss or sheen. To prepare the surface, rent a floor polisher — available from the floor-care center of many grocery stores and at tool-rental outlets. Steel wool pads are an additional cost to the rental fee, but you can use both sides of the pads. The steel wool does a good job of preparing the surface by removing any dirt or grit as it buffs away the top surface.

Inspect the floor for protruding nail heads, and tap them below the surface with a hammer and nail set. You don't want a maverick nail head to chew up the steel wool pad and tear the paint roller. Then use a vacuum cleaner with a crevice tool to remove dirt and dust, paying particular attention to the cracks and crevices between the floor boards and underneath any radiators or heating convectors.

Choose an oil-based porch-and-floor paint, and apply it with a roller with a dense $^3/_4$-inch nap. Use a long extension pole to avoid developing a decidedly Quasimodo posture from stooping over to paint. Roll the paint on the floor going in the direction of the wood grain, and use a 2-inch-wide brush to cut in around the floor and dab paint into any wide cracks or spaces between the floor boards.

Plan the attack so you don't paint yourself into a corner (which could be very embarrassing). First, outline the perimeter of the floor and any spaces between the floor boards; then begin rolling the paint on. Work on an area about 24 inches wide at a time. Paint the entire length of the boards from one wall to the other, using the edge of a board as a stopping and starting place. This technique keeps the wet edge of paint on an even plane, instead of in the middle of a board where lap marks would be visible.

Cleaning Up

Before the paint has a chance to harden, clean off the brush or roller and pan. Cleaning is the final phase of painting, and it's an important step for keeping your equipment in good shape. A utility sink or work area is the best choice for cleanup chores. To clean latex paint off your equipment, use soapy water; to clean up after oil-based paint, use mineral spirits. In either case, don't cut corners on this job because, if you clean up the equipment properly, you'll be able to use and reuse it for a long time.

Paint sticks have a curved end and a straight end. The slight round indentation is for wringing out a paint roller. Scrape the paint off the stick as shown in Figure 4-11, and then rinse the stick in cold water. Wash out the roller as follows:

✔ Use water to clean latex paint from brushes and rollers. Hold the brush or roller under a stream of warm water at a work sink and towel dry or use a paint spinner to remove excess water.

✔ Use mineral spirits to clean up after oil-based paint. When the excess paint is removed, use the spinner to thoroughly dry the bristles until they're supple and clean.

Figure 4-11:
Use the curved handle of a paint stick to scrape off the excess paint, and use a spinner to pull out any excess moisture.

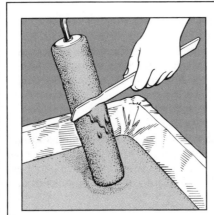

Spray Painting

A few gallons of latex paint and an airless paint sprayer can perform miracles on an unfinished basement with concrete or cinder-block walls. Although the unevenness of these rough surfaces make them difficult to paint with a brush or roller, a power paint system makes short work of the task. And besides, the equipment is fun to use.

For this project, rent a professional-quality airless sprayer. High-powered units put out a lot of paint, which is just what you want when trying to cover rough surfaces. From start to finish, you'll probably spend more time preparing the area than actually spraying. You can break this project down into five easy steps:

- ✔ Preparing the surface
- ✔ Protecting the areas you don't want painted
- ✔ Preparing the spray equipment
- ✔ Spraying on the paint
- ✔ Cleaning up the spray equipment

Preparing the surface

Use a wire brush to scrape the rough surface so that it's free of flaky paint and crusty residue. If you see signs of mildew, scrape them off and wash the stained area with a 50/50 solution of water and bleach. If mildew is a recurring problem, get to the source of the problem and solve it before painting the walls. (See "Avoiding a Wet Basement" in Chapter 16.)

Masking protected areas

Use pretaped plastic dropcloths to protect the furnace, shelving, windows, doors, and anything else that you don't want to get painted. As latex comes out of the airless unit, the overspray dries very quickly. This fine mist is liable to drift throughout the house if you don't seal off the area where you're spraying. Because latex paint dries fast, you can remove the dropcloths right after you finish painting.

Be sure to turn off appliances like the water heater or furnace before you cover them with dropcloths.

In addition to preparing the basement area for paint, you should also prepare yourself. Along with the spray unit, rent a good-quality respirator. Paper masks don't provide enough protection for spray painting. Wear a long-sleeved shirt and a stocking hat pulled way down over your ears and neck or, even better, purchase a disposable painter's hood or use an old nylon stocking cap with cutouts for your eyes, nose, and mouth. (Don't forget to take off the stocking cap before you venture into a bank or convenience store!)

Preparing the equipment

When renting any tool, especially an airless spray unit, describe what you want to paint so that the person at the rental store can recommend the best unit for the job.

Airless sprayers use very high pressure to atomize the paint. These units are not toys, and the business end of the unit, the spray gun, should be treated like a loaded weapon. Airless spray units are capable of injecting paint through your skin right into your hand or, for that matter, into anyone you point the gun at. The nozzle must be quite close to the skin for this to occur, but the danger is always there.

Be sure that you get a crash course in how to operate the unit at the rental store. The important points to know before you leave the store are how to perform the following tasks:

- Start and stop the unit
- Adjust the paint pressure
- Load paint
- Adjust the paint tip
- Adjust the spray pattern
- Clear a clog in the tip
- Clean the gun, hose, and pressure unit

Spraying it on

Operating airless equipment is not difficult, but it does take a bit of practice to be able to apply an even coat of paint. That's why painting a basement is such a great first spray project. How badly can you mess up down there?

Figure 4-12: Under-standing how to use spray equipment properly is key to doing a safe and professional-looking job.

A. Thin paint according to manufacturer's recommendations.

B. Move the spray gun back and forth, keeping it the same distance from the surface.

The controls on the paint sprayer vary by manufacturer, but all airless sprayers operate in basically the same way: A pump sucks the paint out of a bin or bucket and compresses it down the delivery hose to the paint gun. When you pull the trigger, the paint is forced through a small hole in the tip, causing it to break up into tiny particles.

The paint pressure and the diameter of the hole in the tip determine the amount of paint that comes out of the gun and its pattern. Check with the salesperson at the rental store to make sure that the gun is equipped with a tip suitable for spraying latex paint. If the gun has an adjustable tip, make sure that you understand how to adjust it.

Because the hole in the gun tip is very small, it can easily become clogged if the paint isn't clean. Have the salesperson show you how to clear the gun. Some spray guns require that you remove the tip; others, with adjustable tips, can be cleared by opening up the adjustable tip. Understanding how to safely clean the spray gun is important. The paint is under very high pressure as it comes out the tip of the gun, so always be careful.

The best technique for painting rough surfaces is to keep the gun about 18 inches from the wall and move it parallel to the wall. Release the trigger at the end of each pass so that you don't overcoat the edges of the spray area. Work on a 3- to 4-foot-wide area at a time, keeping the gun perpendicular to the wall as you move it back and forth (see Figure 4-12). If you have long arms, you may be able to spray a wider area.

Overlap each pass to avoid leaving light areas. After you complete your first area, stand back and look for light spots between the passes. If the paint appears banded, you're not overlapping the passes enough. Do a little experimenting to get the hang of it.

It is better to put the paint on a little light and have to go back and apply a bit more than to load the wall with a heavy coat of paint that will dry unevenly and, in time, begin to flake off or peel.

As long as you have the spray equipment, consider spraying any exposed floor joists. Spray paint is ideal for these difficult-to-reach surfaces, mired with heating ducts, electrical wires, and plumbing lines.

Cleaning up the equipment

Spraying paint is fast; cleaning up the equipment isn't. But the time you save spraying versus rolling or brushing outweighs the extra cleanup time.

Each unit has specific cleanup procedures, so be sure to have the salesperson explain how to clean the unit you rent. In general, you have to run water through the unit until all the paint is removed from the pump, hose, and spray gun. The spray tip is removable on most sprayers, enabling you to push a larger volume of water through the machine. After you've pumped water through the unit for several minutes, the water should run clean. When the inside of the unit is clean, wash down the outside, especially the spray gun and the hose near the gun, where paint tends to build up.

If you aren't returning the unit right away, run a gallon of mineral spirits through the gun to further clean it out. Because spirits are petroleum-based, they don't cause rust to develop inside the way water can.

Chapter 5

Exterior Painting: Now That's a House of a Different Color!

In This Chapter

▶ Finding the right color, finish, and quantity of exterior paint

▶ Making all the proper preparations

▶ Painting your house from head to toe

*T*o gain a full appreciation of the curb appeal that paint can add, drive through any post-World War II housing development and take a look at the variety, ranging from houses you love to ones you can't stand. Often, all the houses in such developments started out as cookie-cutter look-alikes, but it doesn't take long for individual tastes to surface. Homeowners quickly begin to give their houses distinct personalities, in large part by choosing different colors of exterior paint.

It's never been easier to make color selections, because most of the paint manufacturers have taken the guesswork out of choosing coordinated color schemes. Their brochures put it all together with color samples for siding, and palettes of companion shades to accent the front door, windows, and trim. Just visit the exterior-paint department of any hardware store, home center, or paint outlet — the choices are sure to dazzle you.

Finding a Color That You (And Your Neighbors) Can Live With

You can arrive at the right finish (paint or stain) and color selection for your house in several ways. The first method is to drive through housing developments, and check out the finish and color combinations on houses that appeal to you. Color choices that are the obvious result of good taste can make a house absolutely striking. And notice the negative effect of a house painted with ho-hum or ridiculous colors. Blue siding, white trim, and red shutters may work well for a local restaurant with a patriotic theme, but you can count on gasps, gossip, and perhaps even some spirited complaints from your neighbors as soon as that first brushful of bright blue paint hits the siding of your home.

A tour of any neighborhood reveals that many people don't plan carefully when choosing an exterior finish or color for their homes. Never underestimate the important role that paint and color can play in customizing a house. And remember: Choosing just the right paint or stain for your home can increase its resale value. On the other hand, garish colors can scare away prospective buyers and drive down your asking price.

Another approach to exterior decorating is to seek expert assistance. Most paint companies offer consultants and color-palette brochures that suggest appropriate combinations of colors for siding, trim, and accents. These companies pay color consultants and designers to come up with attractive combinations of their color lines, so don't be shy about asking for ideas. Some paint dealers feature computer-assisted color selection. To use this system, take a color photo of your house to the dealer. The computer can display the photo with a variety of hues, enabling you to see exactly how your home will look in an assortment of new colors.

Creating your own "unique" color scheme is usually not a good idea. There's a perfectly good reason why you never see purple houses with green trim: They would look ridiculous! Stick with the basics.

Make the most of what you already have. Remember to consider components of your house that have fixed colors before you shop for coordinating paint and stain. For example, steer clear of paint or stain colors that may conflict with the color of the roof shingles, or with brick or stone features like a fireplace chimney or planter. Also keep in mind the color of the other houses on the block, especially those right next door. Don't choose a color or finish that's a carbon copy of your next door neighbor's house, or one that is wildly different from others in your neighborhood. Imagine painting your house barn red when the rest of the neighborhood shows a preference for pastels or earth tones. Your house will not only attract attention, but also convince your neighbors that you're about one rosy brick short of a full load.

You have three different areas to consider when painting the house exterior:

- First is the body, or siding, of the house. This is the largest area to be painted.

- The second component is the trim. Painting the trim in a color that contrasts highly with the body color can make your house look smaller because it appears to chop the surface area into smaller bits. To make the house look larger, paint your trim the same color as the siding, or choose a trim paint in a shade that compliments the main body.

> ✔ The third area includes accents such as shutters and entry doors. Keep in mind that you can use a bold paint or finish to emphasize an attractive accent area, and you can downplay unattractive features by painting them to blend in with the body finish.

As with any feature of your house that you want to downplay, you may want to camouflage gutters by painting them the same color as the house. One precaution: Because metal expands and contract with temperature changes, thick house paint often peels when layered on gutters. Thin the paint slightly in the work pail (refer to the sidebar "Getting thinner," later in this chapter), and brush out the paint so that you leave only a thin film on the metal surface.

Choosing a Finish: Latex, Alkyd, or Stain

Paint is a coating that lays a protective film on the surface of the material. As a general rule, paint is the preferred finish for smooth siding, for trim, and for refinishing metal siding like steel or aluminum.

When used on new wood, *stain* penetrates into the material in addition to leaving a protective surface film. Because of this superior penetration, stains just weather away, rather than peeling the way paints can. Stains are commonly used on natural wood siding like redwood or cedar, or for exterior wood projects, such as decks or fences.

Latex paint

In the past, experts advised never to use latex (water-based) paints over alkyd (oil-based) paints. The thinking was that alkyd paints were designed to *chalk,* or erode away with time. But now, through the magic of modern paint technology, you're free to use acrylic latex paints over any exterior siding or trim finish. These exterior acrylic latex paints are easy to work with, resist fading, produce a tough protective film, and cause less air pollution than alkyd paints. For all these reasons, exterior latex is the overwhelming choice of homeowners and professional painters.

Remember that there are many grades of latex paints. To ensure that you're using a quality paint, shop where the professional painters go. The pros have to guarantee their work, so they use paint brands that produce the fewest complaints and callbacks. Another indicator of quality is price: the more expensive paints tend to offer better color retention (resist fading), better elasticity, better warranties, and a longer life. The cost of the paint is a small factor when compared with the labor investment of painting a house, so buy the very best paint you can afford.

Check the annual timing of paint sales in your area. In climates with four distinct seasons, peak consumer paint sales are in the spring, and quality paint brands are often available at reduced sale prices after the Fourth of July.

Glossy exterior paints fade when exposed to the weather, and the finish dulls over time. But if the paint you are covering still has its shine, it is important to break down the smooth glossy surface so that the new paint has something to grab onto. Break down the gloss by sanding the surface with 120-grit sandpaper or wipe the surface with a paint deglosser. Then prime the gloss paint with an exterior alkyd primer before applying the topcoat of exterior latex finish paint.

Alkyd paint

Alkyd paint is a better choice than latex on a few surfaces. Because alkyd paints are generally easier to clean and have more sheen or gloss than latex paints, some pro painters prefer to use a latex paint on the body of the house, and an alkyd finish on trim or accent areas. For example, dirt and grime are easy to remove from alkyd paint that's applied on high-contact components like doors and trim.

Alkyd paint is sometimes preferred for house exteriors in areas where high air pollution levels can damage the paint. Alkyd paint offers a more scrubbable surface than latex paint for anyone ambitious enough to scrub the exterior of their homes. We can't even keep the bathroom clean!

Because foot traffic causes wear to painted surfaces, the best rule is to avoid using latex paint on walkways like wood porches or decks. Paint applied to any frequently traveled path shows wear patterns over time. Some alkyd paint is specifically formulated for deck and porch surfaces to offer better wear qualities than latex paint. Another good choice for a surface that's often underfoot is a tough, oil-based semitransparent stain.

Stains

Semitransparent oil stains are a good choice for new wood siding, decks, and fences. These stains have a linseed oil base, which offers good penetration of the new wood (especially on rough sawn surfaces) while revealing the wood grain and texture. For best protection, use two coats of semitransparent stain on new wood surfaces.

Solid-color oil stains have more pigment than semitransparent stains, and tend to cover and hide the wood grain and texture. Because pressure-treated wood has a green or brown tint, semitransparent stains may not cover the wood color. Use solid-color stains to finish pressure-treated wood projects like decks. When used to finish redwood, semitransparent stains may not stay color-true when they dry because the red color of the wood may show through the stain and change its color. Solid-color stain is a better finish choice on dark red woods.

Latex stains tend to hide the wood grain and texture. Because they don't penetrate into the wood as an oil-based stain does, latex stain products are actually more like paint than stain. Use latex stain to refinish prestained wood where no further stain penetration is possible.

Because exterior painting is so labor intensive, the cost of the paint or stain represents a small part of any job. The first rule of business is that you never get more than you pay for. So don't skimp on quality, buy the best paint or stain available.

Estimating the Amount of Paint You Need

To determine how much paint you need for windows, doors, and trim, refer to the paint calculators in Chapter 4.

Estimating the amount of paint to use for exterior siding can be a bit trickier than for interior walls because siding is usually much rougher. If your house has wood siding, especially lap-type siding (where the horizontal siding overlaps each other), you must also factor in the underside of each piece of siding. On a house with board-and-batten siding, you have many more edges to cover with paint because the joints between the vertical siding boards are covered with another board, which has two side edges to paint. When estimating how much exterior paint you will need for your house, order about 15 to 25 percent more paint than the wall-paint calculator in Chapter 4 calls for.

Getting thinner

Most paint is intended to be used straight from the can. Obviously, circumstances sometimes call for thinning the paint, such as for spray application. Do not overthin paint: Thin only as directed by the label instructions. In most cases, latex paint can be thinned by adding a maximum of one pint of water per gallon of paint.

The proper solvent for thinning latex paints is water. Mineral spirits are the best solvent for thinning alkyd paints, enamels, varnishes or oil-based stains. Note that water used for thinning paint needs to be clean enough to drink. The minerals in hard water may cause color shifts in latex paint. If your water is hard, use distilled water for thinning latex paint.

Tooling Up for the Job

To apply paint or stain, choose from any of the paint application tools, including brushes, pads, rollers, or spray equipment. Be aware that the paint application tool you need is often dictated by the substance you are applying and the surface you're applying it to.

Brushes

Exterior work usually calls for a larger brush. The basic rule is to use the largest brush available for large surfaces. Professional painters use a 4-inch-wide brush to paint lap siding. However, for the weekend painter who isn't blessed with Schwarzenegger-like forearms, a 4-inch brush may be too much to heft all day long. The best brush choice is often the largest one that you can use comfortably for an extended stretch of time. In general, if you need two hands to lift the brush, it's too big.

The advice in Chapter 4 about purchasing a quality brush for interior painting also holds true for exterior work. Use a nylon or mixed-bristle (nylon and polyester) brush to apply latex paint. If you're using alkyd paint, buy a natural-bristle or polyester brush.

The most useful brush styles for exterior painting are brushes with square ends, as opposed to angled sash brushes. You can handle most situations with a set of brushes 2, 3, and 4 inches wide (see Figure 5-1). Paint the outsides of windows and doors and other exterior trim with the same sash brushes (those with the bristles cut at an angle) that we recommend in Chapter 4 for interior trim.

Inexpensive sponge brushes are handy for painting small projects or for touch-up work. For example, narrow sponge brushes are useful for painting or staining in the cracks between deck boards. Sponge brushes are throw-away models, so no cleanup is necessary.

Figure 5-1:
The three most useful brush sizes for outside work are 2-, 3-, and 4-inch-wide brushes.

Painting pads

Painting pads are rectangular paint applicators that come in a wide variety of shapes. The most useful types for exterior painting are the larger ones with heavy painting pads. This type of pad, shown in Figure 5-2, is covered with a plastic sponge or furry fabric. Painting pads don't leave brush marks and are useful for painting not only smooth surfaces, but also rough areas like roughhewn cedar siding or cedar shingles. The paint pad is especially appropriate for painting the bottom edges of lap-type siding or shingles.

Figure 5-2: Painting pads apply paint evenly to a wide area, and are especially useful for covering rough surfaces.

Rollers

Like paint pads, rollers are great for painting large exterior surfaces. The same roller equipment you use to paint your living room can be used outside. Rollers are most effective for painting large open areas that are relatively smooth.

Buying good equipment always pays off, so choose a roller handle that has a heavy, durable wire cage. A handle with nylon bearings permits the roller cage to spin smoothly. Make sure that the roller handle is threaded to accommodate an extension handle.

Extension handles, available in either 2- or 4-foot lengths, permit the painter to cover more area without bending, stretching, or reaching far above ladder height to paint a gable.

Roller covers with $^3/_8$-inch nap are the most effective for covering the slightly irregular surfaces usually found on house exteriors. Use a $^3/_4$-inch or longer nap for painting stucco or concrete.

Paint sprayers

Painting exterior siding usually involves applying the same color paint to large areas, which makes it a perfect candidate for spray painting. For some difficult paint or stain jobs, there's no substitute for spray equipment. If you're staining or painting a large house, a barn, roughhewn cedar siding, wood shingles or shakes, privacy fences, or other difficult surfaces, spraying is absolutely the best approach.

You can rent a high-capacity airless sprayer at any tool-rental outlet. These sprayers are the best choice for any project where you expect to apply a large volume of paint.

Getting good results from any paint sprayer depends on thinning the paint to the right viscosity, using the right spray tip or orifice, and adjusting the gun until you achieve a proper spray pattern.

To fine-tune the spray pattern, use a large cardboard box as a target; alternately test the spray and adjust the spray gun until you produce the pattern that you want. With too narrow a pattern, you'd have to apply too much paint to the area and runs would result; with too wide a pattern, you'd have to make several passes with the spray gun to get good coverage. A pattern that's 8 to 12 inches wide is adequate for painting most exterior surfaces.

Hold the paint gun about 8 to 12 inches from the surface you're painting. Keep the gun parallel to the surface and move it back and forth. First, paint the bottom edge of lap-type siding, holding the gun at an upward angle to direct paint at this exposed edge as shown in Figure 5-3. Then, with a second pass of the spray gun, apply paint to the broad side of the siding.

Figure 5-3: When spray painting lap siding, paint the underside edge of the siding first, and then spray the face of the siding.

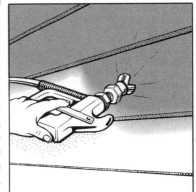

Paint that's sprayed on too thick leaves a textured finish like an orange peel, and paint that's sprayed on too thin doesn't cover well and tends to sag or drip. To get the proper coverage, experiment with the ratio of paint to thinner, and adjust the paint tip or orifice. To be sure that the paint is the right viscosity, you can buy a *viscometer,* a device that measures the viscosity or thickness of the paint.

When you're spraying, the atomized paint (or *overspray*) can become airborne, and this mist can be carried for long distances on a windy day. Floating paint particles pose a threat to neighboring property, because the mist may settle on houses, cars, napping dogs, and so on. For this reason, some city ordinances prohibit the use of paint spray equipment for exterior projects. If you paint your neighbor's new car with exterior latex house paint, your relationship may become more up-close and personal than you ever imagined. Never spray paint on a windy day, or even in calm weather if you live on a city lot where houses are side by side.

Paint, stain, or paint products like solvents and cleaners are all chemicals and are not meant to be ingested. Read and heed the warnings on product labels. Remember that the fumes of poisonous chemicals are also poisonous, and the fumes of flammable chemicals are flammable. Never spray flammable products near an open fire or a standing pilot light. Do not smoke while spraying or otherwise handling paint or paint products. Wear an approved respirator when spraying paints or stains, and wear protective eye goggles to keep paint out of your eyes.

Preparing Surfaces for Paint

Most paint failures are caused by improper preparation, not by poor paint quality. The first step is to find and correct any problems in the area that you plan to paint. If, after five or more years, the last coat of paint is faded but in good condition, you may be able to simply cover it with a new coat and expect it to last for years. However, if the paint is peeling, try to determine the cause and correct the condition before repainting. Figure 5-4 shows a variety of problems you may encounter with old paint.

Alligatoring results from applying an inflexible paint over a flexible one, or from applying a second coat before the first coat dries. *Blistering* occurs when you apply an alkyd paint to a damp or hot surface. *Excessive chalking* is common over time with low-grade paints. *Cracking* or *scaling* commonly results from overthinning paint, applying to heavy a coat of paint, or applying paint to bare, unprimed wood. *Peeling* and *mildew* often result from excessive moisture escaping from inside the house.

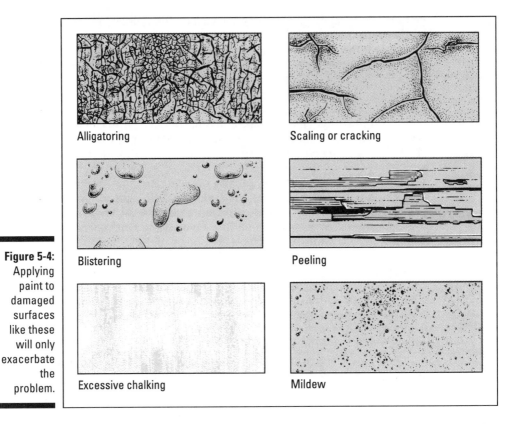

Alligatoring

Scaling or cracking

Blistering

Peeling

Excessive chalking

Mildew

Figure 5-4: Applying paint to damaged surfaces like these will only exacerbate the problem.

As a general rule, the proper sequence for preparing a house for painting is as follows:

1. **Repair loose or missing siding or trim, and correct problems that may be causing premature paint failure.**

2. **Caulk gaps and cracks.**

3. **Pressure-wash the entire exterior.**

4. **Scrape and sand off chipping paint.**

5. **Patch nail holes and small cracks.**

6. **Apply a coat of primer.**

7. **Apply the topcoat.**

Getting to the source of peeling paint

If paint is peeling down to bare wood, the cause is usually moisture coming from inside the house. After repeated recoating, the first coat may fail and peel at the wood level. If this condition describes your home, then you better sit down: The only solution is to scrape, sandblast, or use heat to remove all the old paint . . . *down to the bare wood.* Then apply a coat of alkyd primer, followed by a topcoat of quality latex house paint.

If only the topcoat is peeling, either all over or in patches, the cure isn't quite so bad. The following list describes the possible types of topcoat failure, explains how to handle each case, and provides some tips on preventing these problems in the future:

- ✔ **Complete failure:** If the entire top coat of paint is peeling, suspect that the cause is improper surface preparation during the last paint job. Latex paint may have been applied over a chalking oil-base paint, or the surface may not have been properly cleaned before painting. You must either wait until the paint completely peels off, or remove all the paint yourself.

  To prevent the problem from recurring, be sure to properly clean and prepare the surface before repainting it. If you are painting over a chalking surface, consider using a paint additive that improves paint adhesion. Mix the additive with your exterior latex paint (according to the manufacturer's directions) and apply it with a brush, roller, or spray equipment. If a second coat of paint is needed, apply the paint without an additive. Another way to eliminate peeling due to application over chalking paint is to use a quality latex paint that's formulated as an overcoat for "problem surfaces."

- ✔ **Patches of peeling paint:** If paint is peeling only in random spots, assume that you have a moisture problem and investigate the source. For example, paint often peels near the clothes-dryer exhaust vent because of repeated steam exposure. To prevent future peeling in this case, extend the vent pipe further away from the siding to limit moisture contact with the paint.

- ✔ **Peeling paint on soffits and overhangs:** If paint is intact on the house siding, but is peeling on the underside of the *soffits* (roof overhangs), on porch ceilings, or on siding that covers the gable ends, the problem is too much moisture and too little ventilation. Replacing the randomly placed soffit vents with continuous metal vents that extend along the full length of the roof ridge may be well worth the effort. You can purchase simple-to-install round soffit vents at any home center. Just cut a hole the same size as the vent in the underside of the soffit and insert the vent. These vents allow air to circulate in the soffit and provide a path for excess moisture to exit.

  The failure to clean the surfaces before painting is another cause of peeling paint on soffits or porch ceilings. The sides of the house get regular showers from the rain, but the soffits and porch ceilings that are not exposed to rain can become quite dirty. When scrubbing the house exterior, pay special attention to these unexposed areas, and clean them thoroughly.

✔ **Peeling paint on gables:** If paint is peeling only on the gables of the house, the problem is attic moisture buildup and too little attic ventilation. To increase attic ventilation, install larger gable vents or continuous ridge vents.

✔ **Peeling paint around windows and doors:** Another common point for peeling paint, especially on brick or stucco houses, is the trim around windows and doors. In winter, warm indoor air tends to hold more moisture than cold outside air. In exterior walls, the path of least resistance for moisture migration is often between the window and door units and the rough frames into which they're installed. When the moisture reaches the exterior trim, it condenses beneath the paint and causes the paint film to pull away from the trim.

To block moisture in its tracks, use an acrylic caulk to seal any cracks between the walls and the interior trim. Also remove electrical outlet covers and caulk any cracks between the outlet box and the plaster or wallboard. Filling in gaps retards the flow of moisture through the walls, from indoors to the outside.

Before repainting, remove all the peeling paint from the exterior window and door trim. Be sure to remove the paint beyond the area of obvious peeling because the paint failure often extends into paint that appears to be sound. After the old paint's gone, apply an alkyd primer and then two coats of acrylic latex trim paint; acrylics are more flexible and permit moisture to escape more readily than alkyd paints.

✔ **Peeling paint at siding joints:** Peeling paint is common on the ends of lap siding, at the joints where siding meets siding, and where siding meets trim boards. Water enters the crack between the two pieces of wood, soaks into the end grain of the siding, and causes the paint to peel. To remedy the problem, first use sandpaper or a paint scraper to remove the peeling paint. Then use an acrylic latex caulk to seal the cracks between the siding and trim. Apply a coat of wood primer plus a topcoat, or two coats of exterior latex paint.

✔ **Peeling paint where wooden porch posts meet concrete:** If the paint at the base of your porch posts or columns is peeling, the carpenter probably failed to apply a sealer to the end grain of the posts or columns. Water that falls on the concrete porch can travel underneath the wood posts and wick upwards through the post end grain, causing the paint to peel at the post base.

To fix leaks around posts, first scrape away the peeling paint. Seal the peeled area of the wood with an alkyd primer, then topcoat with the finish of your choice. Or, apply two coats of acrylic latex house paint to the posts. When you're sure that the wood is dry, use an acrylic latex caulk to seal the crack between the wood posts and the concrete porch. The caulk prevents future water entry into the crack.

Caulking the exterior

Caulk is a substance designed to seal the joint between two surfaces. A common cause of paint failure is water getting behind the paint and making it peel, so keeping caulk in good shape makes any paint job last longer.

Scrape away any peeling paint that's adjacent to the caulked areas. Then recaulk all cracks between any two nonmoving materials. No, we don't mean your brother-in-law and the couch. Examples include cracks around exterior electrical outlets, around plumbing pipes including the exterior hose bibs, and between siding and trim (as shown in Figure 5-5) or siding and brick trim, such as a fireplace chimney. Let the caulk cure a few days before power washing the exterior.

Figure 5-5:
Before you paint, use acrylic latex-type caulk to seal cracks in the siding and trim, and any other gaps around the exterior of the house.

Don't caulk the horizontal joints on siding where the siding courses overlap. Each course of siding has a *weep edge* designed to let water fall harmlessly away without penetrating into the cracks between courses. The cracks between two courses of siding provide ventilation points to let moisture escape from inside the wall. For the same reason, don't fill these joints between courses of siding with paint when you're applying paint to the siding.

Cleaning

Modern paint covers so well that you can paint over just about anything, but don't. Paint may cover dirt and grime, but it won't stick to it. Dirt gets between the paint and the surface, eventually causing the paint to peel. The secret to a long-lasting paint job is cleanliness.

Washing your house may seem like an insurmountable job, but a pressure washer can make this project manageable and even fun. Rent a pressure washer at an equipment-rental center, or purchase one at a home center. In fact, this tool is so handy, we happen to include a couple of power-washing projects in Chapter 16.

Power washing your house is the best way to get it clean, and the spray of high-pressure water does a great job of blasting off most of the loose or flaking paint. But you don't have to use a power washer. You can get the job done with nothing but some elbow grease, a bucket of soapy water, and a scrub brush.

Chalking (and how to erase it)

As they age, most paint surfaces chalk slightly, or *oxidize*. Some oil-based exterior paints are intentionally designed to chalk so that the surface can be cleaned and washed away by the rain. But latex paints may peel if you apply them over chalking paint.

To determine whether the surface you want to paint is chalky, wipe it with the palm of your hand. If the paint color comes off on your hand, the paint is chalking. Wash the chalked surface with a strong solution of water and Spic N Span, or use a wood cleaner to remove the chalked paint. Note that you must scrub away the chalk residue: Microscopic chalk particles are so small that water pressure alone cannot lift and flush them away. As you scrub the surface, rinse frequently with clear water. Allow the surface to dry completely before painting.

Fighting mildew

Paint that's applied over grime or mildew peels or fails, so you must remove both grime and mildew from the surface before you paint. Accumulated dirt and grime support mildew growth, so if you have recurring problems with mildew, power wash the house exterior once a year to remove the crud. You can rent a power washer at tool rental outlets.

A brown, gray, or black stain on siding or trim may simply be grime, or it may be mildew. To test whether a stain is grime or mildew, try washing the stain away with water and a detergent such as Spic N Span. If the stain washes away, you're dealing with grime, and you may proceed with preparing the surface. If the stain does not wash away with water and detergent, the culprit is probably mildew.

Because mildew is a fungus growth, it thrives on moisture and heat. (Remember athlete's foot from gym class?) When you eliminate moisture problems, the mildew disappears. To ensure proper air circulation to keep siding dry, do not store firewood or other materials close to the house. To provide good air circulation and to allow sunlight to penetrate and dry the siding and trim surfaces, prune shrubs or hire a tree trimmer to trim and thin the crown of the trees whose branches overhang and shadow the house.

To kill the spores on areas where there's a heavy coat of mildew, wash the house with a 50/50 mix of chlorine bleach and water. The best approach is to wet the mildewed surface with a garden hose or a garden sprayer. To lift and loosen the dirt and mildew, let the surface sit wet for five minutes, then use a garden sprayer to apply the chlorine-water mix. Be sure to wear work clothes that can stand up to the bleach solution, and wear goggles to protect your eyes. Let the bleach solution set for a few minutes, then wash the mildew away with a blast from a garden hose or power washer. Flush the bleach away with lots of water. Let the cleaned surface dry for several days, or longer depending on the weather, before proceeding with painting.

Most good-quality exterior paint contains some form of anti-mildew additive. However, if you have a particularly severe problem with mildew, you can purchase a special additive called a *mildewcide* to mix with your paint. This approach may be the only answer for a mildew-prone north-facing area of your house that receives little, if any, direct sunlight.

Always consider the effect of any project on the environment, and make every effort to limit your use of chemicals. Rather than using a 50/50 solution of chlorine bleach and water for lightly mildewed surfaces, try a more diluted mix. For lightly soiled surfaces, apply a solution of only one cup of bleach per gallon of water. If this diluted solution doesn't do the job, increase the amount of bleach in the solution until the surface comes clean. Always rinse thoroughly after you clean, diluting the bleach completely as you wash it away.

We've had to resort to using a 50/50 solution on siding directly above beds of blooming flowers. The flowers didn't wilt, lose their blooms, or show any other ill effects from the bleach.

Removing peeling paint

If the old paint is failing down to bare wood, you have to remove it all. You can hire professionals to remove the paint by using chemical removers or by sandblasting. We don't recommend that amateurs undertake either of these removal methods: The chemical removers that pros use are too dangerous for the novice to handle, and if the air pressure is set too high on sandblasting equipment, an inexperienced worker may blow the siding right off the house. If you decide to have the paint removed by sandblasting, choose an experienced pro who can offer referrals to satisfied customers, and call or visit those customers to check the references. We emphasize *experienced* pro, because not all professional painters have had much practice sandblasting wood.

If only a small area of paint is peeling, say the patch under a window, then you can undertake the job yourself. But we still don't recommend that you use chemicals or sandblast the area. For removing small areas of peeled paint, the do-it-yourselfer can choose from the following methods (illustrated in Figure 5-6):

- **A belt sander or orbital sander:** You can remove minor areas of peeled paint with a belt sander or orbital sander. These power sanders create enough dust to choke Lawrence of Arabia, but they're fast, easy to use, and sometimes even fun. Use 80-grit open-coat sandpaper to minimize clogging and gomming up the paper. Don't use a rotating sanding disc, because it tends to leave deep swirl marks in the wood.

- **A paint scraper:** Paint scrapers are also available in a choice of sizes. Scrapers are a lot less fun than power sanders, but they're effective tools, especially for small areas. For the best scraper efficiency, sharpen the scraper blade when you bring it home from the hardware store — before you use it. Because scraping old paint quickly dulls the blade, resharpen the scraper often with a small file or a grinding wheel to maintain a good cutting edge.

- **An electric heat gun:** As an alternative to scraping, or in addition to scraping, use a heat gun to remove the really stubborn paint. Heat guns are very effective for removing multiple coats of oil-based paint.

If you choose to use a heat gun for paint removal, remember that air hot enough to melt paint is hot enough to kindle a fire in dry wood or paper products. Use the heat gun with care, keep a garden hose handy for wetting down any burned areas, and keep an eye on the burned area for several hours after you quit working. You want to quickly spot any fire that develops from a smoldering or scorched area, and put the fire out or call for help.

As we mentioned earlier, certain methods of paint removal are best left to the professionals. The following procedures are *not* Dummies Approved:

- **Chemical paint remover:** Messing around with these toxic chemicals in quantities large enough to remove paint from a house is just plain nuts. Rely on a sharp scraper and a lot of elbow grease to get the job done, instead.

- **Rotating sanding disc:** This tool may get the job done, but if you don't have a lot of experience operating the blasted things, you'll gouge the siding. Renting this macho tool may seem like a good idea, but for your house's sake, don't do it.

- **Propane torch:** This is just another type heat gun, but one that can quickly burn you and your house to the ground. When applied over older, dry siding, the heat and open flame from a propane torch can easily start a fire. Be wise; stick with the electric version.

- **Chain saw:** We're just trying to cover all our bases, here.

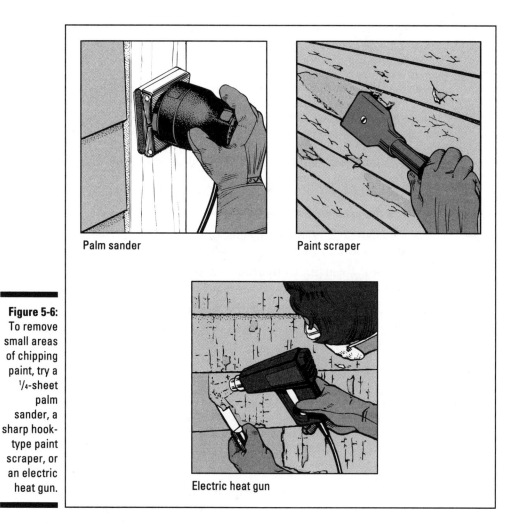

Palm sander

Paint scraper

Electric heat gun

Figure 5-6:
To remove
small areas
of chipping
paint, try a
¼-sheet
palm
sander, a
sharp hook-
type paint
scraper, or
an electric
heat gun.

Before you begin to remove paint by any method, be aware that paint dust is a health hazard. Always wear a dust mask and eye goggles when removing paint, and wear protective clothing to cover up bare skin. Exterior lead-based paints were commonly used before 1978. If you suspect that the old paint contains lead, have paint chips tested by a laboratory. (Refer to the sidebar called "Removing lead paint," in Chapter 4.)

Patching

Filling cracks and holes in the trim and siding of your house before painting not only makes the paint job look better, but it also makes the paint last longer. Cracks and holes in any surface collect water, which eventually causes the paint to fail.

Patching a hole or crack on the outside of the house is not much different than filling a hole in your living room wall. The main difference is that you use materials specially designed for exterior use.

Fill small holes in the siding with an exterior patching compound, available in a premixed form (much like interior spackle) and in a dry powder form that you mix with water. Either type is effective, just make sure that the package states that the patching compound can be used outside.

To patch holes and depressions in any kind of siding, follow these steps:

1. **Clean the hole or depression you plan to fill.**

2. **Fill the area with the patching compound.**

   Apply the compound to the hole or depression and then smooth it so that it's level with the original surface.

3. **Allow the compound to become hard and dry according to the directions on the package.**

4. **Sand the hardened compound smooth.**

   This type of compound shrinks a bit, so a second coating may be necessary. Be sure to remove the dust from sanding the compound before you apply a second coat. After this coat is hard, sand the patch smooth again.

To repair large cracks and damaged trim, use a two-part polyester-based compound, similar to auto-body filler. Two-part fillers come with a thick paste base and a small tube of hardener. Mix the hardener with the paste according to the manufacturer's directions. This type of filler begins to set up quickly (within 3 to 5 minutes), so mix only the amount you can use right away.

Use a putty knife to apply the compound to the damaged area and level it with the surface. This filler doesn't shrink as much as premixed exterior fillers, but you may still need several coats to completely fill a large hole. When the filler hardens, it's suitable for sanding, drilling, or even carving.

Priming

If the paint is generally sound, you need to prime only scraped or repaired areas. If you're painting latex paint over a shiny or gloss-paint surface, prime the entire house. As a general rule, use an alkyd primer and a latex topcoat.

A white primer is difficult to hide with one coat of colored paint. If you plan to use primer as the first coat on a two-coat job, have the paint dealer tint the primer to the approximate color of the finish coat.

Knowing When to Paint and When to Wait

Plan to paint in late spring or early summer, between spring rains, but before insects hatch and dust collects in the air. Don't apply paint on a windy day because strong winds can cause paint to dry too rapidly and can blow dust and insects into the fresh paint. In general, avoid applying latex paint at temperatures below 50°F or above 90°F. Check the label for specific temperature limits for the paint you're applying.

You can apply latex paint on a dew-damp surface, but avoid putting alkyd paint on any surface that's even slightly damp. Never paint on any day following a rain, on any day that's humid, or if afternoon showers are forecast. Do you see pro painters breaking these rules? Yes. But you also see a lot of peeled paint.

You also don't want to paint in direct sunlight. When you apply paint to an area in direct sun, it immediately begins to dry. Then, as you go back to paint the adjacent areas, you end up brushing over paint that has already begun to dry. The result is distinct lap or brush marks. Stay one step ahead of the sun: Start the day by painting on the shady side of the house, and move with the sun so that you're always working in shade.

Remove any shutters from the house and set them aside on a porch or in a garage to keep them out of the weather. If you also store doors and storm windows with the shutters, you can work on them even if it rains.

Getting High on Ladders and Scaffolding

When painting a house exterior, you can reach the top of the job in three basic ways. The first is to use ladders of various heights. The problem with working from a ladder is that you can reach only a small area at one set, then you must climb down and move the ladder. If you use a ladder, never try to overreach or stretch to cover more area at one set. A good safety practice is to crook the elbow of your free arm around the rail of the ladder, and reach out with the free arm only as far as this grip allows. Stretching too far can shift your weight to one side of the ladder, and the ladder may slip. You don't want your last word to be "Timber!"

Set your ladder up so that the bottom of the ladder is a distance of approximately ¼ the overall height of the ladder from the base of the wall. If you place the ladder too far from the wall, the ladder can slip away from the wall at the base. If you place the ladder too close it is unstable and may fall backwards — with you onboard. Correct and incorrect ladder positions appear in Figure 5-7.

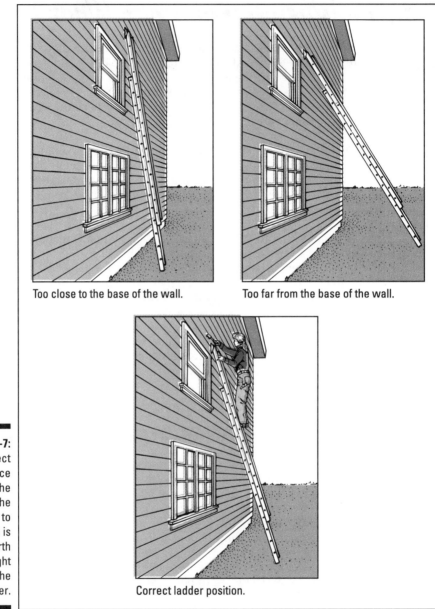

Too close to the base of the wall. Too far from the base of the wall.

Correct ladder position.

Figure 5-7:
The correct distance from the base of the ladder to the wall is one-fourth the height of the ladder.

When buying a ladder, check the label to find its load rating. Common lightweight household ladders are not meant to carry heavyweights, and may collapse or break if they're overloaded. If you weigh 200 pounds or more, buy a commercial ladder with a proper weight rating. (Remember to include your clothes, tools, and paint in that weight!)

Check ladders often to make sure that they're not bent or cracked. Also check the hardware on the ladder and tighten anything that seems loose. Always open a stepladder fully and lock the braces in place before climbing on it. Use a product like WD-40 to lubricate snaps, hooks, pulleys (on extension ladders), and the folding hardware on stepladders. Be careful not to spray any lubricant on the rungs; you don't want to create slippery footing for your climb.

Professional painters avoid frequent moves of their ladders and scaffolding by painting everything within reach at one set: siding, trim, gutters, and all. Homeowners often prefer to paint the siding and trim in two applications: Either paint the trim first and then the siding, or siding first and then trim. If you choose to paint the siding and trim as separate jobs, consider painting the trim first, and then the siding; you won't have to worry about setting your ladder against fresh siding paint when you paint the trim.

If you're painting your house white or gray, you probably want to paint the trim a different color. If you're using any other paint color, consider painting the windows and trim the same color as the siding, using only one kind and color of paint. If you go with the monochromatic look, you only need to carry one work pail of paint, one or two brushes, and you can complete the job as you go.

Invest in a pair of painter's pants or overalls. Not only do they look professional but they also have convenient loops and pockets that allow you to carry all your tools up the ladder or scaffold with you. And you have a ready-made costume for Halloween! The tight-knit canvas clothes are made tough and snag-proof for climbing, and they're also designed to soak up paint spills so that the paint doesn't reach your skin.

Spreading It On

Read the paint label to find the proper coverage rate per gallon for that particular product. The coverage rate varies by job, depending on the condition of the old paint, the porosity of the surface, whether the surface has any texture, and how much you spill on your shoes. Rough or dry surfaces take more paint than a smooth, sound base coat of paint. The label advice may read "will cover 350 to 400 square feet per gallon, when applied to smooth siding." To test the recommendation, apply about a quart of paint and check the area you covered, measured in square feet. A quart of that exterior paint should cover between 90 and 100 square feet; if you covered more square footage than recommended, flow the paint onto the siding more generously.

Don't try to stretch the paint by applying it so thin that it covers more than the suggested area per gallon. The spread rate suggested by the manufacturer is intended to provide full protection of the painted surface, and to provide good *hide,* or coverage of the old paint color.

Most paint is intended to be used straight from the can, without the addition of thinners. If your situation calls for using a paint thinner, refer to the sidebar "Getting thinner," earlier in this chapter.

Paint may show slight color variations from gallon to gallon — especially paints that are custom-mixed. For this reason, professional painters use a technique called *boxing* when painting large surfaces that require more than 1 gallon of paint. Boxing was probably discovered by a painter who applied paint from different gallons of paint and then discovered, when the paint dried, the house was striped like a zebra — a great look if you happen to live in a drive-through safari. When painting the side of a house, take a tip from the pros and figure out how much paint that side will take; then pour that amount into a 5-gallon pail, creating a single color for the entire side of the house. Change to a new pail of paint only at the house corners, where slight color shifts aren't obvious.

Painting Everything Under the Sun

Before you start to paint, remove the window screens, or move the screens behind the glass on combination storm windows — spills on screens are very hard to clean. Drape plastic dropcloths to completely cover the walls on a screened porch. If you do spatter paint on a screen, sell the house and move. Just kidding: Wet a clean paint brush with water for latex paint, or with mineral spirits for alkyd paint, and immediately brush away paint from screens.

Cover foundation shrubs or flower gardens with plastic dropcloths using stones or paint pails to hold them in place. (Don't leave the plants covered too long, or they'll burn.) Trim any shrubs to remove limbs that contact the house siding. Use wooden stakes and clothesline cord to tie back and hold limbs or shrubs away from the surface to be painted.

Use canvas dropcloths or buy heavy paper dropcloths to cover walks, drives, or patios. Plastic dropcloths are slippery to walk on, especially when they're wet. Never carry a large quantity of paint — the cleanup can be a killer. Buy a small plastic pail and fill it with about one quart of paint, or enough to cover the area within reach of the ladder or scaffold. Remember: an ounce of prevention is worth a gallon of scrubbing.

When painting anything, start at the top. Carry sandpaper, a scraper, a wire brush, and wood putty up the ladder with you. As you paint, clean or patch any defects that you missed during preparation.

Painting doors

Doors get a lot of use and abuse, so choose a semigloss or high-gloss alkyd-based paint for best results. Latex enamels also hold up well. If the door was previously painted with a high-gloss paint, use a deglosser to dull the finish and clean the surface.

If the door is flat, you can paint it with a brush, pad, or roller. Any door can be painted using a 2-inch or 3-inch wide brush. If the door is paneled, paint the panels first. Then use a brush to paint the horizontal crosspieces (or *rails*), and finally paint the vertical pieces, or *stiles*. Always sand and paint with the grain. When painting trim, such as doors and windows, check over the work as you proceed and brush away any paint drips.

Painting windows

The strategy for attacking a window with a paintbrush is similar to the one for painting a door: Start from the center and work out. The reason for this approach is that painting the inner portion of a window, the grid that holds in the glass, takes a long time. If you try to paint the jamb and trim first, they will be tacky by the time you finish the interior, and you won't be able to brush into the outer paint without leaving brush marks. Instead, follow this sequence:

1. **First, paint the wood next to the glass with an angled sash brush.**
2. **Next, paint the window sash.**
3. **The *casing,* or trim, comes next.**
4. **Last, but not least, is the window sill.**

When painting a window, leave any previously unpainted surfaces unpainted. Because painted surfaces tend to stick in the frame, the edges of the window are best left unpainted. Coat unpainted edges of the window with a clear penetrating wood sealer to prevent moisture entry into the sash.

Use a *dry brush,* one that has very little paint on it, to coat the outside edge of the sashes. The dry-brush method prevents paint from running into the crack between the sash and stops, where it may cause the window to stick. If you're painting the window sash while it's in the frame, move the window sash frequently to prevent the window from sticking. If the window does stick from paint runs, use a serrated tool called a *paint zipper* to cut away the paint run.

To form a moisture shield between the glass and the sash, overlap the paint about $1/8$-inch onto the glass, as shown in Figure 5-8. To successfully create a straight line, use a quality brush and thin paint as necessary. Wrap a clean cloth over the tip of a putty knife to clean the paint off the glass. To prevent paint smears, rewrap the knife often so that clean fabric covers the tip.

Whether to take the time to use masking tape to protect the glass from excess paint, or to paint carefully and then use a razor scraper to remove any goofs after the paint has dried, is a tough call. Most pros don't use tape on the windows unless they spray on the paint, but you may find that taping works better for you. To mask a window, apply the tape to the glass next to the sash, but leave a tiny gap between the tape and the sash. After positioning the tape, use the tip of a putty knife to press the paint edge of the tape firmly against the surface to prevent paint from seeping under the edge of the tape.

Figure 5-8:
Seal the joint between the window sash and the glass with paint. Apply paint to the wood and overlap on the glass about $1/8$ inch.

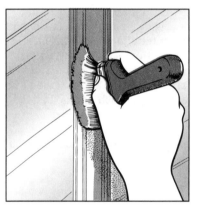

 Apply masking tape only on the day you plan to paint, not before, and remove the tape as soon as the paint is too dry to drip. If you leave the tape in place for a long period, the sun can bake the tape's adhesive, making the tape difficult to remove.

If you decide not to tape the windows, you can use a trim guard to protect the glass from your stray brush, but don't push too tightly against the sash. Remember that you must apply a bit of paint to the glass in order to seal the job.

 Some double-hung windows have removable sashes. If this is the case for the window you're painting, then removing the sashes from the window jamb to paint them will be easier than painting them in place. Follow the same procedures you use to remove the sash for cleaning the window, or consult the owner's manual — if you can find it. After the sash is out of the window, lay it flat on sawhorses or a workbench to paint it.

Painting Other Surfaces

Most of the text so far has covered prep and painting techniques for wood surfaces, but houses are covered with many other materials that can also use a coat of paint from time to time. The following sections discuss how to prep and paint these nonwood surfaces.

Painting aluminum siding

Aluminum siding is often advertised as maintenance-free, but the finish on aluminum siding fades and ages just as any other paint does. If the paint on the surface of your siding is intact but dull, clean the siding using any of the wood-cleaning products designed to renew wood decks.

If the siding finish still looks dull, use a sponge or paint pad to wipe on a coat of Penetrol, which is a paint conditioner. Buy a pint and test the Penetrol in an inconspicuous spot. If the Penetrol renews the luster of the paint, apply a coat over the entire siding surface. If you decide to paint the siding, Penetrol provides an excellent base for the paint. Use a quality exterior latex paint that indicates that it's approved for painting aluminum siding.

If the paint finish on the aluminum siding is excessively covered with chalky particles (refer to "Preparing Surfaces for Paint," earlier in this chapter), wash the surface to clean away as much chalked paint as possible. Then mix one quart of Emulsa-Bond (EB) in one gallon of latex paint, and paint the siding. If one coat doesn't cover the siding, apply a topcoat of latex paint without the additive.

Leave that vinyl alone

Unlike aluminum siding, vinyl siding does not have a surface coating of paint. Instead, the color of vinyl siding is continuous through the product. This peel-proof feature is one of the great advantages of vinyl siding — that is, unless you don't like the color. Because vinyl siding is very flexible and plastic, it doesn't take paint very well.

Don't consider painting your vinyl siding; the paint is sure to peel over time. Instead, clean vinyl siding with a solution of TSP (trisodium phosphate) and water. And whatever you do, never sand vinyl siding — you'll create a conspicuous rough spot.

Painting brick or stucco

You can paint brick, stucco, and the concrete foundation of a house with exterior flat latex paint. First, power wash the masonry surface to remove accumulated grime. Use a sprayer, long-nap roller, or rough-surface paint pad like the one shown in Figure 5-9 to paint a masonry surface.

Figure 5-9: Paint rough surfaces like stucco and cinderblock with a special long-bristled painting pad.

Think before you tamper with unpainted brick. Removing paint from brick or other masonry surfaces is nearly impossible. If you decide to take the plunge, use a flat latex house paint to cover the brick.

Because winter moisture passes through masonry walls and causes any paint to peel, stucco is not a good candidate for painting in cold climates. In many cases, masonry cleaner — available at any janitorial supply store — is all you need to renew a stucco surface. Apply the cleaner to lift the dirt, and then power wash the stucco. If the stucco still looks dingy, consider having a stucco contractor redash the finish. The contractor can either brush or spray a new cement surface onto the stucco. If you live in a warm climate, you can paint stucco with an acrylic latex product. Ask a paint dealer or stucco contractor about painting stucco in your area.

Painting metal surfaces

To prepare new metal for paint, wipe down the surface with mineral spirits to remove any residue left from manufacturing or shipping. Then apply a metal primer and allow the primer to dry. Primer drying time is listed on the label. To topcoat, use an alkyd paint product that's recommended for use on metal. Use a brush, roller, pad, or sprayer to apply the finish coat.

If the metal to be painted is rusty steel, use steel wool or a wire brush to remove any scaling or loose rust, as shown in Figure 5-10. Then prime with a rusty-metal primer. Topcoat with a finish product that's approved for use on metal.

Another option for painting rusty metal is to first apply a paint conditioner that locks down the rust and provides a good base for paint application. In repeated coats, apply as much as the rust can absorb. When the surface is dry, apply a coat of metal primer followed by a topcoat of quality alkyd or enamel paint.

Figure 5-10:
A stiff wire brush with a scraper on the end is great for removing loose or flaking paint from metal. For small areas, use an aerosol paint designed for metal.

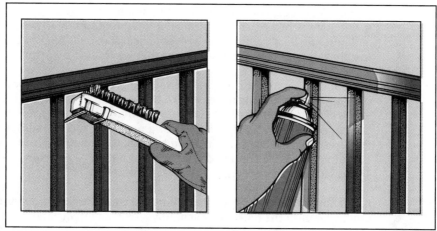

For spraying small metal areas, use an aerosol paint product that's prethinned to the proper viscosity or thickness for spraying. (See Figure 5-10.) Aerosols are almost foolproof if applied according to label directions.

If you're spraying a large metal area and you decide to use a paint sprayer, buy primer and paint that are intended for application on metal. Most oil-based paints must be thinned for spray application. The proper solvent and proportion for thinning is listed on the paint label. For a successful spray job, the nozzle pressure of the gun and the viscosity of the paint must be exactly right; you're wise to practice spraying on a piece of cardboard before starting the spray job.

Remember that metal is an unforgiving paint surface. Unlike wood, metal has no absorption powers. All the paint sprayed on the metal remains on the surface, so if you apply too much paint, expect runs and sags. Lay the paint on the metal in thin applications, making repeated passes over the surface. Don't panic if the metal isn't covered by the first pass of the sprayer: If you're using the paint as directed by the label, repeated coats eventually leave the finish job that you expect.

Whether you're spraying with an aerosol can or a paint sprayer, move the nozzle at a uniform speed parallel with the surface. Keep the nozzle about 8 to 12 inches from the surface, and release the trigger when you come to the edge of the surface. If you hold the trigger down when making a return pass, you double up the coat, spraying more paint on the edges than on the surface. The extra paint then overloads the edges.

Applying exterior varnish

You may choose to use a clear finish, such as varnish or polyurethane, to set off an entry door. This effect may look great, but be aware that any varnished surface that is exposed to direct sunlight and moisture requires more maintenance than a painted surface. It often requires yearly reapplication and periodic finish removal to prevent excessive buildup. Of course, a freshly varnished door looks so good that we think it's worth the effort.

If you have an exterior door whose varnish is peeling, first remove all the old finish. Use a chemical stripper to be sure that every bit of the old varnish is gone, and then sand the door smooth with 120-grit sandpaper. You can choose either a marine varnish or a polyurethane (plastic) finish. Polyurethane finishes contain a combination of radiation absorbers to block ultraviolet rays, plus antioxidants to retard fading — basically, a sunscreen. To provide full protection, apply at least two coats of finish.

If you have an exterior door that's finished with varnish or polyurethane, don't wait until the finish looks shabby to refinish it. Instead, apply a new coat of finish once a year. Just sand the door lightly with fine sandpaper, wipe away the dust, and apply one coat of new finish. If done on an annual basis, the job takes only about an hour.

Cleaning Up

The proper solvent for cleaning up latex paints is warm, soapy water. Mineral spirits or paint thinner are the best solvents for cleaning alkyd paints, enamels, varnishes, or oil-based stains. Use denatured alcohol to clean up alcohol-based coatings, such as some fast-drying primers.

To limit cleanup time, cover any surface that you don't want painted. Clean paint spills and spatters immediately, before they dry. Use a brush or sponge soaked in the proper solvent to pick up any paint spills.

Although soapy water removes most latex paint from brushes or rollers, some paint residue is often left behind. After cleaning latex paint with water, rinse the tool with brush cleaner. You may be surprised by the amount of paint left in the tool after you wash with water alone.

Chapter 6

Refinishing and Staining Wood

In This Chapter

▶ Refurbishing, refinishing, and stripping wood

▶ Cleaning handles, hinges, knobs, and whatnot

▶ Staining, whitewashing, pickling, and painting bare wood

*I*s your house full of woodwork that you're itching to refinish or paint? Do you have a yard-sale desk that's a Cinderella story waiting to happen? Perhaps the seemingly overwhelming prospect of stripping and refinishing these items keeps you from lifting a finger in their direction.

First, don't assume that you have to strip off the old finish; sometimes, a good cleaning is all it takes to restore wood to a like-new luster. If a full-fledged refinishing *is* necessary, don't despair. This chapter contains all the information you need for stripping and staining woodwork and wooden furniture. It also shows you how to create your own special effects with stain and paint.

Refurbishing and Refinishing

The approaches to transforming wood fall into three basic categories:

✔ **Refurbishing:** Renewing or refreshing the existing finish

✔ **Refinishing:** Removing the surface finish and replacing it with another finish

✔ **Stripping:** Taking all the finish out of the wood, leaving no surface color whatsoever

These three processes are progressively more difficult, messy, and time-consuming. So if you can salvage a piece by refurbishing or refinishing alone, consider yourself lucky.

Start with a good cleaning

Over time, both woodwork and furniture can accumulate a buildup of wax, cooking grease, and grime. If wood begins to look dark or dirty, don't assume that you have to strip and refinish it. First, give it a thorough cleaning to determine the condition of the original finish.

To remove old wax and grime, follow these steps:

1. **Soak a clean cotton cloth in a solvent, such as odorless mineral spirits.**

   Mineral spirits, available at any paint store or paint department, are excellent for removing wax and grease. Saturate the center of a clean cotton rag (an old tee-shirt, sock, or washcloth will do) with mineral spirits poured straight from the can.

   If you're working indoors, open the windows to provide cross-ventilation, because the fumes can be irritating to your senses. Built-up fumes can also be explosive, so turn off all pilot lights in the area.

2. **Clean a small area of the wood by wiping on the mineral spirits and then wiping away the residue with a clean, dry cloth.**

   Choose an inconspicuous area, like the underside of a table, to test the results of using mineral spirits before trying it on the rest of the surface.

3. **If the finish appears intact in the test area, proceed with the cleaning until the entire project is renewed.**

   In the case of a heavy wax or grime buildup, you may have to do a second or third application of mineral spirits.

4. **If you see spots where the finish has worn off, apply a coat of matching stain to the worn areas.**

   For the details on this process, refer to "Staining Things . . . on Purpose," later in this chapter.

If you're happy with the results of your work, you can give the wood a topcoat of a clear wipe-on finish that protects the wood while letting the original color of the wood show through. If, after following these steps, the surface still looks a bit shabby, you may have to move on to Plan B: refinishing.

Resigning yourself to refinishing

Sometimes, even a good cleaning isn't enough to bring old wood surfaces back to life. Refurbishing wood takes off the dirt and dull finish, but it doesn't work miracles. If the wood has one of the following problems, you may have to remove the existing clear finish — but not necessarily strip the color (stain) from the wood:

- ✔ The finish is marked by extensive and random cracking, like the skin of an alligator.
- ✔ The surface has white hazing or stains from water damage.
- ✔ The clear finish is peeling from the base coats.

Choosing your poison

To remove finishes from wood, you need a *paint stripper* (also called a varnish remover) or an *antique refinisher* (also sold as furniture refinisher). Paint stripper removes polyurethane or paint finish. Antique refinisher removes shellac, varnish, or lacquer finish. Both products are sold in quart and gallon containers in the paint department of home centers and hardware stores.

To determine the type of finish on the wood, first test the finish in an inconspicuous spot, as shown in Figure 6-1. Pour fingernail polish remover (which contains acetone) or a refinisher product on a cotton ball or clean cloth and apply it to the finish. If the finish softens within a few minutes, it's lacquer, varnish, or shellac. These finishes can be refurbished with one of the many refinisher products. If the finish does not soften from the polish remover, it's probably a polyurethane, and you must use a paint remover to strip the wood.

Figure 6-1:
To determine the type of finish, perform a nail-polish test on an inconspicuous area.

Many refinishers, strippers, and solvents contain mineral spirits and other chemicals that may be hazardous if improperly used. Always read the warnings on the label of any chemical product you use, and keep these safety precautions in mind:

- ✔ If a label says to use the product with *adequate ventilation,* work with this substance only outdoors or in well-ventilated rooms. Most paint-removing products are too caustic to be used in a basement area where there's little ventilation.

- ✔ Do not use these products near flame or fire; be sure to extinguish nearby pilot lights. Remember that the fumes of flammable materials are also flammable.

- ✔ Do not smoke, eat, or drink when using any paint product, and remember that the fumes of toxic materials are also toxic. Wear an approved respirator mask when using materials that produce fumes.

- ✔ Dispose of rags that have come into contact with these substances by placing them in a water-filled metal container. Dispose of leftover materials at an approved disposal location or according to label directions.

Instead of relying on these harsh, toxic products, you can try stripping gels and semipaste removers that are nonflammable, nontoxic, and biodegradable. These environmentally friendly products are designed to remove latex or oil-based paint or varnish. They have no harmful fumes, cleanup is easy with soap and water, and you don't even need to wear protective gloves! Because they wash off with water, these products are often referred to as *water-wash* strippers. Years ago, you had to hunt for these products, but today several brands are available in paint stores and the paint sections of home centers and hardware stores.

Stocking up on supplies

Here's a rundown of the other materials and tools you need to refinish wood:

- ✔ Fine steel wool (0000 grade)

- ✔ Various soft brushes, including a 2-inch brush and old toothbrushes for removing the finish from intricate designs

- ✔ A protective apron made of a heavy fabric like canvas or denim to cover your clothes

- ✔ Clean, lint-free cloths and/or tack cloths

- ✔ Rubber (not latex) gloves

- ✔ Eye protection, such as glasses or safety goggles

- ✔ Sandpaper in 220 and 440 grits

- ✔ A putty knife and/or a plastic stripping tool

- ✔ Dropcloths for protecting walls, floors, and so on from splatters

If you have worn-out white sheets or shirts, cut them into suitable sizes to make paint rags or cloths. To prevent scratching the finish, remove any buttons or zippers from old clothing. You can also buy painters' cloths by the pound from paint stores or home centers.

Refinishing, step-by-step

To avoid a fire or explosion, don't use refinishing products near a flame (including a pilot light or furnace). Also, any paint remover or cleaner product that contains chlorine can damage a furnace if the chlorine is drawn into the combustion chamber. The chlorine may combine with hydrogen during the combustion process, forming hydrochloric acid (HCL), which can destroy the furnace heat exchanger. When using these products, turn off the furnace and open doors and windows. Do not use paint or remover products in a basement or furnace room. If the fixtures you want to strip are located in an unventilated room, remove them and strip them elsewhere and reinstall them when the stripping is complete.

When using any furniture refinisher, always follow the manufacturer's recommendations. Here are some guidelines about what the process involves:

1. **Protect the surrounding area with heavy (4 mil) plastic dropcloths that are covered by unfolded newspaper in layers of five to six sheets.**

2. **Pour about a cup of refinisher in a coffee can.**

   If you stop working, cover the can with a lid to contain the fumes.

3. **Tear a steel wool pad in half, and then dip it into the refinisher.**

4. **Squeeze the steel wool pad to remove any excess refinisher, and then apply it to a square-foot area, working in a circular motion.**

   As you pick up residue, rinse the steel wool in the refinisher and squeeze away the excess.

   To reach into the crevices of moldings or any intricate carvings, use a toothbrush, or twist strands of steel wool around a stout piece of string or twine, as shown in Figure 6-2. For narrow grooves, use the string alone.

5. **Continue cleaning with the steel wool until the old finish is removed.**

   As one area is cleaned move to the next area and repeat the process, overlapping the work areas as you proceed. Replace the steel wood pads as they become worn or saturated with the old finish.

6. **After you remove all the old finish, dip a clean steel wool pad into a clean supply of refinisher and wipe the wood to clean any residue off the surface.**

Figure 6-2:
Use a steel wool pad soaked in refinisher to wipe the surface; twist steel wool into a thin strand or wrap it around a piece of string to clean small grooves and crevices.

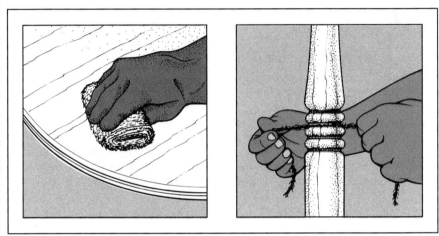

Using long strokes, wipe the surface of wood in the direction of its grain (wood pattern). To lighten the wood tone, use repeated strokes.

7. Allow the wood to dry thoroughly, ideally overnight.

8. Using a clean cotton rag, gently rub one or more coats of antique oil or tung oil into the wood.

These products, available in most paint departments, protect the wood while bringing out its natural color. Follow the specific manufacturer's directions. Some products tell you to apply the oil and then let it dry; others tell you to apply the oil and then buff it with another clean rag to make the wood shine. In either case, as the oil dries on the wood, it creates a hard, protective finish.

The preceding instructions apply to both furniture and woodwork. Follow these steps to refurbish and refinish wood cabinets, trim, ceiling beams, crown or cove moldings, windows, or built-in furniture.

If you're working on a window or molding, choose a gel-like or semi-paste stripper. Unlike liquid refinishers, these thicker products won't drip off the surface and damage surrounding areas.

Stripping Down to the Bare Wood

If you decide to change the wood's finish or tone, you must strip the project down to bare wood. Professional paint strippers have large tanks full of chemical stripper so that they can completely submerge an entire piece of furniture in the liquid. The problem with this approach is that immersing the item may cause a failure of the old glue and loosen the joints like chair rungs or legs. The alternative is to do the paint stripping yourself, in a well-ventilated area.

Stripping paint is never an easy job, but you can reduce the work and the mess by following the manufacturer's directions and reading the following information and advice.

Making repairs before stripping

Before you start stripping furniture, examine the project for any damage. If any regluing is required to repair the object, do so before stripping the finish away. When glue is applied to bare wood, it acts as a sealer; glue spots don't absorb stains. If you reglue the project before stripping, the stripper will remove any residue the glue leaves behind.

If veneer has loosened, you may be able to reactivate the glue with steam. First make a razor cut (with, not against, the grain) to allow steam to penetrate beneath the veneer. Hold a clean cloth over the loose veneer and then apply heat from a steam iron. This trick doesn't always work. If it does, secure the area with a stack of books or any heavy, flat object larger than the repair area.

If heat application does not cure the problem, inject or brush on white carpenter's glue underneath the veneer, as shown in Figure 6-3, and then press the veneer in place. Remove any excess glue from the surface of the veneer. If the repair area is flat, cover the repair area with wax paper or aluminum foil and lay a heavy object over the area until the glue dries, usually overnight. If the repair area is curved, tie a rope tourniquet-style around the project to serve as a clamp.

If the veneer itself is split in several places or has missing pieces, you can take the piece to an expert who replaces or repairs veneer. The price for this service varies, based on the size and complexity of the job. It may be worthwhile for a family heirloom or treasured piece of furniture, but not for your ordinary flea-market finds.

Figure 6-3:
Repair veneer along an edge by lifting it from the base, applying white glue, and laying a heavy object on it until the glue dries.

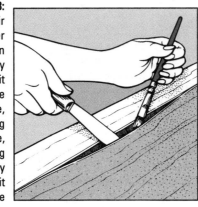

To reglue loose rungs or legs, remove the loose parts from the chair or table and clean away the old glue. You may have to be ingenious if the glue is tucked into a small crevice or difficult to reach. Try using a small piece of sandpaper, a wood scraper, or even an emery board to scrape or sand away the old glue. Recoat the glued surfaces with white carpenter's glue and replace the part. To clamp the piece together, tie a soft rope, such as clothesline, around the legs, making a double loop. Place a scrap of wood between the two loops and twist the wood to tighten the rope clamp, as shown in Figure 6-4. Let the project sit overnight, until the glue is dry.

After you complete all the necessary regluing, you're ready to begin stripping the piece.

Figure 6-4:
Loop a light rope several times around the legs and tie it off. Insert a stick between the loops and turn to tighten them.

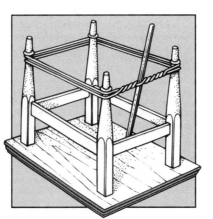

Choosing your stripper (It's not as fun as it sounds!)

Wood strippers come in two basic types, and which one you choose depends on the project you're stripping:

> ✔ *Semi-paste strippers* are the best choice for tough jobs like removing epoxies, polyurethane, enamel, or marine finishes, or when multiple layers of paint or finish must be removed. Use either a brushable semipaste or a heavy-bodied remover for stripping vertical surfaces, such as the side panels of chests or the legs of a chair or table.

> ✔ *Spray strippers* are available in aerosol cans for small projects. They're not a good choice for large projects, but they are useful for removing a finish from a difficult-to-reach area like an intricate molding on a wall. When you use spray strippers on a small area, be sure to carefully mask and protect the adjoining surfaces so that no spray gets on them.

If in doubt, explain your project to the dealer and ask for help choosing the right stripper.

Preparing for the task

To make a project easier to strip, remove any hardware, doors, or legs (if they're attached with hardware rather than glue). Lay doors, panels, and so on a flat surface, such as between sawhorses, for stripping. You can lay smaller pieces on a workbench or old table if you raise them up on scrap lumber or bricks and place a protective dropcloth beneath.

Use plastic dropcloths to protect the floor and other surfaces from the stripper. If you're stripping furniture legs, place the bottom of the legs in shallow cans to catch any sludge that drips down the leg.

Paint stripper must remain wet on a surface long enough to dissolve the old finish. Work outdoors if you can, but never work in direct sunlight or where a breeze is blowing. Sunlight or moving air can dry the stripper before the paint is dissolved.

Laying it on . . . and taking it off

Follow these steps for applying stripper and removing it (hopefully along with the old paint):

1. **Shake the can to mix the stripper.**

   Open the lid very slowly to permit built-up pressure to escape.

2. **Lay on a heavy coat of stripper with a *stripping pad* (an item that looks like a scouring pad) or a soft brush.**

   Don't brush out the stripper as you would paint; instead, flow on a generous amount, stroking in one direction only, and do not brush back over it.

   When you're working on the vertical surfaces of chair or table legs, you may be tempted to skimp on the stripper because you're afraid of messy drips running down the sides. Instead, place wide-mouthed metal containers, such as cat-food cans, under each leg to contain drips; then go ahead and really lay the stuff on. (See Figure 6-5.)

Figure 6-5:
To catch drips of stripper, place table or chair legs in empty cans.

3. **Let the stripper work for the time specified on the label.**

   The amount of time you have to wait is usually between 5 and 45 minutes, depending on the age, type, and number of coats of finish. If you're stripping a small item, you may be able to apply the stripper and then place the piece in a large plastic garbage bag and tie the top to keep the stripper wet for a long time.

   Don't rush the project; let the stripper do its job. It's tempting to begin scraping before the stripper has had time to loosen the paint, but you end up having to do more work that way. Instead, be patient and don't scrape until the paint bubbles up from the surface of the wood.

4. **Test the finish with a paint scraper.**

   Plastic scrapers work best because they don't scratch the wood. You can tell that the paint is ready to be removed when it readily lifts off the surface as you gently push the scraper under it. If the paint doesn't come up easily, it's not ready for scraping. Wait and try the scraper again later. If the paint doesn't budge, apply another layer of the stripper.

5. Scrape, scrape, scrape.

This is the messy tedious part of the job. Push the scraper through the layers of paint, working on one area at a time, like the bottom of a table or the front of a drawer. When stripping vertical surfaces, work from the bottom upwards. As you remove sludge from the wood, deposit it in a metal container. Keep your scraper clean by wiping off the excess into the container.

For spindles or other intricate areas, twist strands of premium-grade steel wool into a rope, wrap the steel wool around the grooves, and use a sawing motion to remove the old finish (refer to Figure 6-2). Check the label to be sure that the stripper you're using doesn't react with steel wool. Optional tools range from an old toothbrush (see Figure 6-6) to specially designed stripping tools available at paint dealers.

Before painting the woodwork in our old house, we had to remove *beaucoup* layers of paint. The woodwork was 4-inches wide and milled with a concave curve and grooved detail. To remove the paint on the uneven surface, we found the handiest tools right in our own wood-working shop: a set of cabinet scrapers. The tools are thin, flat pieces of steel that come in various shapes. After the stripper raised the paint from the surface, the scrapers worked well in removing it.

If the old finish is stubborn, you may have to apply repeated coats of stripper.

6. Scrub away any stripper residue.

- If you used a nontoxic stripping gel (sometimes called *water-wash stripper*), dip a stripping pad or brush in warm soapy water and scrub away the residue. Remember that the water may swell the fibers of the wood or loosen the glue joints. The best approach is to scrape the old finish away first, and then use a wash product to remove any remaining residue.

- If you used a standard chemical stripper, remove the residue with an after-wash product. Like mineral spirits, after-wash removes the residue left by paint removers and is best applied while the surface is still damp from stripping. Pour some after-wash liquid into a wide-mouthed container and dip a piece of fine-grade steel wool into it. Wipe the steel wool back and forth on the surface, following the grain of the wood.

7. Clean up your tools and remove all the materials you used, including dropcloths, and rags.

Remember that materials soaked in paint chemicals can ignite spontaneously. Leave used rags, steel wool, papers, or other materials outside in the open air to dry. Only after they are dry, place them in a metal container that has a tight-fitting lid. Follow label directions or call the refuse or garbage disposal department of your town or county office for instructions about disposal of used or leftover stripper.

Figure 6-6:
Allow the stripper to soften the finish and then scrape off the loose paint or varnish. An old toothbrush works great for removing finish from hard-to-reach areas.

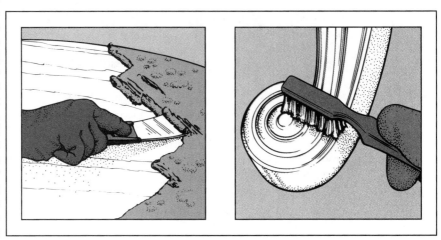

Making repairs after stripping

After you strip the wood, but before you begin refinishing it, inspect the surface for any damage. If the wood is dented, you can often lift the wood fiber to reduce or eliminate the dent. Try laying a cloth over the dent and then heating the area with a steam iron, as shown in Figure 6-7. Or spray a few drops of hot water into the dent and let it stand. If the dent is deep, fill it with wood putty or a patching compound. After the patch has hardened, sand it smooth.

Figure 6-7:
To raise a shallow dent in a wood surface, place a damp rag on the area and heat with a hot iron.

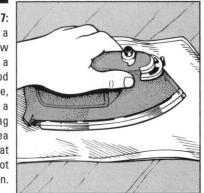

Wood putty and filler are pastelike substances that fill in gaps between the fibers of the wood, blending with the fibers to create a smooth surface. Use a 1½-inch putty knife to apply the substance and gently work it into the wood fibers. Tinted wood putty is also available in a variety of woodlike shades to help blend with the existing color. To tint putty yourself, take a small paint stick and drag it across the bottom of a can of stain to remove some of the pigment that has settled there. On a trial-and-error basis, blend the pigment into putty until you create a good match with the wood.

Another alternative is a wood-putty marker, similar in design to familiar ink marking pens. Wood-putty markers have the same angled felt-tip applicator, and are a good choice for filling in thin gaps in the wood's surface.

If dark stains appear on the wood (usually the result of water damage), first try removing them with another application of stripper. If the stain persists, you can use oxalic acid (available at paint stores) to bleach it out. Be aware that oxalic acid causes wood to lose all its natural color. Instead of a dark stain, you end up with a colorless patch of wood that you have to stain to match the original wood. So if you have dark stains to remove, plan on restaining the whole piece for a uniform look.

Mix the oxalic acid crystals with water according to the manufacturer's directions, soak a clean cloth in the acid solution, and lay the cloth on top of the stain. Wait ten minutes for the bleach to work and then lift the cloth to see whether the stain is gone. If it isn't, replace the cloth and repeat the treatment until the stain is removed.

Oxalic acid is poisonous, so store any leftover crystals in a safe place away from children, or dispose of the product completely. Wear heavy rubber gloves to protect your hands when working with this product.

Sanding down the surface

After the old finish is stripped away and repairs are complete, examine the project. If you find nicks or scratches, or if the wood grain feels fuzzy or rough, now's the time to sand away these problems. In addition to smoothing scratches, sanding also removes the very thin top layer of wood so that stains can penetrate more evenly.

Use a fine (120-grit or finer) garnet paper to sand the piece. Follow the pattern of the wood as you sand; if you sand across the grain, you may scratch the surface. Cut sandpaper into strips to sand round leg spindles, as shown in Figure 6-8. Cover your free hand with a sock or a pair of pantyhose and wipe it over the surface as you sand. The sock or hose will snag on rough spots, letting you know which areas need more attention.

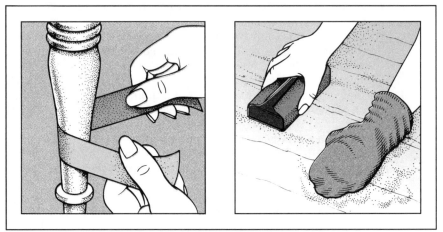

Figure 6-8:
Make a narrow strip of cloth-backed sandpaper to get into small areas. Run a sock or nylon over the surface to catch rough patches.

You can make your own hand-sanding block with a piece of wood that fits comfortably in the palm of your hand. Cut a piece of sandpaper (approximately 3 inches wide by 12 inches long) to wrap around the wood block. When one section of the sandpaper is used up, refold it and use the other section.

An electric palm sander (or *random-orbit* sander) is an ideal tool for flat surfaces like the top of a table or the sides of a chest of drawers. This hand-held specialty sander costs around $30 or more, but is well worth the investment if you have a great deal of sanding to do. Electric palm sanders are designed to use a quarter of a sheet of sandpaper, and most have an attached dust bag that helps contain the sanding particles.

If you're refinishing a piece of fine furniture, avoid sanding unless absolutely necessary. Sanding removes the fine patina of age, and may lower the piece's value.

Staining Things . . . on Purpose

Stains are available in a wide variety of wood tones, as well as pastels. Your paint dealer probably has samples so that you can see how the various stains look on real wood. Let your décor and your tastes determine which is stain is best for you. For nicely grained wood such as oak, a good choice is to use a stain that enhances the grain pattern. For furniture made of less attractive wood or mismatched pieces of wood; pastels are a good choice, because they conceal the grain of the wood.

Also, you can mix different wood stains together to make your own unique stain. If you decide to experiment by mixing stains together, mix enough stain to do the entire job. Measure the proportions carefully, because if you run out of custom stain in the middle of a project, it's difficult to match that color or tone exactly. If you accurately measure the proportions, you can remix another batch of the stain without trying to reinvent the recipe.

You can make your own stain by thinning any alkyd paint with mineral spirits. For example, for a deep black stain, thin flat black alkyd paint with mineral spirits. Start with a quart of black paint and a quart of mineral spirits, and then add more mineral spirits, testing often on scrap wood until you get just the result you want.

Pine and other softwoods tend to have uneven grains that absorb stain unevenly, creating a blotchy appearance. To prepare softwood for staining, first apply a coat of wood conditioner designed to control stain penetration and help you achieve a uniform stain job.

The way you apply the stain depends on the results you want to achieve. One option is to use a sponge or folded cloth to wipe on a stain product, and then apply a finish or topcoat of sealer, varnish, shellac, or polyurethane. Polyurethane is quick drying and provides a durable finish, so it has become the popular choice, replacing the varnishes and shellacs of yesteryear. Polyurethane is available in both satin and gloss sheens.

Another wood-finishing option is to use a product that combines a stain and a durable polyurethane finish in one application. Multiple coats of this product give the wood a deeper color and a more durable finish. Sand lightly between coats. Other options include using polyurethane finish alone, for a natural wood tone on bare wood. Or you can apply a stain, followed by a topcoat of tung oil or paste wax, both of which provide a durable finish that protects the wood and its finish.

When finishing furniture or cabinets, coat all wood surfaces including the inside of drawers and doors to prevent the wood from warping. If you have warped cabinet doors, try this painter's trick: Lay the door on a flat surface, with the bowed side up, and stack books or other weights on the door. Leave the weights in place until the door straightens. Then apply an extra coat of finish to the inside of the door to prevent moisture from penetrating into the surface of the wood and causing warpage.

The process for staining and finishing wood is the same whether the wood is new or stripped:

1. **Wear rubber gloves to protect your hands from the stain.**

2. **Pour a small amount of stain into an open pan or a paint roller tray.**

3. **Dip a clean sponge, cloth, or paintbrush into the stain and squeeze out the excess.**

   The pigment in the stain settles to the bottom of the can after several hours. For a more uniform stain job, stir the stain at regular intervals.

Assembly-line staining for new woodwork

If you're adding new trim or molding to a house, or installing wood ceiling beams, try this trick to reduce staining time. First lay all the trim or molding across two sawhorses. Using the sponge- or cloth-wiping method described in the previous steps, wipe the stain on the pieces and then nail them into place. This way, you can avoid working overhead with messy stain, and you can get the job done without having to protect walls, ceilings, or other surfaces from drips or spills. You can also apply the polyurethane finish at this point, or use a combination stain/polyurethane product.

After you install the trim or molding, use a small brush to touch up at cut ends. Also, after you nail the trim in place, mix a small amount of stain with the wood putty you plan to use to fill nail holes. This ensures that the wood putty matches the stain on the wood.

4. **Using long, continuous strokes, apply the stain to a small area at a time, following the grain pattern of the wood as shown in Figure 6-9.**

5. **Wipe the wet stain with a clean, dry cloth to even out the application and to remove excess stain.**

   Repeat for a darker tone.

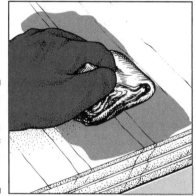

Figure 6-9:
Apply stain in the direction of the wood grain.

Cleaning the Hardware

Wood isn't the only part of furniture that needs cleaning and refurbishing. The metal knobs, pulls, handles, hinges, and other goodies attached to wood furniture and doors and windows also become mired in paint, grime, or varnish.

Remove the hardware to refurbish it — you may need a screwdriver for this job. If the hardware is small and intricate, have an old toothbrush on hand to use as an applicator. Choose between using a brass refurbisher or paint stripper; both products remove tarnish, grime, clear finishes, and paints from brass, copper, and bronze. Prepare a work area where you can keep the pieces of hardware together and protect the surrounding area from the remover. We like to use a tray made of a heavy box with the sides cut down.

Follow these steps to clean hardware with brass refurbisher:

1. **With a bristle brush, apply a good coating of liquid brass refurbisher to the hardware.**

2. **Let refurbisher work for 5 to 10 minutes.**

3. **Wipe off the refurbisher with a clean rag or cotton ball, as shown in Figure 6-10.**

   You may need to make more than one application to remove several layers of paint or grime.

4. **When all the residue is removed, buff the hardware dry with a clean cloth.**

Figure 6-10:
Spruce up old hardware by stripping off paint or grime with a brass refurbisher.

Follow these steps to clean hardware with paint stripper:

1. **Soak the hardware in paint stripper.**

2. **Wait until the stripper begins to bubble up or pull away from the surface.**

3. **Wearing rubber gloves, use a stiff brush to remove the old paint or finish.**

   This process is similar to stripping wood, except that pieces of hardware are usually smaller and, therefore, require more intricate work.

 4. Use an after-wash product to remove the stripper residue.

 5. Let the hardware dry thoroughly.

 6. Buff the surface with a clean, dry cloth.

Both of the preceding treatments work for cleaning any hardware that's *solid* brass, copper, or bronze. To test whether the piece is solid metal or plated steel, hold a strong magnet near the item. Solid brass, copper, and bronze do not attract magnets; plated steel does. If you determine that the piece is plated steel, test a small area with the brass refurbisher. If the refurbisher cleans the piece without removing the plating, continue to clean the piece. If the refurbisher removes the plating, use ordinary metal cleaners, instead, to clean the piece. Copper, bronze, and brass finishes are also available in aerosol cans if you find that you need to replace some of the plating.

If the hardware doesn't seem worth cleaning and refurbishing, spring for new hardware to dress up the furniture.

Adding Special Finishes for Decoration

You can't walk into a furniture store and not notice the dramatic change. Never before have so many styles and colorful finishes been available. Sure, manufacturers still sell wood-tone furnishings, but now they also offer a wide range of special finishes.

Some popular finishes make it easier than ever to disguise an inexpensive piece of unfinished furniture into a showpiece. We've had success using two such finishes — whitewashing and pickling — when a project called for something special.

The two treatments in this section are not like the typical stains we discuss elsewhere in this chapter. They're less-than-ordinary finishes that are great for transforming unfinished or bare wood. *Whitewashing* produces a fresh-from-the-country, washed-out appearance. *Pickling* produces the same weathered effect, but it uses dye to add color. Both finishes are easy to apply, and they create an attractive alternative to paint, stains, and finishes.

Whitewashing bare wood

To add a pastel or white shade to bare wood, whitewash it with alkyd paint and give it a topcoat of polyurethane. Wear rubber gloves and old clothes — this is a messy project.

The washed-out, weather-beaten effect is easy to achieve, but you may want to experiment with the look you want, first. Practice on the bottom or back of the wood so that you know how much pressure to apply on the real thing.

Working in small sections, no more than 3 feet wide, apply the paint with a wide brush and then quickly rub it off with burlap rags. The rough surface of the burlap gives the wood a sort of skim coat of color. Work from the top to bottom, following the grain of wood, and wipe away the excess paint while rubbing the color into the surface. When the wood has just the right splash of color, allow it to dry completely. Then apply a topcoat of polyurethane for protection.

Fabric stores sell burlap in 48- to 54-inch widths. Half a yard is plenty for whitewashing a chest of drawers; you can buy less if you're doing a smaller project. Choose the colorless natural shade of burlap so there's no chance of the cloth's color bleeding into the paint.

Pickling bare wood with dye

You can achieve a colorful finish by using dye to glaze, or *pickle,* the wood. You apply the dye over a base coat of flat, white latex paint, so the effect is more subtle and softer-looking than using wood stain. Like whitewashing, pickling works best when you start with bare wood, unfinished wood, or old wood that's been stripped of its paint or varnish.

To achieve a pickled finish, follow these steps:

1. **Use a 3-inch-wide foam brush to apply a coat of flat, white latex paint.**

   The thinner the paint you use, the more wood grain you can expect to show through on the final product.

   Foam brushes resemble regular paint brushes, but have a tapered foam applicator. Because they're inexpensive and disposable, foam brushes are ideal for touching up small areas and for decorative finishes like this one.

2. **Immediately after applying the base coat of paint, wipe it off with a rag.**

   Wipe off the paint before it starts to get tacky on the surface of the piece. You want to remove most of the paint leaving only a translucent white film on the wood. See Figure 6-11.

3. **Allow this first coat to dry overnight.**

4. **Pour liquid dye into a Styrofoam food tray.**

   Liquid dyes come in a rainbow of colors, and are available at hardware stores, craft centers, and even some groceries.

5. **Apply the dye with a foam brush, and immediately wipe off the excess with a dry rag.**

   Apply the dye following the direction of the wood grain and turn the rag frequently. Replace the rag with a fresh one when it fills up with dye. Use a small, angled foam brush to dab the dye into tight spaces like corners and grooves, and use another brush to remove any excess.

6. **Let the dye dry completely.**

7. **Apply a topcoat of polyurethane for a hard, protective finish.**

Figure 6-11:
Before pickling wood with dye, paint on and wipe off a light coat of white latex paint.

A. Apply a light coat of white latex paint. (Step 1)

B. Use a clean, dry rag to wipe off the paint before it gets tacky. (Step 2)

Stenciling walls and furniture

Introduce color and design to your walls, floors, or furniture by using an artform called *stenciling.* For a simple first-time job, stencil a pattern on top of a bench or door. Or stencil a simple border at the ceiling of a room or around a fireplace, or as wainscoting over the painted walls. The opportunities are endless.

To create the design, first choose a stencil pattern that's cut out on a clear acetate sheet. A simple design may involve only one sheet; more complicated artistry requires several overlays. You can find ready-made stencils in a wide variety of patterns and designs — including geometric shapes, flowers, and wildlife — at paint, decorating, and craft stores. These precut acetate stencils not only give you a design, but also show registration holes where you align the pattern as you relocate the stencil along the wall.

Use any quick-drying paint — acrylics are a good choice because they come in many colors and are quick to dry and clean up. And while you're shopping, pick up a stencil brush, drafter's masking tape, and spray-mount adhesive. You also need Styrofoam food trays and some scraps of felt or paper towels.

Don't forget to put dropcloths down where you're working — in case your brush drips.

Here are the basics of stenciling a room border:

1. **Beginning at a corner of the room, measure down from the ceiling to the point where you want the top of the stencil to be.**

   With a light pencil, mark this point on each wall.

2. **Use a carpenter's level to draw a level line connecting these marks around the room, as shown in Figure 6-12.**

   If you live in an older house where the walls are way out of kilter, measure the same distance from the ceiling and connect the lines with a straight edge, rather than relying on a level.

3. **Align the edge of the acetate with the pencil line and attach it to the wall with spray adhesive or masking tape.**

   To ensure that you begin a new section where the last one ended you can cut a small V-shaped nick in the acetate and use it as an easy reference point as you make your way around the room. Some acetates have precut registration holes, which makes aligning them easy.

4. **Pour each color of paint into a readily available foam tray.**

   You actually use very little paint as you stencil, but most patterns require more than one color. For example, a floral design may use green for the leaves, two shades of pink for flowers, and brown for the stem.

5. **Begin by dipping the brush in the paint and blotting it in felt or paper toweling to remove the excess.**

6. **Dab (don't brush) the paint inside the cutout of the design, working your way in from its edges and filling the center of the design last.**

   The stencil brush is round and squat, making it easy to dab paint inside the cutout design, as shown in Figure 6-12.

   Don't drag the stencil brush over the stencil or you may drive paint under the stencil.

7. **When you finish painting in all the cutouts, remove the acetate from the wall.**

   The paint dries very quickly, but still use caution when removing the acetate to avoid smudging.

8. **Wipe off any paint from the backside of the acetate, and then realign and mount the stencil on the wall with the adhesive.**

9. **Repeat this process until the design is complete.**

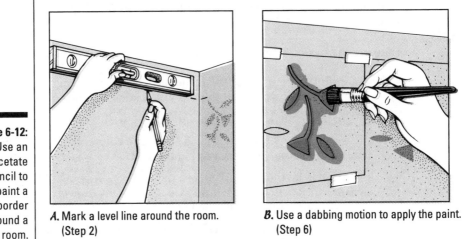

Figure 6-12:
Use an acetate stencil to paint a border around a room.

A. Mark a level line around the room. (Step 2)

B. Use a dabbing motion to apply the paint. (Step 6)

Furniture-Painting Primer

You can find real bargains at yard sales and unpainted-furniture stores. New furniture is easy to paint, because it doesn't have any problem surfaces or coatings to interfere with the application. But painting old furniture has its advantages because you don't have to strip off the old finish first. Alkyd (oil-based) paint is more resistant to wear than water-based latex paint, making it a better choice for layering onto your prized finds.

Alkyd paints are available in flat, semigloss, and gloss sheens. Choose the sheen to match or contrast with other furniture in the room. Remember that flat finishes do not reflect light and can therefore help conceal blemishes; gloss paints are durable and easy to clean, and notorious for highlighting any nicks or tool marks in the wood.

Painting unfinished wood

When painting wood, be sure to keep your work area clean. Choose a place that's free of drafts and airborne dirt to prevent dust and lint from settling on the wet paint surface. If you're painting indoors in cold weather, heat the room up to a comfortable working temperature and then turn off the thermostat. Doing so prevents the furnace from cycling on and causing dust-laden drafts from the furnace blower.

Painting bare wood may sound like a no-brainer, but getting professional-looking results calls for a lot of prep work, as shown in Figure 6-13. For a stellar paint job, follow these steps meticulously:

1. **Use fine 220-grit sandpaper to buff any smudges or tool marks off the wood.**

2. **Clean off any dust and grit left by sanding.**

   Wipe the piece down with a rag lightly dampened with mineral spirits or with a *tack rag* (a sticky cheesecloth designed to pick up dust and lint).

3. **Apply an alkyd primer to seal the grain of the wood.**

   By priming the wood first, you ensure that the final coat of paint is absorbed uniformly over knots and open or soft grain. For a topcoat with an even sheen free of brush marks, use a 2-inch-wide brush or painting pad to apply both primer and paint.

4. **Let the primer coat dry completely per the label directions.**

5. **When the primer is dry, sand the surface with 220-grit sandpaper.**

6. **Again, use a tack cloth to remove any dust.**

7. **Apply the first coat of paint, and allow it to dry.**

8. **After the first coat of paint is dry, again sand the project and wipe it clean.**

9. **Apply a second coat of paint.**

   Choose a fast-drying finish to reduce drying time and exposure to dust.

Figure 6-13:
Before painting bare wood, buff all the surfaces with sanding block, clean off the dust, and seal the surface with a coat of primer.

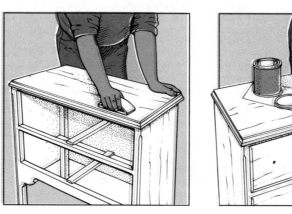

For best results, set up your work area in a room with good overhead lighting. Add side lighting with a portable lamp to highlight any flaws or missed spots as you apply the paint as shown in Figure 6-14. Strong side lighting is important because paint often runs at corners on furniture or at the junctures between two members, like where the rungs meet the legs on chairs. As you paint, frequently inspect areas you already painted; check for runs and catch them with the brush.

Figure 6-14: Strong side lighting helps highlight flaws as you paint.

Painting over already-painted furniture

The procedure for painting already-painted furniture is basically the same as for painting bare wood. If the old paint is in good condition, you can simply sand it thoroughly with medium-grade sandpaper and then apply the first paint coat over the old finish. If the old finish is chipped or cracked, first sand the damaged areas to smooth them.

If sanding doesn't level the surface, use wood filler to even the gap. After the filler dries, sand it smooth and then apply a coat of primer over the entire project. Follow with two coats of finish paint, always sanding between paint coats. For a lacquered look, use high-gloss alkyd enamel. For an extremely smooth and shiny finish, thin the enamel to the maximum allowed on the label and apply several thin coats, sanding between each.

The consistency of the enamel is the key; if it's too thick, it will sag and leave brush marks. We like Penetrol for thinning; add it according to the directions on the can. Don't add the thinner to the paint can; it's better to pour the paint (in the amount suggested in the directions) into a new container and then add the thinner to it, creating just the right consistency. This approach lets you thicken the mixture with more paint, or thin it with more Penetrol, without affecting the rest of the paint in the can.

Chapter 7
Wallpapering Projects

● ●

In This Chapter

▶ Repairing wallpaper quickly and easily

▶ Decorating with borders

▶ Hanging wallpaper

▶ Removing wallpaper

● ●

*W*allpaper can have a profound effect on your daily life. The room papered with your favorite pattern is a welcome sight that draws you inside; just seeing it makes you smile. Yet even a quick glimpse of the wallpaper-from-hell hung by a previous owner can make your anxiety level soar.

In this chapter, we leave the psychological impact of irksome wallpaper to therapists, and focus instead on hanging the wall coverings you want and getting rid of those you don't want. For people who like their wallpaper but have run out of pictures to hang over all the tears and stains, we include a few quick, easy wallpaper repairs. By following the simple instructions in this chapter, you can make your home a more pleasant place to be.

Performing Wallpaper First Aid

Nothing seems to scream out for attention more than a patch of damaged wallpaper. The eye is inevitably drawn to the point where the pattern is broken by a tear or blemish.

The harsh truth is that wallpaper can tear. Seams pull away from the wall if not enough paste was applied, and bubbles that weren't removed when the wallpaper was hung don't just go away. Maybe a budding artist in the family used the dining-room wallpaper as a canvas for a permanent-ink display. Whatever caused the damage in your wallpaper, read on to find out how to fix it.

The right tool for the job

For under $15, you can buy a wallpaper-tools kit that includes a tray, trim guide, seam roller, smoothing brush, and razor knife — nearly everything you need for a wallpapering project. You also need a measuring tape and scissors. A plumb line comes in handy to establish a straight horizontal layout line (for a chair rail), and a carpenter's square is helpful to determine a straight vertical line in a room.

Use the following checklist to assemble your own wallpaper tool kit:

- **Bucket and wall sponge:** Use these to wash the new wall covering to remove excess paste that oozes out from the edges.

- **Carpenter's level:** This measuring tool lets you determine a straight vertical or horizontal line in a room.

- **Paint roller or paste brush:** Use either one to apply adhesive to the back of wall covering.

- **Plumb line:** This tool comes in handy when you need to establish a straight horizontal layout line. You can make your own plumb line by attaching a weight to the end of a string. Tie the string to a nail near the top of the room and drop the weighted end — you want a string long enough to almost, but not quite, reach the floor. When the plumb line stops swinging, align a ruler with the string to establish a perfectly vertical line, and mark it on the wall.

- **Razor knife:** Key to the operation is a sharp razor cutter with breakaway blades used with the trim guide to cut off excess paper at the ceiling and floor molding and to make trim cuts around obstructions.

- **Scissors:** Choose a good pair of sharp scissors to cut wallpaper strips to size.

- **Seam roller:** This tool looks like a pastry roller and is used to press down wallpaper seams where two edges meet. You can find this $2 item wherever wallpaper is sold.

- **Smoothing brush:** This brush usually has a single layer of flexible bristles that help smooth the wall covering so that it's free of bubbles or wrinkles.

- **Tape Measure:** Used to measure and cut strips of wallpaper.

- **Trim guide:** You can use a broad knife or a painting edger that has a heavy metal blade. Use it to press the wet wallpaper into a ceiling or wall joint and then trim the paper with a razor knife for a precision cut.

- **Water tray:** Use this narrow plastic tray to hold water for soaking prepasted wall covering. If you're working near the bathroom, you can soak wallpaper in the bathtub, too.

- **Ladder:** Okay, this item may not fit in a tool kit, but you'll probably need one for the job. Choose a ladder that's sturdy and safe to work on, preferably with a shelf for holding your tools.

Patching a tear

A tear in wallpaper is like a run in pantyhose: Both are eyesores that never go unnoticed. The most common culprit for a tear occurs when a door is carelessly slammed into the wall or the sharp corner of a piece of furniture pierces the wall and cuts through the wallpaper. The good news is that, despite how awful a tear looks, you can repair the damage quickly and easily. (We're talking about a tear that's less than 12 inches in width or height. For anything larger, you're better off replacing the full roll of wallpaper.)

To mend a tear or hole in wallpaper, you need a scrap piece of matching wallpaper large enough to cut out a patch. Stand back and take a look at the wall to judge how and where the pattern runs in relation to the tear. Then follow these steps, which are illustrated in Figure 7-1:

1. **Unroll a piece of matching wallpaper on a flat surface and find an area large enough to cover the damage to make a patch piece.**

2. **Use masking tape — or better yet, drafting tape, which doesn't stick as tightly as other tapes — to secure the scrap piece over the damaged area.**

   The trick is to align the pattern carefully so that the patch piece matches the pattern.

3. **After you're satisfied with the pattern match, use a sharp utility or razor knife to cut through both the scrap piece taped to the wall and the paper underneath.**

   Use the design of the pattern to determine the shape of the patch. If the pattern is a check or stripe pattern, cut along a vertical line to conceal the seams. For a print or floral pattern, use a less defined or irregular cut line. When you finish cutting, carefully remove the patch piece and peel away the rest of the taped-on paper.

   Be sure to cut through both pieces at the same time so that the finished product is a perfect match.

4. **Use a spray bottle filled with water to dampen the damaged wallpaper and loosen the adhesive behind it.**

   Check out the "Removing That Horrid Wallpaper" section, later in this chapter, for some tips.

5. **Use a small putty knife to scrape off the damaged wallpaper, but be very careful not to gouge the surrounding paper.**

6. **Clean the damaged wall area so that it's free of any old wallpaper paste.**

7. **Coat the back of the patch with either wall-covering adhesive or seam sealer and position it carefully.**

8. **Hold the patch in place until it feels secure, and use a wet sponge to wipe away any excess.**

9. **Use a wallpaper seam roller to seal the edges of the patch.**

Hold the seam roller as though it's a pizza or pastry cutter, and press it firmly and equally along the mating edges of the wallpaper. After the patch dries, the seam will be undetectable.

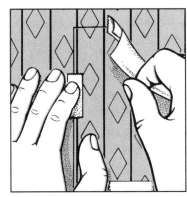

A. Cover the damaged area with a large scrap of wallpaper, lining up the patterns, and affix it with drafter's tape. (Steps 1 and 2)

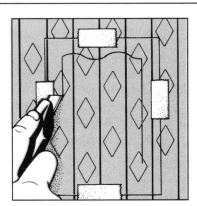

B. Cut around the damage with a razor cutter, pressing through both sheets. (Step 3)

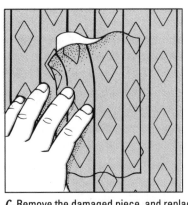

C. Remove the damaged piece, and replace it with the new cutout. (Steps 4 to 9)

Figure 7-1:
Patching
damaged
wallpaper.

Fixing loose seams

If you don't apply enough glue when hanging wallpaper, the edge eventually loosens and pulls away from the wall. To reseal an edge, apply *wall-covering seam sealer* to bond the overlapping edges of paper. Wall-covering seam sealer comes in a small, squeezable tube with an applicator at the tip.

Follow these steps to refasten the wallpaper edge:

1. **Very carefully peel back the loose wallpaper.**

   Don't stretch the paper — go only as far as you can without tearing the wallpaper.

2. **With a wet rag or sponge, carefully dampen the adhesive side of the paper (the side against the wall) and the wall to soften the old glue.**

   Wait a couple of minutes for the paste to soften and then wipe as much of the paste as possible from the paper and the wall behind the paper. Clean both surfaces several times to make sure that they're adhesive-free.

3. **Open the tube of seam sealer, put the nozzle behind the paper, and squeeze the seam sealer onto the wall.**

   Try to get the seam sealer as far back under the paper as possible.

4. **Reposition the edge of the wallpaper so that it matches the pattern of the adjacent paper. Hold it carefully and firmly in place for a few seconds.**

5. **Wipe the wallpaper with a clean rag to remove any excess sealer.**

   The sealer dries clear, mending the loose wallpaper.

6. **Use a wallpaper seam roller to seal the edges and wipe away any excess sealer with a damp rag or sponge.**

Sometimes, two edges pull away at the same seam, giving you a clear view of the wall behind. To fix this problem, clean the exposed wall surface so that it's free of old glue (or anything else). Then apply the sealer to the wall behind both pieces of pulled-away wallpaper. After you apply the sealer, carefully position both pieces so that they align, and smooth the edges.

Bordering on Beautiful

To give a room a quick facelift, consider adding a wallpaper border. A border is like the ribbon wrapped around a package: It isn't functional, but it adds a special touch. Borders provide a decorative trim around the windows, doors, or ceiling — they can even serve as a chair rail. You can apply a border to any painted wall or on top of a wall covering.

Adding a border is an ideal job for a first-time paper hanger: It gives you a chance to practice using basic tools, and the investment in time and equipment is minimal. A seasoned do-it-yourselfer can enjoy this project, too, because a border transforms the look of a room with so little effort and expense.

Borders range in size from a few inches to a foot wide, and come in a variety of styles and patterns. Modern borders are prepasted and strippable, and some now have laser-cut edges, for a decorative scalloped effect.

Wallpaper borders have become quite popular, and are available almost anywhere that sells home-decorating products. Wallpaper books are also filled with samples of wall coverings, many with their own coordinated borders. Expect prices upwards of $8 per 15-foot roll. Measure the perimeter of the walls and add a few extra feet to determine how many rolls of border you need.

You don't need fancy tools to hang a border. All you need is a tape measure, a seam roller, a razor knife, scissors, a bucket, a wall sponge, a carpenter's level, and possibly a ladder. For details about these tools, refer to the sidebar called "The right tool for the job," earlier in this chapter.

Getting the border straight

Because most rooms aren't truly square, hanging border paper sometimes calls for an imaginative approach. Being flexible is important when planning a border-hanging project. Borders look best if they are hung level, unless the room is way out of square. Hanging a truly horizontal border paper close to a sloping ceiling only emphasizes the fact that the ceiling is not level.

In newer houses, you can usually establish a horizontal line and hang the border along it. When hanging a border in a room that has ceiling molding, you can use the molding as your guide, even if the walls aren't level, by butting the top of the border to the bottom of the molding. If the room doesn't have a molding, plan on hanging the border flush against the ceiling.

If the ceiling-to-wall joint is very rough, or just for a different look, you can place the border a couple of inches below the ceiling. If you hang the border any farther down the wall, you have to decide whether to use the ceiling as a guide or establish a level line below the ceiling by which to hang the border. In deciding whether to go for a ceiling-level border or a mid-wall border, consider the effects you want:

✔ A border that runs just below the ceiling defines the space and accentu-
ates the shape of the room. If the room is small, a ceiling-level border
can help expand the space.

✔ A border that divides a wall in the same manner as a chair rail tends to
make a room appear smaller.

If you're hanging the border mid-wall, you need to establish a horizontal
layout line. Use measuring tape and a carpenter's level to establish guidelines around the room, as follows:

1. **Decide where you want to position the top of your border and mark
   the location on the wall.**

   You can measure down from the ceiling or up from the floor, depending
   on which distance is shorter.

2. **At the point you marked, hold the level flat against the wall, adjusting it until the bubble is centered.**

3. **Use the level as a straight edge and draw a line along the wall.**

4. **Move the level to the end of the line, center the bubble, and continue
   the line.**

5. **Walk the level around the room, repeating Step 4 until you've
   marked the entire room.**

6. **Hang your border, with the top edge just covering the level
   layout line.**

When running borders around windows and doors, use the woodwork as your
guideline — even if the woodwork is a little crooked. You want the border to
be in alignment with the windows and doors, not emphasizing the fact that
the doors and windows may have moved out of plumb over the ages.

Hanging the border

Before you hang the border, check to see that your walls are clean and dust-
free (especially in the corners). If the border is going to pass through any
light switches or electrical outlets, remove the covers and screws and store
them together in a plastic sandwich bag.

When you hang a border, start and end in the least conspicuous corner of
the room so that it will be less noticeable if the pattern doesn't match up.
Above the entry door is usually a good spot. If necessary, trim off the end of
the paper a bit so that little or no pattern is close to the end. Starting and
finishing is much easier when the ending strip doesn't have to match the
pattern where the border begins.

To hang a border, follow these steps:

1. **Activate the adhesive backing.**

   Most borders are prepasted, and you generally activate the adhesive by soaking the border in water. Follow the directions provided by the manufacturer.

   If the border you've chosen isn't prepasted and you're hanging it on painted walls, use any premixed wallpaper adhesive. If you're hanging the border (prepasted *or* non-prepasted) on top of a wallcovering, use a vinyl-to-vinyl adhesive. Use a clean paint brush (foam or bristle) to spread the adhesive on the back of the paper, being careful to apply it evenly from edge to edge.

2. **Fold the pasted sides together.**

   This step, called *booking,* keeps the adhesive moist.

3. **Align the top edge of the border on top of the layout line (to conceal it) and gently but firmly smooth the border onto the wall.**

4. **Butt the joints together as you continue to hang additional rolls of the border.**

Miter corner cuts

For a neat, precise cut at right angles, such as where a horizontal border joins a vertical strip of border, you use a *miter cut,* also called a *double cut* because you cut two overlapping pieces at once. You make an outside-corner miter cut for a border that outlines a window or doorway at the top corners. You use an inside miter cut where a chair-rail border turns and runs vertically up a window or doorway. Simply follow steps, as shown in Figure 7-2:

1. **Apply the horizontal border a few extra inches beyond the corner of the window or door so that it will extend a few inches past the vertical border (which you apply next).**

   You're going to trim off the border, so don't press it too firmly in place.

2. **Hold another strip of border vertically so that it overlaps and covers the horizontal border.**

   The two strips form a small cross.

   If the paper has a bold pattern, you may want to cut both these strips a bit long so that you can move the vertical strip up and down, or the horizontal strip back and forth, to match up the pattern. You can get a hint of how the joint will look by lifting up the top strip and visualizing how the patterns will match up after you make the miter cut. (The miter cut starts at the corner of the trim and extends out diagonally, cutting off a portion of both strips.)

A. Apply a horizontal border and lay a vertical border over it. (Steps 1 and 2)

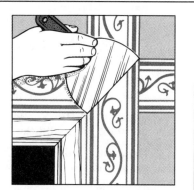

B. Align a straight edge diagonally across the intersection. (Step 3)

C. Cut through both layers with a razor knife. (Step 4)

D. Remove the cut-away pieces and apply the vertical border. (Steps 5 and 6)

E. Seal the edges with a seam roller. (Step 7)

Figure 7-2:
Use a miter cut for a border that outlines a window or the top of a doorway.

3. Lay a straight edge, such as a wide putty knife or ruler, on a diagonal line connecting opposite corners.

4. Cut through both layers of the border with the razor knife, using the straight edge as a guide.

5. Lift up the vertical border and remove the triangular cut-away piece of the horizontal border.

6. Gently apply the vertical border so that it forms a perfect 90-degree, or *miter,* joint with the horizontal border.

7. Firmly press the two joining edges together and seal them with a seam roller.

   The seam roller presses the edges tight against the wall. For details about this tool, refer to the sidebar called, "The right tool for the job," earlier in this chapter.

8. After about a half-hour, lightly rinse the border edges with a damp sponge to remove any adhesive that may have oozed out from the seam.

Picking a Peck of Paper Patterns

For some people, choosing wallpaper can be more difficult than hanging it — the choices are daunting! Just lifting the enormous books of samples is a challenge, not to mention actually sifting through the pounds of pages in search of the perfect wallpaper. But wallpaper can do so much for the look and feel of a room that the selection process is worth enduring.

Choosing a material

In spite of its name, wallpaper isn't always made of paper. Various materials and features differentiate the kinds of wallpaper you can buy. Vinyl and vinyl-coated wall coverings are the most popular types because they're easy to put up, to clean, and to take down. Both choices come in various textures, styles, and patterns.

Other types of wall coverings include foils and mylars, which have a thin, shiny metal coating; grasscloths, which are woven with natural fibers and richly textured; and velvety flocked papers with raised patterns. The foils and mylars aren't good choices for hiding imperfections, because their shiny surfaces accentuate small bumps and holes in the wall.

Anaglypta wallpaper

Deep-relief wallpaper, called *Anaglypta*, has covered the walls of houses since the turn of the century. If you want to renovate an old house to its original status, consider using this material. But Anaglypta is not advisable for a first-time paper hanger because the installation is more complicated than hanging vinyl wall coverings.

For one thing, Anaglypta is white and embossed with a pattern. You paint it after hanging it. Because it's heavy, the preparation is more involved. And if you're covering walls that are painted, you have to first test the wall for paint adhesion. Often, sanding the walls or removing the paint is required.

Before you hang Anaglypta, you must make sure that the wall is clean and dry and primed with a coat of water-based primer/sealer designed for wall covering. Use a clay-based vinyl wall-covering paste as the adhesive.

The National Guild of Professional Paper Hangers, Inc. has a free brochure with its official hanging instructions for Anaglypta and Lincrusta papers. Write to NGPPH, Inc., 136 S. Keowee St., Dayton, OH 45402 or call 513-222-9252.

Even though hanging reflective wallpaper on rough walls isn't a great idea, you can improve the results by first covering the walls with a heavy liner paper designed to bridge small cracks and imperfections. Foil and mylar papers are expensive, and liner paper can be a bit advanced for the everyday do-it-yourselfer, so we recommend that you call in a pro for this job.

If you're a first-time paper hanger, go for the vinyl papers. The selection is staggering, and handy little samples are usually available so that you're not tempted to tear the page out of a sample book. (Oh, admit it. Those big wallpaper books just beg you to snip off a scrap!) If you're not particularly fussy and just want a moderately priced wall covering, head for the ready-to-hang vinyl or vinyl-coated wallpapers sold off the floor. Because only in-stock patterns are displayed, you don't have to order ahead and wait around for your shipment to come in.

Picking a pattern

Here are some basic guidelines to consider when selecting a pattern:

- ✔ Vertical stripes make the ceiling appear higher, and horizontal strips seem to widen a room.

- ✔ Large patterns don't look good in a small room; a mini-print or a paper with a small pattern or geometric design suits smaller dimensions.

✔ Dark colors make a room seem smaller; wallpaper with a light background makes the room look larger.

✔ A large, open pattern looks best in a larger space; if used in a small room, big designs overpower the space and make it seem smaller.

Hanging a paper with a short pattern repeat is easier, and you waste less paper.

Considering quality

Which style, color, and pattern to buy and whether to opt for prepasted or non-prepasted aren't your only decisions when shopping for wall coverings. You also have to consider the quality or stamina of various coverings.

The term *washable* on a wall covering means that you can sponge the paper down occasionally with soap and warm water, but *scrubbable* coverings are made of tougher stuff and can be washed more frequently. Scrubbable wall covering is ideal for kitchens, bathrooms, and hallways, where spills and smudges are inevitable.

Buying and measuring

You can purchase your wallpaper from a number of sources:

✔ **Wallpaper outlets:** These stores offer the largest selection of carryout, ready-to-hang paper because they maintain a large inventory of in-stock designs.

✔ **Home centers and paint stores:** Most of these retailers offer wallpaper-to-go, as well as a complete library of manufacturers' books to choose from.

✔ **Mail-order catalogs:** Some manufacturers publish catalogs with pages of actual wall coverings that you can order by phone. Look through advertisements in decorating magazines for information on ordering these catalogs.

On in-stock patterns, the roll price is noted on the package. In a wallpaper book, pricing of patterns is noted by a key usually found on the front or back cover. For example, "A" may represent $12.95 per roll, and "B" may be $17.95 per roll.

Even though it's priced by the single roll, wallpaper is sold in double rolls. We know it makes no sense, but that's the way it is. Apparently a marketing department somewhere decided that wallpaper sounds less expensive when you only advertise the price of *half* the minimum purchase. Go figure!

Also check the packaging or catalog entry for the wallpaper's drop pattern, dye lot, and total coverage — all important information. The *drop pattern* tells you how frequently the pattern on the wallpaper is repeated. The lower the number, the more easily you can match patterns. A paper with a large drop pattern, like 15 inches, requires you to moves the paper up or down as much as 15 inches to align the pattern for the adjacent drop. If you have to move the paper up or down significantly to adjust the pattern match, you'll waste a great deal of paper when you align one sheet next to another one.

When you get an order of wallpaper, make sure that the *dye lot* of all the rolls is the same so the coloring matches. If you have to order additional paper, be sure to request the same dye lot. Otherwise, the colors may not match exactly.

To estimate how much wall covering you need for a room, look for the total square footage of paper required. Follow these steps to determine the total coverage you need:

1. **Measure the length of each wall.**

2. **Add the lengths together and multiply by the height of the room.**

3. **Because you won't be applying wallpaper on the doors and windows, measure the area of these openings and then subtract the amount from the room total.**

4. **When you have your room total, find the square foot coverage on the package, and divide that coverage figure into the room's total square footage.**

   Most likely, the answer won't be an even number, so round up to the next highest number for the number of rolls you need to buy. In this equation, you have to also consider the waste factor, which is about 20 percent.

Hanging Wallpaper Step by Step

If you're hanging wallpaper for the first time, we recommend tackling a back bedroom, not a bathroom or kitchen where you have many cutouts and the working area is small and confining.

Wallpapering with a spouse can pose a dangerous threat to a relationship. After 30 years of blissful marriage, we attribute our successful partnership to having avoided the stress and conflicts involved in sharing the precision art of hanging wallpaper. Our decision is based on one wrenching experience, and we've since vowed never again to make wallpapering a team sport.

Preparing the room for wallpaper

To prepare a room for wallpaper, remove as much furniture from the room as possible. Ideally, you want to have a good 3 feet of work area in front of the walls. Having a long work table set up where you can roll out and measure the strips of wallpaper as you cut them is also handy.

Remove the covers on electrical receptacles and light switches, and put a small piece of masking tape over the electrical outlets. Also remove any heating grates or plate covers from the walls. Clean any dust from around these wall openings.

Do a quick once-over to dust and clean the walls and woodwork. Remove fuzzy-wuzzies and cobwebs from corners and, if the woodwork is dirty or greasy, wash it in a solution of phosphate-free household cleaner according to the directions.

You want the walls to be clean and dry and in good shape, without any holes or cracks. Patch any holes with wallboard compound. After the compound dries, sand the patched areas smooth. Apply *wallpaper sizing* to the walls to make them tacky so that the wallpaper paste or adhesive has a good surface to bond with. Pour the sizing into a paint pan and use a paint roller to apply it to the wall. When the sizing is dry, you're ready to hang paper.

A primer on primers

The key to good wallpaper adhesion is the condition of the wall to which you apply the adhesive. If you start with a perfectly clean painted wall, you're likely to get good results with any prepasted wallpaper. However, you're *guaranteed* to get good results if you prime the wall first.

If you're papering over new drywall, applying a coat of primer is a *must*. If you don't start with a primer-sealer, which soaks into and coats the drywall, you'll never be able to re-move the wallpaper without gouging the dry-wall. It's a good idea to tint the primer-sealer in the shade of the paper so that the white primer won't show through if the seams don't align perfectly.

Pigmented acrylic all-surface wall-covering primer helps to cover dark surfaces and pre-vent them from showing through the paper. *Acrylic all-surface wall-covering primer* goes on white but becomes clear as it dries. Both primers perform equally well on porous and nonporous surfaces.

A coat of wall-cover primer takes two to four hours to dry, so paint it on at least a few hours before you hang the wallpaper. Ironically, not only does a primer coat promote adhesion, but it also makes the wallpaper easier to strip off when you get tired of it.

If you're planning to paint the woodwork and trim in the room to match the new wall covering, paint *before* hanging the wallpaper. Getting wallpaper glue off a painted surface is easier than removing paint from wallpaper.

Laying out a starting line

After you prepare the room, choose a starting point to begin papering. You're best off starting and ending in the least conspicuous corner of the room, where it's less noticeable if the pattern doesn't match perfectly. The corner beside an entry door is usually a good spot to start. If necessary, trim the end of the paper a bit so that little or no pattern is close to the starting point; starting and finishing is much easier when the final strip doesn't have to match up with a pattern on the first strip.

Use a plumb line or a carpenter's level to create a straight vertical starting point on the wall, as shown in Figure 7-3. To use a plumb line, drive a small nail into the wall near the ceiling and hang a weighted string line from it. When the string stops swinging, mark its position with a pencil; this line becomes your starting point. Align the edge of the first strip of wallpaper with this starting line, and the remaining strips will be straight.

Figure 7-3:
Use a plumb line to create a starting point.

Even when your walls are not straight, you're better off aligning the wallpaper with a plumb line rather than the ceiling or corner. Otherwise, you'll end up with mismatched patterns at the corners and seams.

In our kitchen, we have paper with a simple pattern of taupe and gray wandering sheep. The sheep are grazing in a straight horizontal pattern, so if you look at the ceiling in one corner and follow the line of grazing sheep across the walls, you quickly see that some walls are much higher than others — part of the charm of living in an old house! In some places, a whole new line of sheep appears; in other places, the sheep gradually graze into oblivion. But the advantage of following a true horizontal line is that the pattern matches in the corners and seams. If we had aligned the paper with the walls or ceiling instead of a vertical layout line, the sheep pattern would be parallel to the ceiling, but would be way off at each wall junction.

Cutting the first drop

Cutting the first strip (also called a *drop*) is easy, but you must take the pattern repeat into consideration if the pattern is large. For a pattern repeat of less than 3 inches, measure the height of the wall from ceiling down to the floor and add about 5 inches to that figure. Then cut the first drop from the role of wallpaper. Simply unroll the wallpaper and cut a strip to size using scissors. This cut can be rough, because you'll trim off both the top and bottom after you hang the drop.

If the pattern repeat is over 3 inches, carefully unroll enough paper to reach the ceiling and hold it in place against the wall. Move the paper up or down to adjust the pattern for best looks and then mark the paper at the ceiling and floor, take it down and cut this length from the roll. This strip will give you a good idea how you will have to cut the other strips to maintain pattern alignment.

Sticking it on the wall

After you cut the first drop, soak the cut wallpaper strip in water following the manufacturer's suggested time and water temperature. Then *book* the strip by loosely folding the backsides together so that the pasted sides touch each other. Fold the strip in half again and let it set while the paste is activated. The booking process lets the strips relax and the paste penetrate the wallpaper so that it doesn't dry out.

To hang the strip, open it at the first fold and then pull it apart so that it's free from the end. Hold the drop up to your starting point at the ceiling, with the pasted side facing the wall. Position the top of the strip at the ceiling joint of the wall and carefully align its side with the vertical starting line, as shown in Figure 7-4. Leave a few inches of extra paper at the top; you'll trim this part off later.

Use the smoothing brush and your hands to smooth the paper at the top, also shown in Figure 7-4. Unfold the bottom section of the paper and smooth it into position on the wall. Positioning and smoothing the first strip takes a little finesse. When the strip is straight, brush the entire surface smooth to remove wrinkles and bubbles.

Hang subsequent strips, one next to the other. Make sure that the seams (where the edges of the strips meet) are aligned so that they just touch, without overlapping or leaving a gap. Then use the seam roller to press them in place. Don't press the roller too heavily against the seam, because you don't want to squeeze out the adhesive. Even when you use a soft touch to seal the seam, paste sometimes oozes out. Gently remove the excess paste with a wet sponge.

Wiping up wet paste from the front of the wallpaper is easier than waiting until after it dries. So as you hang each drop of wallpaper, use a wall sponge to wipe off any excess adhesive. Also be careful to wipe up excess adhesive from any molding and trim.

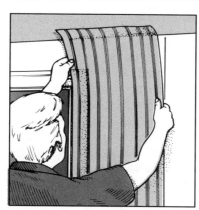

Figure 7-4: Hanging the first drop.

A. Align the first drop with your starting line.   *B.* Brush out bubbles and wrinkles.

Trimming the paper

Use the trim guide and razor knife to make a neat cut along the joint where the top of the strip meets the ceiling. Then do the bottom cut. With one hand, hold the trim guide in the joint and cut away the excess with the razor knife, as shown in Figure 7-5. This feels awkward at first, but the more you do it, the more at ease you'll feel.

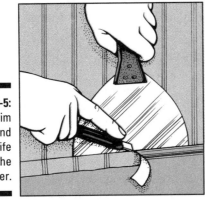

Figure 7-5:
Use the trim guide and razor knife to cut the paper.

Repeat this process for each of the wallpaper strips, always taking time to stand back and look at the overall effect.

To make trim cuts around doors and windows, try these techniques:

✔ When you wrap a strip of wallpaper around an inside or outside corner, snip the top at the corner joint to ease it around. This technique, called a *relief cut,* enables you to manipulate and smooth the wallpaper without tearing it. Then use the smoothing brush and your open hand to smooth out wrinkles.

✔ To negotiate wallpaper around an inside corner, measure the distance from the end of the nearest drop to the corner and add 2 inches. Then cut the next drop to that width and save the cut-off piece. Hang the drop, working it into the corner with a smooth brush. Then measure the width of the cut-off piece and, on the adjoining wall, snap a plumb line that distance from the corner. Align the cut-off piece with the plumb line and continue with full-width drops around the room.

✔ Butt the edge of wallpaper directly up to woodwork. Then use a trim guide and razor knife to cut away the excess paper. At the corners of woodwork, cut an angle into the wallpaper with scissors and then trim the cut with a razor knife.

✔ To trim wallpaper around an electrical outlet or switch, *turn the electricity off.* Hang the wallpaper over the outlet or switch, and then make short diagonal X cuts to reveal the outlet. Then trim around the opening with a razor knife. The plate covers will conceal the rough edges.

Take a break when you get tired. Don't rush the job.

To trim the final drop to size, allow it to overlap the first drop and then cut through both pieces of paper along a plumb vertical line. Let the cut-away strip of the final drop fall away, and then gently pull the edge of the drop away so that you can peel off the cut-away strip from the first drop. Seal the seam with a seam roller and wipe off any excess adhesive. (See Figure 7-6.)

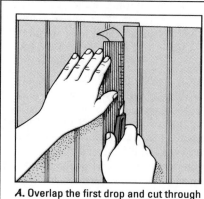

A. Overlap the first drop and cut through both pieces.

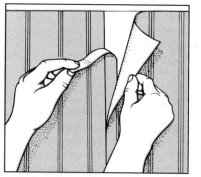

B. Peel off the cut-away pieces of both drops.

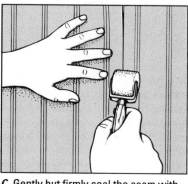

C. Gently but firmly seal the seam with a seam roller.

Figure 7-6: Trimming the final drop to make a seam with the first drop.

Removing That Horrid Wallpaper

The task of removing wallpaper doesn't have to be dreaded. But it can be mind-numbing to stand in a large room with the world's ugliest wallpaper and know that only you can change its destiny. Although taking down wallpaper isn't fun, it's a good example of grunt work any do-it-yourselfer can accomplish. The downside is that it's a messy and time-consuming job; the upside is that it's a no-brainer and doesn't require expensive tools or even talent.

In a perfect world, you'd be able to gently pull at a loose seam and the old paper would miraculously peel off the wall, leaving no residue or adhesive, just a nice clean surface. In the real word, that scenario is very unlikely. What's more likely to happen is one of the following:

- ✔ The paper won't come off at all because it requires steam to break down the adhesive.

- ✔ As you pull the wallpaper, the top coating, or *face,* of the paper comes off. However, the thin (usually white) backing paper remains on the wall. Removing this backing usually requires the use of steam to break down the adhesive. Sometimes you get lucky, and a good soaking with a wallpaper-removing solvent or a household cleaning solution is enough to take it off. But if you use the soaking technique, you'll probably need a 4- or 5-inch-wide putty knife to scrape off the goo.

The real challenge is removing more than one layer of wallpaper, or removing wallpaper that's been painted. In these situations, you're talking major work. But the work is more messy than difficult. For these tough jobs, you're best off renting a wallpaper steamer (about $15 for a half day) or buying one (about $50). A wallpaper steamer, shown in Figure 7-7, is basically a hotplate that's attached to a hose that's attached to a hot water reservoir that heats the water and directs steam to the hotplate.

For most ordinary wallpaper removal jobs, all you need is a dropcloth, a perforator, a bucket of water, a paint roller, and a scraper. The idea is to score the paper with holes or slits and then apply moisture to break down the adhesive.

Water is a key reason that so much preparation work is necessary before removing wallpaper. Protect the floor and molding from water damage with pretaped plastic dropcloths taped to the top of the baseboard floor molding, as shown in Figure 7-8. Stick these cloths around the perimeter of the room and then unfold them into the room to cover the floor.

Use a 3- to 4-inch razor scraper and change the razor as soon as it appears too dull to score the wallpaper with holes. This tool looks like a putty knife but has a slot for replaceable blades so you can always have a sharp edge.

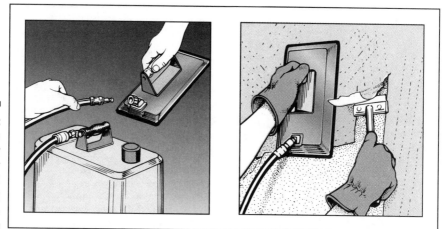

Figure 7-7:
Filling a
wallpaper
steamer
and
steaming
away.

A *Paper Scraper,* shown in Figure 7-8, is a nifty gadget for removing wallpaper from walls made of wallboard or gypsum drywall. It has a round knoblike handle attached to a scraping blade that doesn't damage the paper face of the wallboard the way a sharp razor knife does. Its rounded edges help ensure that you won't have to repair the walls after removing the wallpaper. Use the paper scraper before soaking the walls to keep the blades from penetrating the wallboard. Look for this gadget with the wallpaper removal tools in home centers, wallpaper outlets, and hardware stores.

The cuts you make allow the moisture to get behind the paper and dissolve the adhesive on the wall. Mixing wallpaper-remover solvent into the water helps speed the process. The solvent breaks down the adhesive so that the wall covering loosens and can be scraped off the wall.

Here are two home brews for wallpaper-remover solvents:

- ✔ A 50/50 combination of vinegar and water
- ✔ A 25/75 solution of liquid laundry softener and water

Apply the wallpaper solvent with a paint roller or a liquid sprayer (as shown in Figure 7-8) to a 3-foot-wide section of wallpaper and wait for it to work. Make more than one application of moisture to the wallpaper, soaking it as much as possible each time. After a few applications and enough soaking time, the wallpaper should peel off easily with a razor scraper. Work on a 3-foot-wide section of the wall at a time, and then move on to the next area.

As you scrape off the old wallpaper, let it fall onto the plastic dropcloth. When all the wallpaper is removed, simply roll up the entire mess — wallpaper, dropcloth, and all. Use a wall sponge and warm water to remove any excess paste from the walls.

A. Protect molding and floors with pretaped dropcloths.

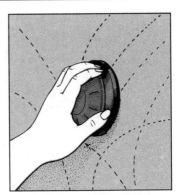

B. Score the paper with a razor-scraper or a perforating gadget.

C. Mix wallpaper-removing solvent with water.

D. Apply the solution with a paint roller or liquid sprayer.

Figure 7-8: The low-tech wallpaper removal system.

E. Peel and scrape off the wet paper.

F. Clean off residual glue and scraps with a wet wall sponge or sponge mop.

Part III
The Nuts and Bolts of Carpentry

The 5th Wave   **By Rich Tennant**

"Oh Dave is very handy around the house. He manually entered the phone numbers for the electrician, the carpenter, and the plumber on our speed dial."

In this part . . .

Doors and windows and floors, oh my! The road to renewal is wide open for your best do-it-yourself efforts. Pack up some courage and take heart: Understanding the mechanics of your windows, doors, and floors is a solid first step to keeping them in good working order and fixing them when they need it. This part doesn't call for major brain power, just attention to a few details that may remind you, there's no place like an improved home!

Chapter 8
Walking the Floor Over You

· ·

· ·

Floors in today's homes have the life expectancy of a fruit fly. Whether they're covered with carpet, tiles, or hardwood, the pathways underfoot are subjected to considerable use and abuse every day. Muddy traffic, pet scratches, and drips, drops, and spills all contribute to the need for frequent repair, rejuvenation, and replacement of indoor flooring. This chapter deals with common flooring fix-ups and explains what's involved in getting those jobs done.

Repairing Damage

Sure, the floor under your feet is made of tough stuff, but it's not indestructible. And when flooring gets damaged or torn, it can look awful. No matter how small the damage, all eyes go right to the flaw!

If the damage is in a floor tile, the solution is pretty easy: Remove the individual floor tile and replace it with a new one. The job gets a little trickier when the problem is in sheet flooring or carpeting, because you have to make a patch. Surface damage to good old-fashioned hardwood is usually only skin-deep, so it's easy to fix.

Replacing damaged vinyl floor tiles

Vinyl tile is the easiest type of flooring to repair. If a tile is damaged, simply replace it with a new one. Of course, you do need a few extra tiles stashed away somewhere. When positioning the replacement tile, make sure that it follows the pattern. Nothing is more obvious than a mismatched pattern.

Follow these steps to replace a vinyl tile:

1. **Remove the damaged tile.**

   Use a clothes iron or an electric heat gun to soften the adhesive so that you can lift the tile away, as shown in Figure 8-1. Move the hot air stream over the entire tile, making sure that you don't keep the heat in any one area too long — you don't want to scorch the tile and stink up the house with the aroma of cooked vinyl. Take your time: The tile and underlying adhesive needs a couple of minutes to heat up.

   When the tile is hot, gently push a thin-bladed putty knife or scraper into the tile joint and pry upwards. If the tile doesn't lift easily, stop prying and apply more heat. Repeat the prying action and lift the damaged tile away.

Figure 8-1:
Carefully move the iron over the tile to soften the adhesive so that you can pry the tile loose.

2. **Remove the old adhesive from the subfloor.**

   Depending on how much dried adhesive is stuck to the floor, you may need to use a cloth soaked in solvent, a scraper, or both.

3. **Use a notched trowel to apply new tile adhesive to the back of the replacement tile.**

   The best offense for combating a damaged floor is a good defense. When you're installing new flooring, plan ahead: Save leftover materials for repairs. Wrap extra tiles in the original box or packaging, and store them in a dry place.

4. **Press the tile firmly into place and secure the adhesion.**

   You can secure the tile in place by rolling a rolling pin (borrowed from your kitchen cupboard) across the tile, or by placing a flat wood block over the tile and tapping it gently with a hammer.

5. **Use mineral spirits or other solvent (see directions on the adhesive label) to clean up any adhesive that oozes up through the tile joints.**

Use a cloth that's damp, but not wet, with solvent to clean the tile face or joints. Don't let solvent run into the tile joint because it may dilute the adhesive and cause a bond failure between the tile and the floor.

If you don't have a replacement tile, steal an existing tile from an inconspicuous spot, such as inside a closet or beneath an appliance. Follow Step 1 of the preceding instructions to pry up the hidden tile, and then use this tile to replace the damaged one. Be sure to clean off the old adhesive from the back of the tile before you apply new adhesive. You can purchase a new tile of the same size and as close to the original pattern as possible for the spot where you stole the replacement tile. Then shut the closet door or roll the refrigerator back over the tile, and your secret is safe.

Fixing damaged vinyl sheet flooring

Use the *double-cut method* to repair a hole or tear in a sheet vinyl floor. Figure 8-2 illustrates the following steps:

1. **Position a scrap of flooring over the damaged area, making sure that the pattern on the scrap piece matches the floor pattern.**

2. **Tape the scrap firmly in place with masking tape so that it doesn't slip when you cut the patch.**

3. **Cut completely through both the patch and damaged flooring with a sharp utility knife, making the cut lines entirely outside the damaged area.**

Because you're cutting both the patch and the floor at the same time, you can expect an exact fit even if the cuts aren't perfectly straight.

4. **Remove the tape and set the newly cut patch aside.**

5. **Remove the damaged area and replace it with the cut-out patch by following the instructions for replacing a floor tile.**

Fixing the damaged hardwood floors

If a hardwood floor shows signs of extensive wear and tear, the solution may be to sand and refinish the entire floor. But if the damage is limited to a small gouge or slight crack in the flooring, use a wood-patch compound, which is kind of like wood-tone Play-Doh. Remove any dirt or wood splinters from the damaged area and smooth the patching material with a small putty knife so that it's level with the floor surface. When the material dries, sand the patch with fine sandpaper.

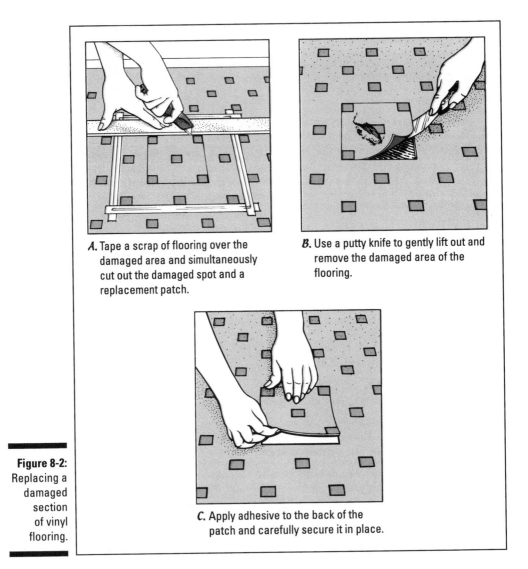

A. Tape a scrap of flooring over the damaged area and simultaneously cut out the damaged spot and a replacement patch.

B. Use a putty knife to gently lift out and remove the damaged area of the flooring.

C. Apply adhesive to the back of the patch and carefully secure it in place.

Figure 8-2: Replacing a damaged section of vinyl flooring.

If the floor is stained, brush a matching stain on and beyond the repair area, blending the new finish into the old. Let the stain dry and then coat it with the same finish used on the floor.

For surface scratches, use Minwax Wood Stain Markers to fill in blemished areas. These felt-tip pens come in various wood shades and are available in home centers and paint and hardware stores. Choose a shade that's closest to the color of your floor.

Patching a hole in the carpeting

Cigarette burns and tough stains can cause permanent damage to carpeting. If the blemish is on the surface fiber only, use a nail clipper or small manicure scissors to clip away the damaged fiber. Remember to remove only a small amount of fiber at a time; unlike your hair, this stuff won't grow back if you cut it too short.

If the damage is deep or the carpet is torn, replace a section of the carpet as shown in Figure 8-3. Cut a replacement patch using a straightedge and a utility knife to make a straight cutout around a damaged area. Then install a replacement patch cut to the same size, using double-stick cloth carpet tape to hold the patch in place.

The tape, sold in widths of $1^1/_2$ inches and 2 inches, is available at home centers and hardware stores. Cut the tape to size to outline the perimeter of the patch area. Peel the protective paper from the face of the peel-and-stick tape and press the patch of carpeting into the repair area to ensure full contact between the carpet patch and the adhesive tape. Carefully separate the carpet fibers between the patch and the surrounding fibers. Give the adhesive time to set and then use a comb or brush to blend the carpet pile between the carpet and the patch.

Figure 8-3: With careful measuring and cutting, you can replace a patch of damaged carpet without leaving a trace.

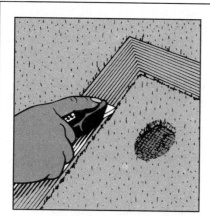

A. Use a framing square to guide the utility knife as you cut an area around the damaged carpeting and a patch from a matching piece of scrap carpet.

B. Outline the bare spot with double-stick cloth tape to hold the replacment patch securely in place.

Rather than cutting your own patch, you can take out the guess work by using a doughnut. A *doughnut* is a circular cutting tool with a razor blade cutter fixed to the perimeter, and a center rotating pin to anchor the cutter in place. The tool cuts shapes that are 3 inches in diameter and it costs about $12.

Refurbishing a Hardwood Floor

If your hardwood floor needs refurbishing, first clean the floor and remove any wax. Vacuum away all dirt and grit, and then apply a floor cleaner or mineral spirits to strip away any wax buildup. Use adequate ventilation when you clean the floor, and observe precautions listed on the product label.

Next, inspect the floor for damage. If the wood has gouges or scratches, use fine sandpaper to remove the old floor finish. Always sand *with* the grain of the wood; cross-grain scratches are tougher to remove than old tattoos. Do not extend the repair area beyond the damage: Sand only an inch or two beyond the perimeter of the damaged area.

Use a putty knife and latex wood patch, available in various wood tones, to fill deep gouges. Let the latex patch set until dry, usually for 24 hours, and then sand the patch smooth. If the floor is stained, apply stain so that the repair area matches the surrounding floor. Then apply a finish to match the finish on the existing floor: Use varnish for varnished floors, polyurethane for floors with a polyurethane finish. Using a natural bristle brush, carefully blend the new finish into the old.

If the floor has a varnish finish, apply a coat of floor wax over the entire area. Do not wax any wood flooring that has a polyurethane finish.

You can remove light scratches by sanding the surface with fine sandpaper or with steel wool — always working in the direction of the wood grain, not across it. After you remove the scratches, follow steps for fixing damaged hardwood floors, found earlier in this chapter.

Repairing water damage on a hardwood floor

Always use a solvent-type cleaner on hardwood floors. Water-based cleaners can stain or darken the wood. Never wet-mop hardwood flooring, because water can penetrate into cracks and stain or warp the flooring. Stains and a damaged finish can also result from pet urine or from spilled liquids. To avoid stains, wipe up any spills or pet accidents immediately.

If you find dark or black stains on the floor, first sand away the old finish. Then mix oxalic acid crystals with water as directed on the product label. Oxalic acid is available at paint stores or home centers. Be sure to follow the directions on the package and wear acid-resistant rubber gloves, eye goggles, and protective clothing when working with this caustic product.

Soak a clean white cloth with the oxalic acid, press the cloth on the stained area, and let it set for about one hour. Lift the cloth and check the stain. If the stain has not been bleached away, apply more acid to the cloth and replace it over the stain. Repeat the process until the stain disappears, and then rinse the stain area with ordinary household vinegar to neutralize the acid. Wipe away any moisture and let the area dry. Be careful that you don't get oxalic acid anywhere else, because it can damage the finish or surface. And whatever you do, don't drip any acid on the sofa, drapes, rug, or family cat (even if she is the source of the original damage).

After you remove the discoloration, apply a matching oil-based wood stain to the bleached area. Apply the stain lightly — you can always apply another coat of stain to darken the area, but you can't lighten the area after the stain dries. If the stain appears too dark when you apply it, wipe the area immediately with a cloth dampened with mineral spirits to remove some stain and lighten the area. After the stain dries, apply another coat of stain to the area if you want to darken it more. Allow the area to dry overnight, and then coat the entire surface of the floor with a floor restorer to create an even finish.

Refinishing a hardwood floor

Did you hear about the guy who was sanding his dining room floor and blew a fuse? When he threw the switch in the fuse box in the basement, his sander started up again. By the time he got back upstairs, the sander was running wild all over the room like some sort of crazed rhinoceros, sanding a path behind it. We mention this happy little moment to underscore the serious damage that not-so-handy homeowners can do when they boldly choose to sand their own floors — a classic example of the Do-It-Yourself Damage Factor.

Badly worn or damaged hardwood floors may require refinishing — not a particularly pleasant solution, but perhaps the only solution. The refinishing part is easy, sanding is the dreaded part because the fine sawdust raised in the process permeates the house, no matter how painstaking your preparations. Keep in mind that excessive sanding can remove part of the thickness or stock of the wood, making the flooring more flexible and prone to squeaking. If the floor is not badly damaged, consider stripping the finish, repairing minor scratches, and refinishing rather than sanding.

If the hardwood floor shows extensive damage, or if you want to change the tone or shade of the wood, you have no other choice but to sand the floor first. The sander runs continuously, so you must keep the machine moving at a uniform speed. If you stop the machine in one spot for too long, it'll grind its way right down to the basement. Okay, we may be exaggerating just a tad, but anything less than an even pass across the floor can gouge the wood at that spot and make the sanded floor uneven. If you have any doubts about tackling the job yourself, hire a professional to sand your hardwood floors.

Insist on doing it yourself? Here are the basic steps:

1. **Rent a drum sander for the floor and an edger to sand close to the walls, inside closets, and on stairs.**

2. **Tape dropcloths made of heavy vinyl at doorways to seal off the work area.**

3. **Remove base shoe moldings around the walls with a pry bar and hammer, being careful to gently ease the molding away from the walls without breaking the wood.**

   Carefully drive the pry bar between the floor and the molding and lever the molding away from the wall a bit. Peek between the molding and wall and find the closest nail. Remove the pry bar and reinsert it as close to the nail as possible. Pry the molding loose at each nail to avoid breaking the molding. If a nail refuses to budge, use a nail set to drive the nail through the molding.

4. **Open the windows and get everyone out of the house.**

   Sawdust can be very damaging, especially to kids and folks with respiratory conditions. Wear a dust respirator, as well as ear and eye protection.

5. **Use an *edge sander,* which is a smaller hand-held disc sander, to refinish the perimeter of the room and inside closets, where the large drum sander is too big to operate.**

6. **Use the drum sander to sand the floor with a medium paper.**

   Several passes may be necessary.

7. **Follow up with fine sandpaper to remove any sanding marks and to leave a perfectly smooth floor.**

8. **Carefully vacuum up dust and grit from the sanding process and then wipe the floor down with a tack rag to pick up any remaining dust.**

9. **Apply a penetrating stain that doesn't raise the grain of the wood so that you don't have to sand the floor after applying the finish.**

10. **Use a rag or paint roller to apply the finish, following the grain of the wood.**

    Try to apply as even a coating as possible.

11. **When the stain is dry, use a brush or roller to apply a coat of poly-urethane finish.**

    Let the first coat dry for six to eight hours, and then sand lightly. Apply a second coat of polyurethane.

Polyurethane is fast-drying, so airborne dust and lint are less likely to accumulate on floor surfaces during the drying process. It's durable and provides a glass-smooth finish. Liquids spilled on a polyurethane finish bead up and can be easily wiped away. Do not use floor wax on polyurethane finishes.

Silencing Squeaks

Floor squeaks are among the more common and irritating homeowner annoyances. That torturous noise comes from two strips of hardwood flooring moving against each other — for example, when loose hardwood flooring rubs against the subfloor, or when floor bridging between the floor joists moves or rubs against the other bridging members.

Floor bridging is used to transfer the floor load over more joists and stiffen the floor, or to prevent floor joists from warping. Floor bridging may be two wood or metal members nailed to form an X between joists, or solid wood bridging like a 2-x-10-inch block cut to bridge between 2-x-10-inch joists. Solid wood bridging rarely creates a squeak problem.

Poor installation techniques are the main cause of most floor squeaks. If you're nailing down hardwood floors, be sure to nail every strip at each juncture between the flooring strips and the floor joists, or at 12-inch intervals. If you're using an adhesive to lay hardwood flooring, be sure to apply the adhesive at the rate recommended by the manufacturer.

If you have carpet on floors, or you're replacing vinyl floor covering, plan to eliminate floor squeaks before you install the new floor covering. With carpet or floor covering removed, you can renail the floor from the topside to eliminate the squeaks.

Locating a floor squeak

If the basement ceiling is unfinished, or is finished with acoustic tiles set in metal grids, you can gain access to the underside of the floor and quiet the squeaks from below. If the ceilings are finished with plaster or wallboard, you must wait until you're ready to recarpet or replace the floor covering, and renail the subfloor or underlayment plywood from the room side of the floor. The same is true for a multistory house where the upstairs floor is covered with carpet and the bottom side of the floor is the finished ceiling of the room below.

To pinpoint the location of a floor squeak, have a heavy-footed helper walk slowly across the floor while you listen from below, in the basement or crawl space area. As your assistant steps across the floor, note where the squeak is coming from. Have the helper step forward and back over the squeaking area so that you can note the exact spot. Carry a piece of chalk to mark the location of the squeak. Repeat this procedure over the entire floor, marking all the squeaky spots. Sounds like a great way to spend a Saturday night, doesn't it?

Stopping the squeak

After you pinpoint all the squeaky spots, inspect the area to see if you can identify the problem. Many houses have a subfloor of plywood or 1-x-6-inch tongue-and-groove boards nailed to the floor joists, then hardwood flooring nailed over the subfloor. The squeak may be caused by movement either between the subfloor and the hardwood flooring, or between the subfloor and the joists. Try the follow three techniques, illustrated in Figure 8-4, to silence the squeak underfoot:

- ✔ If you find a gap between the subfloor and the floor joists, coat a tapered wood shim with carpenter's glue and drive it between the subfloor and joist until the shim fits tightly in the space. You want the shim to restrict movement between the subfloor and the floor joist. Cedar shims are available in bundles at home centers or lumberyards.

- ✔ If the squeak is coming from your hardwood flooring, use a screw gun to drive drywall screws upward through the subfloor and into the flooring strips above. Be sure that the screws you're using are long enough to penetrate the subfloor and go into, but not completely through, the hardwood flooring. For most subfloor/flooring jobs, a $1^1/_4$-inch-long screw serves well; if the subfloor is $^1/_2$-inch-thick plywood, use a 1-inch-long screw.

 After you drive screws into the squeaking area, have the helper walk over the spot again to be sure that you have silenced the squeak. If the squeak persists and you can't get at the floor from below, drive in more screws over a slightly larger area until the floor is squeak-free.

- ✔ If you have a squeaky second-story floor and you can't get to the underside because of the finished ceiling below, try driving #8d finish nails through the floor at an angle into the floor joists. Use a nail set to drive the heads of the finish nails below the surface of the flooring.

Other sources of floor squeaks may be plumbing pipes that are held tightly against the floor joists with wire pipe hangers. If the pipes are rubbing against the underside of the joist when the floor is flexed by the weight of the helper, loosen the pipe hangers and reset them. You can also quiet the pipe squeak by placing foam pipe insulation around the pipes at the pipe hanger locations.

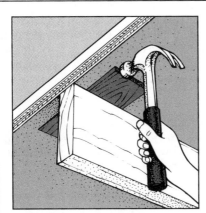

To stop a squeak, apply glue to a wood shim or shingle and drive it between the floor joist and subfloor.

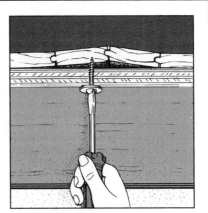

Driving a screw through the subfloor into the finished flooring can pull the boards together, stopping a squeak.

Figure 8-4:
Three ways
to squelch
a squeak.

If the underside of the floor is inaccessible, drive finish nails through the flooring at an angle to silence a squeak.

Squeaking stairs

A staircase consists of the *stringers* (the notched boards that provides the support for the stairs), the *treads* (steps that you walk on), and the *risers* (boards that enclose the space between the treads). If any of these components is improperly nailed or fastened, the stringers, treads, and risers may rub against each other and cause squeaks.

Have a helper walk slowly up and down the stairs while you listen for squeaks beneath the stairs. (At this rate, your friend may lose so much weight that the floor stops squeaking all by itself.) Many stairs have three stringers: one on each end and a third down the center of the staircase. The first step is to check the stringers to be sure that they're securely fastened to the wall framing, if the stairs are against the wall, or to the header joist at the top of the stair landing.

If the center stringer sags (drooping lower than the side stringers), purchase a couple of 8-foot-long two-by-fours. Cut the boards long enough to span the width of the staircase and screw them to the two side stringers and the sagging center stringer, perpendicular to the three stringers, at about the midpoint of the stair run or length. Then cut two-by-four braces and place them beneath the two-by-fours you just installed and the floor to prop up the stairs.

If the treads and risers are rubbing against each other, and you have access from the underside of the staircase, coat wooden shims with carpenter's glue and drive the shim between the riser and the tread. Or, cut small rectangular wood blocks and coat two adjoining sides with carpenter's glue. Screw the wood blocks in place with one glued side against the tread and the other glued side against the riser, as shown in Figure 8-5.

Figure 8-5: Two methods for controlling squeaky stairs.

Stop squeaking stairs by gluing and then screwing wood blocks between the risers and treads.

If you can't get to the underside of the staircase, drive finish nails into risers at an angle to help silence squeaks.

If these techniques fail, or if the staircase is not accessible from the underside, drive flooring nails from the top of the treads down into the risers. Drive these nails at an angle, or slightly toenailed, to prevent them from working up and out, as shown in Figure 8-5. Carpenters use this technique to drive a nail into wood diagonally where there's little wood surface, such as on a stair tread and riser. Two nails driven in at an angle hold boards together better than nails driven in straight. Use a nail set to drive the heads of the nails below the surface of the treads.

Laying Resilient Floor Tiles

Resilient floor tiles are available in a wide variety of attractive patterns, and in 9- and 12-inch squares. Because the tiles have joints at all four sides, they're not suitable for installation on floors that are exposed to water, such as a bathroom or laundry room floor. The water may enter the joints between the tiles and destroy the bond between the adhesive and the tiles.

Some tiles have peel-and-stick adhesive backs, so you don't need adhesive or trowels to lay the floor. Other resilient tiles are dry-back, requiring that you trowel a coat of adhesive onto the floor before laying the tile.

To estimate how many tiles are needed for a room, multiply the room's length by its width, and ta-da! You have the square footage. Because the tile may vary slightly from one tile run to another, buy enough tile to complete the job and to keep some leftovers for later repairs. If you're not confident with calculating square footage, draw a sketch of the room (preferably on graph paper) showing dimensions; take the floor plan to a tile dealer, who can help you figure out how much tile and other supplies to purchase. You can use our floor tile estimator on the tear-out reference card in the front of this book to find out how much you need.

The most difficult part of laying floor tiles is the grunt work you have to do first: carrying the heavy boxes of tiles home, removing all the furniture in the room, and rolling up the carpeting. After you finish all the hard labor, follow these steps for the fun part of this project — laying the tiles:

1. **Remove the base shoe molding around the walls with a pry bar and hammer, being careful to gently ease the molding away from the walls without breaking the wood.**

   A *pry bar* is a flat steel bar with beveled edges in its ends and a hole in one end. Its design gives you leverage to slide one end in between the molding and wall while you use the other end to force the molding away from the wall.

2. **Pull out the nails from the wall and molding and clean the existing floor covering.**

   Be sure to remove all dirt and wax; the adhesive on the tiles won't stick to a waxed or a dirty surface.

3. **When the floor surface is clean and dry, measure to the center of the room along both the length and width of the room.**

   Use a chalkline to mark the centerline of the room going both ways. You will begin laying the tile at the center of the room, where the two chalklines cross, to ensure that the border tiles along the width and length of the room are equal (shown in Figure 8-6).

4. **Before starting to lay the tiles, open several cartons and lay out loose tiles from each carton so that all are within your reach.**

5. **Lay the tiles alternately (one from one pile, then one from another, and so on) so that slight color variations in the tiles between cartons won't be noticeable.**

   Follow the arrows on the paper that you peel off the back of the tiles to be sure that the tile is headed in the right direction for a continuous pattern.

6. **Lay all the full-sized tiles first; then do the border tiles that require cutting, which you can do with a sharp utility knife and straightedge.**

Figure 8-6:
Accurate layout lines assure a good-looking floor. Begin laying tiles where the two chalklines intersect.

The procedure for laying dry-back tiles is the same, except that you have to use a notched trowel and spread tile adhesive on the floor. The proper adhesive choice depends on the surface that you plan to cover, so be sure to tell your salesperson what sort of surface you're covering so that you go home with the correct adhesive.

Your chalklines divide the floor into four equal sections. To double-check your layout, go to the center of the room, where the chalklines intersect; begin laying tiles from that point all the way to the wall. The distance from the last full tile to the wall needs to be at least a quarter-tile in width. If the last tile is only a slim sliver, adjust the position of the layout lines. Using a larger section to fill the gap makes your tile job easier and more professional-looking.

Apply adhesive to only one quadrant of the floor at a time and block the doorway to keep kids and pets from running in and getting stuck — not a pretty sight. Most installations require you to wait until the adhesive is dry to the touch, or *tack-free,* before you can lay the tiles. First, position three or four tiles along the chalklines in two directions; then go back and lay tiles next to these. Finally, fill in the area between these rows. This approach helps to ensure straight rows as you progress toward the walls.

To lay the border tile that goes around the perimeter of the room, position a full tile squarely atop a tile in the last full row. Then position a second tile above the first, with the front edge of the tile $^1/_4$ inch away from the wall (or base trim, if the shoe molding only has been removed). With a pencil, mark the front edge of the border tile on the face of the tile beneath (shown in Figure 8-7), and use a utility knife to cut the tile. Then position the cut tile so that you have a tight seam where the tiles meet. Continue in this way until you lay all the border tiles.

To ensure a good bond between adhesive and tiles, rent a heavy floor roller and, after you finish laying the tile, roll it over the entire floor, being careful not to miss a spot.

Figure 8-7:
Laying border tiles around the perimeter of the room requires careful measuring and cutting.

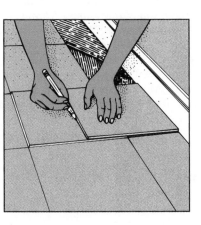

The backer paper that you peel off tiles is slippery. Throw it away so that you don't slip on it and fall — you wouldn't want to dent your brand-new floor.

Laying Parquet Tiles

Parquet tiles are usually 12-x-12-inch tiles made of small wood strips bonded together in an alternating pattern. Some versions of parquet are composed of a veneer laminated to a plywood backing. The solid-wood type is usually made up of individual pieces of wood held together with a wire backing.

Laying parquet is similar to laying resilient floor tiles, but you want to pay special attention to placement because the tiles are made of four smaller squares of alternately oriented strips. Lay them so that the parquet squares form a pattern. They look best in parallel, woven, or herringbone patterns — depending on the look you want. Use a trowel to apply *plank parquet acrylic urethane adhesive,* available where the tiles are sold, usually at home centers or tile stores.

Because parquet is real wood, it is more sensitive to moisture than resilient flooring materials. We don't recommend that you install parquet on a below-grade basement floor. It can be done, but it's a project best left to a professional.

The preparation for laying parquet tiles is the same as for laying resilient tiles. Use a sharp hand saw to undercut the bottom edge of door casings, or to trim and cut out a $\frac{1}{2}$-inch-wide section of the door casings so that you can slip the edge of the tile under the casing. Prepare the room by thoroughly cleaning the floor so there's no grit or dirt.

The right time to renail squeaking floors is when you're laying a new floor or floor covering. Before beginning any flooring project, walk over the floor(s) to test for squeaks. If you locate a squeak, drive spiral-shank flooring nails through the floor/subfloor and into the joists. (*Spiral-shank* nails have a twist in their shaft that enables them to act more like screws than nails.) Drive these nails in at an angle — or, as a carpenter would say, *toenail* them. Nails driven in at an angle hold two boards together better than nails driven straight into the wood. Walk over the floor to be sure that all squeaks are silenced before proceeding with your new flooring project:

1. **Measure out from the starter wall a distance of 4 or 5 tile widths. Mark this distance on each end of the room.**

2. **Find the centerline for the length and width of the room and use a chalkline to mark these two lines.**

   Begin installation in one quadrant, at the corner, formed where the two chalklines intersect.

3. Use a notched trowel to spread adhesive on the existing floor.

The type and size of the proper notched trowel is noted in the instructions, often the best choice is a trowel with a $3/32$-inch notch. To ensure that you're applying the adhesive at the right spread rate, push the trowel against the floor and hold it at a 45-degree angle as you smooth out the adhesive. You generally want to apply the adhesive to a 3-foot-square area at a time so that the adhesive doesn't dry out, but be sure to refer to the instructions on the can. As you apply adhesive, be careful not to cover the layout lines.

4. Lay all the full-size tiles first; then cut and install the border tiles.

5. Cut border tiles to the proper size.

At the borders, lay a full tile face up and centered over the last full tile that you laid. Then take a second tile and position it on top of the first tile with the back edge of the second tile about $1/2$ inch away from the wall or base trim. The $1/2$-inch gap allows for expansion of the wood tiles. Make a pencil mark on the first tile using the front edge of the top tile as a guide. Use a hand saw to cut the lower tile along the pencil mark and then install it at the border. Proceed in this manner until you finish cutting and laying all the border tiles.

Parquet tiles are factory-finished with a tough polyurethane coating. Do not use floor wax over any flooring that has a polyurethane finish; the wax interferes with refinishing when the floor must be renewed.

Concrete floors that are at or below *grade level* (the level of the soil on the outside of the building) are prone to moisture from absorption or condensation. The moisture can destroy the bond between the adhesive and the tiles, and may warp or stain wood flooring. For this reason, don't install parquet or strip-wood flooring directly on any concrete floor that's below grade level. If you want to install a wood floor over a concrete basement floor, consult the manufacturer about using their product on concrete floors that are below grade. Some manufacturers prohibit any such installation; others require that you first waterproof the concrete slab, lay down a plastic vapor barrier film, and then glue or nail wood strips or sleepers at intervals 16-inches OC *(on center)* — that is, measuring 16 inches from center to center. Then install a subfloor of $1/2$-inch-thick exterior plywood, and install the wood flooring atop the plywood.

Laying a Vinyl (Sheet) Floor

Sheet flooring is a resilient material that withstands continual use and washings. If you're setting out on a first-time project, installing sheet flooring is a good choice, so long as it's for a small room rather than a large area. The sections of material for a large room can be cumbersome and difficult to manage. You can install either 6- or 12-foot widths of this flooring with adhesive, or you may choose to allow the sheet to lay unglued on the surface of the floor, only fastened around the perimeter of the room when base shoe molding is nailed in place.

Use a sharp hand saw to undercut the door casing or trim moldings, so that the vinyl can slip easily beneath the casing, as shown in Figure 8-8.

Figure 8-8: To assure proper clearance when cutting door molding, place your saw on top of a piece of the vinyl flooring, or under-layment and flooring.

To prepare for new floor covering, first consider the old flooring. If the existing floor covering is vinyl, the best solution is to install a layer of $3/8$-inch-thick lauan mahogany plywood over the existing floor. The new underlayment eliminates the frustrating task of removing the old floor covering and conceals any pattern that may show through.

When laying the plywood, stagger the end joints and make sure that they're all positioned over a floor joist. Use nails or screws driven into floor joists to anchor the plywood in place. Then trowel a floor filler over the joints and nail or screw holes to level and smooth the underlayment.

Floor fillers are available at dealers who sell materials to professional installers and at home centers and flooring stores. Fast-setting Patch & Skim Coat by Armstrong is one popular brand of floor filler. Follow the directions for mixing and application and let it dry before installing the new vinyl floor covering.

If increasing the floor height by the thickness of the plywood underlayment causes problems along cabinets or at doorways, you can install the new vinyl over the existing vinyl. Check the old vinyl to be sure that it's tight to the floor, and use a wax remover product to take off old wax and grime from the existing vinyl. Then trowel two coats of floor filler over the entire floor.

If the old floor covering is embossed, the pattern may show through the new vinyl. Buy an embossing compound from a dealer, and trowel two coats of the compound over the existing floor to cover the embossing pattern and to smooth the floor.

Because a wrong cut can be an expensive mistake, you're wise to make a paper template of the room so that you know where to cut the flooring — an especially important step if the room is irregular in shape, or has many corners. Use masking tape and sheets of heavy building or butcher's paper taped together to form a pattern of the floor plan, and cut holes in the paper so that you can tape it to the floor to hold it in place (shown in Figure 8-9). You can also use photographic backdrop paper, called *no-seam,* to completely cover the floor and make a new pattern. You can also find template paper at home and floor centers where floor coverings are sold.

Figure 8-9:
Make a paper pattern of the room by taping together pieces of butcher paper or newspaper.

Overlap the edges of the adjoining sheets of paper a few inches and tape them together. In creating the pattern, subtract $^1/_8$-inch margin away from the wall and other cutout areas to allow for fitting the sheets into place. Use a combination square to measure distances from the wall and cabinets or whatever else is permanently installed (pipes, for example). We know that it's tempting to cut around a refrigerator or other heavy object, but don't. Move it out of the way; the same goes for your lazy brother-in-law.

A *combination square* is a steel ruler that has a movable slide with a 90-degree and 45-degree surface. This type of ruler is handy for transferring measurements from one area to another.

When the paper template is complete, unroll the sheet flooring with the pattern side up and position the paper template on top of the flooring. Use a water soluble felt-tipped marker to trace the outline of the template onto the flooring. Then cut the sheet flooring with a utility knife along the outline marks. Replace the knife blade frequently with a sharp one for clean cuts.

If the room has straight walls with few offsets, you can simply lay the covering in place and position it so that the covering overlaps about three inches up each wall. Then carefully cut the covering to fit. (Some manufacturers offer a marking tool that you move along the wall, marking the cut line.) Then cut away the excess along the line, using sturdy scissors.

If you must have a seam in the floor covering, use vinyl seam sealer to secure and weld together the edges of the covering to prevent water entry and damage to the flooring.

At the edges, you can cover the crack between the floor covering and the base trim with base shoe or other molding. Or use a quality caulk, like a latex tub-tile caulk, to seal the edge seams.

 Renail squeaking floors when you're laying a new floor or floor covering. Before beginning any flooring project, walk over the floor(s) to test for squeaks. If you locate a squeak, drive hardened flooring nails through the floor/subfloor and into the joists. Toenail or drive the nails at an angle to prevent withdrawal. Then walk over the floor to be sure all squeaks are silenced before proceeding with your new flooring project.

 What is the most likely time for damage to occur to your new floor covering? When you're moving heavy appliances or furniture into place on the new covering. To avoid floor damage and injury to your back, rent an appliance dolly and use it to move the appliances out of the room, and to reposition the appliances atop the new floor covering.

 For any flooring work, invest in a pair of knee pads — wear them and save your knees!

Laying a Prefinished Wood Floor

Prefinished wood flooring is an ideal material for the do-it-yourselfer. The flooring is seasoned, sanded, and finished at the factory, under ideal conditions, so none of these critical steps is left for the amateur. The product is ready for installation right out of the box. The finish is either a combination of wood stain plus durable polyurethane, or a clear polyurethane that protects and enhances the natural wood tone. Prefinished flooring is available in oak, birch, hard maple, or pine.

The method of installation depends on the type of flooring and the manufacturer's specifications:

✔ Some hardwood flooring is laid over a subfloor on which adhesive has been spread with a trowel.

✔ Some flooring is nailed in place, or joined with tongues and grooves.

✔ Some brands of flooring are laid over a resilient base, with the individual flooring strips glued together at the edges, instead of being glued to the subfloor.

Buy enough flooring at one time to do the job. Be aware that you must make some allowance for end-matching and waste. The easiest way to estimate your flooring needs is to carefully measure the floor size in square feet (room width multiplied by room length) — take the measurements to your flooring dealer for an accurate estimate of the amount of flooring needed. Use our project calculator on the Quick Reference Card at the front of this book to find out how much flooring material you'll need for a room.

When you choose a flooring, read and heed the manufacturer's directions for installation. For adhesive application, use *only* the adhesive or mastic suggested by the manufacturer. Substitution of a cheaper adhesive may lead to job failure and void the product warranty.

Because of the danger of moisture damage to a wood floor, most manufacturers prohibit the use of wood flooring over any concrete floor that is below grade; that is, lower than the ground level at the exterior foundation. Check with the manufacturer for further advice on below-grade wood floor applications.

Wood flooring is properly dried at the factory, and is relatively stable, but any wood product is subject to some expansion and contraction as the temperature and humidity changes. Many experts suggest putting the wood flooring in the room where it's to be laid, and left for two or three days to acclimate to the temperature and humidity conditions there.

Instructions for installing prefinished wood flooring are supplied by the manufacturer. The following general directions apply to any installation of prefinished wood flooring:

1. **Remove all the base shoe molding on the walls.**

   If your walls are wearing sock molding, remove it, too.

2. **Clean the subfloor with a shop vacuum and crevice tool for removing dust and debris.**

3. **If you plan to nail the flooring in place, first cover the subfloor with builder's paper, sometimes called *red rosin paper*.**

   This step helps prevent future squeaks and retards the passage of moisture from below, a source of warping.

4. **Position the first strip of flooring $^3/_4$ inch from the wall, with the groove side of the strip toward the starter wall.**

   The $^3/_4$-inch space, which will be hidden by base trim, allows the wood flooring to expand without buckling. Lay the flooring in the direction of the length of the room.

5. **Make a mark along the edge of the tongue at both ends of the room, and then use a chalkline to make a continuous mark that extends the length of the room.**

6. **Nail the first row of flooring so that the tongue edge of the flooring aligns with the chalkline.**

   Face nail the groove side of the flooring in place. You just drive the nails through the face of the flooring board to face nail, as shown in Figure 8-10.

7. **Blind nail the rest of the flooring in place.**

   No, *blind nailing* doesn't mean closing your eyes; it means that you drive the nails through the tongue on the front side of the flooring strip. The nails are then hidden by the next strip of flooring. To blind nail, position the nail at a 45-degree angle on the corner at the top of the tongue. Use 7d hardened (spiral-shank) nails. Don't drive the nail home so hard that the hammer damages the edge or face of the flooring. When the nail is almost home, raise the hammer handle so that the hammer face strikes both the head of the nail and the tongue of the flooring. Then lay another nail flat, with its head over the head of the driven nail, and strike the horizontal nail head to sink the driven nail. You can also use a nail set to drive nails the last little bit into the tongue.

Figure 8-10: Use spacers to position the first floorboard; rent a floor nailer to nail down subsequent boards.

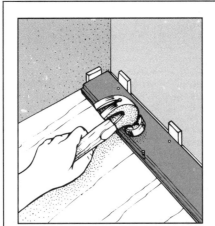

A. Use 3/4-inch spacers between the first floorboard and wall.

B. A floor nailer positions the nails so that one blow from the mallet drives the nail into the flooring at the correct angle and depth.

Putting power into your nailing

If you're nailing down the flooring, you can proceed with hand nailing or you can try a quicker, easier way: Rent a power nailer, which holds a magazine full of nails. Power nailers are so darn easy to use, they make the job fun. Simply strike the plunger with a hammer to drive the nail home. (Refer to Figure 8-10.)

The power nailer has a double-faced hammer: The steel face is used to strike the plunger; the rubber face is used to tap the flooring strip tight against the last strip. If you're using a power nailer, strike the flooring strips on both the tongue edge and the ends to drive the flooring strip tight along both the edge and the ends.

Practice with the power nailer to be sure that you're using it properly. The first blow must be sufficiently heavy to drive the nail in, because a second nail drops into position behind the first (sort of like a stapler).

If you're using a power nailer, you must face-nail the first few rows against the wall until there's room to position the power nailer. (*Face-nailing* means to drive the nail into to top surface of the floor board, and not into the tongue.) After you establish the starter rows,

cut and lay out six or eight rows of flooring, a process called *racking the floor*.

Racking lets you arrange the floor pattern and do most of the cutting in one operation, saving you time and energy. The flooring strips are bundled in random lengths. As you rack the floor, stagger the end joints so that they're at least 6 inches apart. Alternate the strips by length. Set aside the shortest strips for use in closets or for filling small spaces. Scatter the rest of the short lengths so that they fall randomly over the floor. As you install the flooring that's already racked, move out and rerack more flooring.

When you get to the end of a row of flooring, use the cutoff piece (if it's at least 6 inches long) to start the next row at the opposite end of the room.

When you reach the opposite side of the room, you must hand-nail the final three or four strips because there's not room to use a power nailer. If necessary, rip cut the last row of flooring for width. Then use a pry bar set against a block of wood on the wall to pry the last flooring strip tightly against the laid flooring and face-nail it in place.

 If you're laying wood flooring in more than one room and have to change the direction of the flooring strips, the tongues and grooves may not match up. In this case, you can cut a thin wood strip, called a *spline*, the thickness of the groove in the flooring. Insert the spline into the groove edge of one board to act as the missing tongue and fit into the grooved ends of the opposite flooring.

Laying Carpeting

The key to laying carpeting is to make sure that the fuzzy side faces up. The next most important step is to figure out how to operate the glue machine that seams carpet edges together. You also need to master the stretching tools that keep the carpet wrinkle-free. Lighter weight, less expensive carpeting is your best bet if you're attempting installation for the first time. If the room is less than 12 feet wide (standard width of carpeting), no seaming is needed — definitely doable. The problem is that heavier, better quality carpet is much more difficult to stretch out to lay flat. Light- to mid-weight carpet is easier to lay, cut, fit, and stretch than heavier quality carpet.

Getting rid of the old stuff

Your first job — removing the existing carpeting — is a simple but dirty task, perfect for a homeowner with limited carpentry skills but plenty of brute strength.

Some really old wall-to-wall carpeting is stapled directly into the floor with U-shaped staples; you simply have to pull up the carpeting and roll it in small bundles to remove it. But most wall-to-wall carpet is held in place by wooden hook strips nailed to the floor around the perimeter of the room. *Hook strips* are narrow strips of plywood that have small hooks or nails that protrude upward at an angle. The carpet is stretched into position, then pushed over the nails that protrude upward from the hook strip.

To remove the carpet, look at the corners of the room: Often, you find that the old carpet's stretched enough to loosen the corners of the carpet. Grasp the corner of the carpet and pull upward to release the carpet edges from the hook strip. To make the old carpet easier to handle, use a sharp razor knife to cut it into more manageable pieces. Roll the old carpet tightly and secure the roll with twine or duct tape for disposal. If the existing pad shows little wear and isn't completely flattened or "bottomed out," you can reuse it.

If the carpet pad's in a deteriorated state, replace it with *rebond* padding, which is made from multicolor foam particles, bonded together by adhesives. Rebond pads offer a good combination of performance and economy. Choose a 6- to 8-pound rebond pad for most carpet installations.

To remove an old carpet pad, just pull up the staples that hold the pad in place. Use a staple gun and $1/2$-inch staples to secure the new pad to the wood floor.

Using carpet strips and tools

If you're recarpeting, the hook strips are already in place. If you're carpeting over a wood or concrete floor, you must install new hook strips around the entire room perimeter. To install hook strips on a wood floor, just drive in the anchor nails that are already started in the hook strips, as shown in Figure 8-11. If you must install hook strips on concrete floors, you can use adhesives to secure the strips to the concrete, or use a power nailer to penetrate the concrete.

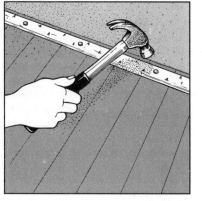

Figure 8-11:
Hook strips nailed around the perimeter of the room hold carpeting in place.

You can rent carpet tools at most tool rental outlets. To install a room-sized carpet, you need a pole stretcher, knee kicker, wall trimmer, and utility razor knife. If you have seams to match, you also need adhesive-coated seam tape and a heating iron.

✔ Use a long *pole stretcher* to brace against the baseboard on one wall while the carpet is stretched toward the opposite wall. The stretcher head has protruding teeth at the working end that hook into the carpet. The carpet pole can be adjusted for length. Hook the teeth of the stretcher head into the carpet and pull back on the handle to stretch the carpet until it's tight, and then push the carpet over the teeth on the hook strip.

✔ A small stretching tool, called a *knee kicker,* can be used for stretching the carpet edges in limited spaces like hallways. To use the knee kicker, just hook the teeth in the head in the carpet, and then drive the kicker by bumping the padded end with your knee. When the carpet is stretched, press the carpet edge over the hook strip to secure the carpet in place.

✔ You can rent a *wall trimmer,* which has a handle to guide you as you cut the edge of the carpet. If you push the trimmer along the wall or baseboard, you get a straight cut that fits neatly along the baseboard.

Laying it down

Position the carpet on the floor so that the carpet edges overlap on all walls, as shown in Figure 8-12. Stretch the carpet until it's taut and wrinkle-free, and then secure the edges over the tack strips. Use a knee kicker or carpet trimming tool to cut away the overlap.

Unmatched carpet edges produce visible seams and rapid wear. Carpets that are improperly stretched tend to wrinkle. As people walk across the carpet, their feet slide across the peaks of the wrinkles, causing premature wear.

To make a seam in the carpet, fit the two edges of the carpet together. Insert a strip of adhesive tape under the carpet so that it's centered at the seam. Plug in the electric iron and let it heat up. Then pull back one edge of the seam and insert the heating iron to melt the adhesive on the tape. Press both edges of the carpet into the adhesive tape, as shown in Figure 8-12.

To make trim cuts around outside and inside corners, first measure and cut the carpeting with several inches excess in each direction. Lay the piece down and make relief cuts with a razor knife to cut away excess carpet.

Laying Foam-Backed Carpet

Foam-backed carpet, often used on porches or basements, incorporates both carpet and pad and is relatively inexpensive and easy for the handyperson to install. At the risk of stating the obvious: Buy a piece of carpet that's slightly larger than the room. Although there may be some advantages to buying a piece of carpeting that's smaller than the room (it costs less, it's lighter, you don't have to deal with that fussy trimming), the finished product will look a tad funny.

Unroll the carpet on the floor and position it so that it overlaps all the walls. Let the carpet lay or relax for 24 hours to get the wrinkles out. You can spend the same time resting your own wrinkles.

You can secure foam-backed carpet to the floor with carpet adhesive or with double-faced carpet tape (shown in Figure 8-13). Both products are sold at carpet dealers and home centers. To make future removal easier, apply a trowel-width of glue on the floor, along the walls, so that it contacts only the four edges of the carpet.

You can rent carpet installation tools, such as the knee kicker, which helps stretch the carpet tight.

Seams in carpeting are joined together with heat-activated tape. Rent a seaming iron or use an old iron to melt the adhesive on the tape and then press carpet in place.

Figure 8-12:
Three tricks to laying down carpeting like a professional.

Cut carpet several inches larger than needed; make relief cuts in the corners so that carpet lies flat and then trim to fit room.

As you secure the edges of the carpet to the adhesive, pull the carpet taut to eliminate any wrinkles. You may want to rent a knee kicker to make stretching easier. (This tool is designed to stretch and force carpeting for a tight fit. While you're down on your hands and knees, you apply pressure to the padded end of the tool, forcing the other end of the tool to drive the carpeting against the wall.) When the carpet is secure, trim the edges with a sharp utility knife, carefully fitting the carpet against the wall or base trim, as shown in Figure 8-13. An even better approach is to rent a carpet-trimming tool for cutting and fitting the carpet edges.

 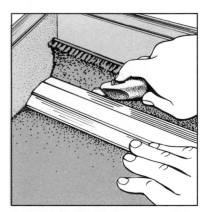

Figure 8-13:
Attach and trim your foam-backed carpet.

A. Use double-sided carpet tape around the perimeter of the room to hold foam-backed carpet in place.

B. To trim foam-backed carpet, push the straightedge tight against wall and then cut carpet with a sharp utility knife.

Chapter 9

Windows Don't Have to Be a Pane

● ●

In This Chapter

▶ Keeping all your windows in good working order

▶ Conserving energy with caulking and weather stripping

▶ Treating your windows to shades, blinds, and curtains

▶ Protecting your windows from thieves in the night

● ●

*T*he windows in a house are designed to bring sunshine and fresh air inside and make a dreary room cheerful. Unfortunately, in some homes, windows have broken glass panes and rotted wood, or they rattle like a bag of bones and let in cold drafts. This chapter is a crash course in the basics of window maintenance and repair. Read on to discover how to improve or upgrade your windows, and even how to decorate them with shades and miniblinds.

Know Your Window

Not all windows look and work alike. Some windows slide, crank, or swing open and close; others, such as picture windows, have no working parts. The window frame, which encloses all the basic parts of the window, may be made of wood, vinyl, or metal. Wooden window frames require painting, but those made of vinyl or aluminum are maintenance-free. Because metal conducts cold, wood windows are preferred in climates with cold winters.

The most popular window style is the *double-hung window,* shown in Figure 9-1. Double-hung windows have an upper and a lower *sash* (the inner frame that holds the glass panes in place) that move vertically in separate channels. The sashes are separated by a small piece of wood called a *parting strip.* The upper and lower sashes have *meeting rails* — that is, the top rail of the bottom sash and the bottom rail of the upper sash meet and are slanted to form a tight seal between the rails. A locking mechanism secures the sashes together at the two parting rails to create a tight seal and to minimize air infiltration and heat loss.

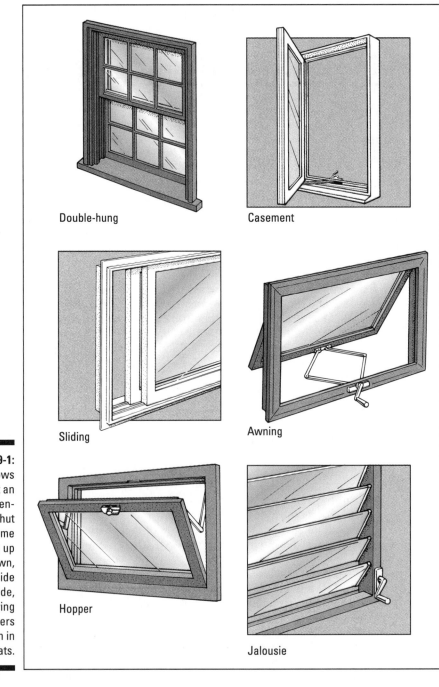

Double-hung

Casement

Sliding

Awning

Hopper

Jalousie

Figure 9-1:
Windows
aren't an
open-
and-shut
case; some
slide up
and down,
others side
to side,
some swing
out, others
open in
slats.

Other common window styles, also shown in Figure 9-1, include the following:

- ✔ *Casement windows* have hinges on one side of the sash, and swing outward when you activate a lever or a crank. Because the entire casement sash swings outward, these kinds of windows provide full ventilation and unobstructed views. Casement windows are easy to open, so they are commonly used where humidity or heat can build up, such as above kitchen sinks, in bathrooms, and on walls that connect to porches.

- ✔ *Sliding windows* open horizontally and bypass each other in separate tracks mounted on the header jamb and sill.

- ✔ *Awning windows* are hinged at the top and swing outward via a crank or lever.

- ✔ *Hopper windows* are hinged at the bottom and swing inward.

- ✔ *Jalousie windows* are made of a series of horizontal glass slats that are joined so that all the glass slats open or close together when the crank is turned. The drawback to jalousie windows is that there are cracks between all the slats, and these cracks offer an avenue for air infiltration.

Although all these windows differ in design, the basic maintenance is the same for all types of operable windows. By figuring out how your windows are supposed to work, you can maintain them in top shape and detect any problems before they become serious.

To make window maintenance and repair easier, take time to familiarize yourself with the windows in your house. We once spotted a neighbor teetering precariously on a 24-foot ladder, washing a second story double-hung window. He had been at it all day, and was tired from climbing and balancing on a ladder. He was flabbergasted when we walked up the stairs and, using a sideways motion, snapped the sash out of the window he was washing. If our neighbor had only known the features of his windows, he could have easily removed and washed the windows from the inside, without having to set foot on the ladder.

Window Maintenance

At least once each year, put together a maintenance kit and inspect, lubricate, and clean each window. We admit that window duty is not a particularly pleasant way to spend a weekend, but annual maintenance adds years to the life of your windows. Be sure that your maintenance kit includes the following items:

- A small paintbrush for cleaning dirt and debris from the window channels
- A handheld, battery-powered vacuum for sucking up loose dirt
- A roll of paper towels
- An aerosol can of spray lubricant, such as WD-40, for lubricating channels and locks
- A selection of both Phillips and flat-head screwdrivers for tightening any loose screws

First, open the window and use a hand vacuum or small paintbrush to clean the debris from the window sill. Then wet a paper towel and wipe down the sill to remove any residual dust.

Inspect the window unit for any loose hardware. Metal window channels or guides are attached to the side frames via small brads or screws. Renail or tighten loose guides. Check the window locks to be sure that screws are tight: If they aren't, retighten them. Lubricate the locks with a shot of spray lubricant.

If window locks are fouled with paint, remove the locks and soak them in paint remover; then clean, polish, lubricate, and replace the hardware. Use paper towels to wipe away any excess lubricant.

Modern double-hung windows don't have ropes and sash weights, the way older model windows do. Instead, the sashes travel vertically in metal channels that are positioned on both sides of the window. The channel on one side is spring-loaded, and the spring tension holds the window in position. But when you move the window sash to the middle of the frame, and then pull sharply to the spring-loaded side, the sashes slip easily out of the frames, ready for repair or cleaning. This easy-access feature has been available on double-hung windows for several decades. To check your own windows, press against the metal channel on both sides of the frame. If one side yields to hand pressure, your window sash can be snapped out of the frame. Use graphite or any other dry lubricant to grease the metal window channels in double-hung windows.

Casement or awning windows are operated with a crank or lever. The windows open via an arm, which may be either a single linkage arm, double sliding arms, or a scissors arm. By opening the windows fully, you can disengage the arm from the track, which permits you to lubricate the arm and track, or to free the window sash for easier washing.

If you have casement windows that are hinged on one side and swing out via levers or crank handles, open the windows fully and use spray lubricant to oil the hardware, including the crank or lever, the hinges, and the lock.

With the arm disengaged, you can also service the operator mechanism. Check the owners' manual provided with the windows for instructions on how to remove the cranking mechanism cover. Of course, owners' manuals, like able-bodied teenagers, have a way of disappearing when you need them. If you can't find the official instructions, look for a couple of screws on the housing cover to which the crank or lever is attached and remove them. Lift off the cover, apply a bit of light grease to the crank gears or the opening levers, and then replace the cover.

Unsticking a stuck window

If a window is stuck, the problem may be simply that the window channels need cleaning and lubrication, but the odds are that paint has run into the cracks between the window stops and the sash and is binding the window. Either problem usually yields to a simple solution.

The first rule of unsticking is this: If the window doesn't budge, *don't force it*. You may break the glass and cut yourself, or damage the window beyond repair.

First, check to be sure that the window is unlocked and that you're not lifting up on the sill. If the window is unlocked, place a block of wood against the sash frame and, moving the block along the entire length of both stiles, tap the block lightly against the stiles with a hammer. This trick may loosen up the window so that you can open it. Whatever you do, don't pound on the block or you may crack the glass.

If your double-hung window still refuses to open, use a small pry bar to remove the stops along both side stiles of the sash. You can then remove the window sash. Use fine sandpaper or a paint scraper to clean the edges of the sash and the edges of the stops. To lubricate the sash, rub a block of paraffin or a wax candle stub along the edges of the window sash and the stop.

If the window resists your best open-sesame efforts, check for paint in the crack between the window sash and stops. Insert a serrated tool, called a *Paint Zipper,* into the crack, as shown in Figure 9-2. Using a light sawing motion, move the Paint Zipper in the crack along the entire length of the window sash, on both sides. Then use the Zipper to cut any paint bond between the bottom rail and the sill. Now try again to open the window. In most cases, the window will open. (A pizza cutter has been known to work just as well as a Paint Zipper; don't hesitate to experiment!)

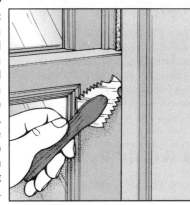

Figure 9-2:
Use a special tool with a serrated blade or a putty knife with a thin, flexible blade to open painted-shut windows.

Replacing the sash cords

The sash weights in old double-hung windows are intended to provide balance so that, when the window is open to the desired position, it stays there. If the sash cord (or chain) breaks, the window can't stay in place. If you have to use a stick to prop open your double-hung window, chances are that the sash cord is broken and the window operates with all the controlled restraint of a guillotine.

To replace the sash cord, follow these steps (illustrated in Figure 8-3):

1. **Use a razor knife to cut the paint line where the stop is attached to the frame.**

   Cutting this paint seal prevents the stop from breaking when you pry it off.

2. **Using a thin pry bar or a stiff putty knife, gently pry out the stop at each nail location.**

3. **At both sides of the frame, along the upper sash, use the pry bar or putty knife to remove the parting strip.**

4. **Raise the lower sash so that it clears the *stool* (or sill); then swing out the sash.**

5. **Disconnect the sash cords from the slots at each side of the sash.**

   With the sash removed, you can see the sash weight access panels on each side of the jamb.

6. **Use a screwdriver to remove the retaining screws, and then pull off the panel cover.**

7. **Remove the sash weight from its space.**

8. **Use an aerosol lubricant such as WD-40 to lubricate the pulley above each access panel.**

9. **Feed the new sash cord over the pulley and downward, until you can see the end of the cord through the hole at the access panel.**

10. **Tie the sash cord to the weight.**

    Pass the end of the cord through the hole in the top of the sash weight and then tie a figure eight knot in the end of the rope.

A. Gently loosen the window stop before pulling out the nails. (Step 2)

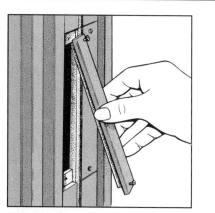

B. Access the window weights by opening the small door in the base of the jamb. (Step 6)

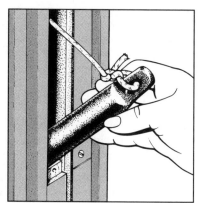

C. Remove the weight from the hollow area behind the window jamb. (Step 7)

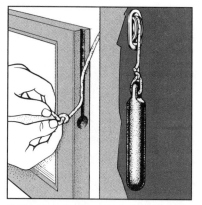

D. To reinstall the sash, tie a knot in the end of the cord and push the knot into the recess in the side of the sash. (Step 12)

Figure 9-3:
Replacing a damaged sash cord in a double-hung window.

11. **Replace the weight in its compartment.**

    Pull the other end of the rope tight so the sash weight stands up straight in the compartment.

12. **Attach the sash rope to the sash**

    The end of the rope you have in your hand attaches to the window sash. Most sashes have a groove milled in the side that fits the diameter of the sash rope. At the end of the groove is a recess that holds the knot. Tie a knot in the cord so that the sash weight hangs about 3 inches above the bottom of the compartment when you put the knot into the recess and raise the sash all the way up.

While you have the window sash removed, replace *both* sash cords, not just the broken one. Follow the preceding steps to replace the sash cords in both sides of the window. After you replace the cords, position the window sash back in the frame and renail the window stops.

Modern double-hung windows have metal channels in which the sash sides, or *stiles,* move. These channels are spring-loaded, and one channel has tension screws that can be adjusted to hold the window in any open position. If your double-hung window refuses to stay open at the chosen position, adjust the tension on the channel. Inspect the window channels to find the adjustment screws. To increase the tension on the stiles, use a screwdriver to turn the screws counterclockwise. When properly adjusted, windows open easily, but remain firmly in place at any open position.

Replacing a broken window pane

Replacing window glass is not a difficult task. Repairing the damage is only slightly more difficult than breaking the glass in the first place. Just gather the appropriate materials and tools and follow the steps for the type of window you're repairing.

You need the following materials to replace a broken pane:

- **Replacement glass:** Ask the salesperson at a hardware store or home center to cut a piece of glass exactly to size. Follow the steps later in this section to make sure that your measurements are accurate.

- **Latex glazing putty:** This material, available by the can in the glass and painting departments, forms an airtight, watertight seal while allowing the pane to expand and contract in changing temperatures.

- **A box of metal glazing points:** Sometimes called *glazier's points,* these tiny T-shaped metal pieces have pointed ends that you force into the frame and two small flaps that hold the pane of glass in place.

You also need the following tools:

✔ A heat gun (available from rental outlets) to soften the old glazing if it's still intact and as tough as cement

✔ A flexible putty knife

✔ A 1- or 2-inch stiff steel putty knife

✔ A flat-head screwdriver

When you work with broken glass, wear safety goggles to protect your eyes and gloves to cover your hands.

Wood-frame window

To replace a broken glass pane in a wood window, first measure the size of the pane. Measure the exact length and width of the grooves in which the pane will fit, and then have a new piece of glass cut so that it measures $1/8$-inch short of the exact dimensions on both the length and width, leaving a $1/16$-inch gap on all four sides between the edges of the pane and the rabbetted groove cut into the edge of the wood where the glass pane rests. This gap between the wood sash and glass is necessary because it allows room for the glass to expand when weather changes.

When you have all your tools and supplies ready, follow these steps (illustrated in Figure 9-4):

1. **Remove any remaining glass shards.**

2. **Use the heat gun to soften the old glazing putty.**

   Heat the glazing putty and try to scrape it away with a putty knife; if it does not lift off easily, apply more heat and try again. You may find that the putty around really old windows is as hard as concrete. Be patient — the heat eventually softens all putty. Don't be tempted to chisel out the old putty, unless you don't mind wrecking the window and creating even more work for yourself!

   As you remove the old glazing putty, you can see small triangular metal *glazing points,* which are used to hold the glass in position until the glazing putty is applied.

3. **Use the putty knife or the tip of a screwdriver to remove the old glazing points.**

4. **Clean and inspect the rabbet groove to be sure that no glazing putty, glass shards, or glazing points remain.**

   Be sure to wear safety goggles as well as gloves because small chips of glass can cause permanent eye damage.

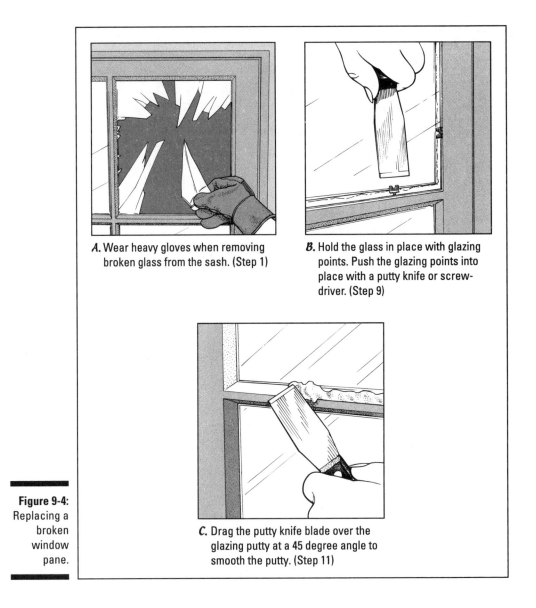

Figure 9-4:
Replacing a broken window pane.

A. Wear heavy gloves when removing broken glass from the sash. (Step 1)

B. Hold the glass in place with glazing points. Push the glazing points into place with a putty knife or screw-driver. (Step 9)

C. Drag the putty knife blade over the glazing putty at a 45 degree angle to smooth the putty. (Step 11)

5. **Squeeze out a $^1/_{16}$-inch bead of putty on the glass side of the rabbet groove between the edge of the glass and the window frame.**

6. **Press the glass down gently at the edges to bed the glass into the putty.**

   Allow the putty bed to spread out and form a moisture seal on the inside of the window, between the glass and sash.

7. Position the new pane in the rabbets so that a ^{1}/$_{16}$-inch gap remains between pane and sash on all four sides.

8. Place at least two new glazing points in each section of the window sash surrounding the new glass.

    Space the points evenly around the perimeter, about 6 inches apart.

9. Using the flat side of the putty knife or the screwdriver blade, push one corner of each triangular glazing point into the wood sash.

10. Roll a glob of putty between your bare hands to form a ^{1}/$_2$-inch-thick rope and then press the length of putty along all four sides of the glass.

11. Holding the putty knife at a 45-degree angle, press and smooth the glazing putty against the glass and sash.

12. Allow the putty to dry and then repaint the putty and repair area.

    Don't use masking tape on the glass before painting because you want the paint to form a moisture seal between the glass pane and the sash. Allow the paint to overlap about ^{1}/$_8$ inch onto the glass.

Metal-frame window

Some steel or aluminum window frames, such as those you find in many basements, are welded together in one piece at the factory. The other common type of metal-frame windows are storm windows. The glass is held in place either by glazing putty or by some sort of gasket. Except for some minor points, which we explain, replacing a broken pane of glass in either type of metal-frame window is basically the same as for wood windows.

To replace the pane in a one-piece steel window, follow the instructions for replacing glass in a wood window with the exception of the glazing points. The glass pane in steel casement windows is held in place by glazing putty and spring clips, rather than glazing points. When you remove the broken glass from the metal frame, save these clips so that you can reinstall them later.

On some one-piece aluminum windows, such as metal storm windows, the glass is held in place by a vinyl strip called a *spline.* This spline acts as the seal between the metal and glass, eliminating the need for glazing putty. Use a screwdriver or putty knife to pry out the spline. Carefully remove any broken pieces of glass from the frame and then replace the pane with new glass. Reverse the process and push the spline back into the frame with a putty knife or screwdriver.

Some metal window frames, including sliding sashes, are held together by screws placed at each corner of the frame. Remove the screws, slide out the broken pane, slide in a new pane, and redrive the corner screws.

Other metal frames may be held together by L-brackets placed at the four corners. The faces of these frames are dimpled over the L-brackets. To take these frames apart, you only have to remove one side. To do so, follow these steps:

1. **Drill a hole in the depression at both ends of one side of the frame.**

   Use a bit slightly larger than the diameter of the depression.

2. **Pull the sides of the frames apart and carefully remove any broken glass from the frame.**

3. **Replace the pane, making sure that the new glass is fully seated into the gasket surrounding the glass.**

4. **Push the corners together so that the L-brackets are in place and the joint is tight.**

5. **Use a small nail set or a punch and hammer to dimple the metal back over the L-brackets and lock the frame together.**

Repairing a rotted window sill

Window sills are sloped outward so that water can run off the sill. Brilliant, huh? Still, if the paint is peeling and the sill is left unprotected, the wood may rot. For some reason, although this condition is caused by moisture, it's called *dry rot.* Go figure.

If you have a window sill that's rotted or decayed, first use an ice pick or carpenter's awl to probe the wood. Wherever the awl penetrates easily, the wood is rotted. When you hit a point where the wood is difficult to penetrate with a probe, you've reached solid wood. If the wood is completely rotted out, you'll have to replace the entire sill with a new piece of wood — probably a job best left to a skilled carpenter. If the rot is limited to a small area, you can make repairs by following these steps (illustrated in Figure 9-5):

1. **Using a wood chisel or sharp knife, cut away any soft wood.**

   Remove all the damaged wood down to the rot-free portion.

2. **Fill the damaged area with a wood filler.**

   Filler bonds to sound wood and is very durable.

3. **Use a putty knife or a small broad knife to shape the wood filler so that it matches the contours of the old sill.**

4. **Wait for the filler to set and then sand it smooth.**

   Follow the directions on the container; you want the filler to be rock hard to the touch before sanding. Sand the repair area so that the new surface is smooth and level with the adjoining surface.

5. **Apply wood primer and paint to the repair area to match the existing finish.**

We use Minwax's High Performance Wood Filler and Wood Hardener to patch everything from rotted windows to wooden boats. You mix the wood filler together, apply it, wait for it to harden, and then sand it smoothly to shape. For deep holes, pour in the wood hardener first to stabilize the surrounding wood. Then apply the wood filler.

A. Chisel away all soft, rotten wood. (Step 1)

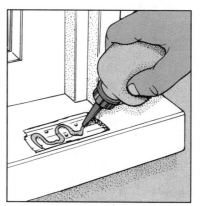

B. Apply the wood filler to the damaged area. (Step 2)

C. Smooth the filler and allow it to harden before sanding. (Steps 3-4)

Figure 9-5: Use wood filler to repair small patches of rotted wood on the window sill.

Replacing window channels

If your sashes let in drafts and rattle in their channels, you may want to consider window replacement. However, a less expensive solution is available: You can install replacement channels in your double-hung windows.

Replacing window channels is no walk on the beach, but it does give you an opportunity to clean and repair the windows while they're apart. (Okay, so doing those jobs is no picnic, either.) But by replacing the channels, you can have windows that operate more freely, waste less energy, and save you hundreds or thousands of dollars compared to the cost of buying new windows.

Buy your new channels at a home center or glass company. They are sold in kits that range in sizes from 3 to 5 feet long, so they fit most sizes of windows. Measure the window opening from the top of the upper sash to the bottom of the lower sash for the correct dimension. Then choose a channel kit that is slightly larger than that dimension. Because a typical sized channel kit is under $50, replacing the channels is a very reasonable way to fix a drafty window.

The following steps walk you through installing new window channels. Consult Figure 9-6 if you aren't sure about what some of the terms in these steps refer to.

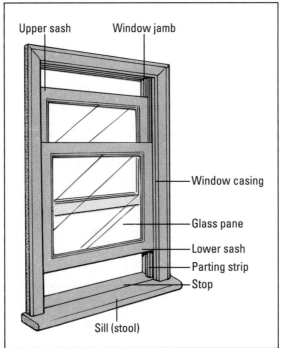

Upper sash   Window jamb

Window casing

Glass pane

Lower sash

Parting strip

Stop

Sill (stool)

Figure 9-6:
All the bits and pieces that go into a window.

1. Remove the window stops.

If the window stops are painted, use a razor knife to cut through the paint film along the line where the stops meet the jambs. To avoid breaking the stops, use a thin pry bar, pry only at nail locations, and work carefully.

2. Pull out the lower sash and then pry out the parting strip to remove the upper sash.

Set the sash aside for later, when you can clean it, repaint it, or install new weather stripping.

3. Release the sash cords from the slots in the sash.

Pull the sash cord out of the groove in the edge of the sash. Sometimes, the knotted end is held in place by a small nail. If this is the case, pull the nail out to remove the sash cord.

If you're replacing the channels in a double-hung window, this is a good time to replace the sash cords, as well. (See the "Replacing the sash cords" section earlier in this chapter.) If your replacement channels are spring-loaded, the sash weights are no longer necessary. In this case, remove and discard the old sash weights and cord.

4. If necessary, cut the new channels to length with a hacksaw.

Remember: Old windows may not be square. Carefully measure each side of the window jamb and cut channels to fit. Note that the bottom of the channel is cut at a slight angle to match the slope of the sill. If the precut angle matches the slope of your window sill, trim the top of the channel; if the angle is different, cut the bottom of the channel to the same angle as your sill.

5. Inspect and clean the sash and stops.

If paint is peeling, now is the time to repaint the windows, while they're out of the frame. To prevent paint runs, lay the sash flat on a workbench or across two sawhorses. Sand the sash carefully to remove any dried paint runs or other roughness from the frames and stops. You want to apply only a thin film of paint on the sash, so thin the paint a bit by adding a small amount of water (if the paint is latex) or mineral spirits (if it is alkyd).

Surfaces that are painted do not slide easily against each other. For this reason, some parts of the window sash, such as the backside of the meeting rails and the inside edges of the stops, are left unpainted. Because painting channels or the edges of the sash may cause them to stick, don't paint any exposed bare wood.

6. Reassemble the window, as shown in Figure 9-7.

Figure 9-7:
Place the window sashes in the replacement channels and then slide the assembly into the jamb.

Replace the upper sash first — it goes in the outside channel — and then place the lower sash in the inside channel. Hold the channels against the sashes and place the bottom of the channels into the window jamb. Then push the assembly into the jamb so that the channels rest against the outside window stop. The unit will stay in place while you install the inside stops.

Before you nail the stops permanently in place, test to make sure that the windows operate freely. Don't push the stops too tight against the channels, or the windows will be hard to open.

Energy-Saving Projects

Two of the easiest projects you can do around the house happen to be improvements that shave down your heating and cooling bills. Weather stripping and caulking fill in gaps and holes around the doors, windows, and other places that leak air. Buttoning up the holes and plugging the leaks are must-do projects, and they couldn't be easier.

Weather stripping, step by step

Weather stripping is any material that seals the cracks between moving components, such as the crack where the window sash meets the frame or the stop. In addition to saving energy, weather stripping blocks drafts and keeps out dust and insects. The thin barrier also blocks outside noise, including the sound of your neighbor's yapping pooch.

Weather stripping comes in many shapes. It's available with a felt, vinyl, or foam-rubber edge on a wood or plastic strip that you attach to the edge of the door or window with small brads. Some versions have an adhesive back so that you can install them without nails.

The easiest type of weather stripping to install is the adhesive-backed V-seal type, available in a peel-and-stick roll. This type of weather stripping is inexpensive and easy to install. To apply adhesive-backed weather stripping to a double-hung window, just follow these steps (illustrated in Figure 9-8):

1. **With a damp rag, clean the window jamb or any surface where you plan to apply the weather stripping; allow these areas to dry completely.**

2. **Cut the strip to the length you want.**

   Use a measuring tape to find the length you need, or place the weather-stripping in position and cut a piece slightly longer. To fully seal up the window, you need strips for each side of the inner and outer sash, the bottom of the inner sash and the top of the outer sash, and the outer meeting rail.

3. **Raise the inner sash as far as it will go.**

4. **Peel away the backing of the strip, except for a inch or so at the top.**

   Later, you have to push this part of the strip up between the sash and jamb, which is easier to do if you leave the backing in place.

5. **Press the strip in place with the V facing inside.**

6. **Install the strip on the opposite side of the jamb in the same way, and then close the window.**

7. **Remove the backing from the top of the weather stripping that protrudes above the sash and press it in place.**

8. **Lower the outer sash as far as it will go and install the weather stripping in this sash in the same way as you did on the inner sash.**

   The only difference here is that you should leave the backing at the bottom of the strip in place until you raise the window.

9. **Raise the inner sash and apply a strip of weather stripping to the bottom of the sash; then lower the outer sash and put a strip on the top.**

10. **Lower the outer sash far enough to expose the inside face of the bottom of the sash; clean this surface and then apply a strip of weather stripping with the V facing down.**

Modern windows often have a *kerf* — a slot into which the weather stripping fits. The weather stripping for these windows has a tubular edge on one side, with a felt or vinyl lip on the opposite side that closes and seals any crack. To replace this weather stripping, pull or pry the tubular retaining edge from the slot in the window and then press the new weather stripping into the slot.

A. Raise the inside window sash and apply the weather stripping with the V facing towards the inside of the jamb.

B. Lower the sash and remove the backing from the top inch or so of the weather stripping and press it in place.

Figure 9-8:
Installing adhesive-backed V-seal weather stripping.

C. Lower the outer sash and install the weather stripping in the jamb with the V facing inside.

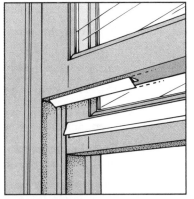

D. Install weather stripping on the bottom of the inner sash, the top of the outer sash, and the inside face of the lower portion of the outer sash.

Caulking, step by step

Caulk is a filler material used to seal a crack where two nonmoving components meet, such as where a house's siding meets the exterior window trim. Caulk seals the crack against air infiltration, prevents drafts, and keeps moisture from entering the crack and causing the paint to peel or the wood to rot.

Caulk is available in many formulations, including latex, acrylic latex, and silicone. Unlike traditional oil-based caulks that are known to crack and fail within a very short time, modern caulks are warranted for 25 or more years. To avoid having to recaulk each summer, choose a quality paintable silicone or acrylic latex caulk product. These caulks are *elastomeric,* which is a fancy word meaning that they remain flexible after drying and don't crack when weather changes cause either of the two joined components to expand and contract.

Caulk is available in tubes that hold 10 ounces of product, enough to caulk around the average size door or window. At one end of the caulk tube is a cone-shaped plastic nozzle. Because the nozzle gradually decreases in size from its base to the tip, you can squeeze out a bigger bead of caulk by cutting the nozzle shorter. How much coverage you get from a tube of caulk depends on the size of the caulk bead.

The caulk tube fits into a caulk gun. The gun has a trigger handle that you squeeze to apply pressure to the tube, forcing the caulk out the nozzle. Caulk guns are available at home centers, hardware stores, and paint outlets, usually hanging right next to the display of caulk.

To seal the exterior of a window with caulk, follow these steps:

1. **Use a putty knife or scraper to clean away any old caulk remaining on the outside of the window.**

2. **Cut the tip off the caulk tube nozzle at a point where it produces a bead large enough to fill the crack.**

   A $1/4$-inch bead is large enough for most cracks. To avoid too large a bead, cut the nozzle tip near the end, test the bead for size, and then cut off more tip if you need a larger bead.

   After you cut the tip, you have to puncture the seal in the end of the caulk tube before any caulk will flow. To puncture this seal, insert a stiff wire, such as a piece of metal clothes hanger or a long nail, into the nozzle and push it into the caulk tube until you feel it puncture the seal.

3. **Apply the bead of caulk, moving the caulk gun at a measured pace along the crack and using continuous light pressure on the gun trigger.**

   Caulk on all four sides of the window trim to seal the crack between the trim and the siding.

4. **Smooth the caulk.**

   You can use a Popsicle stick, plastic spoon, or wet finger to create a smooth surface.

5. **Wash away caulk remaining on the gun, your hands, or other unwanted spots before it dries.**

Window Enhancements and Add-Ons

To avoid living in the proverbial fish bowl, most people want some kind of cover for their windows. For rooms where privacy is a prime concern, such as the bathroom and bedroom, window covers are more important. In other rooms, you may need them mostly for protection from bright sunlight. Whatever the motivation, basic window cover-ups are easy to install, even for the not-so-handy.

Installing a window shade

Window shades are spring-loaded so that they can roll up or down and lock in a chosen position. The hardware consists of round support brackets at each end of the shade, as shown in Figure 9-9. You mount the brackets on the inside of the window stops. One bracket has a hole into which a round shade support is inserted; the opposite bracket has a slot to receive the flat support on the other end of the shade. Shades are so easy to install and remove that even a child can do the job; problem is, there's never a child around when you need one.

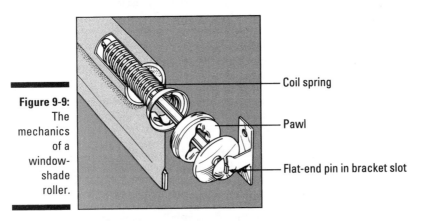

Figure 9-9:
The mechanics of a window-shade roller.

Coil spring

Pawl

Flat-end pin in bracket slot

If you're replacing an old shade, measure the width of the old roller from end to end, including the metal tips, and then measure the length of the shade fully extended. Order a new shade of the same width and length.

To measure for a new shade, hold a rigid measuring stick across the top of the window. Place one end on the inside upper window stop and carefully extend the rule across to the stop on the other side. Order a shade $1/8$ inch smaller than the measurement.

Measure the inside of the jamb and then subtract $1/8$ inch to find the proper length. You can purchase shades that are easy to cut to the exact length you need.

To install the shades, follow these simple steps:

1. **Position the metal support brackets on the two window stops at opposite sides of the window, and use a sharp pencil to mark the brad hole positions on the stops.**

   Allow enough room between the top of the window jamb and the shade for the roller to turn freely, remembering that, when the shade is fully rolled up, it grows in diameter. Hold the shade up where you plan to install it. When you find the correct position for the first bracket position, make a pencil mark for the location of the brad hole. Measure the distance from the top and sides of the window frame and then use that measurement to locate the bracket on the opposite side.

2. **Secure the window-shade brackets to the window stops with small brads.**

   Use a carpenter's awl or an ice pick and hammer to make starting holes in the stops. Hold the shade bracket in position and use a tack hammer to drive in the brads.

3. **Slide the ends of the shade into the slots in the brackets.**

   Make sure that the shade is fully wound up when you install it, or it may not retract properly. If you pull the shade down and it does not fully roll up by itself, pull the shade down a foot or so and take it off the bracket. Rewind the shade on the shade roller and then reinstall it in the bracket.

To remove the shade, just push upward on the slotted end of the shade to free it from its bracket, and then pull the round support from the hole in the opposite bracket.

Installing a miniblind

A miniblind has narrow slats that you can adjust with a wand to let in the amount of sunlight you want. Miniblinds are mounted in U-shaped brackets that have snap-on covers to provide a finished look. Miniblinds are now a mainstream decorating choice for a window treatment because they're attractive with just about any decor. Use them alone or with a fabric valance or cornice board covering the top of the window.

You can mount most miniblinds outside the window frame (on the outer trim of the window), on the wall (so that they cover the window trim), or on the inside of the frame between the window stops. Because of all these options, most mounting brackets have predrilled holes on both the ends and the backs of the mounting brackets. You only use one set of holes, depending on how you mount the miniblinds.

Trim-to-fit shades

Many large retailers sell inexpensive window shades that you can cut to fit almost any window. These shades are lightweight and flimsy (what do you expect for about $8?), but they may be just right for a quick-fix or when you're on a strict budget.

You can't do anything about the length of these shades, but you can custom-cut the width by using the score lines as guidelines on the shade. The steel shade roller slides together to fit the new width.

Install the brackets as we describe for regular shades, and insert the shade in the left bracket. Remove the plastic hem slat from the pocket and notice its score lines that match up with the score lines running the length of the shade. Hold the shade level under the right bracket so you can determine the correct width. Then mark the width with a light pencil mark at the closest score line on the shade. Carefully begin to tear the length of the shade at its score line until the entire shade is done. Adjust the shade roller to fit the new width by pushing the end plug until it reaches the end of the shade. Then snap off the plastic hem slat to the same width and install it.

Before you purchase miniblinds, first decide whether you want to mount the blind inside or outside the window frame, and then measure your windows using a folding wooden measuring rule or a wooden measuring stick. Manufacturers of blinds have specific directions for measuring on their packaging or brochures, but the general procedure is to measure the width at the top, middle, and bottom of the window and use the smallest dimension for its width. Measure the length of the window to get the correct extension of the blind.

If you order custom blinds, you can also indicate the length that you want the blinds to be. If you buy blinds off the rack, you have to cut the blind cords to the proper length; usually you want the bottom edge of the blind to rest on or slightly above the window sill. Directions for cutting the blind cords for length are included in the miniblind package.

You can install small clips on both sides of the window to act as hold-down brackets to secure the bottom of the blinds so that they don't sway freely. These clips, secured with a small brad or finishing nail, are easy to reach but not noticeable.

To install the blinds on the inside of the jamb, follow these steps:

1. **Measure and mark the locations for the U-shaped mounting brackets.**

   Position the mounting brackets at the top corner of the window jamb. Hold the brackets in place (paying attention to which is the right and left bracket) and use them as a template to mark the location of the mounting screws with a pencil.

2. **Drill a pilot hole for the mounting screws through the pencil marks on the window jamb.**

   Use a $^1/_{16}$-inch drill or a carpenter's awl to make starter holes for the screws.

3. **Use a screwdriver to install the mounting brackets with the screws provided.**

4. **Push the blind's header bar into the brackets, as shown in Figure 9-10, and secure it by closing each bracket.**

   Some designs simply slide into the bracket.

5. **If necessary, cut the blind cords to length.**

Figure 9-10:
To install miniblinds inside the jamb, screw the brackets to the top or side of the jamb.

Driving small screws while reaching upwards is an awkward and frustrating job that may introduce new and colorful words into your vocabulary. To make the job easy, use a cordless screwdriver. A cordless screwdriver is small, lightweight, and has a toggle switch to provide drive or reverse power. This tool is ideal for installing window blinds, curtains, or drapes.

Installing curtain rods and hardware

Rods for lightweight curtains often are held in place by rod-mounting brackets that are simply nailed to the window trim or stops. To install curtain rods, refer to the directions for installing window shades, earlier in this chapter.

Installing rods to support heavy curtains or drapes can be a horse of a different color. If you're mounting drapery hardware on the window trim or on the wall at the window edge, you can drive the hardware screws into wood. But you may encounter difficulties mounting rods that extend onto the walls if the @*!&* builder failed to install nailing blocks beyond the header to provide something into which you can screw the rod brackets. In this case, you must install hollow-wall fasteners like Molly bolts in the walls, and then secure the drapery hardware with the fasteners.

If the wall is plastered over a wood lath base (rock lath became standard for plaster in 1950), you can drive screws through the plaster and into the wood lath. Predrill the screw holes. To be sure that you drill into the wood lath, and not through the gaps or key strips between the laths, check the drill bit as it penetrates the plaster. If you penetrate the wood lath, you can see wood chips in the plaster dust as the bit bores into the wood. If you don't see wood chips, plan on using a Molly bolt. If you see water, call a plumber.

Molly bolts include a metal shaft or sleeve into which you can insert a small machine screw, as shown in Figure 9-11. As the machine screw turns in the Molly shaft, the shaft collapses against the back side of the plaster or wallboard, providing a secure support for the weight of the rods and the drapes. Other types of fasteners are also available for this purpose: Ask your hardware or home center clerk to suggest a fastener for your project.

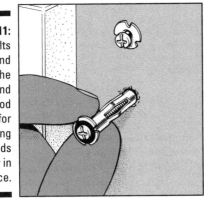

Figure 9-11: Molly bolts expand behind the wall and are a good choice for holding curtain rods securely in place.

To install a Molly bolt, drill a hole at the rod hardware location, through the wallboard or plaster. Insert the Molly screw into the hole and tap it lightly to seat it against the wall. Place the rod mounting bracket in position so that the screw holes line up with the Molly bolt(s), and use a screwdriver to drive the screw home. To test the installation, pull firmly on the mounting bracket. If the bracket moves, tighten the screw a bit more until you're sure that the screw is securely anchored.

Child-safety miniblind alert

Vinyl miniblinds pose a risk to children under the age of 6, who may ingest lead by touching the blinds and then putting their fingers in their mouths. When exposed to ultraviolet rays, vinyl miniblinds deteriorate, eventually causing poisonous lead from the vinyl to end up as a chalk dust on the surface of the blinds. Aluminum miniblinds and vinyl vertical blinds are not affected. When selecting a miniblind, choose one that specifies that it's lead-free.

Miniblinds also can be a cause of strangulation when their long cords are within the reach of children. Choose a blind with a breakaway device that reduces the risk of injury. When installing a miniblind, make sure that its cord is safely attached to the window out of a child's reach.

Installing a Window Lock

If the lock that came with your window gets broken, you can usually find the right replacement lock at a home center. But these standard-feature locks permit you to secure the window only in the fully closed position. For security *and* ventilation, you can purchase optional locks that permit you to lock the window when it's partially open.

With a minimum of effort and money, you can rig your double-hung window so that you can lock it while it's in a partially open position. Here's how:

1. **Open the window a bit, say 6 inches, for ventilation.**

2. **Circle masking tape $2^1/_2$ inches from the tip of an $^{11}/_{64}$-inch drill bit to mark a depth guide on the bit.**

3. **Drill a hole at a slight downward angle through the top rail of the lower sash, and into (but not completely through) the stile of the upper sash.**

   Stop at the $2^1/_2$-inch depth guide.

4. **Insert a 16d nail into the hole.**

   The nail prevents the window from being raised any higher: The nail head protrudes slightly for easy removal when you want to open or close the window.

We know a woman who, fearing burglars, drilled nail holes through both sashes and inserted a nail through the hole to prevent the window from being raised. By spring, she had forgotten about the security nails and, when she tried to open the window, she pushed upwards so hard that she broke the parting rail. Sounds like the burglars should have feared *her!*

Installing a window air conditioner

If your house lacks central air conditioning, you can install a window air conditioner to cool the rooms that you use most often. Measure the square footage of the area you want to cool and then bring the figures to the appliance dealer, who can help you calculate the size of the air conditioner you need. Follow the instructions that come with the unit.

Remember that an air conditioner uses a compressor, and compressors pull a heavy electric load when they're under pressure. For this reason, never use an extension cord with an air conditioner. Choose a window that has an electrical outlet nearby, one that can be reached using the appliance power cord only. High-capacity air conditioners run on 220 volts: If necessary, hire an electrician to run a 220-volt power outlet to the chosen window.

Because air conditioners also dehumidify, they generate water. When you position the unit in the window, be sure that the unit is level or tilted slightly away from the room — that is, the outside of the unit is a bit lower than the inside of the unit. This placement assures that the water that condenses on the cooling coil runs outside. Some units have a drain tube, which you position so that it leads outside.

Adjustable panels are available to fill the space on either side of the air conditioner. Use weather stripping to ensure a tight seal between the panels and the window frame. You can also purchase an insulated cover to protect the outside of your air conditioner during winter weather.

This do-it-yourself lock works, but it can be defeated more easily than a commercial version. For a few dollars, you can purchase an inexpensive add-on lock that includes both a keyed lock and a steel bolt that protrudes through a steel strike plate, as shown in Figure 9-12.

Follow the full step-by-step instructions that come with these locks. The following steps provide a general outline of the installation:

1. **Install the lock body on the top of the lower sash.**

2. **Place the strikeplate against the outside window sash and position it so the plunger from the lock aligns with the hole in the plate when it is fully extended.**

   Use the strikeplate as a template to locate the position of the mounting screws. Mark the screw location on the outside jamb with a pencil.

3. **Drill a pilot hole through the pencil marks on the outside window jamb and then install the strikeplate with the screws provided.**

4. **Install the second strikeplate about 6 inches above the one you just installed.**

   This feature allows you to lock the window in the closed position and then raise the window until the lock is aligned with the upper strikeplate and lock the window in an partially open position.

Figure 9-12: A keyed window lock can have two strike-plates: One locks the window shut, and the other, installed above the first, locks the window while it's open a crack.

Installing a Motion Sensor

Window security sensors range from battery-powered motion detectors costing around $10, up to the Fort Knox-type hard-wired total security systems that must be installed by pros and cost thousands of dollars.

The security industry estimates that a home is broken into every ten seconds: Now isn't that a comforting thought? Ten percent of the burglaries are committed by pros, but 90 percent are committed by amateurs who live within three miles of the target house. A determined professional burglar can defeat all but the most sophisticated alarm systems, but amateur burglars can be deterred by the presence of an inexpensive alarm system.

The simplest motion sensor is a battery-powered alarm that detects any motion of the window and sounds a 90-decibel alarm. One such unit is called Glass Guard. The small disk has a peel-and-stick backing adhesive. To install the unit, just clean the glass pane and then peel off the disk's adhesive backing. At a corner of the pane, press the detector firmly onto the glass surface. If the window is opened or the glass is broken, the alarm will sound. To discourage break-ins, a warning label on the exterior side of the disk announces to burglars that the home is protected by electronic security — assuming, of course, that these dolts can read.

Homeowners can install more elaborate do-it-yourself security systems. One such unit is called The Safe & Sound Wireless Home Security System. This radio-operated unit doesn't require any wiring, and you don't need any tools to install it. See Figure 9-13 for an illustration of this unit.

Figure 9-13: Battery-operated wireless security systems are easy to install. If the window is opened or the glass broken, an alarm sounds.

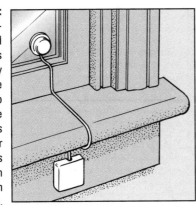

The heart of the unit is a radio-operated control console and a remote-power alarm. All family members can carry small arm/disarm transmitters that turn the system on or off. You can plug the control console into any 110-volt outlet, usually at a central point in the house. The console has a 100-foot range. Miniature radio transmitters and magnets are mounted with adhesive on the trim and sash of windows and doors. If the window is opened, the transmitter sends a signal to the control console, which sounds a 112-decibel alarm.

Buy the basic unit and then add only the accessories you need. Options include the following:

- ✔ A plug-in lamp flasher that causes a light to flash when the alarm is sounded. This item is useful for hearing-impaired homeowners, and it may also attract the attention of neighbors in the event of a break-in.

- ✔ An outdoor alarm and siren to alert neighbors.

- ✔ An interior motion sensor that has a *pet-alley lens,* which prevents the unit from being activated by Fido or Fluffy.

- ✔ A glass-break detector that ignores vibrations caused by the wind, and sounds only if the glass is broken.

Chapter 10

Doors: An Open and Shut Case

*T*hey swing open; they slide shut — simple acts you probably take for granted. But when they squeak or refuse to budge, you start to notice the doors in and around your house. To keep everything in good working order, follow the typical door maintenance and repair jobs in this chapter. They may be all you need to know to keep your home safe and secure.

Maintaining Your Locks and Hinges

You probably don't spend a whole lot of time thinking about your doors — and if you do, you may want to seek professional help — but consider that a family may open and close entry doors thousands of times each year. The hinges and locks on the doors can take a real pounding, so plan to lubricate them at least once per year. To lubricate door hardware, you need a can of aerosol lubricant such as WD-40, paper towels, slot- and Phillips-head screwdrivers, and a hammer.

Lubricating hinges

Interior doors typically have two or three hinges. Exterior doors are heavier than interior doors, so they have three or four hinges. To lubricate door hinges, first remove one hinge pin. Some hinge pins extend through the hinges, so you can use a large nail to tap them up from the bottom, as shown in Figure 10-1. Other hinges may require you to insert the blade of a slot screwdriver under the head of the hinge pin, and then tap the handle of the screwdriver with a hammer to drive the pin up and out of the hinge.

Figure 10-1:
Hinges with an open bottom have hinge pins that you can remove by tapping a large nail into the bottom of the hinge, driving the pin up and out.

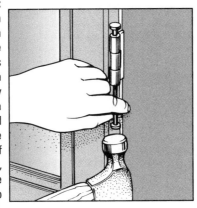

After you remove one hinge pin, drop a large nail in the hinge to temporarily replace the removed pin and prevent the door from sagging off its hinges. Lay the hinge pin on paper towels and remove any dirt. Then spray the pin with a light coating of lubricant and replace the pin in the hinge. Repeat this procedure for all the hinges, one at a time.

Lubricating door locks

Many people put up with the aggravation of a sticking door lock for years — an annoyance that would even try the patience of Harry Houdini. Ironically, you can fix most stubborn locks in a matter of minutes.

Clean the keyhole with a penetrating lubricant like WD-40. (Don't apply household oil to the key or cylinder, because it attracts dirt and eventually gums up the lock.) Spray the lubricant into the keyhole itself, and then spray it on the key. Slide the key in and out of the lock several times to spread the lubricant.

If this superficial cleaning doesn't free the lock, eliminate the aggravation altogether: Take about ten minutes to disassemble, clean, and reassemble the entire door lock. Here's how to remove the most common type of door lock:

1. **With the door open, use a Phillips screwdriver to take out the two connecting screws that are located by the doorknob on the inside of the lock.**

2. **Next, remove the two screws that hold the lock faceplate on the edge of the door.**

3. **Slide the doorknob off the spindle, pull out the lock mechanism, and remove the latchbolt from its hole in the edge of the door, as shown in Figure 10-2.**

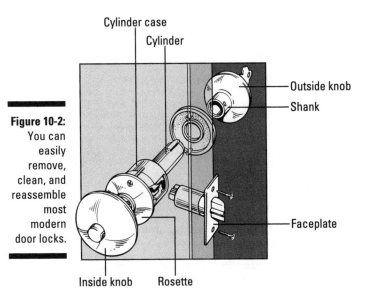

Cylinder case

Cylinder

Outside knob

Shank

Faceplate

Inside knob   Rosette

Figure 10-2: You can easily remove, clean, and reassemble most modern door locks.

4. **Lay the disassembled lock parts on layers of newspaper or paper toweling.**

5. **Spray a light all-purpose household lubricant or a silicone lubricant on all moving parts of the lock, flushing out the latchbolt. Use powdered graphite to lubricate the lock cylinder.**

   Spray until all dirt is flushed from the assembly and then let the latchbolt assembly lie on the toweling until all the excess lubricant has dripped off.

To reassemble the door lock after cleaning and lubricating it, follow these steps:

1. **Insert the latchbolt assembly into its hole in the edge of the door.**

2. **Insert the exterior doorknob and spindle into its hole, aligning it so that the spindles and connecting screws pass through the holes in the latchbolt assembly, as shown in Figure 10-3.**

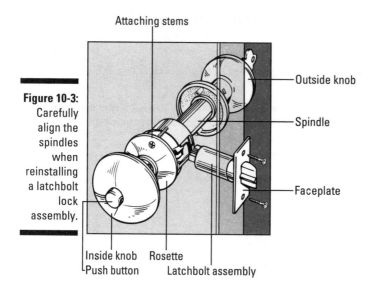

Attaching stems

Outside knob

Spindle

Faceplate

Figure 10-3: Carefully align the spindles when reinstalling a latchbolt lock assembly.

Inside knob   Rosette
Push button   Latchbolt assembly

3. **Drive in the latchbolt screws, but don't tighten them until the lock is completely assembled.**

4. **Slide the interior doorknob onto the shaft, aligning the screw holes, and then drive in the screws.**

   Turn the door knob back and forth to check that the cylinder and latch bolt are engaged and in proper alignment.

5. **Tighten the screws on the latchbolt and recheck the alignment by turning the knob.**

   If you have any parts left over, guess what? You goofed somehow. Disassemble the lock and replace all the pieces.

6. **Test the lock by turning the knob and locking the lock.**

   If the lock doesn't work smoothly, loosen the screws, realign the cylinder and latchbolt, and try again.

You can lubricate deadbolts in the same way as other locks. Remove the connecting screws, the faceplate screws, and then the knobs. Next, pull out the latchbolt assembly and clean and lubricate the lock as described earlier. To reassemble the lock, reverse the procedure.

Tightening loose hinges

Loose hinges can cause a door to stick or bind or scrape the floor. Lucky for you, this is another common, easy-to-solve problem. First, check that the hinge screws are tight. Open the door, grasp it by the lock edge, and move it up and down. If you encounter movement at the hinge screws, they need to be retightened.

If the hinge screws have been loose for only a short time, you may only need to tighten them with a screwdriver. But when hinge screws are left loose for a long time, the constant movement of the hinge plate and screws enlarges the screw holes. Eventually, the holes become so large that the screws can't stay tight. The result: stripped screws that are completely useless!

If the door still moves even a tiny bit after you tighten its hinge screws, you have to repair the enlarged screw holes. Repair one screw hole at a time so that you don't have to remove the door. Here's how:

1. **Remove the loose screw.**

2. **Dip the bare end of a wooden match in some carpenter's glue and tap it with a hammer as far into the screw hole as it will go, as shown in Figure 10-4.**

   If the screw is large, you may have to put several glue-coated matches in the hole.

Figure 10-4: Tighten a loose hinge screw by driving a glue-coated wooden match or small dowel into the screw hole and then reinstalling the screw.

3. **Break or cut off the matches flush with the hinge plate and discard the heads.**

4. **After you've filled the void in the screw hole with the wooden match stick(s), use a screwdriver to drive the screw into the hole.**

5. **Remove the next screw and repair its hole, continuing the process until you fix all the enlarged screw holes.**

In place of a matchstick, you can also use wooden golf tees coated with glue to plug a stripped screw hole. Golf tees are tapered, so they fit easily into the screw hole. Let the glue dry and cut off the protruding part of the tee.

Fixing Problem Doors

The following sections cover two of the most common door problems:

- ✔ Moisture can warp a typical hinged wooden door so that it changes shape and doesn't correctly swing on its hinges or open and close in its frame.
- ✔ Bifold doors have another chronic condition; they tend to jump off their tracks or become misaligned and, consequently, don't open or open only partially.

If you have a door with either of these problems, read on for easy repair tips.

Straightening a warped wood door

If you have a warped sense of humor, we can't help. But if your solid wood door is warped, then try this trick: Lay the door across two sawhorses, one at each end of the door, with the convex side (the side that makes a hill, not a valley) up. Spread an old towel across the center of the door and lay heavy objects, such as concrete blocks, on it. Check the warp now and then over the course of a couple days; when the door is straight, remove the weights and reinstall the door.

 After the door straightens out, give it an extra coat of finish on the side that was convex, or outwardly curved. Also coat all exposed wood at the edges and ends of the door with a water repellent to prevent water from soaking in and causing future warpage.

Fixing bifold doors

Bifold doors are arranged in hinged pairs that fold like an accordion toward both sides of the door jamb, or frame, when opened. Because bifold doors permit you to fully open the doors and provide access to all storage, they are often used on closets. They move via nylon rollers or pins mounted on the top of the doors, and travel on a track mounted at the top of the door jamb, as shown in Figure 10-5. The doors nearest the side jambs swing on pivot blocks installed at the top and, on some models, at the floor to secure the bottom of the doors from swinging outward. To keep bifold doors operating smoothly, clean and lubricate the track, rollers, and pivot blocks at least once each year.

Rollers   Track

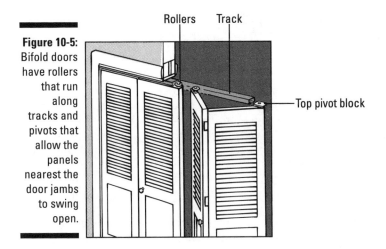

Figure 10-5: Bifold doors have rollers that run along tracks and pivots that allow the panels nearest the door jambs to swing open.

Top pivot block

To tune up bifold doors and lubricate the top track, open the doors. Wipe the track with a clean cloth to remove dust. Use an aerosol lubricant to spray the track and rollers or pins. Apply the lubricant sparingly and be careful not to spray any clothes hanging in the closet. Leave only a light film of lubricant on the parts; use paper towels to wipe away any excess lubricant.

If your bifold doors *bind* (don't open or slide on their tracks easily), first check to see whether all the hardware is secure and working properly. If the parts are broken, replacement hardware is available at home centers. Check the hinges between each pair of doors. If the hinge screws are loose, use a screwdriver to tighten them. If the screw holes are stripped so that you can't tighten the hinge screws, remove the hinges and plug the screw holes following the steps we suggest earlier in this chapter for door hinges.

Sometimes, it's easier to work on bifold doors if you remove them from the door frame. To do so, unfold the doors and carefully lift them up and out of the frame. You may find this easier to do if you stand inside, not outside, the door. For example, to remove a bifold closet door, you may have to take some items out of the closet so that you can stand inside and see how the door sits in its track so you can lift it out.

If, when you rehang the doors, the gap between the door and jamb is not even, use a screwdriver or a wrench to adjust the top pivot blocks and make the gap even. Some bifold doors have adjustable pivot blocks at the bottom corner.

Maintaining Combination Storm/Screen Doors

Combination storm/screen doors relieve you of the seasonal hassle of taking down screen doors and putting up storm doors, taking down storm doors and putting up screen doors. These units come with both a screen and storm insert that you can install and remove, depending on the season. Combination doors can have any variety of screw-in or bolt-in systems that hold the screen or storm panes in place. Some newer versions have a groove in the frame that the screen or glass fits into, and a gasket to hold it in place. The doors themselves may be made of wood or metal, usually aluminum.

To keep these doors in top condition, provide maintenance service at least once per year. Spray an aerosol lubricant on the door lock, hinges, and closer mechanism. Also lubricate the push buttons that hold the glass or screen units in place. These buttons are located on the bottom edge, at both sides of the unit.

If the lock isn't working properly, the easiest solution is usually to replace it. You can purchase replacement locks at home centers and hardware stores.

Replacing the screen

If you have a door with a loose or damaged screen (a given if you have kids or pets), don't fret. Replacing screens is relatively easy, and it's a useful skill to have, considering that you're likely to be doing it for many years to come.

Both aluminum and fiberglass screening is available at home centers and hardware stores. The screening fabric comes in prepackaged sizes of 25 inches wide by 32, 36, and 48 inches long; and 84 inches long by 32, 36, and 48 inches wide. It is also sold by the foot from bolts in the following widths: 24, 36, 48, 60, and 72 inches.

Take a measurement of your window before shopping for a replacement screen. Measure the length and the width of the window opening, and add a few extra inches to both dimensions.

If solar heat or bright light is a problem, consider using a special screen material like Phifer's Sunscreen to block out the sun. Black and dark-colored screens are easier to see through than bright reflective aluminum.

The screen is held in a frame by a rubber or neoprene *spline,* which looks like a thin cord pressed into grooves. To replace an aluminum screen, you use a *screen-installation splining tool.* The tool looks like a pastry cutter with a convex roller on one end, and a concave roller on the opposite end.

Installation steps are basically the same for aluminum or fiberglass screen, with slight variations.

Aluminum screens

To replace an aluminum screen, follow these steps:

1. **Remove the screen in its frame from the door and lay it flat on a workbench or a set of sawhorses.**

2. **Use small pliers or a carpenter's awl to pry the spline out of the groove and then lift out the screen.**

   To navigate around tight corners, use a screwdriver to ease the spline out of the frame, as shown in Figure 10-6. If the spline appears to be in good shape, set it aside for use with the new screen. If the spline is brittle or cracked, replace it with a new spline (available at hardware stores everywhere).

Figure 10-6: Pry out the old spline from the groove in the frame of the aluminum screen. Work carefully, and you can reuse the spline.

3. **Wipe the spline groove clean, making sure to remove the tiniest grit.**

4. **Lay a new aluminum screen over the frame so that it overlaps the groove by at least $1/8$-inch on all four sides.**

5. **Cut off the corners of the screen at a 45-degree angle, just inside the outer edge of the spline groove.**

6. **Use the convex end of the splining tool to press the screen into the groove of the frame.**

   Hold the roller at a 45-degree angle toward the inside edge of the groove, and then roll downward to press the screen into the groove. Be sure to hold the screen taut across the frame as you roll it into place. Sags and wrinkles are about as attractive on screen doors as they are on people.

7. Use the concave end of the roller to press the spline into the groove.

Do not cut the spline at the corners: Instead, bend the spline around the corners and install it in one continuous piece. When you position it tightly in the groove, the spline holds the screen in place.

8. Use a sharp razor knife to trim away any excess screen.

Place the tip of the knife between the spline and the outside edge of the spline groove and pull the knife slowly along the entire groove perimeter.

Fiberglass screens

To replace a fiberglass screen, first remove the old spline and clean the spline groove. Lay the fiberglass screen over the frame so that it overlaps about $1/2$-inch on all four sides. Now use the concave end of the roller to roll both the screen and spline into the groove at the same time, as shown in Figure 10-7. Be careful to hold the screen straight while you work on the first two sides, and then roll in the last two sides. To cut away excess screen, position the razor knife tip between the spline and the exterior side of the spline groove.

Figure 10-7:
Installing a new fiberglass screen.

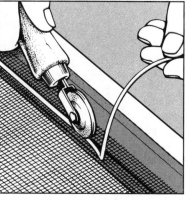

A. Lay the fiberglass screen over the frame so that it overlaps about $1/2$-inch on all four sides.

B. Using the concave end of the roller, roll both the screen and spline into the groove at the same time.

Tightening loose storm-door panels

You want your storm-door panels to sit firmly in their channels, secured against air infiltration by weather stripping that's tucked into the grooves on all sides of the panel. When panels become loose from wear or weathering and begin to rattle in your door, it's time for new weather stripping.

The weather stripping in your storm door may be felt strips (common on older models) or rubber or vinyl gaskets. Replacement weather stripping, especially the felt kind, may be difficult to find. Look in large home centers for storm-window or storm-door repair kits, or check out the weather-stripping department. Chances are, you'll find something that comes close to the original.

Follow these steps to replace worn-out weather stripping:

1. **Remove the panels.**

   Most panels slide into channels in the frame and are held in place by thumb screws. Loosen these screws, turn the brackets that hold the panel in place, and lift out the panel.

2. **Remove the old weather stripping.**

   Pull up the weather stripping at one end and work it out of its groove. You may need to use a flat-head screwdriver to begin the job if the material is stuck in place.

3. **Press the new weather stripping into the groove at one corner and slide it down the groove.**

   Depending on the type of weather stripping, you may have to use a screwdriver to push it into place.

4. **Replace the panel by reversing the actions in Step 1.**

Sliding By with Sliding Doors

The two types of doors that are easiest to open don't have hinges at all; instead, they slide on tracks. Sliding glass doors are a popular feature in rooms with decks or patios, because their full-length glass panels open the room visually to the great outdoors, while providing access to the outside, too. Interior sliding doors are frequently used for closets and pantries, and sometimes to conceal hot water heaters and furnaces. You can remove sliding-door panels easily to gain complete access to what's behind them.

Follow simple repairs and maintenance to keep your sliding doors on track.

Getting your patio door to slide better

Patio doors slide horizontally — or at least, they're supposed to. All too often, these big, pesky contraptions stubbornly resist opening, and getting outside becomes about as easy as dragging a refrigerator through a sandbox.

The most common cause of sticking patio doors is debris in the lower track. This channel is easily clogged with dirt, leaves, and such because people and pets walk over it whenever they go in or out. Each time you vacuum your floors, use a small brush attachment or cordless vacuum to clean the sliding-door tracks. Apply a lubricant to both upper and lower tracks to keep the door hardware clean and operating freely.

In addition to cleaning and lubricating the sliding-door tracks, you also want to lubricate the door lock. The best way to lubricate any lock is to disassemble it and use an aerosol lubricant to flush away grime and to coat the moving parts of the lock.

Sometimes, patio doors become hard to open even when the track is clean. In these cases, the problem is usually that the rollers at the bottom of the door have started rubbing against the track. The rollers at the top can also wear down, lowering the bottom of the door so that it rubs on the track.

Most sliding doors have a mechanism called an *adjusting screw* located at the bottom of the door ends. Turning this screw raises or lowers the roller, as shown in Figure 10-8. Give the screw a clockwise turn and test to see whether the door slides easier. If the door becomes even harder to open, turn the screw in the opposite direction. After a bit of adjustment, the door should roll easily without rubbing on the bottom track.

Figure 10-8:
A screw at the base of the door controls the clearance between the bottom of a patio door and the track.

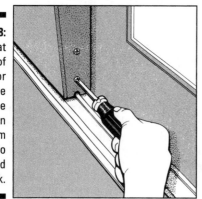

Maintaining sliding closet doors

Sliding closet doors operate on rollers that are positioned in tracks at the top jamb and floor, allowing the doors to bypass each other in the tracks (see Figure 10-9). Because sliding doors don't fold out the way bifold doors do, they only allow access to half the width of the opening at a time.

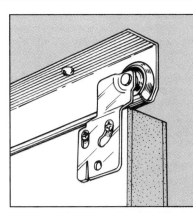
A simple roller-and-track assembly.

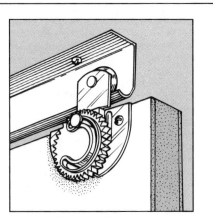
A roller with adjustable clearance.

Figure 10-9:
Periodically
clean and
lubricate
the tracks
and roller
assembly of
sliding
closet
doors.

A two-track sliding door.

Removing a sliding door by lifting it up
out of its tracks.

To clean and lubricate the hardware for a sliding closet door, use a stiff
brush, a toothbrush, or a cordless hand vacuum to clean dust from the
tracks. Use an aerosol lubricant to lubricate all the door rollers. If the rollers
are damaged, install replacement rollers (available at home centers).

If the door doesn't hang level, leaving an uneven gap between the door and
door frame, look for an adjustable mounting screw at the inside top of each
door. Use a screwdriver to adjust the mounting screw.

Locking It Up

If a door in your house is looking good, but its lock wobbles or shows signs of wear, consider replacing the lock. Standard interior locks come in a variety of styles and finishes that can improve the look of the door as well as provide security.

Replacing standard door locks

If your locks are becoming worn or damaged, replace them with new units. Because door locks vary somewhat in design, remove the lock and take it with you to a home center so that you can compare it to the selection for sale there. By choosing an exact match, you don't have to redrill the lock holes.

To replace standard door locks, see the directions earlier in the chapter under "Maintaining Your Locks and Hinges."

Installing a deadbolt

Many exterior doors are fitted with an ordinary cylinder lock, which has the key in the door knob. This type lock offers little resistance to a determined burglar (and what other kind of burglar is there?). The latchbolt of most standard locks extends only into the door frame, and a stiff kick from a booted foot can splinter most door frames. And thieves can wrench out the exterior knobs of passage locks by using a pipe wrench. For more security, install a deadbolt lock on all exterior doors.

Deadbolt locks have latchbolts that extend through the door frame and into the wall stud next to the frame. A deadbolt lock has no exterior knob, so it's impossible to wrench the lock from its hole in the door. From the inside, you operate a deadbolt lock by turning either a thumb-turn lever (if you have a single-cylinder lock) or a key (for a double-cylinder lock). If you have small children in the home who may not be able to find the key in an emergency, choose a thumb-turn lock.

Deadbolt locks are relatively inexpensive and come complete with a cardboard template that shows where to drill the cylinder and latchbolt holes. Follow these general steps, illustrated in Figure 10-10, to install a deadbolt lock:

1. **Choose a position on the door for the lock.**

   Most standard locks are set at or near 36 inches up from the bottom of the door. Install the deadbolt lock above the standard lock, or about 44 inches above the bottom of the door. If you have a combination storm door, position the deadbolt lock so that it doesn't interfere with the operation of the storm doorknob or lock.

2. **Use masking tape to stick the template on the door edge and face.**

3. **Use an awl, nail set, or large nail to mark the center of the holes for the lock cylinder (through the face of the door) and the latchbolt (into the edge of the door).**

4. **Use the proper size hole saw to bore the hole for the lock cylinder.**

   Some manufacturers offer a kit that includes a hole saw with the lock set. Drilling the hole from both sides helps prevent the door from splintering. The hole saw has a center pilot bit to guide the saw through the door. From one side of the door, drill until the tip of the pilot point pokes through the opposite side of the door, and then pull the hole saw out and position the bit in the hole and finish boring the hole from the opposite side of the door.

5. **Use a 1-inch spade bit to drill the latchbolt hole into the edge of the door.**

   The *spade bit* is an inexpensive wood-boring instrument that looks like a paddle with a triangular point on the end. Attach it to your drill to cut a perfectly round hole into the wood.

6. **Cut a mortise, or recess, in the wood for the latchbolt faceplate.**

   The latchbolt faceplate must fit into a shallow mortise in the edge of the door. Cutting out this mortise is not nearly as difficult as it sounds. All you need is a sharp 1-inch chisel and a hammer.

   To cut the latchbolt mortise, place the latchbolt into the hole and mark around the faceplate with a knife to indicate its outline on the end of the door. Use the chisel to deepen the marks about $1/8$-inch. Then, starting at the top of the faceplate outline, make a series of closely spaced chisel cuts inside the marks. A 1-inch-wide chisel blade will fit inside the outline. Use a hammer to tap the chisel so that it makes $1/8$-inch deep cuts.

   Remove resulting wood chips with the chisel blade. Then use the chisel to smooth the bottom of the mortise. Place the latchbolt in the door and check the fit of the mortise. If the faceplate is not flush with the door edge, chisel away a bit more wood.

7. **When the faceplate fits flush with the door edge, hold it in place and use it as a template for installing the two mounting screws.**

8. **Before installing the lock, apply a thin film of aerosol lubricant to all the moving parts.**

9. **Place the latchbolt in its hole and then insert the keyed portion of the lock so that the tailpiece extends through the hole in the latchbolt.**

10. **From the inside of the door, fit the inside cylinder so that the holes for the retaining screws are aligned with the exterior portion of the lock.**

11. **Use the two retaining screws to secure the two sides of the lock together.**

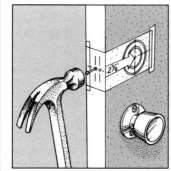

A. Drive a nail through the template layout marks to indicate the position for the lock-set holes. (Step 3)

B. Use a hole saw to bore the large hole for the lock cylinder in the side of the door. (Step 4)

C. Use a wood-boring spade bit to drill the latchbolt hole in the edge of the door. (Step 5)

D. Use a utiltity knife to mark the outline of the faceplate on the edge of the door and then make the shallow mortise to recess the plate. (Step 6)

E. Insert the keyed portion of the lock into the hole in the latchbolt. (Step 9)

Figure 10-10:
Install a deadbolt lock for extra security.

12. Shut the door and use a pencil to mark the spot on the door jamb where the latchbolt meets the jamb.

13. Use the strikeplate as a template cutting a mortise on the door jamb; then use a sharp chisel to dig out the mortise.

14. Use a spade bit to bore a latchbolt hole in the center of the mortise.

15. Use the screws provided to install the strike plate into the mortise.

16. Shut the door and test the fit by operating the deadbolt lock. If necessary, you can loosen the screws and adjust the lock set slightly so that the latchbolt passes easily into its hole.

 If you replace entry door locks on several doors, buy locks that are keyed alike, so that one key can be used to open both or all entry doors. If you're replacing only one lock, ask the dealer to rekey the existing lock so that one key can open both back and front doors. If you use separate keys for your home's entry locks, you can have a locksmith rekey the locks so that one key fits all.

Securing the patio door

Because they're large and easy to force open, patio doors are common targets for intruders. Safeguard your residence by buying a locking device that blocks the track, preventing outsiders from forcing the door to slide open. Or create your own device by cutting a length of wood (such as a 2-by-2-inch board) to fit snugly between the door frame and the stile of the operable door.

You can enhance this safety feature by drilling a hole through one door and into the other, and then inserting a long nail through the holes: This setup prevents intruders from prying the door up and swinging out its bottom to gain entry. If the existing lock doesn't work, check out home centers for replacement locks.

To prevent a break-in through the door pane, install a tough window film (sold at local glass installers) that prevents the glass from shattering and resists forced entry.

Installing a Doorstop

A doorstop prevents the door from striking and damaging the wall or base trim. Doorstops are available in a variety of designs, including stops that you install on the hinge pin, stops that you screw to the floor, and stops that you screw into the base trim, where an open door strikes the trim.

Hinge stops

Hinge-mounted stops, like the one shown in Figure 10-11, are the easiest doorstops to install. Just remove the hinge pin, slip the pin through the doorstop, and reinstall the hinge pin in the hinge. Then adjust the stop by twisting the threaded screw until the doorstop contacts the door and wall when the door is fully open, preventing the doorknob from hitting the wall.

Heavy exterior doors require a hinge stop on every hinge to avoid collision with interior walls.

Floor stops

In some instances, a stop is best installed directly in the floor so that it can keep a door from swinging too close to the wall. For example, if you have a china cabinet behind a swinging door, you may want to install a floor stop slightly in front of the cabinet for protection.

To determine the location for the floor stop, slowly swing the door and notice where the doorknob contacts whatever's behind it. Install the stop on the floor before the knob can do damage to what's behind it.

To install a floor-mounted doorstop, open the door as fully as possible and mark on the floor where you want the stop. Predrill a screw hole into the floor and then screw the stop into the floor.

Figure 10-11: Both hinge stops (left) and screw-type stops (right) are easy to install and prevent the doorknob from hitting the wall.

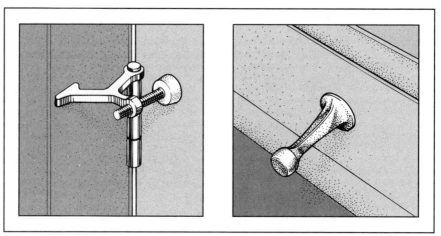

Don't just rely on doorstops — bring in reinforcements

If you don't have doorstops, your walls are likely to get damaged from the doorknob striking the wallboard or plaster. If the knob strikes the wall with force, it may even penetrate through the wallboard or plaster and leave a gaping hole. Doorstops guard against this kind of damage, but for extra protection, you can install a metal foil, peel-and-stick patch on the wall *before* it becomes damaged. This tip is especially useful if you have children running around the house.

To reinforce the wall against damage from the knob, open the door and mark the spot where the knob contacts the wall. Peel the backing from a metal foil patch (available in most paint stores) to expose the adhesive, and center the patch over the spot. Use a broad knife or trowel to apply a thin coat of wallboard compound over the patch. Let the first coat dry and then apply a thin second coat. Paint over the patch to match the wall. Now, if the doorstop fails, the knob won't make a hole in the wall.

Baseboard stops

Some doorstops have a screw built into the end of the stop. This type of stop screws directly into the wooden baseboard behind the door and is very easy to install.

Screw-type stops like the one shown in Figure 10-11 are not adjustable, so be sure to position the stop behind the door such that, when you open the door, the doorknob doesn't hit the wall.

To install a screw-type stop on the base trim, open the door toward the baseboard and mark the spot where it strikes the trim. Bore a pilot hole (about 6 inches inward from the mark, towards the door) in the trim and screw the stop into the hole. Open the door again to check that the stop strikes the edge of the door before the door can strike and damage the trim or the wall.

Replacing a Door Threshold

Most residential entry doors swing inward. The *threshold* is the part of the frame that meets and seals the bottom edge of the door. On some doors, the threshold is shaped from one piece of wood (usually oak, because of its durability); others, like the one being installed in Figure 10-12, have an additional weather stripping of aluminum or vinyl to seal the crack between the lower edge of the door and the threshold.

A. Remove nails and pry up the threshold. If necessary, cut the threshold into three pieces to remove it. (Steps 1 and 2)

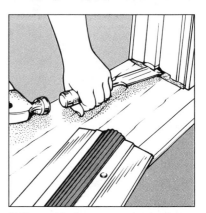

B. Use a chisel or saw to trim the door stops so that the new threshold can fit flush against the sides of the jamb. (Step 3)

C. Screw the threshold in place and then install the vinyl weather stripping into the channel in the center of the threshold. (Steps 4 and 5)

Figure 10-12: Installing a weatherproof threshold.

If the threshold becomes worn by traffic, replace it with a new one to keep a tight seal at the bottom of the door. A good threshold keeps bugs and insects out, and keeps your energy bills down.

The first step to replacing a threshold is to measure the width of the door. On older houses, the width of the door and threshold may vary; in modern houses, the standard exterior door width is 36 inches. Buy a new threshold to match the old one or choose one slightly wider and then cut it to size.

To replace a standard threshold with a weather-stripped aluminum version, follow these steps, illustrated in Figure 10-12:

1. **Remove any nails or screws from the piece with a *cat's paw,* a tool with a hooked end and a nail claw.**

   Removing nails or screws that have been deeply worn into the surface can be difficult. If you run into especially stubborn nails, you can use a nail set to drive them completely through the threshold, rather than trying to pry them out.

2. **Pry up the old threshold.**

   If the threshold doesn't extend under the side of the door jamb, you can pry it up without too much trouble. Otherwise, use a backsaw to make a cut through each end of the threshold. Use a pry bar to remove the center section of the old sill; then pry out the end piece from under each jamb.

3. **Cut the new threshold to the width of the door jamb.**

   The new threshold fits under the door stops, which are nailed to the side of the door jamb. Use a chisel or backsaw to cut these stops so that the new threshold slips under them and is flush with the sides of the jamb.

4. **Position the new sill and secure it with the screws or nails provided.**

5. **Caulk the joint between the ends of the new threshold and the door jamb with acrylic latex caulk, and then install the vinyl weather stripping in the center groove of the threshold.**

Maintaining Your Garage Doors

Because garage doors are especially exposed to weather extremes, you should inspect and service them at least once each year. Most modern garage doors consist of four or more panels that are hinged so that they can travel in a pair of tracks, as shown in Figure 10-13.

Use an aerosol spray lubricant and wand to clean and lubricate all the following moving pieces:

- ✔ **The combination hinge and rollers:** These gizmos are located at either side of the door, between each pair of panels. Apply lubricant to the roller and the hinge to which the roller is attached. Use the lubricant sparingly; too much lubricant doesn't make the door work better, it just attracts dirt that will eventually gum up the works.

- ✔ **The hinges in the field or center of the door panels:** The hinges that hold the center of the door panels together don't have a roller. Apply lubricant to these hinges and then operate the door several times to distribute the lubricant to all moving surfaces of the hardware.

✔ **The lock mechanism on the door:** Spray lubricant into the keyhole and work the key several times to distribute the lubricant to the lock's moving parts. If your door is manually operated, lubricate the pair of locking latches at each side of the door.

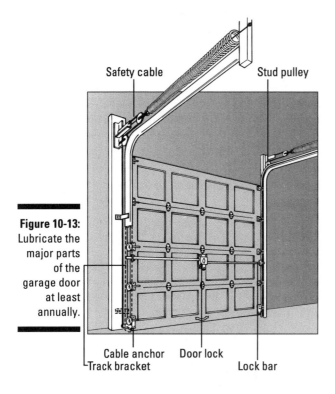

Safety cable   Stud pulley

Figure 10-13: Lubricate the major parts of the garage door at least annually.

Cable anchor   Door lock
Track bracket   Lock bar

If your garage door operates with an automatic opener, be sure that it's equipped with a safety-stop feature that prevents damage to the door and protects young children from being trapped and injured under the door. The safety-stop mechanism on older doors causes the door to reverse direction if it meets any resistance as it closes. Newer models have a safety-stop mechanism that causes the door to stop closing if anything interrupts a beam of light directed across the door threshold. Refer to Chapter 14 for information on how to test old and new automatic garage doors.

Part IV
Plumbing and Electricity

The 5th Wave   By Rich Tennant

"It's a thank-you note from the plumber's kid. He says our bathroom repair paid for his next two years of college."

In this part . . .

*W*e could all use some pointers on how to unclog a drain or stop a running toilet, especially when you have to chase it all the way to the next block. Put on your gear and plunge into this part, where you can expect to find out how to survive some deep plumbing dilemmas.

Plug into the chapters on electrical repairs and discover how to accomplish everything from resetting breakers and replacing fuses to installing a smoke detector and maintaining your clothes dryer.

Before you know it, you'll be on your neighborhood's who-to-call list — remember, most telephones run on electricity.

Chapter 11

Becoming Your Own Plumber

Many plumbing emergencies are the result of poor operating and maintenance procedures. By following good maintenance practices, you can avoid such common plumbing problems as plugged drainpipes in the sink, toilet, or bathtub; a backed-up sewer resulting from a clogged main drain; and burst water pipes. This chapter not only shows you how to fix these problems if you encounter them, but also gives you tips on proper maintenance so that you can avoid most of these water hazards in the first place.

 Later, if not sooner, all homeowners require the services of a good plumber. If you don't have a regular plumber, ask friends, coworkers, and relatives to refer you to one. Just as with a doctor, the best time to find a good plumber is *before* an emergency.

Locating Your Water Shutoff Valves

The first rule of good plumbing maintenance is making sure that every member of your family knows the locations of the main water shutoff valve and all sink or fixture shutoff valves (shown in Figure 11-1):

> ✔ The *main valve* is usually a gate valve that allows a full flow of water through the pipe when its open. This valve is located near the water meter (or pressure tank, if you rely on well water). Turning this valve clockwise cuts off the water supply to the entire house.

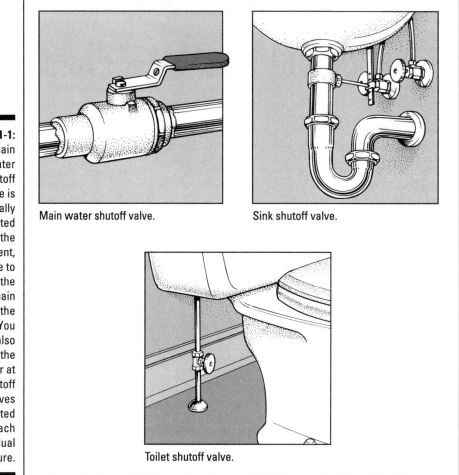

Figure 11-1:
The main water shutoff valve is usually located in the basement, close to where the water main enters the house. You can also turn off the water at shutoff valves located under each individual fixture.

Main water shutoff valve.

Sink shutoff valve.

Toilet shutoff valve.

✔ Most houses have *fixture shutoff valves* at the toilet and at each sink. These valves let you shut off the water supply to one fixture without halting water service to other fixtures. The water shutoff valves to the kitchen sink are inside the cabinets beneath the sink; the bath lavatory valves are usually concealed in the vanity cabinet beneath the lavatory. For the toilet, the water shutoff valve may be on either side, or beneath the water closet or tank.

✔ In the basement or crawl space, you can find water shutoff valves to the outside, or *bib,* faucets. Some newer houses have frost-proof bibs or faucets to the outside to prevent the faucets from freezing in winter. If you have frost-free bibs, you don't have to shut off the water at the valves inside the basement or crawl space in winter. The shutoff valve for frost-free bibs is located inside the house, at the end of a thick pipe that connects to the water supply pipe outside.

If your house doesn't have frost-free bibs, look for a shutoff valve in the pipe leading to the outside bib. During freezing weather, turn this valve off and then open the bib valve to allow the water between the shutoff valve and bib to run out.

All Clogged Up and Nowhere to Drain

Nothing good comes from a clogged drain — except, of course, the relief you feel when you get all systems working again. With a little care and common sense, you can avoid most clogs altogether. If a drain does become clogged up, read on to find ways to solve the problem.

Avoiding clogs

You can count on a life free of clogged drains if you follow these simple preventative measures. That is, of course, assuming that your kids don't try to flush Raggedy Ann down the toilet.

- **Kitchen:** A clogged kitchen sink is usually the result of garbage or foreign objects entering the drain. Use the sink strainer to prevent garbage from entering the drainpipe and be mindful of any small items you're washing.

  If you have a garbage disposer, run cold water at full volume while the machine is chopping the garbage; leave the water running for a full minute after you shut the disposer off. This precaution flushes the garbage completely out of the small-diameter sink drainpipe and into the larger main drainpipe, where it's less likely to cause a clog.

- **Bathroom:** Lavatory and tub drains clog up with soap scum and hair. As a defensive measure, fit strainers over the drains to catch debris before it can enter and clog the drain. Keep the strainers in place and clean them after each use. You can find replacement strainers in the plumbing section of home centers. Measure the diameter of the drain to find a strainer that fits exactly and then simply place the strainer in the drain.

- **Laundry:** Drains in the laundry tub usually become plugged as a result of two things: lint buildup from the washing machine, and leftover building materials flushed down the drain by do-it-yourselfers (the most common offender is plaster or wallboard compound, which seems innocent enough going down, but can harden in the drainpipes and clog them). To prevent these clogs, install a slip-on filter on the washing machine drain hose to catch lint before it enters the drain, and never dispose of leftover building materials in tub drains.

✔ **Main sewer:** Have you ever experienced the mess, smell, and damage caused by a main sewer backup? If so, you probably agree that cleaning the main sewer drain should be regarded as a regular maintenance procedure, not as an emergency measure. Depending on the length of the main sewer drainpipe and the location of your house, you can have the main sewer drain cleaned for $100 to $200. A service person from the sewer company can advise you on how frequently you need to have the drain cleaned. The interval for drain-cleaning maintenance depends on the number of people using the system, whether you have trees over or near the drainpipes (tree roots can penetrate and clog drainpipes), and how often you serve chili for dinner.

✔ **Septic system:** The sewer line to a septic system is no different from one leading to the city sewer; the same preventive maintenance goes a long way to keeping this line clear. You can also keep the septic field itself open with minimal maintenance. When rainfall is the heaviest, a septic system is most likely to fail; other problems can occur if a house has an inadequate gutter and down-spout system so drainage goes directly onto the leach fields. A wet basement or tree roots can also clog the leach field. Never try to flush disposable diapers or other nonbiodegradable items into a septic system. You can use a garbage disposal with a septic system, as long as the tank is pumped regularly.

Unclogging a sink

Your sink seems to be draining slower and slower, or maybe it has completely stopped draining and now resembles a stagnant pond. What's going on? You have a clogged drain; more precisely, your *sink* has a clogged drain. (For help with personal blockages, you need another book.)

The easiest solution for common clogs is to use any of a wide range of chemical drain uncloggers, available in solid and liquid form at supermarkets, hardware stores, and plumbing supply dealers. You pour the product in, wait for it to dissolve the blockage, and then flush the drain with running water.

Be aware that some chemical drain cleaners can damage the plastic or rubber parts of a garbage disposer and cause injury if the cleaner splashes into your eyes or onto your skin. If you use chemicals, read package directions and precautions carefully and follow them precisely; the directions vary according to manufacturers. If the blockage doesn't clear after a couple of tries, you're ready for a more hands-on approach.

Trap removal

If the sink or toilet drains are clogged, your first line of defense is the *trap* (the U-shaped pipe located under the sink). Some traps have a clean-out plug that you can unscrew to access clogs, as shown in Figure 11-2. If yours doesn't have such a plug, remove the entire trap and scrape out any material that you find there. Sink traps are easy to remove. Use a wrench or slip-joint pliers to unscrew the metal slip nuts about half a turn or so; you can loosen them by hand the rest of the way. To protect the chrome finish on the slip nuts, wrap tape around the jaws of your wrench or pliers.

Clean any blockage from the trap and then reassemble the trap. Tighten the slip nuts with your hands first, to be sure that they are threaded on the trap correctly, and then tighten with the wrench or pliers. A half a turn is usually all that's necessary to stop the trap from leaking; don't overtighten.

Figure 11-2: Some traps have a clean-out plug so you don't have to remove the entire trap to access the blockage.

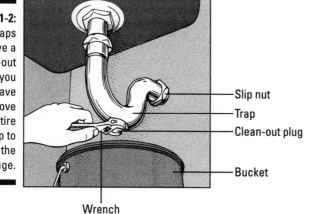

Slip nut

Trap

Clean-out plug

Bucket

Wrench

Some folks may advise you to try unclogging the sink drain with a plunger before you resort to removing the trap. We believe that cleaning the trap first is a better approach, because using a plunger can push the clogged material out of the trap and further into the drainpipe, where it's more difficult to remove.

The trusty plunger

The plunger is your friend. (If it's your *only* friend, then you may want to re-examine your life.) This common tool is capable of unclogging a drain that chemicals cannot budge. Unlike chemicals, the plunger uses suction to alternately push and pull the clog within the pipe until the force dislodges the blockage.

Remove any standing water that may contain chemicals before you start whaling away with the plunger. Splashing even diluted chemicals into your eyes can cause severe damage.

Remove the stopper first, if there is one. Fill the sink with enough clean water to cover the rubber portion of the plunger to assure good suction. Place the plunger over the drain, as shown in Figure 11-3, and vigorously push down and pull up several times. If you're successful, you'll notice a sudden quick emptying of the sink.

Stuffing a wet washcloth into the overflow hole, usually located on the side of the sink, is a good way to improve suction.

Figure 11-3:
Push down slowly on the plunger and then pull up with a quick motion to loosen the clog.

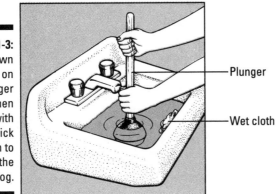

— Plunger

— Wet cloth

The snake

If the plunger doesn't do the job, try your next best friend: the drain auger, or *snake*. You can rent a manually operated or electrical drain auger for a few bucks at a rental center. The equipment is easy to use, but you still want to ask your dealer for instructions about how to operate it. A drain auger is a coiled spiral cable, usually about $1/4$ inch thick, with a handle on one end. You push the cable into the clogged drain and crank it further to dislodge the obstruction. Some units come in the form of attachments for an electric drill, giving them more power to force through the clog.

The basic process is to push the end of the snake into the drain opening and turn the handle on the drum that contains the coiled-up snake. The auger then begins its journey down the drain. Keep pushing more snake into the drain until you feel resistance, as shown in Figure 11-4. You may have to apply pressure while cranking the handle to get it to bend around the tight curves in the trap under the sink. After clearing the curve, the snake usually slides through easily until it hits the clog. Snakes are especially handy because they're long enough to reach clogs deep in the drainpipe.

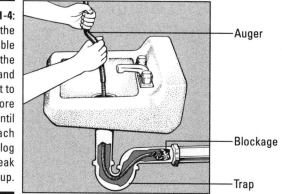

Figure 11-4:
Push the auger cable into the drain and turn it to feed more cable until you reach the clog and break it up.

Auger

Blockage

Trap

Rotate the auger cable against the blockage until you feel it feed freely into the pipe. The rotating action enables the tip of the snake to attach to the clog and spin it away or chop it up. If the clog is a solid object, the auger head will entangle it. If you don't feel the auger break through and the twisting get easier, pull the auger out of the drain and, most likely, the offending object will come out with it. Run water full force to be sure that the drain is unclogged.

If the snake doesn't fit down the drain or stops a short distance in the trap, you need to open the trap beneath the sink. Put a bucket under the trap and avoid contact with the water that comes out, as it may contain chemical drain opener. Some traps have a clean-out plug that you can unscrew with a wrench. Remove the plug and insert the snake going either up toward the sink or down the drain until you reach the clog. If your trap doesn't have a clean-out plug, you must remove the trap itself by unscrewing the large slip nuts at both ends. Insert the snake in either direction, as shown in Figure 11-5, until you reach and clean out the clog.

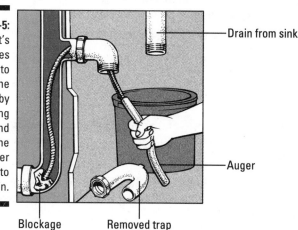

Figure 11-5:
It's sometimes easier to reach the blockage by removing the trap and feeding the auger directly into the drain.

Drain from sink

Auger

Blockage   Removed trap

Unclogging a bathtub drain

Just like your sink, your bathtub drain can become clogged. Your tub, however, usually doesn't provide the option of working from an accessible trap. Instead, you must apply all your efforts from above.

Calling on chemistry

Your first and easiest approach to clearing the clog is by pouring a chemical drain opener down the drain, waiting the specified period of time, and flushing the drain thoroughly with running water. You may have to repeat this procedure a few times until the chemicals dissolve the blockage enough to dislodge it. With each application of more chemicals, you may see incremental improvement in the tub's drainage. Chemicals are especially effective for clearing bathtub drains because they contain protein-dissolving elements that can work wonders on the most common cause of bathtub clogs — accumulated masses of hair. As always, follow product directions carefully.

Taking the plunge

If chemicals don't unclog your bathtub drain, it's time to call your old friend, Mr. Plunger. Plungers work pretty much the same way on a tub as they do on a sink:

1. **Remove the stopper, if there is one.**

   The stopper is a pop-up plug that alternately seals or opens the drain. To remove it, push and pull it up and then down until it is released. If your drain doesn't have a stopper, simply lift the strainer up and out of the drain opening.

2. **Stuff a wet washcloth in the overflow holes to plug them up and improve suction.**

3. **Fill the tub with a couple of inches of water, enough to partially submerge the plunger head, to assure air-tight suction.**

4. **Push the plunger down and pull it up forcefully.**

   You know that the blockage is dislodged when the water begins to drain much more quickly than it did before.

Resorting to the auger

If the plunger doesn't work, try using an auger, or *snake,* to unclog the tub drain, just as you would for a sink drain. (See "The snake" section under "Unclogging a sink," earlier in this chapter.)

1. **Remove the tub stopper or strainer and then push the tip of the snake into the drain opening, continuing to feed the coil through until it meets an obstacle.**

Push the cable all the way to the clog and then crank it farther to dislodge the obstruction. To remove a clog that's not in the trap, but beyond it under the tub, rotate the snake while you push it into the pipe.

2. **If the snake continues to resist passage through the trap, remove the overflow cover (usually located in the end of the tub directly above the drain and below the faucet).**

   As you remove the screws that hold the cover in place, be careful not to drop the screws down the drain. If the drain-closing mechanism is attached to the cover, pull up on the cover; the linkage comes out of the overflow hole with the cover.

3. **Push the snake directly down into the hole, bypassing the trap, as shown in Figure 11-6.**

   Note that this approach doesn't help clear a blockage stuck in the trap.

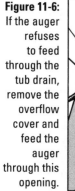

Figure 11-6: If the auger refuses to feed through the tub drain, remove the overflow cover and feed the auger through this opening.

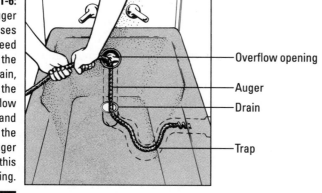

Overflow opening

Auger

Drain

Trap

If the blockage is past the trap, somewhere down the drainpipe, reaching it may take some time. The cable stops feeding in when it hits the blockage. You must work the snake against the blockage until the cable freely feeds in the drain; then you know that the clog is clear. Flush the drain with water to confirm that the blockage is gone.

Unclogging a toilet

So, you flushed the toilet and the usual thing didn't happen. Don't take it personally. Instead, put on your detective cap and figure out what's wrong. When you flush, which of these results do you see?

✔ The water is not swirling down as usual. Consider yourself lucky; this is a sign of an easy-to-fix problem.

✔ The water level lowers slowly and only weakly flushes the bowl.

✔ The water level barely drops (if at all) and then begins to rise past the normal full-bowl level. In the worst cases, the water continues to rise until it overflows onto your bathroom floor. To experience such an event is to understand the true meaning of the word *panic*.

Don't flush again if the bowl level rises past the normal height. You may be inviting an overflow.

If your toilet plays any of these tricks, you have a clogged or partially clogged toilet bowl. Often, the clog is caused by a blockage in the built-in trap of the toilet bowl. Partial or total blockage requires one of three solutions:

✔ Your old pal the plunger is your first choice to attack the problem.

✔ The second line of defense is using a toilet auger (also called a *closet auger*) designed specifically for dislodging a toilet clog.

✔ If all else fails, get a snake.

Before you attempt to unclog the toilet, clean up any overflow so that you can work in clean, dry surroundings. Be careful when you handle toilet water and waste; it's laced with bacteria. Thoroughly wash the area, your hands, and your clothing with a disinfectant soap.

The toilet plunger

The ball, or cup-type, plunger is designed specifically for toilets. The rounded lower surface nests tightly in the bowl, giving the plunger greater suction to dislodge the blockage. The trick to using this baby is properly positioning it completely over the hole in the bottom of the toilet bowl, as shown in Figure 11-7. With the plunger in place, push down gently and pull up quickly to create suction that pulls the blockage back a bit and dislodges it.

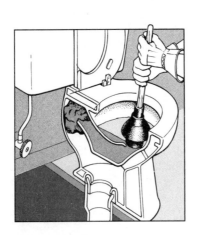

Figure 11-7:
Push the plunger down gently and then pull it up quickly to loosen the clog.

Another advantage of the ball plunger is that it doesn't splash as much water around as regular plungers because the ball of the plunger covers the entire hole. However, if all you have is a small sink-type plunger, try using it. It can't hurt, and it just may work.

The toilet auger

A more aggressive solution is to use a toilet auger. A toilet auger is a short, manually turned clean-out snake designed specifically to fit in a toilet bowl and clean out clogged toilet traps. Insert the rigid, hollow rod all the way in the bowl. Turn the crank while slowly pushing the flexible shaft through the hollow rod until it hits the blockage, as shown in Figure 11-8.

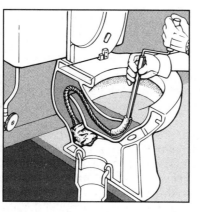

Figure 11-8: Feed the end of the toilet auger into the bowl and crank as you push the coil into the toilet until it snags the blockage.

Although the thought of renting or buying a toilet auger may not thrill you, the idea seems amazingly wise when you're faced with a clogged-up toilet. Toilet augers are inexpensive, and they make a particularly handy investment because most toilet clogs occur in the built-in trap — exactly where this tool delivers its punch. Buy one *before* you experience a problem and have to explain to your dinner guests that the bathroom's temporarily closed for repairs.

The heavy artillery

If the toilet auger doesn't do the trick, you probably have a blockage somewhere farther down the line, past the trap in the toilet and beyond the reach of the auger's coil. Your last hope for repairing the problem yourself is to rent a snake.

Make sure that the snake's small head fits past the tight curve in the toilet trap. The only thing worse than having a clogged toilet is having a clogged toilet with a snake stuck in the bowl; it's tough to explain to the guys at the rental shop why there's a toilet stuck on the end of their snake. Feed the flexible snake into the toilet until you feel it engage the clog — when the cable becomes harder to turn or refuses to move another inch into the toilet. When this happens, pull the snake back a bit to dislodge the clog. The water level should go down, signaling that the clog is loose. Then flush the toilet to push the clog down the drain line and, hopefully, out to the sewer or septic system. If the clog is a diaper, rubber ducky, or something else substantial, you may have to pull the offending item all the way out of the toilet to clear the line.

Unclogging the main line

Sometimes, the clog is so far from the toilet or fixture that you can't reach it with the snake. If you've fed the snake through the toilet or drain to its full length and still haven't reached the clog, your last resort before calling in the pros is to feed the snake through the main clean-out plug in the sewer line leading out of your house.

A clean-out plug is usually located at the base of the main soil pipe (a large-diameter cast-iron, copper, or plastic pipe), where it enters the floor of the basement or takes a 90-degree turn to pass through the foundation wall.

Look for a round plug with a square lug on it. You can unscrew the plug to push a snake into the line, as shown in Figure 11-9. The biggest problem here is that, unless the plug is brass, it has most likely rusted in place and will have to be broken into pieces. This is a standard practice with plumbers, but it may seem a bit extreme for you. Another point to consider before you bust open this plug is that there may be water standing in the pipe just waiting for you to crack the plug so it can come gushing out.

If you do decide to open the plug, and it isn't a brass one, go to the hardware store or home center and purchase a new plug so that you can close up the opening after you remove (read "destroy") the old plug. Then feed the snake directly into the drainpipe until it engages the plug.

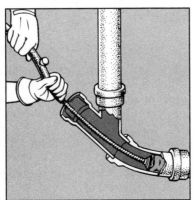

Figure 11-9: Clean out a blockage that is not right at the toilet or fixture by removing the clean-out plug in the main sewer line.

Unclogging a faucet aerator

New faucets usually come with an *aerator*, a device that conserves water and keeps it from splashing all over the place, while still providing a steady stream and good water pressure. If one faucet seems to be running slower than normal, the aerator may be clogged.

Aerators are simple inserts that fit inside the faucet's little chrome cap. Tiny holes in the aerator restrict the water flow and mix air into the water stream, providing a nice, soft flow of water. The little air bubbles prevent the water from splashing when it hits something. Without an aerator, your faucet would deliver water with all the subtlety of a fire hose.

The problem is that the minuscule holes in the aerator eventually become blocked by small particles in the water; even the ones that get through the aerator itself may be trapped by the aerator screen. The water restrictor inside the aerator has only seven or eight holes. If two of them become clogged, your water flow is cut about 25 percent.

Cleaning the aerator is a simple task:

1. **Place a towel or rag over the faucet cap, or cover it with a bit of masking tape.**

   This protective barrier keeps the surface from being marred when you strong-arm the cap off.

2. **Using a wrench or pliers, turn the cap counterclockwise until it separates from the faucet.**

3. **When the cap is off, remove the aerator screen and restrictor.**

   Pay attention to the way the inserts are arranged. When the time comes to put the aerator back in place, you have to replace these parts in the same sequence and position. Figure 11-10 shows a typical placement for these bits and pieces.

4. **Clean the screens and water restrictor by flushing them with water or use a brush; push through the tiny holes with a needle or pin to unclog them.**

5. **Reassemble the aerator in the reverse order that you took it apart.**

Expect a marked improvement in your water flow after you reinstall the cleared screen and restrictor.

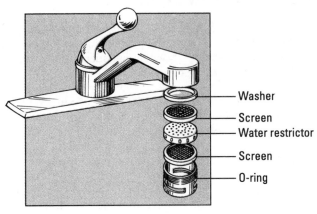

Figure 11-10:
The aerator located at the end of most faucets can become clogged. You can greatly improve water flow by cleaning out the aerator screens and restrictor.

Washer
Screen
Water restrictor
Screen
O-ring

Living a Leak-Free Life

The continuous drip, drip, drip of a leaky faucet, pipe, or toilet can be annoying to hear, let alone to pay for in high bills for wasted water. In this section, we take you through the steps involved in stopping the most common leaks in faucets, pipe joints, and the toilet — all very important parts of the plumbing system of your house.

Fixing a leaky faucet

A leaky faucet is one of those little annoyances that tortures you over time — even if it does reassure you that the plumbing still works!

Before you do anything to repair the leak, turn off the hot and cold water shut-off valve under the sink. (Refer to "Locating Your Shutoff Valve" at the beginning of this chapter.)

Stopping a stem leak

If you have a leaky handle, rather than a drippy faucet, the water is leaking past the stem packing or washer. Older faucets have a stringlike substance wrapped around the handle stem to hold the water back. This packing eventually wears, and water can sneak between the stem and packing. Newer faucets stop the water leak with an O-ring, or *washer*.

The following steps are for fixing older faucets with packing, which are the most likely to leak:

1. **Remove the handle from the shaft.**

2. **Before you replace the packing, try tightening the packing nut by turning it clockwise about a half turn.**

   This may be all that is necessary to stop the leak. If so, skip to Step 6.

3. **Loosen the packing nut with slip-joint pliers or a wrench and then unscrew the nut by hand and remove it.**

4. **Remove the old packing from around the stem.**

5. **Replace the old packing with new.**

6. **Reassemble the faucet.**

Keep a supply of various sized O-rings, packing washers, packing rope, and washers handy to save you a trip to the store when these problems arise.

Stopping a washer-type faucet leak

A *compression faucet,* shown in Figure 11-11, is often called a washer-type of faucet because rubber, and sometimes metal, washers are part of its design. The washers are discs that restrict the flow of water as the handle is turned.

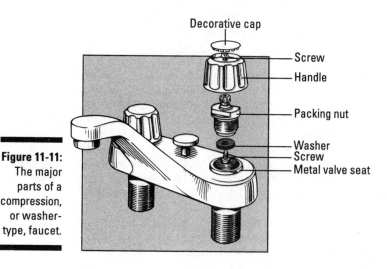

Figure 11-11: The major parts of a compression, or washer-type, faucet.

Decorative cap
— Screw
— Handle
— Packing nut
— Washer
— Screw
— Metal valve seat

If a faucet uses washers, a leak means that the rubbery gasket that is supposed to stop water from seeping through the faucet when the handle is shut has worn away. Less common is a worn metal seat that the washer presses against when it's closed. Seals can become damaged if you don't change the washer before it's too worn, so that metal grinds against metal and chews up the seat. Hard foreign matter can become trapped between the seat and the washer, so that closing and opening the faucet grinds the particles inside, damaging the seal beyond simple washer replacement.

To replace a worn washer, follow these steps:

1. **Remove the decorative cap, if there is one, atop the faucet handle.**

   Depending on its design, this cap either pulls or screws off.

2. **Unscrew the handle and remove it.**

   If the handle sticks, gently nudge it up with a screwdriver. Wrap the screwdriver edge with a rag to prevent marring the finish.

3. **Unscrew the packing nut and remove the valve stem.**

   Most older faucets have a cover over the actual valve. If, after removing the handle, you don't see a large packing nut with the valve stem protruding from it, you have to remove the decorative cover. Some types unscrew; others are held in place by set screws.

   Under this cover, you will find the packing nut that holds the body of the valve in place. Unscrew this large nut (turning it counterclockwise), and the valve stem should come out of the base of the valve. You may have to twist the body of the valve stem several turns after you loosen the large nut and the valve stem. If the valve stem is difficult to un-screw, put the handle back on the stem and give it a twist; the stem should then come out of the valve more easily.

4. **Unscrew the retaining screw and replace the washer.**

   On the other end of the stem is a rubber washer that is held in place by a screw. These valve washers come in many shapes and sizes; your best bet is to take the valve stem to the hardware store or home center and get a washer that matches the old one. This may be harder than it sounds if the old washer is damaged and deformed. The best clue to the original shape of the washer is to look into the valve body. Look for the metal opening, called the *valve seat,* that the washer presses against. If the side of the valve seat is angled, find a cone-shaped replacement washer; if the seat is flat, get a replacement washer that's flat.

If the faucet still leaks after reassembly, the seat may be damaged. You can purchase a simple, inexpensive seat-grinding tool at a plumbing supply store or home center. The tool comes with instructions and is easy to use. Disas-semble the unit again. This time, after the stem is removed, place the grinding tool over the metal valve seat (where the washer usually rests) and grind the seat with the tool. The idea is to reshape the damaged seat to accept the new washer. Then replace the assembly.

Stopping a washerless-type faucet leak

The newer variety of washerless faucets are easier to fix than the old washer-type. The hardest part of this project is figuring out what type of faucet you have. In this section, we explain how to fix the three main types of single-handle faucets currently on the market. It doesn't matter whether the faucet is in the kitchen or in the bath, the valve mechanism will be the same.

The best tip-off as to what type faucet you have is how the handle that controls the water moves:

- ✔ If the control handle moves in an arch (up and down and sideways) and is attached to a dome-like top of the faucet with a small set screw in the base of the control handle, then you have a *ball-type faucet*. See Figure 11-12.

- ✔ If the handle seems to move up and down to control the water flow, and right or left to control temperature, then you have either a cartridge faucet (Figure 11-13) or a disk-type faucet (Figure 11-14).

If you can find the user manual that came with the faucet (small miracle) you will find the manufacture name and model number. Most manufacturers offer a repair kit that has all the necessary parts, including any special tools you need to take the faucet apart.

Repairing a ball-type faucet

Follow these steps to fix a single-handle ball-type faucet:

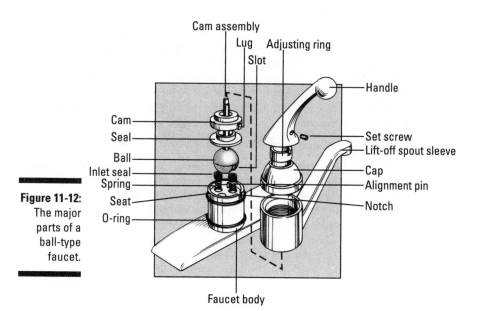

Figure 11-12:
The major parts of a ball-type faucet.

1. **Remove the handle by loosening the set screw that secures it to the shaft coming out of the ball valve.**

   The screw head is on the underside of the lever, and requires an Allen wrench to loosen. An *Allen wrench* is an L-shaped hex wrench that fits into the recessed socket in the head of the set screw. You can purchase a set of Allen wrenches at any hardware store or home center.

2. **Remove the ball valve and spout.**

   Wrap tape around the jaws of your wrench or slip joint type pliers to protect the valve parts. Loosen the cap assembly (the dome-shaped ring at the top of the faucet) by turning the adjusting screw counterclockwise. Grab the shaft to which the handle was attached and move it back and forth to loosen the ball-valve assembly; then pull it straight up and out of the faucet body.

3. **Replace the valve seats, springs, and O-rings.**

   Look inside the faucet body for the valve seats and rubber O-rings; behind them are springs. Remove the seats, O-rings, and springs from the faucet body and take them to the hardware store or home center to be sure that you get the correct repair kit. Replace the parts and reassemble the faucet in the reverse order that you took it apart or follow the directions in the repair kit. Be careful to reinstall the ball in the same position it was in when you removed it.

Repairing a cartridge-type faucet

Follow these steps to fix a single-handle cartridge-type faucet:

1. **Remove the handle.**

   Remove the cover on the top of the handle to expose the screw that holds the handle to the valve stem. You can pop off the cover by placing the tip of a screwdriver between the cover and the handle housing and then prying upwards. To remove the handle, turn the screw in the center of the cap counterclockwise, remove the screw, and then pull the handle up and off the valve assembly. The valve stem is now visible coming out if the valve cartridge.

2. **Remove the pivot on faucets that have movable spouts.**

   Use an adjustable wrench or slip-joint pliers (turning counterclockwise) to loosen and remove the pivot nut at the top of the faucet body. This nut holds the spot sleeve in place and prevents water from coming out the top of the faucet. Remove the spout assembly by twisting it back and forth as you pull up.

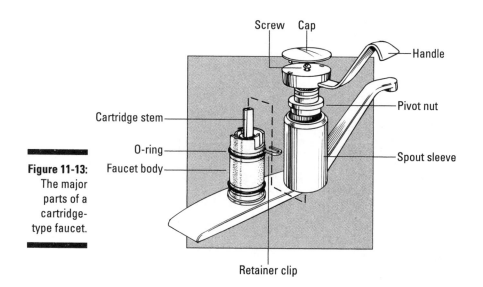

Screw Cap

Handle

Pivot nut

Cartridge stem

O-ring

Spout sleeve

Faucet body

Figure 11-13:
The major
parts of a
cartridge-
type faucet.

Retainer clip

3. **Remove cartridge clip and replace cartridge.**

After removing the pivot nut, you can see the cartridge. To remove the cartridge, pull out the small U-shaped clip that holds the valve cartridge in the faucet body. Pry the clip loose by placing the tip of your screwdriver between the faucet body and the U-shaped section of the clip. Twist the screwdriver until the clip comes out, and then grab the clip with your pliers and remove it. Pull up on the cartridge stem with a twisting motion. If it doesn't twist out easily, reinstall the handle so that you can get a good grip on the shaft to pull the cartridge out.

Take the old cartridge to your hardware store or home center and purchase a replacement kit. Reassemble the faucet according to the directions.

Be sure to replace the cartridge in the correct position. The cartridge fits into a notch in the valve body. How you insert the cartridge into the valve body determines which side the hot and cold water are on. Traditionally, you move the lever right for the cold and left for hot. If you reverse the position of the cartridge, the hot and cold will be on opposite sides. How embarrassing!

Repairing a ceramic disk-type faucet

The ceramic disk-type faucet is very reliable and usually doesn't require much maintenance, but it can be a bit tricky to take apart. Older models are held together by screws underneath the faucet. So if you can't figure out how to get the handle off, look under the counter for a couple of brass screws. Loosen these screws, and the whole cover and handle come off the faucet, revealing the valve cartridge.

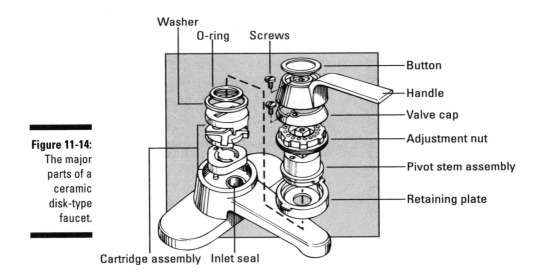

Figure 11-14:
The major parts of a ceramic disk-type faucet.

Washer
O-ring   Screws
Button
Handle
Valve cap
Adjustment nut
Pivot stem assembly
Retaining plate
Cartridge assembly   Inlet seal

No matter how you get it apart, follow these steps to replace the valve seals and cartridge:

1. **Remove the handle and button.**

   Use an Allen wrench to loosen the control lever set screw, usually located under the handle arm. Remove the handle and pull the decorative trim cap up and off the cartridge body.

2. **Remove and replace the valve seals and cartridge.**

   Loosen the two long screws on the top of the valve cartridge and lift the assembly off the faucet body. You'll find several rubber seals under the cartridge; replacing these seals is usually enough to solve minor leaking.

   If you replace these seals and the faucet still leaks, then the valve cartridge is worn. Take the cartridge assembly to your local hardware store or home center and purchase a replacement kit. Install the new cartridge according to the instructions in the kit. This kit will contain new O-rings to seal around the faucet body; be sure to replace these rings even if the old ones appear to be in good shape.

Fixing a leaky pipe

Home plumbing pipes come in four broad material categories: threaded (brass, galvanized, black pipe), copper (rigid and flexible), plastic, and cast iron. What all these kinds of pipes have in common is that they all can leak. Even a slow, insignificant, teardrop drip may foreshadow a more pronounced leak down the road.

Pay strict attention to any signs of wetness in your home. A musty odor or obvious moisture or stains may signal that a pipe is leaking behind a wall or ceiling where you cannot see it.

Before attempting any plumbing repairs, you must turn off the water-supply lines so you can work on the pipes without water flowing through them. All the pipes that supply water to the fixtures in your house are connected to the water main coming into your hose from the city water supply or from your well. You can turn off the water supply to all these pipes by turning off the main shutoff valve. See "Locating Your Water Shutoff Valves," in the beginning of this chapter.

Don't forget to tell the family when you plan to work on waste pipes. The last thing you need is someone flushing a toilet and causing waste water spilling out on you as you work. Gentle reminders include placing a masking tape "X" across the sink and duct-taping the toilet seat to the bowl.

Stopping pipe leaks

Leaks along the length of a pipe are the quickest and easiest to fix. Kits are available for repairing most types of pipe. The kit is basically a wide clamp whose two semi-circular sides match the diameter of the pipe you need to mend. You insert the rubbery gasket, included with the kit, between the pipe and the clamp as shown in Figure 11-15. When the clamp is tightened, the leak stops. These fast fixes have been known to last for years — some for over a decade — but don't rely on them to last that long. They're not designed to be a permanent repair.

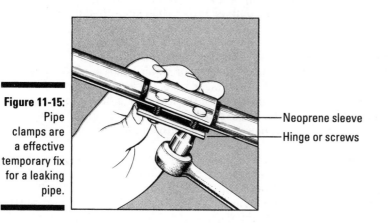

Figure 11-15: Pipe clamps are a effective temporary fix for a leaking pipe.

— Neoprene sleeve
— Hinge or screws

Knowing when to call a plumber

No one enjoys inviting a plumber out for a housecall. But a pipe or pipe joint that leaks more than a drip usually must be replaced, and trying to fix it yourself can result in a larger leak and a more expensive repair bill. No leak ever fixes itself, and they all eventually get worse — and, of course, they get worse at the worst possible time.

Leaks in threaded-pipes (the old-fashioned galvanized steel piping found in most older homes) are difficult to fix and are often better left to a professional plumber. To permanently fix a leaky joint in a threaded pipe, you need two pieces of pipe cut to precise lengths and then threaded on a threading machine, a universal joint, and a collar (coupling or elbow that matches the leaking one). Threaded pipe is a complete system: You can't just unscrew a single piece. The pipe has to be cut and these new parts used for the replacements.

Copper pipe also requires cutting because it works as a completely soldered system. A leaky joint requires lengths of pipe, two couplings, and a new coupling or elbow. And because copper pipes have no threads, they must be cut in two places — one on each side of the leaky coupling or elbow.

Plastic joint leaks are a lot easier to fix, but you're still better off leaving the job to a pro.

Stopping pipe-joint leaks

Okay, we told you to call the plumber for a pipe leak, but there are some emergency measures you can do yourself. You can handle a simple pipe leak at the joint, but the fix will be temporary at best. Pipe joints pose a special problem because the surface is complex rather than smooth and level, like the pipe.

The old standby for this job is applying plumber's two-part epoxy putty generously around the leaky joint. This type of repair is not a permanent fix if the leak occurs in the joint of a galvanized pipe, because it can't make a tight bond to the usually rusty steel. But if the leak is in a drainpipe, then have at it with the epoxy putty. There's little water pressure in the drain pipe, so this type of surface repair is more effective there.

Before you begin repairs, be sure to turn off the water (or at least announce that no one should use a fixture connected to the drainpipe). Carefully read the directions on the package of the putty and follow them. Allow the leaky joint to dry thoroughly before you apply epoxy putty. Mix the two-part putty as directed and apply it to the joint as shown in Figure 11-16. Before the putty sets, wrap the pipe in plastic electrical tape. When the putty is thoroughly dry, turn the water back on. The repair may or may not work, depending on the intensity of the leak and the pressure in the line. If the repair doesn't work, call a plumber.

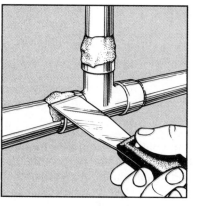

Figure 11-16:
Apply epoxy putty to the pipe joint with a putty knife to temporarily stop a leak.

If you repair a joint leak with epoxy putty, remember to check the spot regularly. Epoxy putty on a joint is much more likely to fail over time than a line-clamp repair made in a straight section of pipe.

Thawing frozen pipes

Not surprisingly, the easiest fix for a frozen pipe is to prevent it from freezing in the first place. Water pipes that run through poorly insulated outside walls or between an un-heated basement-level garage may freeze in cold weather. To prevent this problem

✔ Use heating cables on exposed pipes.

✔ Leave water running slightly in plumbing fixtures whose water pipes run through cold spaces. Running water does not freeze as readily as still water.

✔ Remove and reroute water pipes through heated spaces.

✔ Keep kitchen or bathroom cabinets on north-facing walls of a house open during freezing temperatures. Doing so allows warm air from the room to circulate around the pipes.

If a pipe does freeze, use a hair dryer or heat gun to thaw it. Before you start heating the pipes, open the fixture or faucet to allow any steam you generate by thawing the pipe to escape. Then play the heat flow over a large area, moving it slowly over the entire length of the pipe to prevent pressure buildup in the pipe. The idea is to *gradually* warm the entire pipe, so don't hold the heat source at one location. Be patient; the pipe will thaw in time. And heating it slowly reduces the danger of damage to you or to the plumbing.

Fixing a leaky toilet

One day you casually look down and notice a little water on the floor around the bottom of your porcelain toilet bowl. Water belongs inside, not outside the toilet; the floor at the base should be clean and dry. Most likely, your toilet has a damaged wax gasket seal. To replace the leaking wax ring, you have to remove the toilet bowl from the floor. This job requires much more work than it does money.

Before you begin this project, go to your home center or hardware store and buy a replacement wax seal and small tub of plumber's putty. Having your tools and supplies assembled in advance minimizes the time that the toilet is out of service. As a general rule, never attempt a toilet repair after a holiday feast, Super Bowl party, or chili cookout.

Many older toilets, and most new ones, have a shutoff valve located low on the wall under the tank. Before you begin repairs, turn this valve clockwise to shut off the water supply to the toilet. If your toilet doesn't have a shutoff valve under the tank, you have to turn off the water at the main valve. See "Locating Your Water Shutoff Valves," in the beginning of this chapter.

After shutting off the water, follow these steps to fix a leaky toilet:

1. **Flush the toilet to empty the reservoir.**

2. **Remove as much of the clean water from the toilet tank as possible.**

   First use a small cup, and then sop up the rest with a sponge. (Don't worry; tank water is relatively clean.)

3. **Use a small cup or can to bail out the toilet bowl.**

   Remove as much water as possible. This water is not clean, so wash your hands after this part of the job.

4. **Place a pan under the shut-off valve to catch any dripping water and then use a wrench to disconnect the *riser tube* (which brings the fresh water to the toiler tank) leading from the shutoff valve to the tank.**

   Don't just loosen the nut holding the riser to the bottom of the tank, remove the tube completely so that it doesn't get bent or damaged.

5. **Loosen and remove the bolts that attach the toilet bowl to the reservoir tank.**

   These bolts are located in the bottom of the tank (see Figure 11-17) and extend through the tank into holes in the body of the toilet bowl. You can loosen them from the underside of the toilet bowl with a wrench.

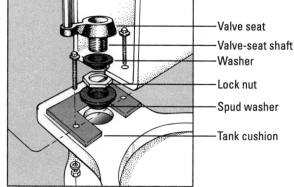

Figure 11-17:
The toilet tank is held to the bowl with bolts. Replace all hard or cracked rubber washers and gaskets.

Valve seat

Valve-seat shaft

Washer

Lock nut

Spud washer

Tank cushion

6. **Lift the tank off the bowl.**

   If the tank is wall mounted, you don't have to take the tank off the wall; simply remove the wide pipe leading from the tank to the bowl. This pipe is held in place with a large nut at each end. Use slip-joint pliers to loosen the nuts and then remove the pipe.

7. **On each side of the base of the toilet bowl, unscrew the nuts that hold the bowl to the floor.**

   These two nuts are usually hidden by decorative caps. Simply pull these caps off to access the nuts.

8. **Gently rock or otherwise tilt the bowl back and forth until the seals loosen enough that you can remove the bowl.**

   Even with the nuts removed, the putty along the bottom edge of the bowl and the wax ring (even though it's leaking) still form a strong bond between the heavy toilet bowl and the floor. You may need help freeing. But don't hit the bowl or try to pry it off the floor with a large screwdriver or pry bar, because you may chip the porcelain or crack the bowl.

9. **With the bowl removed, thoroughly clean off all putty and wax from the bowl, the waste pipe (called the *closet bend pipe*), and the floor.**

   Be sure that the floor is thoroughly clean and dry.

10. **Insert the new wax ring over the closet bend and apply a new 1-inch-wide band of putty under the outer perimeter of the bowl rim.**

11. **Lift the bowl, position it over the opening, and gently lower it down.**

   Apply pressure in a rocking or circular motion to push the bowl fully down. The bowl must squeeze the wax ring and putty for good adhesion. Keep pushing the bowl until it rests firmly on the floor, as shown in Figure 11-18. The wax ring creates a waterproof seal and assures that the bowl won't shift around during use.

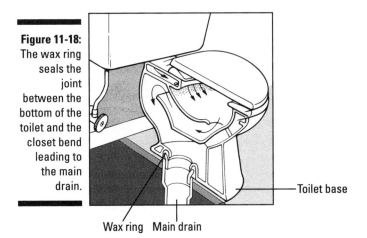

Figure 11-18:
The wax ring seals the joint between the bottom of the toilet and the closet bend leading to the main drain.

Toilet base

Wax ring   Main drain

12. **Reattach the nuts to the floor bolts and replace the decorative caps.**

13. **Reattach the reservoir tank or connection pipe and connect the water supply line to the reservoir tank or shutoff valve.**

    If the toilet has been in service for a long time, the rubber parts of the tank may be hard and cracked. If this is the case, purchase the necessary replacement parts. As long as you have the toilet apart, now's probably a good time to replace the rubber components.

14. **Turn on the water supply, and you're all set to go — so to speak.**

Repairing a Run-On Toilet

A toilet that runs continuously wastes hundreds of gallons of water a week — water that you pay for. And the constant sound quickly wears down your nerves. Repairing the problem quickly is well worth the effort. The only tool you need to fix a constantly running toilet is a screwdriver.

The first step to repairing a run-on toilet is to identify the parts of a toilet (refer to Figure 11-19) and how they all work. All tank-type flush toilets operate the same way. You can observe the toilet's inner workings by removing the top of the tank. Set the lid in a safe place, laying it flat so that it doesn't fall and break. Push the toilet's flush lever and peek inside the tank to observe the intricate ballet that takes place every time you flush the toilet:

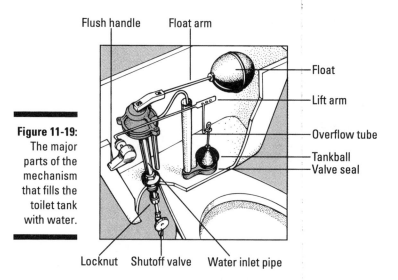

Flush handle   Float arm

— Float

— Lift arm

— Overflow tube

— Tankball
— Valve seal

Figure 11-19:
The major
parts of the
mechanism
that fills the
toilet tank
with water.

Locknut   Shutoff valve   Water inlet pipe

1. The flush handle lifts a round rubber *tankball* (or a rubber flapper) to let water flow into the toilet bowl.

2. As the tank empties, the large ball, called a *float,* attached to the end of a long rod falls with the water level in the tank.

3. At the other end of the float arm is the *intake valve,* which opens as the float moves down.

4. Water feeds into the tank as the intake valve opens.

5. When the tank is almost empty, the tankball falls into the outlet, stopping the flow of water to the bowl.

6. The tank then begins to fill from the open inlet valve.

A run-on toilet is usually caused by a malfunction in the tankball, the inlet valve, or the float. After you find the source of the problem, the next step is to get in there and fix it.

If the water keeps running into the tank and spilling out of the overflow pipe after the tank refills, the float mechanism and the inlet valve are likely suspects:

✔ The floatball should, well, *float* in the water and resist any pressure to push it under. If the float remains partially submerged, then you have a Titanic float: It's taking on water. Time for a new float. Unscrew the damaged float from the rod by turning it counterclockwise, as shown in Figure 11-20. Then visit a home center or hardware store for a plastic or copper replacement float mechanism.

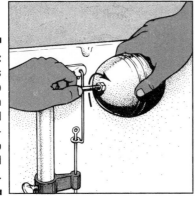

Figure 11-20:
Tank floats can develop leaks. Turn the ball counter-clockwise to loosen and remove it.

✔ If the water in the tank continues to run, but the floatball is floating as it should be, lift up on the ball. If the water stops, you need to bend the float arm down, as shown in Figure 11-21, lowering the floatball and creating more pressure to close the valve as the water rises. After bending the arm slightly, release the ball and check for running water. Repeat the process, increasing the bend in the arm, until the flow stops. Flush the toilet and check for leaking.

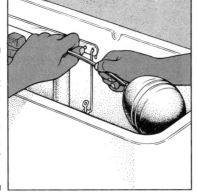

Figure 11-21:
Bend the float arm a bit to lower the float-ball and stop the toilet from overfilling or running on.

Some toilets don't have a float ball on an arm, but rather have a float that surrounds the fill pipe, as shown in Figure 11-22. To adjust this type of float, loosen the screw on the side of the float and lower the float a bit on the connecting rod that leads from the float to the fill valve arm.

✔ If you bent the float arm several times and the toilet still leaks, the problem is in the intake valve. Leave intake-valve repairs to your plumber; intake valves vary too much for a do-it-yourselfer to quickly diagnose and repair the problem.

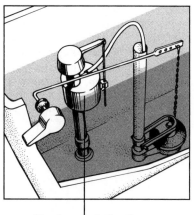

Figure 11-22:
To adjust a floating-cup ballcock valve, loosen the set screw on the side of the float and adjust the position on the connecting rod.

Floating-cup ballcock

If the tank doesn't fill after you flush, or if you have to wiggle the handle up and down to get the tankball to fall into the outlet pipe, the problem is with the tankball mechanism. Reach into the tank and pull up on the wire that the tankball is attached to. The wire and tankball should slide up and down easily and drop straight down into the outlet pipe. To make repairs, bend the tankball wire and the wire leading up to the arm that connects to the flush lever until the tankball works freely. Check your work by flushing the toilet and making sure that the tank refills.

If you can't get the tankball to fall into the outlet pipe and stop the water flow, buy a flapper-type tankball. Remove the old tankball by unscrewing it from the end of the brass rod. Install the replacement according to the manufacturer's directions.

Replacing a Faucet

The procedures for installing bath and kitchen faucets to water pressure lines are similar. If the kitchen faucet has a spray unit, it attaches to the faucet, not the pressure lines.

Before you go shopping for a new faucet, you need to measure the exact center-to-center distance between the holes in the sink through which the faucet stems connect to the water-supply lines. These distances are standard, but the dimensions come in many combinations; some sinks have a single hole, others have two or more.

You can find these measurements on your sink in several ways. The most accurate way is to remove the faucet and measure the distance between the holes in the sink through which the faucet stems connect to the water-supply lines. Put a measuring tape in the center of one hole and measure the distance to the center of the other hole. Better yet, take the old faucet with you to the store so that you can compare the spacing of the new faucet stems. If you can't go without water while shopping, leave the faucet attached and measure the handles, from center to center, as shown in Figure 11-24. Because the stems go straight down, this approach should give you an accurate measurement.

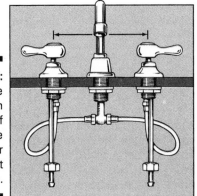

Figure 11-23:
Measure faucets from the center of one handle to the center of the next handle.

Getting this measurement is a little trickier if you have a single-handle faucet. In this case, you have to measure from underneath the sink, which is a cramped and difficult place to operate. Even if you can manage to squeeze in there without getting stuck, the existing plumbing makes taking a straight measurement difficult. Because plumbing faucets are manufactured to standards, you only need to worry about getting an approximate measurement. If the sink that your faucet is mounted on seems to have holes spaced about $3^3/4$ inches apart, you may only find faucets designed to fit sinks with holes on 4-inch centers — close enough! If the holes are widely spaced, as on a kitchen sink, chances are they're 12 inches apart. After you have a good idea of the spacing of the mounting holes in your sink, finding a valve that fits is easy.

While you're out shopping for that faucet, pick up a basin wrench (also called *faucet wrench*). This inexpensive tool, shown in Figure 11-24, is specially designed to work in tight spaces under a sink. It lets you tighten and loosen pipes in places that were otherwise impossible to reach.

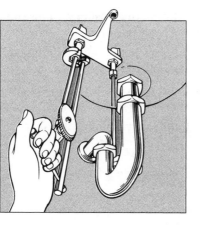

Figure 11-24: With a basin wrench, you can reach up under the sink and tighten compression nuts and hold down bolts without skinning your knuckles.

Over time, the nuts become difficult to loosen, even if you're working with a basin wrench. If your sink is easily removed, you may find it more convenient to take the sink out with the faucet still attached. If you do remove the sink, the only other connection you have to loosen and reconnect is the waste pipe leading to the trap. Now removing the old faucet from the sink and installing the new one becomes a much easier task.

The process for detaching and installing any faucet is very straightforward. All replacement faucets come with installation directions furnished by the manufacturer. Here are the major steps involved in swapping that old leaky faucet for a new one:

1. **To avoid a sudden shower, be sure to turn off the water-supply lines at the shutoff valves under the sink before disconnecting the faucet.**

2. **From underneath the faucet, use a basin wrench to loosen the compression nuts that secure the water-supply tubes to the faucet.**

3. **With the basin wrench, loosen and remove the large lock nuts that are threaded on the valve bodies, or the mounting bolts that hold the faucet to the sink.**

4. **Remove the faucet from the sink and clean up any hardened putty or old gasket remains from the top of the sink.**

5. **Assemble the new faucet according the manufacturer's directions.**

6. **Apply plumbers' putty to the underside of the faucet body or install the rubber gasket supplied by the manufacturer instead of the putty.**

7. **Place the faucet on the sink.**

8. **From underneath the sink, thread the washer and locknut onto the inlet shanks of the faucet.**

   Some faucet types are held in place with brackets or mounting screws. Follow the manufacturer's installation instructions.

9. **Reconnect the water-supply tubes to the faucet inlets and tighten the compression nuts with the basin wrench.**

10. **Turn on the water at the shutoff valves under the sink.**

Chapter 12

Maintaining and Upgrading Plumbing Appliances

In 1742, poet Thomas Gray penned the now-famous phrase, "ignorance is bliss." Well, that may be true in poetry, but when it comes to maintaining plumbing appliances, ignorance can be very costly. Repair bills for home appliances are expensive. But plumbing appliances have become a necessity: Garbage disposer, dishwasher, ice-cube maker — no modern kitchen is complete without them. This chapter is a primer on how basic appliances operate, so you can maintain and repair them yourself — and save a bundle.

Believe it or not, the folks in the appliance repair business tell us that the most common causes of appliance service calls are unplugged appliance cords, blown fuses, or tripped circuit breakers. Check to be sure that the appliance in question is plugged in, that the fuses are good, and that circuit breakers are on before you call for service or start fixing the appliance yourself.

If you want to make a full range of appliance repairs, buy a *multitester,* a handy device that allows you to measure the voltage, amperage, or the resistance of an electrical circuit to check motors, On/Off switches, and various valves.

Unclogging a Garbage Disposer

Garbage disposers are not goats — they can't eat everything. Clogs can and do occur. Most clogs are caused by dropping something like a spoon or fork into the disposer, by feeding garbage in too rapidly, or by failing to run enough water to completely flush out the drainpipes while the garbage is being processed.

Avoiding clogs in the first place

Read the owners' manual and follow the instructions for the types and amount of garbage that the unit can process. Feed in the waste slowly, and be careful to keep foreign objects out of the disposer, including your fingers.

Use only cold water to flush the garbage away; cold water helps solidify grease so that it's easier to flush away. Turn the water on full blast and keep it running until you're sure that all the chopped garbage is flushed out of the small-diameter drain pipes under the sink and into the larger main sewer drain. Let the cold water run for a full minute or more after turning off the disposer.

Throw in a tray of ice cubes every so often to keep the disposer blades sharpened.

Loosening that clog

Never use chemical drain cleaners in a disposer because they are highly corrosive and may damage rubber or plastic parts.

To unclog a disposer, follow these steps:

1. **Shut off the electrical power switch, which is located under the cabinet near the disposer.**

   If you don't find a switch, go to the main power panel and turn off the breaker or remove the fuse that powers the unit. See Chapter 13 for information about locating the main power panel in your house.

   Never put your hand into the disposer. Remember that the switch may be defective, so keep your hands out of the disposer even when the power to the machine is turned off.

2. Take a look in the disposer.

A flashlight may shed some light on the problem if you don't have an overhead light above the sink.

3. If the stoppage was caused by an object, use a pair of pliers to reach into the disposer and remove the object.

4. Wait 15 minutes for the disposer motor to cool.

5. Turn on the power and push the reset or overload protector button that is located on the bottom side of the disposer.

6. Push the reset button to set the disposer to operate.

If the disposer is still clogged, follow these steps:

1. Turn off the power and insert a long dowel, a wooden spoon, or broom handle — never your hand — into the drain opening.

2. Push the bottom end of the wooden probe against the impeller (the blades that grind up the garbage), as shown in Figure 12-1, and rock it back and forth to free it.

Figure 12-1:
Never reach into a disposer; use a broom stick or a large wooden spoon to free a clog.

3. When the impeller moves freely, wait 15 minutes for the motor to cool, turn on the power, and push the reset button.

Some disposer models come with a large L-shaped hex wrench. If you have such a model, turn off the power, insert the hex wrench into the opening in the center of the disposer's bottom (see Figure 12-2), and turn the wrench back and forth until the impeller is free. Again, wait until the motor has cooled, press the reset button, and then try operating the disposer.

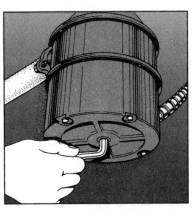

Figure 12-2: Some disposers have a hex-shaped opening at the bottom of the unit where you can unstick the impeller by inserting and turning an Allen wrench.

Getting More from Your Dishwasher

A modern dishwasher like the one shown in Figure 12-3 is a complicated appliance with more bells and whistles than a fire truck. However, a handy homeowner can correct the most common dishwasher problems — not cleaning the dishes or not filling and emptying properly.

Prerinse and load properly

Not all dishwashers are created equal. Your model may require more pre-rinsing than you think, or you may be loading dishes improperly in the racks. Get out the owner's manual and follow the instructions about properly loading the unit and rinsing before loading. If you don't have a manual, ask for one from a local retailer who sells that brand, visit the manufacturer's Web site, or call their toll-free number. The manual contains guidelines about the number and placement of dishes and utensils to get the best washing results.

Check water pressure

Water pressure that's too low may contribute to the dishwasher's failure to clean the dishes. If you have a city water supply, the water pressure should be adequate for proper cleaning. If you have a private water well, the pressure may be low.

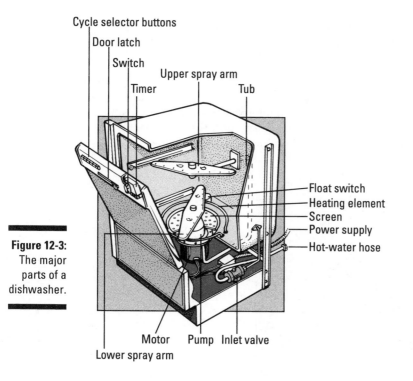

Cycle selector buttons
Door latch
Switch
Upper spray arm
Timer
Tub

Float switch
Heating element
Screen
Power supply
Hot-water hose

Figure 12-3:
The major
parts of a
dishwasher.

Motor   Pump   Inlet valve
Lower spray arm

Follow these steps to check for adequate water pressure:

1. **Turn on the machine and let it run until it reaches the first wash cycle.**

2. **Open the door to stop the machine.**

3. **Use a cup to bail the water from the machine and dump it into a gallon container to measure the volume.**

   The machine should contain about $2^1/_2$ gallons of water. If you find much less water, then your water pressure is too low.

If water pressure to your washer is too low, you can often correct the problem by not using other water faucets or flushing the toilet while the dishwasher is filling.

Low water pressure to the machine may also be caused by a blocked screen in the water inlet valve. To service this valve, you have to remove the front cover of the machine. Unless you have an owner's manual that clearly identifies all the parts of your machine, this job is best left to the appliance repairperson.

If the dishwasher is a portable model, the plugged screen may be at the faucet connector. Clean any filter screens on the faucet itself (see "Unclogging a faucet aerator," in Chapter 11) and on the dishwasher hose connector.

Dishwashers have an overflow float switch that can become stuck and prevent the unit from filling with water — a detriment to dishwashing if ever there was one. The float, which looks like a round knob sticking out of the floor of the dishwasher (see Figure 12-4), should move up and down freely. If it doesn't, remove any buildup of detergent that may be obstructing it.

Figure 12-4:
Remove soap scum buildup or any debris from around the overflow float so the switch has free movement.

Adjust the water temperature

To thoroughly clean food and dissolve grease from dishes, the water temperature in the dishwasher must be at least 140°F. To test the water temperature, run the machine to the end of the first wash cycle and then open the door. Use a cooking thermometer to measure the temperature of the water in the machine. If the water temperature is less than 140°F, turn up the thermostat on the water heater to at least 120°F. If the water temperature remains below 140°F, have a repairperson replace the dishwasher heating element.

If the water heater temperature is higher than 130°F, a child can suffer deep third-degree burns from just two seconds of exposure. If you have small children in the house, set the water heater thermostat at no higher than 120°F.

Try new detergents

How clean your dishes are depends, in part, on the detergent you're using. If your detergent leaves dishes dirty, experiment with other brands of detergent until you find one that works well in your dishwasher.

Powder dishwasher detergent can harden in the dispenser and prevent proper feeding of the detergent into the machine. Clean any crusty detergent residue from the dispenser, and check to be sure the dispenser is operating freely.

If you have soft water, you can use less detergent; if your water is hard, you may have to add extra detergent to the dishwasher.

Unclog the spray arm

Incomplete cleaning of the dishes may be due to a faulty or clogged *spray arm,* that long wand-like device with holes in it to spread the spray of water. Use a screwdriver to remove the spray arm, and lay the washers or gaskets aside in the same order that you remove them. If the spray arm is bent or damaged, replace it.

If your machine has a strainer beneath the spray arm, remove the strainer, as shown in Figure 12-5, and clean it. If your machine has a telescoping spray tower, which rises up to clean the upper tray of dishes, pull up on the top of the arm to be sure that it telescopes freely. To remove the spray tower, unscrew it from the spray arm. Check the tower for blockage and clean it to remove any trapped debris.

Use a stiff wire, such as a paper clip, to clean out the holes in each spray arm, as shown in Figure 12-5. Rinse the strainer, spray tower, and arms under running water and then reassemble them.

Figure 12-5: Most dishwashers have a filter in the base to collect large food particles. Remove and clean the filter and unclog any blocked holes in the spray arm.

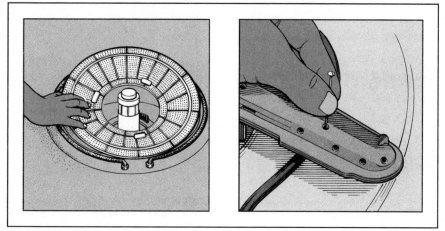

Clear the drain

If a dishwasher drains during the fill cycle, the problem is a faulty drain valve. Have a professional replace the valve.

If the dishwasher doesn't drain properly, the problem may be with the *air gap,* shown in Figure 12-6. The air gap, which is located by the sink faucets, prevents water and waste coming from the sink from flowing back into the dishwasher. Remove the cover and unscrew the cap from the air gap. Wash the cover and cap, and remove any debris from the center tube in the air gap.

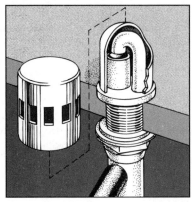

Figure 12-6: Soap scum and food particles can clog the dishwasher's air gap.

If cleaning the air gap doesn't solve the problem, clean the spray arm and filter screen as detailed in the previous section. Also check the drain hose and replace it if necessary. If the problem remains, suspect a faulty timer or a broken pump impeller, and call a service person.

Fixing a Washing Machine

Washing machines are durable and relatively trouble-free. The first rule is to read the owner's manual, and the second is to avoid overloading the machine. Follow the manufacturer's recommendations for load limits and detergent use. If you have heavy loads, such as rugs, take them to a Laundromat and use their heavy-duty commercial equipment.

Even if you do follow all the recommendations in the manual, you may someday be faced with a cranky washer. Clothes washers are complicated machines; many models have sophisticated electronics that require NASA training to understand. But some of the more common washing-machine problems are easily fixed. So before you run off to call for help, try a few of these do-it-yourself repairs.

Washing machine hoses

Rubber supply hoses for hot and cold water are located at the back of the washing machine. Also back there are two shutoff valves that permit you to cut the water supply to the machine during replacement or repairs.

Turn off the water supply faucets when you go on vacation or anytime you leave the house unoccupied for an extended period. The rubber hoses are not intended to serve as water pipes, under constant water pressure. If the supply hoses burst when you're not home, the laundry room will be flooded and no one will be around to turn off the water.

If the washer won't start or run, first check to be sure that the unit is plugged in. Then check the fuse or the circuit breaker to be sure that it's not tripped. Replace a blown fuse, or flip the circuit breaker off and then back to the on position. (See Chapter 13 for more on circuit breakers and fuses.)

When the motor overheats, the heat-activated circuit breaker on the motor opens. Turn off the washer and let the motor cool for one hour, and the breaker will reset itself. Then turn the machine on and see if it will resume the wash cycle.

Before repairing the washer, or any other appliance, turn off the machine and disconnect the power cord. If the appliance uses water, make sure to disconnect the water supply hoses, too.

Washer doesn't fill

If the power source is okay and the motor is cool, yet your washer still doesn't fill with water, try the following:

- ✔ Be sure that the water-supply faucets behind the washer are turned on, straighten out any kinked hoses, and replace leaking hoses.

- ✔ Check that the lid switch is activated when you push the top of the washer shut. The lid switch is located around the edge of the opening and is triggered when the lid pushes on it. If this switch is not working, the washer won't run. Call a repairperson to replace the switch.

Another possible cause of little or no filling action is a clogged water inlet hose screen. To remedy this problem, do the following:

1. **Turn off the water and disconnect the hoses from the washer.**

2. **Use long-nosed pliers or a screwdriver to pull or pry the screens out of the water inlet (located in the end of the hoses) or in the input fitting (on the back of the unit).**

   See Figure 12-7.

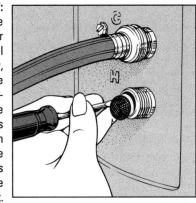

Figure 12-7: If the washer doesn't fill properly, clean the water-intake screens located in the intake hoses behind the unit.

3. **Clean the screens with a stiff brush and replace them if they're damaged.**

If your washer still doesn't fill properly, call a service person.

Washer doesn't drain

If the water doesn't drain out of the washer, first check the drain hose for kinks and, if you find any, straighten them out. If the end of the drain hose is too high, try lowering its position on the drainpipe or laundry tub.

Thick suds may clog the drain and prevent water from draining. If you see heavy suds, reduce the amount of detergent you use.

If you've tried these tricks and the machine still isn't working right, call a service person. The problem may be a faulty water pump, loose drive belt, or a bad solenoid — all jobs for a pro.

Washer doesn't agitate or spin

Most of the time when the washer refuses to toss the clothes around, it's not because your wardrobe is hopelessly out of style; you are faced with a more serious problem. Spinning clothes requires motors, drive belts, and transmissions — and repairing any or all of these parts takes the talents of a service person.

You can, however, check out a couple of simple things before you call for help:

✔ Check that the unit has power and that the lid is closed and make sure that the timer dial is pulled out or pushed in, depending on your model, so the timing cycle is running.

✔ Check that the clothes have not bunched up on one side of the drum and caused the tub to vibrate so much that it has shut down the machine.

✔ Check that the unit is level. Adjust the washer's feet by turning them with an adjustable wrench (see Figure 12-8): counterclockwise to lower the feet, and clockwise to raise the feet.

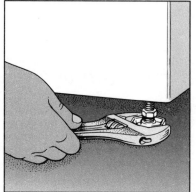

Figure 12-8:
To prevent vibration of the washer during the spin cycle, level the unit by adjusting the feet.

If these three points check out, you can look at the problem in two ways. You can unplug the unit, turn off the water, remove the supply and drain hoses, and then remove the back and mess with the drive belt . . . or you can call for help. We suggest you do the latter. Fooling around with a washing machine's innards can cause more damage, leading to an even costlier repair.

Fixing the Refrigerator's Ice-Cube Maker

Once you get used to an automatic ice-cube maker, your household can be thrown into a state of panic if the machine stops churning out ice. Before you rush out and purchase a new refrigerator, here are a few simple points to check out:

- ✔ Be sure that the refrigerator is plugged in.
- ✔ Check the fuse or circuit breaker.
- ✔ Check that the water supply to the icemaker is on. This supply usually takes the form of a saddle valve clamped to a cold-water pipe close to the refrigerator.
- ✔ Re-examine your family's dependency on chunks of frozen water.

Ice doesn't freeze

If the ice-cube maker doesn't freeze the cubes, test the temperature inside the freezer. Place a food thermometer in a cup of cooking oil (the oil won't freeze) and leave the thermometer in the cup for several hours. The freezer temperature should be between 0 and 8°F. If the freezer temperature is too high, turn the dial down.

Ice cubes come out too small or too large

Most icemakers have an adjustment that controls the amount of water that flows into the ice cube mold. If the cubes are too large or if the water overflows, turn the control to make smaller cubes. If the cubes are too small and turning the control does not seem to work, you may have a clog in the water supply. If not enough water is entering the icemaker to fill the ice-cube mold, the ice cubes will be small or possibly non-existent.

If this is the case, do the following:

1. **Turn off the water at the saddle valve (usually located under the sink or in the basement).**
2. **Unplug the refrigerator and pull it away from the wall.**
3. **Look for the supply tube, which is either a thin plastic or copper tube.**
4. **Follow the tube to the inlet valve and use an adjustable wrench or pliers to disconnect the tube from the valve.**

5. Loosen the screws or bolts holding the valve to the mounting bracket.

Inside the valve is a filter screen that is probably clogged with sediment or small pieces of dirt. Remove the screen as shown in Figure 12-9:

Figure 12-9: If too little water is entering your icemaker, the problem may be a clogged water-supply screen.

6. Clean the screen, replace it inside the valve, and then reassemble the valve and reconnect the water supply tube.

7. Plug in the refrigerator, turn on the water supply, and test the icemaker.

If these steps don't solve the problem, the trouble may be in the On/Off switch, the holding switch, the thermostat, or the motor. Fixing these problems requires some specialized tools, so remove the icemaker and take it to your local dealer for service, or purchase a replacement unit.

Fixing a Water Heater

Water heaters are either electric or gas. The electric heater is less complicated and easier to maintain than the gas heater, but several maintenance procedures are common to both types of heaters.

Water and electricity are a dangerous combination. When working on an electric water heater, always turn the power off at the main panel, not at the switch.

Draining the water heater — annual maintenance

At least once a year, turn on the drain valve and drain the heater tank to remove any sediment. If the drain valve leaks, repair or replace it.

To drain a water heater, do the following:

1. **Turn off the valve on the cold water supply pipe, located above the heater.**

2. **Connect a hose to the bottom drain valve (as shown in Figure 12-10) and direct the end of the hose to a floor drain or out a window.**

Figure 12-10:
Attach a garden hose to the drain valve on the side of the water heater to drain sediment from the bottom of the heater.

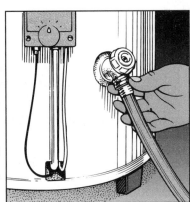

3. **Turn on the drain valve, and open the hot water faucet at the bathtub or laundry tub.**

To refill the heater after servicing, follow these steps:

1. **Shut off the drain valve and the tub faucet.**

2. **Open a hot water faucet that is far from the heater.**

3. **Turn on the cold water supply valve above the heater.**

   When water runs from the open water faucet, you know that the heater is full of water.

Fixing a leaky drain valve

If you see water on the floor around your water heater, it may be coming from a leak in the *drain valve,* the valve used for draining sediment from the bottom of the heater tank. Your water heater may have a metal drain valve, called a *sillcock valve,* with a screw in the handle. The sillcock valve has a replaceable washer, so repair is possible. Some heaters have a plastic drain valve that must be replaced when it leaks.

To replace the drain valve, simply turn the valve counterclockwise with a pipe wrench to remove the sillcock valve. Always wrap a layer of Teflon pipe tape around the threads on any plumbing repair item. Use the pipe wrench to tighten the sillcock valve.

Follow these steps to remove and replace a plastic drain valve:

1. **Using hand pressure only, turn the valve counterclockwise through four revolutions.**

2. **Pull on the handle while you turn the valve clockwise through six revolutions until the valve comes free from the tank.**

3. **Take the valve with you to a hardware store and buy a duplicate replacement valve.**

4. **Push on the handle while you turn the new valve six counterclockwise revolutions, and then clockwise through four revolutions.**

   Spin your partner 'round and 'round.

Checking for and repairing a leaky pressure relief valve

Both electric and gas water heaters have a pressure relief valve located either on the top or side of the unit. This safety valve releases the pressure and prevents an explosion if the heater controls fail and pressure starts to build up in the heater tank. Kind of a nice feature, don't you think?

At least once a year, place a pail under the discharge opening of the valve, (some heaters have a pipe screwed into this opening) and lift the lever on the relief valve. Allow at least a cup of water to run out of the valve to help remove any sediment. Open the valve fully by lifting the valve lever several times. When you release the lever, check to be sure that no water is dripping from the valve.

If no water comes out of the valve, or if the valve leaks after you release the lever, you must replace the relief valve. Here's how:

1. **Shut off the power at the main fuse panel, or turn off the gas valve and the water-supply pipe to the heater.**

2. **Drain enough water from the heater so the water level in the tank is below the relief valve.**

   If the relief valve is top-mounted, open the drain valve at the base of the tank and drain a gallon or two of water from the heater; if the valve is mounted on the side, drain down about five gallons of water, or until the water level in the tank is below the relief valve.

3. **Using a wrench, remove the discharge pipe and the relief valve.**

   Turn the old valve counterclockwise to remove it, as shown in Figure 12-11.

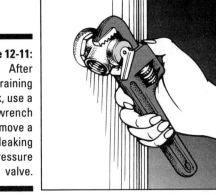

Figure 12-11:
After draining tank, use a pipe wrench to remove a leaking pressure valve.

4. **Take the old valve to the hardware store and buy an identical new relief valve.**

5. **Wrap pipe Teflon tape around the threads of the pipe that the new valve screws on to; thread on the new valve and use a pipe wrench to tighten it.**

6. **Replace the discharge pipe in the new valve, refill the heater, and turn on the power (electric heater) or restart the pilot light (gas heater).**

Replacing the anode rod

Another common repair for both gas and electric water heaters is replacing the anode rod, which is designed to protect the tank from corrosion. If your tank is more than ten years old, chances are that this rod is worn down.

Replacing the anode rod can extend the life of your water heater.

To replace the anode rod, do the following:

1. **Turn off the water supply.**

   If you have an electric or oil-fired heater, turn off the electric power at the main power panel. If the heater is gas powered, turn off the gas supply valve located in the gas pipe leading to the water heater.

2. **Drain about three gallons of water from the tank.**

   Be careful, it's hot!

3. **Use an adjustable wrench or a socket wrench to remove the 1-inch hex plug on top of the heater.**

   You can rent a large wrench at any tool rental center.

4. **Turn the wrench counterclockwise to remove the rod plug.**

   After loosening the old anode rod, pull it out by hand as shown in Figure 12-12. Be sure that the new anode rod is a duplicate of the old one.

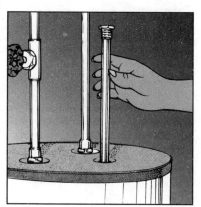

Figure 12-12: The anode rod of most water heaters is located in the top of the tank. Unscrew and replace the rod after ten years of service.

5. **Wrap the end thread of the rod with pipe tape and insert the anode rod into the hole.**

6. **Hand-tighten the rod as far as you can, in a clockwise direction, and then use the wrench to snug up the rod.**

Gas water heaters

In addition to our advice for all water heaters, gas heaters (shown in Figure 12-13) require some extra maintenance procedures. For example, gas water heaters have vents to let exhaust combustion gases outdoors. You must periodically inspect these vents to be sure that they're clean and functional.

Before you inspect the vent, let the water heater run for several minutes. Then insert a lit match under the draft hood. If the vent is clear, the match flame gets pulled upward by the vent gases. If the match goes out or is blown away from the draft hood, you need to clean the vent.

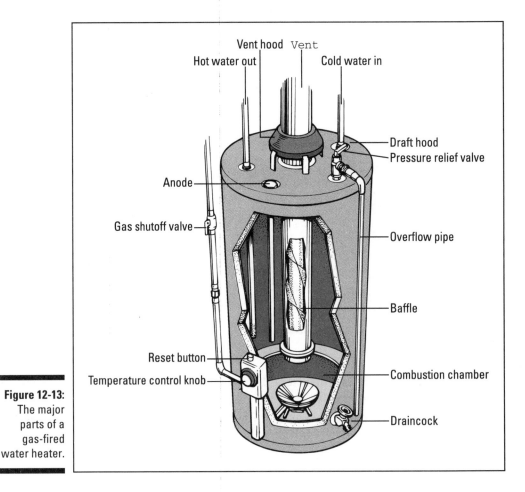

Figure 12-13:
The major parts of a gas-fired water heater.

To clean the vent, follow these steps:

1. **Turn off the gas by turning the handle of the gas valve perpendicular to the gas pipe.**

2. **Remove the vertical vent pipes and unscrew the draft hood.**

3. **Use a wire brush to remove soot from the hood and vent pipes.**

4. **While the vent hood is off, pull the *baffle*, which is a spiral metal insert inside the heater flue, out of this pipe and clean it with a wire brush.**

   If you don't have enough clearance above the heater to completely remove the baffle, give it a good shaking to dislodge any soot buildup.

5. **Replace the baffle, vent hood, and vent pipes.**

6. **Remove the burner access panel at the bottom of the water heater.**

7. **Use a vacuum to clean any debris from the combustion chamber, and clean the burner and the pilot light with a stiff brush.**

8. **Light the pilot light (some heaters have electronic ignition, not a standing pilot light) and turn on the gas.**

   Using a match as described earlier in this section, check to be sure that the vent is operating properly.

Fixing a Sump Pump

Sump pumps are devices used in conjunction with drain pipes to remove water that collects around the foundation of a house. In some houses, especially ones that have septic systems, a basement sump may be used only to collect and remove water from laundry tubs, where the drain pipe exits the house through the wall, above floor level.

Sump pumps come in two basic types, as shown in Figure 12-14. The one on the left has a pedestal where the pump motor sits above the sump; the pump on the right is submersible, meaning that the pump motor sits under-water in the sump.

Because of the danger of mixing water and electricity, always turn off the pump at the main electrical panel and then disconnect it before you begin work on it.

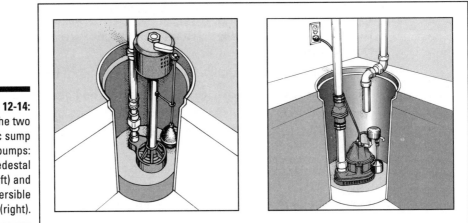

Figure 12-14:
The two
basic sump
pumps:
pedestal
(left) and
submersible
(right).

Sump pump tune-up

Most houses have a *sump pit* where water from around the foundation is directed. The sump pump pumps this water into the main sewer line. With either type of sump pump, pedestal or submersible, the sump or basin may become filled with silt, dirt, and other debris. Frequent maintenance keeps your sump pump pumping.

To confirm that the pump is working, fill the sump pit with buckets of water, enough to activate the pump. The pump should start right up and remove the water. Repeat this procedure several times to test the pump and to clean the yucky water out of the sump pit. If the pump does not work, see the troubleshooting section next in this chapter.

To clean the pump, follow these steps:

1. **Disconnect the power cord from the electrical outlet.**

2. **Put on rubber gloves and, if the sump pit is smelly, pour a little chlorine bleach into the sump and then refill it with water so the pump empties the pit.**

3. **Reach into the sump pit and remove any debris from the bottom of the pit and around the pump base.**

4. **Check that the switch float moves freely.**

   Pedestal pumps have a float that slides up and down a rod; submersible pumps have a float attached to the end of a cord. Both should move freely. If the pedestal pump's float hangs up, check that the rod it runs up and down on is clean and straight. On a submersible pump, check that the float is not stuck between the pump body and the wall of the sump. Also, with either pump, check that the float hasn't sprung a leak and become full of water. Remember: If the float flops, the pump stops. (What, you were expecting Shakespeare?)

A sump pump that doesn't

If your sump pump refuses to pump, check to be sure that power is running to the electrical outlet. First, check at the main power panel to be sure that the fuse or circuit breaker has not failed. Then disconnect the power cord to the sump pump and use a circuit tester to be sure that the receptacle is working. If you don't have a circuit tester, plug in a lamp or radio. If no power comes from the receptacle, replace it as described in Chapter 13.

Bad switch

If power is flowing to the receptacle, but the pump isn't working, check the pump switch. Use a broom handle or wood stick to raise the float switch. On a pedestal pump, slide the float up the rod until the float lifts the rod. On a submersible pump, just raise the float until it is facing up. The pump should start. If it doesn't, the switch is bad and should be replaced by a repairperson.

If you want to replace the switch yourself, check your owner's manual. Unscrew the clamp that holds the float and replace the float switch with a duplicate model.

Clogged pump or pipes

If you hear a humming sound, and the pump is not running, the problem may be a clog. If the pump runs but does not pump water, you've got blockage at the base of the pump or in the piping. To fix the problem, follow these steps:

1. **Clean the bottom of the sump and make sure that the slots in the base of the sump pump are clear and open.**

   Some pumps have a screen at their base. In any case, you want to clear the space at the base so that the water can get to the pump.

2. **Clean the check valve.**

   The check valve is usually located above the pump in the discharge line leading from the pump to the drain pipe or outside the house. This valve is designed to prevent water from running back into the sump after it is pumped out. But if the flapper inside the check valve gets clogged, the water can't leave the sump in the first place. Scoop out the crud with your hands. (Wear gloves!)

Most check valves have a clean-out cover that you can unscrew. Use a pipe wrench or large adjustable wrench to unscrew it, and then clean out any blockage you find.

3. **Check to see that the flapper valve moves freely, and then reassemble the valve.**

Sump pump replacement

Replacing a sump pump is a straightforward project — honest! The pump is connected to the house by a single electrical cord and a drain line. To make this project as easy as possible, purchase a new sump pump that is the same type as the one that you're removing. You may have to remove the old pump (as described in the following steps) before you know which replacement pump to buy.

1. **Unplug the pump.**

   This step seems obvious, but forgetting to pull the plug can be deadly.

2. **Loosen the pump from the drainpipe.**

   If the old pump has galvanized steel threaded drainpiping, use a pipe wrench to loosen the coupling that joins the pump to the discharge pipe. Many pumps are installed with plastic pipe, which may also have a coupling or may be connected with hose clamps, which you can loosen with a screwdriver.

3. **Hoist the pump out of the sump pit.**

4. **Write down the manufacturer and the model number, or note the motor horsepower (HP) and especially the size of the discharge pipe.**

Buying a new sump pump of the same type as the old one saves you from having to replumb the drain line to accept the new pump. Along with the new pump, purchase the necessary plumbing fixtures to reconnect the new pump to the existing drain pipe.

Plastic pipe and the matching fittings tend to be easier to work with than galvanized pipe, and plastic pipe is easy to attach to the existing galvanized pipe. You can also use a piece of flexible rubber hose and some hose clamps to connect the new pump to the existing plumbing, making the new pump easier to install.

5. **Install the necessary piping in the discharge port of the pump and place the new pump in the sump and connect the pump to the drain line, as shown in Figure 12-15.**

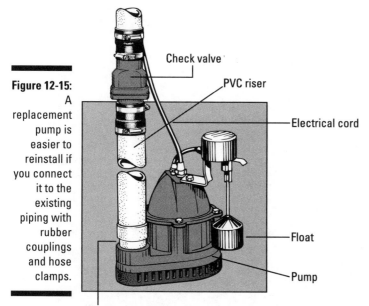

Check valve

PVC riser

Electrical cord

Figure 12-15:
A replacement pump is easier to reinstall if you connect it to the existing piping with rubber couplings and hose clamps.

Float

Pump

Plastic male adapter

6. **Plug the pump into the power source.**

   Dump several buckets of water into the sump pit or place a garden hose into the pit and turn on the water to raise the float and start the pump. The pump should pump most of the water out of the pit and then stop.

7. **Adjust the float so that the pump starts pumping when 6 to 8 inches of water are in the sump, and stops before the pumps starts to draw in air.**

Adding an Outdoor Sprinkler System

A lawn sprinkler system is a labor-saving addition to your home. As with an automatic garage-door opener, after you install a sprinkler system, you'll wonder how you ever lived without one. No longer do you have to drag hoses around the yard, move sprinklers, or try to estimate whether you've given the lawn and garden enough water. You can install either a manually controlled sprinkler system or an automatic one that includes a timer, as shown in Figure 12-16.

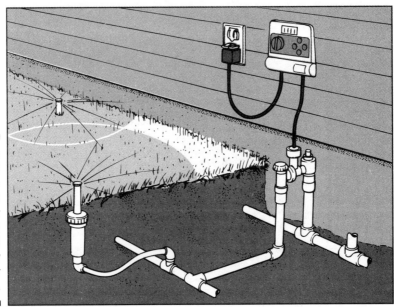

Figure 12-16:
A typical below-ground sprinkler system has a timer control and a variety of sprinkler heads.

You need the following items to install a lawn sprinkler system:

- A yard plan (not to mention a yard)
- Plastic (PVC) piping to reach all the circuits
- A variety of pipe fittings to join the pipe (elbow, four-way, and T-fittings)
- Sprinkler heads
- An anti-siphon valve
- A control valve for each sprinkler circuit
- Miscellaneous electrical wires, an electrical junction box, and fittings

Sprinkler systems are becoming so popular that manufactures are continually coming out with new easier-to-install products. Most large home centers carry several brands. Some systems are more complete than others, so do a bit of window-shopping and tire-kicking before you make a purchase. You may also find that, with a little bit of ingenuity, you can take a special module from one manufacturer to work with another's system.

Drawing a plan

When you shop for a sprinkler system, take along a plot diagram showing the dimensions of your lawn and the location of the house, garage, and driveway. Let the dealer help plan the system, figuring out how many sprinkler heads and how many circuits you need.

If you have a large yard, the house water supply will not have sufficient pressure to water the entire lawn at one time. In this case, you must divide the area into separate watering circuits. A control valve on each circuit provides water to alternating sections of the lawn.

Setting it up

Follow these basic steps to set up your sprinkler system:

1. **Consult your plan and then lay out the route the pipe will travel.**

   Mark this route by driving stakes into the ground and then stretching string from stake to stake.

2. **Bury the pipe in a shallow trench, about 6 to 10 inches deep.**

   Measure the length of your sprinkler head to determine how deep the trench should be. You want the top of the sprinkler head to be flush with the ground. You can dig the trench with a spade, or you can rent a trenching machine.

   Before trenching, first use a spade to cut away a foot-wide line of sod along the string layout line and set the sod aside for replacement after the pipe is laid.

   If the ground is hard and digging is difficult, lay a hose on the trench path and soak it well with water. After soaking the trench area, turn off the water overnight so you won't be digging in mud.

3. **Roll out the PVC pipe in the trench.**

4. **Consult your layout plan and place the sprinkler heads next to the trench at the points where you plan to install them.**

5. **Follow the manufacturer's instructions for installing the devices.**

6. **At the house, install PVC pipe to connect the water supply to the sprinkler system.**

7. **Mount the anti-siphon valve and connect it to the house water supply.**

   This valve prevents polluted water from the sprinkler system from being drawn back into the house water supply.

8. **Inside the garage or the basement, mount the sprinkler timer.**

9. **Connect the wires from the anti-siphon valve to the timer, and set the timer so that the system turns on at desired intervals.**

   By calculating the water flow through the sprinkler, you can set the timer so that it stays on long enough to apply at least 1 inch of water per interval. Most turfs require an inch of water per week, and applying an inch or more of water at one time ensures that the water will reach the roots of the grass. If you have a 1-inch rain during the 2-week period, you can reset the timer to provide only an additional inch of water in that period.

TIP

Getting the help you need

Depending on your time and talent, you may choose to hire a contractor, or do all or part of the sprinkler-system installation yourself. Full installation instructions are available from manufacturer's brochures found at home and garden centers.

You can save money by doing the grunt work — digging the pipe trenches and installing the pipe, sprinkler heads, and circuit controls — yourself. Then hire a plumber to do the tough stuff, like installing the anti-siphon device and the timer, and hooking up the unit to the water supply.

Chapter 13

Light Up Your Life with Electrical Repairs and Replacements

• •

In This Chapter

▶ Dealing with blown fuses and short circuits

▶ Wiring light switches and electrical outlets

▶ Bringing a broken lamp back to life

▶ Replacing a ceiling fixture

▶ Fiddling with faulty phones

▶ Installing a security light in place of your porch light

▶ Adding low-voltage outdoor track lighting

• •

*E*ver since that grand moment when Ben Franklin decided to go fly a kite in an electrical storm (what was he thinking?), civilization has had a curious fascination with and addictive dependency on electricity. But what happens if you're suddenly thrown into darkness by interrupted electrical service? What do you do then? Going to a friend's house to watch TV isn't the response we're looking for, here.

Replacing a Fuse and Resetting a Circuit Breaker

You plug in the rockin' new stereo, flip the switch, and suddenly the whole house goes dark. Sure, you've *heard* of blown fuses and short circuits, but how do you fix them?

The first step is to locate your electrical panel and open it. (See the nearby sidebar, "When it comes to electricity, always be prepared" for tips on finding and labeling your electrical panel.)

Electricity flows through a pair of wires called a *circuit*. Electrical energy flows out one wire (the *hot* wire) through the light, stereo, or whatever you're running, and then returns to the main power panel through the other wire (the *neutral* wire). These wires are sized to carry a certain amount of electrical energy without overheating. But if you plug too many appliances into a circuit, so that the total energy required by the appliances is too much, the wires supplying this energy get very hot. And if the wires supplying the energy touch each other, they create a short circuit — a shortcut for the electrical power to flow — and the wires begin to glow in a matter of seconds.

Each circuit is protected either by a *fuse* or a *circuit breaker* (both of which are shown in Figure 13-1). If a short circuit occurs anywhere in the wiring, if the wires overheat, or if an appliance malfunctions or catches fire, the fuse or circuit breaker shuts down power to that circuit.

✔ **Fuses:** Older houses (more than, say, 30 years old) often have fuses, rather than circuit breakers, to protect the wire circuits. To shut down a circuit in these homes, you have to remove the fuse. Shut off the power to the electrical panel before replacing fuses. Look for a fuse labeled *Master* or *Main* (usually located at the top of the electrical panel); pull this handle and remove the rectangular block containing the main fuses to shut down the electrical power to the entire house.

If the fuses aren't labeled, look into the glass window of each fuse to determine which one is blown. Good fuses show a solid metal bar; bad ones usually show either a broken bar or a discolored glass window. Unscrew the blown fuse and replace it with one of equal amperage. Restore the power by replacing the main fuse.

Have extra replacement fuses on hand at all times.

✔ **Circuit breakers:** Newer homes have circuit breakers: protective switches that enable you to fix short circuits without turning off the power. Circuit breakers simply switch off when they become over-loaded, but the breaker doesn't flip fully to the Off position. To reset a circuit breaker, flip it fully to the Off position and then flip it fully in the opposite direction, to the On position.

Working with live wires is never a good idea, and sometimes wires from more than one circuit may be present in a single outlet. So to make sure that the electricity is turned off on every circuit you come in contact with, purchase an inexpensive neon voltage circuit tester. This little device lets you know whether a circuit has power running to it. The tester's not a loud, dust-spewing, macho tool, but it may save your life.

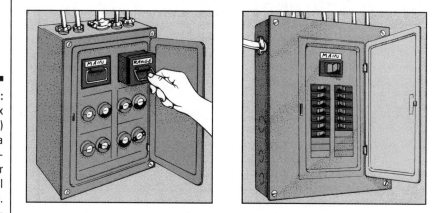

Figure 13-1:
A fuse-box panel (left) and a circuit-breaker panel (right).

TIP

When it comes to electricity, always be prepared

To prepare for electrical emergencies, familiarize yourself with the electrical entrance panel — the circuit-breaker box usually found in the utility room or basement. Have a flashlight with good batteries somewhere near the electrical panel to give you good light for looking inside the panel — remember, the overhead light may not be working when you need to change a fuse.

The electrician who wired your house should have marked each circuit on the panel with a label telling which lights or appliances it controls. But things don't always happen the way they should, and you may find yourself with a panel of unlabeled breakers. Before a short circuit leaves you in the dark trying to guess

which fuse or breaker controls what, get down to business and label those breakers yourself.

To label the breakers, turn on all the lights in your house and plug a lamp into each receptacle. Then go to your electrical panel and turn off each circuit breaker, one at a time. Have a helper call out which lights or appliances shut down and are, therefore, on that circuit. Label all the breakers with lists of what they control.

Labeling the circuits *can* be a one-person job. Plug a radio into the outlet you're testing and turn up the volume so that you can hear it from the electrical panel. When the radio stops playing, you know that you've found the circuit that connects to that fuse or circuit breaker.

Wiring Switches and Receptacles

Switches do just that, switch open and close electrical circuits that power all lights and electrical appliances throughout the house. *Receptacles,* commonly called *outlets,* provide a place to plug in lights and appliances. You may want to replace an old switch or receptacle to upgrade it.

Most modern switches and receptacles have screw terminals on each side and holes in the back to accept the end of the wire. (See Figure 13-2.) You may find that someone has attached the wires to the back of the device instead of to the screws on each side. This technique is called *back-wiring* the device.

Loosening the screws on the side of the device is easy with a standard screwdriver (turning counterclockwise), but getting the wires out of the back of the device is tricky. To remove these wires, insert the blade of a small screwdriver into the slot under the hole into which the wire is inserted and push in as you pull the wire loose. Pushing the blade of the screwdriver into the slot releases the grip on the inserted wire.

Figure 13-2:
Single-pole switches have two screw terminals on the side and a possible third green terminal for the ground wire. The backside of the switch has holes for back-wiring the device.

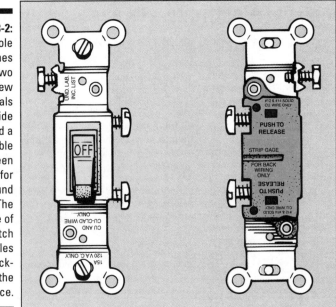

When replacing a switch, you can save some time by back-wiring the replacement device. But the connection won't be as reliable as screwing the wire down.

- ✔ The white *(neutral)* wire connects to the silver screw or is placed in the back wire hole on the same side of the device as the silver screw.

- ✔ The black *(hot)* wire goes to the brass screw or into the hole in the back of the device on the same side as the brass screw.

- ✔ The green or bare copper *(ground)* wire, if the device has one, attaches to the green screw terminal on the switch or to the electrical box.

TIP

Making a wire-to-wire splice

You sometimes find that the existing wires are very short and difficult to work with (kind of like 2-year-olds). You can make the job easier by splicing on an additional length of wire.

You may also have to join the ground wire of an appliance (these are usually bare copper or green) with other ground wires in the electrical box. The easiest way to do this is with a twist-on wire connector, called a *wire nut.*

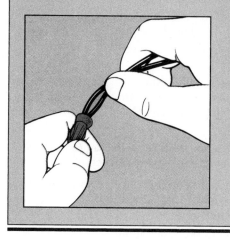

Strip off about a 1 inch of insulation from the end of the wires and use pliers to twist their bare ends together. Then take a plastic wire nut and screw it down over the twisted wires until it is tight.

Wire nuts come in many sizes, and using the proper size is important. If the nut is too small, you won't be able to screw it down over the wires and provide an insulated shield. If the nut's too large, it will screw down over the wires but may shake loose. Look on the wire-nut package for the number of wires of a given size that this wire nut can join. For example, a wire nut could join four #14 wires, but only three #12 wires. (The number refers to the gauge of the wire — the smaller the number, the thicker the wire.)

Swapping a light switch

Most kitchen and bedroom switches are the single-pole type and are designed to control a light or receptacle from a single location. Hallways, on the other hand, usually have three-way switches that are designed to control a light or receptacle from two locations. Sometimes, a four-way switch is placed between three-way switches to allow control of lights or receptacles from three separate locations.

Turn off the circuit breaker or fuse to a light receptacle before you unscrew the switch plate. Then test the wires with a voltage circuit tester to make sure that power isn't flowing to them.

Replacing a single-pole switch

If the switch has *On* and *Off* embossed on its body, and it is the only switch that controls lights or receptacles, it is a *single-pole switch.* To replace this kind of switch, follow these steps:

1. **Turn off the power to the switch at the main circuit breaker or fuse panel.**

2. **Unscrew and remove the switch plate; then use a voltage tester to make sure that the circuit is dead.**

3. **Unscrew the switch from the electrical box and pull it out with the wires still attached, as shown in Figure 13-3.**

   Two or three wires will be attached to the switch: a hot wire, which is black; a colored switch-leg wire, which may be black, red, or any other color except green; and sometimes a ground wire, which is green or bare copper.

   If the switch is connected with nonmetallic cable, you may find a white wire that has black tape on it. This tape indicates that the white wire is being used as a black or colored wire in the switch leg, so it's not neutral.

4. **Compare your new switch with the one you're replacing to find the corresponding locations for the electrical screw connectors.**

   Because the power is off, you can match up the connectors the easy way: Instead of disconnecting all the wires at once and possibly getting totally confused, unscrew and connect one wire at a time.

5. **Attach the first wire you unscrew to the same-colored screw on the new switch as it was on the old; do the same with the second wire and then the third, if there is a third.**

   Attach the wire to the device screw by looping the end of the wire in a single hook clockwise around the screw. When you tighten the screw with a screwdriver, the force of the tightening screw makes the loop wrap tighter around the screw.

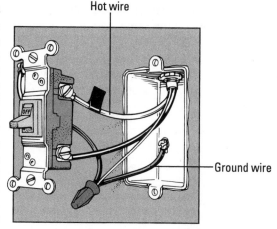

Hot wire

Ground wire

Figure 13-3: Both wires leading to a single-pole switch are hot. If wired with two conductor cables, the white wire is marked with black tape.

Although the connection won't be as reliable, you can also back-wire the switch by straightening the end of the wire and then pushing the end into the hole in the back of the switch closest to the same-colored screw on the old device.

6. **Push the new, wired switch back into the electrical box and screw it in place.**

7. **Screw on the switchplate and turn on the power.**

Replacing a three-way switch

A *three-way switch* is a handy convenience to control a light from two locations, such as at the top and bottom of a staircase. If the words *On* and *Off* aren't embossed on the switch, and it's one of two switches that control a single light or receptacle, you have a *three-way switch*. Seems like it should be called a two-way switch, right? The name refers to the fact that these switches have three terminal screws.

To replace a three-way switch, follow these steps:

1. **Turn off the power to the switch at the circuit or fuse panel.**

2. **Unscrew and remove the switchplate; then use a voltage tester to make sure that the circuit is dead.**

3. **Unscrew the switch from the electrical box and pull it out with the wires still attached, as shown in Figure 13-4.**

   A three-way switch has at least three wires and possibly four, depending on whether it has a ground wire. Two wires attach to brass screw terminals, which are usually at the top of the switch, and an additional wire attaches to a dark-colored (not green) screw terminal, which is usually at the bottom of the switch. Mark this third wire with a piece of tape and also mark the wire on the same side of the switch directly above it with a piece of different-colored tape.

The new switch may have the electrical screw connectors in slightly different locations than the switch you're replacing. Most switches have a pair of terminals on opposite sides of the switch top, and a single terminal at the bottom.

Figure 13-4:
Three-way switches control a light from two locations. The common screw terminal is wired to the light or to the source of power.

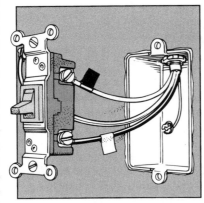

4. **Remove the wires from the switch.**

5. **Attach the tagged wires to the corresponding terminals of the new switch.**

Of course, you can also back-wire the device if the switch design allows it. Be sure to insert the bare ends of the wires into the holes in the back of the switch that are closest to the screw terminal you would attach the wires to. Be aware, though, that this connection is not as reliable as using the screw terminals.

6. **If the existing switch has a green ground wire, attach the wire to the green screw terminal on the new switch or to the electrical box.**

7. **Push the new, wired switch back into the electrical box and screw it in place.**

8. **Screw on the switch plate and turn on the power.**

Replacing a four-way switch

If the switch doesn't have the words *On* and *Off* embossed on its body, and it is the center switch of three switches that control a single light or receptacle, it is a *four-way switch*. Figure 13-5 shows a typical four-way switch.

Figure 13-5:
A four-way switch is placed between three-way switches to control light from three locations. It has four screw terminals plus an optional grounding screw.

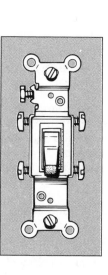

To replace a four-way switch, follow these steps (here we go again):

1. **Turn off the power to the switch at the circuit panel or fuse box.**

2. **Unscrew and remove the switch plate; then use a voltage tester to make sure that the circuit is dead.**

3. **Unscrew the switch from the electrical box and pull it out with the wires still attached.**

   This switch has at least four screw terminals. It may also have a fifth ground terminal (green).

4. **Mark the location of the four wires with tape so that you can replace them on the new switch; then remove the wires from the switch.**

   Alternatively, you may choose to transfer one wire at a time from the old switch to the new stitch.

5. **Attach the wires to the corresponding terminals of the new switch.**

   If the existing switch has a green ground wire, attach it to the green terminal on the new switch or to the electrical box.

6. **Push the new, wired switch back into the electrical box and screw it in place.**

7. **Screw on the switchplate and turn on the power.**

Replacing a standard switch with a dimmer switch

Replacing a standard single-pole or three-way switch with a dimmer switch is no different than replacing a standard switch. You only have one restriction: Dimmer switches don't work on most flourescent fixtures, just regular incandescent lights.

Be sure to check the rating of the dimmer switch you purchase. Most dimmer switches can handle 600 watts of power. Count the number of bulbs that the switch controls and add up the wattage of each light bulb. For example, if the switch controls a light fixture with two 100 watt bulbs (200 watts total) a 600-watt dimmer will have no problem; but a string of seven recessed lights could overload the dimmer.

To replace a standard switch with a dimmer switch, follow these steps:

1. **Turn off the power to the switch at the circuit or fuse panel.**

2. **Unscrew and remove the switchplate; then use a voltage tester to make sure that the circuit is dead.**

3. **Unscrew the switch from the electrical box and pull it out with the wires still attached.**

4. **Remove the wires from the old switch.**

   Dimmer switches are usually connected to the house wiring by short lengths of wires coming out of the switch body, instead of by screw terminals.

5. **Use the connectors *(wire nuts)* supplied with the fixture to attach the black wires coming out of the dimmer switch to the colored wires that were attached to the terminals on the old switch, as shown in Figure 13-6.**

   First twist the wires together, and then screw on the wire nut. Remove and replace one wire at a time.

6. **Push the new switch back into the electrical box and screw it in place.**

7. **Screw on the switch plate.**

8. **Push the control knob, if there is one, onto the shaft protruding from the switch.**

9. **Turn on the power.**

Replacing duplex receptacles

The procedure for replacing *duplex* (two-outlet) wall receptacles is the same as for replacing a switch. The only difference is that, depending on where the receptacle is located in the wiring scheme of a house, it may have more wires attached to it than are attached to a light switch.

Figure 13-6:
Some dimmer switches have screw terminals and are wired like a single-pole switch; others have wire pigtails that are spliced with wire nuts.

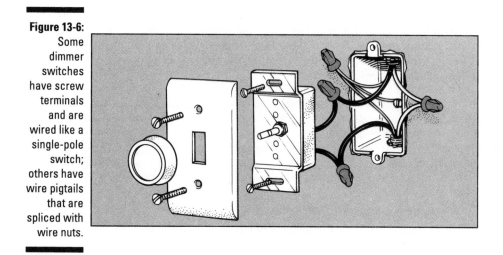

Look closely at the terminal screws of the new duplex receptacle. On each side of the receptacle are a pair of terminal screws. The upper screw is connected to the upper outlet, and the lower screw services the lower outlet. Connecting these screws is a thin metal break-off tab. This tab allows you to attach a single wire to either screw and feed electricity to both outlets of the receptacle. If the tab is broken off, then the upper and lower outlets can be connected to separate wires and controlled independently.

If the receptacle is wired to the end of a series of receptacles, it usually has only two wires, and possibly a third ground wire. If it is not the last receptacle, two additional wires may be connected to it in order to carry current to the next receptacle. Just rewire the new receptacle the same way that the old one was wired. (See Figure 13-7.)

Figure 13-7:
A receptacle in the middle of a series (left) and a receptacle at the end of a series (right).

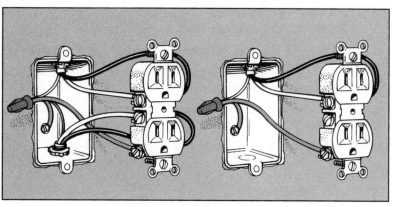

The receptacle may also be wired so that the upper outlet is controlled by a switch and the lower outlet is on, or *hot,* all the time. In this case, the break-off tab connecting the two sets of like-colored terminals on each side of the receptacle is missing. Otherwise, the tab is intact, and you can see a metal bridge connecting the terminals.

The important point to keep in mind is that hot (black or colored) wires attach to the brass-colored screws, and neutral (white) wires attach to the silver-colored screws. If the unit is back-wired, the colored wires will be located in the holes behind the brass screws and the white wires in the holes behind the silver screws. If you attach a white wire to a brass screw, or a colored wire to a silver screw, you may get fireworks.

Replacing a standard receptacle

To replace a standard duplex receptacle, follow these steps:

1. **Turn off the power to the receptacle from the main fuse or circuit panel.**

2. **Unscrew and remove the cover plate; then use a voltage tester to make sure that the circuit is dead.**

3. **Unscrew the receptacle from the electrical box and pull it out with the wires still attached.**

   Note where the white and black wires are attached to the old receptacle.

4. **Remove the wires.**

5. **Carefully inspect the old receptacle to see if the break-off tab connecting the two sets of terminals on each side of the receptacle is broken off. If it is, remove the corresponding tabs from the new receptacle.**

   If you see a gap between the like-colored terminal screws where the break off-tab has been removed, remove the corresponding tabs from the new receptacle. Grip the tab with long-nose pliers and bend it back and forth until it breaks off.

6. **Attach the wires to the terminals of the new receptacle.**

   If a green ground wire is present, attach it to the green terminal on the receptacle or to the electrical box.

7. **Push the new receptacle back into the electrical box and screw it in place.**

8. **Screw on the cover plate and then turn on the power.**

Replacing a receptacle with a GFCI

A GFCI (ground fault circuit interrupter) receptacle is the same as an ordinary receptacle, except that it has a built-in circuit breaker and reset switch. Building codes require this type device be installed in outlets located in areas prone to dampness such as bathrooms, outdoors, and kitchens.

Normally, the amount of current flowing in an electrical circuit is the same in all the wires. For example, if your hair dryer takes 10 amps (a measure of the amount of electricity flowing in a circuit) to run, then 10 amps of current flow into the dryer through the hot (black) wire, and 10 amps flow out of the dryer through the neutral (white) wire. If the dryer experiences a short, current could flow through your wet hand to, say, the faucet handle as you turn off the water. If this happens, the amount of current going into the dryer will be more than the amount coming out, because some of the electricity is going through *you*. The GFCI senses this discrepancy and trips open to instantly stop everything before you turn into a French fry.

We're sure that you don't have any "crash-test dummies" in your household foolish enough to volunteer to stick a finger in a receptacle to test the GFCI. Fortunately, these devices have a Test button on them so you can check that they are functioning properly, instead of finding out the hard way. Press the Test button, shown in Figure 13-8, and the device trips and shuts everything down. To reset the device, press the Reset button.

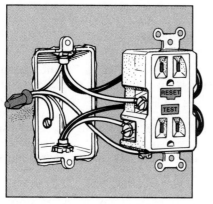

Figure 13-8:
A ground fault circuit interrupter (GFCI) is wired like a standard receptacle.

Get the shocking feeling, or lack of it, that a GFCI is a good thing to have in the kitchen, bath, and outside? You can install a GFCI receptacle the same way you install an ordinary receptacle. To replace a standard duplex receptacle with a GFCI receptacle, follow these steps:

1. Turn off the power to the receptacle from the fuse or circuit panel.

2. **Unscrew and remove the cover plate; then use a voltage tester to make sure that the circuit is dead.**

3. **Unscrew the receptacle from the electrical box and pull it out with the wires still attached.**

4. **Note where the white and black wires are attached to the old receptacle and then remove the wires.**

5. **Transfer the wires from the old receptacle to the GFCI.**

   GFCI receptacles are connected to the house wiring either by short lengths of wires coming out of the receptacle body or by screw terminals.

   • If the GFCI receptacle has wires, use the wire connectors (*wire nuts*) supplied with the fixture to attach the black wires coming out of the GFCI receptacle to the colored wires that were attached to the terminals on the old receptacle. Twist the wires together first, and then screw on the wire nut.

   • If the GFCI receptacle uses screw terminals, attach the colored wires to the terminals of the new receptacle. If a green ground wire is present, attach it to the green terminal on the receptacle or to the electrical box.

6. **Push the new receptacle back into the electrical box and screw it in place.**

7. **Screw on the cover plate and turn on the power.**

Repairing a Faulty Lamp

As electrical appliances go, lamps are very reliable. But after a while, the socket may act up and cause the lamp to flicker, to be difficult to turn on, or to just flat out refuse to light. If this sudden impertinence gives you the perfect excuse to get the hideous thing out of your living room, do it. But if you aren't ready to part with the little feller, you can replace the socket and give the lamp a new life. Replacing a socket is so easy that, even if it's not your favorite lamp, you may want to fix it and give it to someone else, like your nosy neighbor.

You can purchase replacement lamp parts at any hardware store or home center. These parts are standard; lamp cord is sold by the foot, and you can use just about any type plug to replace the one on your old lamp.

Several varieties of lamp-socket switches are available; some are controlled by pushing a short shaft on the side of the switch, other styles are controlled by turning a knob, and still others turn on and off with a pull chain. The other point to consider is whether your present lamp has a three-way bulb in it. If you were able to turn the lamp on to several degrees of brightness, then be sure to purchase a socket switch that is designed to control a three-way bulb.

Probably the easiest way to get the right replacements parts is to take the lamp apart (according to the following directions) and then take the bad parts to the store so that you can find matching replacements.

To replace a lamp socket, follow these steps:

1. **Unplug the lamp.**

2. **Remove the shade, bulb, and harp (the wired shape that holds the shade).**

3. **Snap off the socket shell from the socket shell cap, as shown in Figure 13-9.**

   Most sockets have the word *Press* stamped in two places on the shell. Squeeze the shell at those points and pull up to remove it. If the shell doesn't budge, push the end of a screwdriver between the base of the socket and the side of the shell, and then pull the shell up and off the socket base.

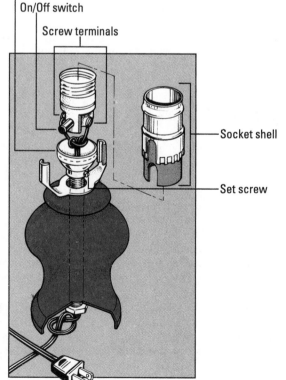

Figure 13-9:
Removing the socket shell.

4. **Pull the socket switch up out of the shell base to expose enough of the switch to reveal the two wires attached to it.**

If the screws are loose, tighten them and reassemble the lamp. Loose screws may have been the lamp's only problem. If the lamp works after tightening up the screws, great! If not, take it apart again and proceed with the following steps.

5. **Unscrew the wires.**

Lamp switches have a brass screw to which the hot (black) wire is attached and a silver screw to which the neutral (white) wire is attached. Lamp cords, however, don't have colored wires in them. So before you remove the wires from the old switch, note which color screw each wire is connected to.

6. **Loosen the socket-cap set screw and then unscrew and discard it along with the old socket shell and socket.**

7. **Screw the wire leads to the new socket.**

8. **Place the new socket shell over the socket and push the cover down until it snaps into the new socket shell cap.**

9. **Replace the harp, light bulb, and shade.**

If, after you follow all the preceding steps, the lamp still doesn't work, you can still give it to your nosy neighbors. Let *them* figure it out.

Replacing a Ceiling Fixture

Residential ceiling fixtures come in many different shapes, and people have devised many different ways to attach them to the ceiling. (See Figure 13-10.) Most of the time, chandeliers are held in place by a central, threaded hollow rod. Ceiling fixtures hang by two screws that attach the fixture base to the outlet box or to a mounting strap in the outlet box.

No matter how a fixture is suspended from the ceiling, the wiring is simple. Other wires may pass through the box, but you only have to deal with three wires: a colored wire (usually black), a white wire, and a green ground wire. These three wires are joined together with twist-on wire connectors.

Get someone to help you with the project of replacing a ceiling fixture. After you loosen the screws that hold the old fixture to the ceiling box, you have your hands full holding the fixture and trying to work on the wires. You may be able to pull off this juggling act with a light fixture, but if you're messing with a chandelier, you need another pair of hands to help.

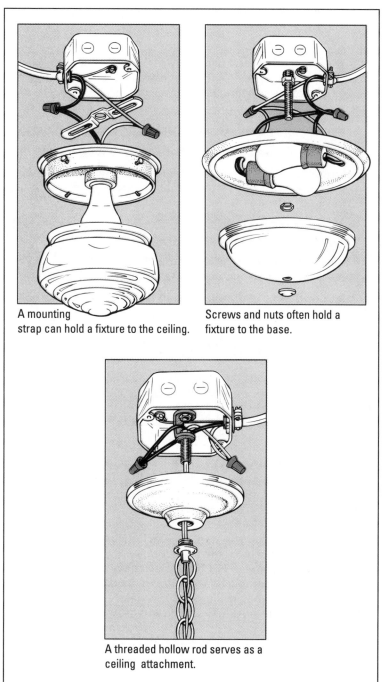

A mounting strap can hold a fixture to the ceiling.

Screws and nuts often hold a fixture to the base.

Figure 13-10: Ceiling fixtures stay secure with different mounting hardware.

A threaded hollow rod serves as a ceiling attachment.

To replace a ceiling fixture, follow these steps:

1. **Turn off the power.**

    You may find several pairs of wires in the ceiling box. Some of these wires may be wired to different circuits than the fixture you are working on. Be safe: Use a circuit tester or turn off the power to the whole house to be certain that all the wires in the box are dead.

2. **Remove the light-bulb cover and bulbs from the fixture.**

3. **Unscrew the screws or nuts holding the fixture base to the ceiling box.**

4. **Lower the fixture base and remove the electrical tape or wire nuts from the black (hot) wire, white (neutral) wire, and, if present, green (ground) wire.**

5. **Attach the wires from the new fixture with wire nuts to the corresponding wires in the electrical box.**

6. **Raise and position the new base plate so that you can screw the new bolts through it to attach to the mounting strap.**

7. **Screw in new light bulbs, install the cover, and turn on the power.**

Installing a ceiling fan

A ceiling fan is a stylish and functional addition to any room. Wiring a ceiling fan is the same as wiring any ceiling fixture, if the room already has a ceiling outlet. If there is no overhead box, hire an electrician to install the box and fish the wires through the walls and across the ceiling. Save the fun of installing the actual fan for yourself.

Because ceiling fans are so heavy, the National Electrical Code (NEC) prohibits attaching a ceiling fan to a standard ceiling box. Before you purchase the fan, check the manufacturer's installation instructions and purchase an approved electrical ceiling box.

If the ceiling on which you want to attach the fan is accessible from the attic or from an overhead area, then you have several choices in the type of box you install (see Figure 13-11). If the area above the box is not accessible, you have to use an adjustable hanger bar designed to be installed through the hole left by the existing ceiling box. If you have no idea whether your house has an attic, maybe you shouldn't be playing with wires.

Figure 13-11:
Attic access allows options in electrical boxes for attaching your ceiling fan.

To replace a ceiling fixture, follow these steps:

1. **Turn off the power at the fuse or circuit panel.**

   You may find several pairs of wires in the ceiling box. Some may be wired to different circuits other than the fixture you're working on. Be safe: Use a circuit tester or turn off the power to the whole house before attempting to install the ceiling fan. That's the only way to be certain that all wires in the box are dead.

2. **Remove any light-bulb cover (such as a globe) and bulbs from the fixture.**

3. **Unscrew the screws or nuts holding the fixture base to the ceiling box.**

4. **Lower the fixture base and remove the electrical tape or wire nuts from the black (hot), white (neutral), and, if present, green (ground) wires.**

5. **Remove the existing ceiling box.**

   Examine the type of box you have to determine the best way to remove it.

6. **Follow the manufacturer's directions to install the adjustable hanger bar and ceiling box.**

   You install most hanger bars by pushing them through the hole in the ceiling left by the old electrical box. When the hanger bar is completely through the hole, rotate it until it's perpendicular to the ceiling joists. The bar expands until it engages the ceiling joists. The ends of the hanger bar are equipped with sharp steel pins that dig into the wood joists when the hanger bar is expanded, as shown in Figure 13-12. You then attach the special ceiling box to the hanger bar, locking it in place to provide a secure base for the fan.

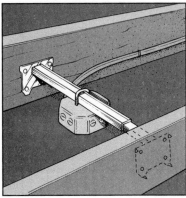

Figure 13-12:
The hanger bar holds the fan firmly within the framing of the ceiling.

7. **Assemble the fan according to the manufacturer's directions.**

   Fan kits contain a ceiling hanger bracket designed for that particular model. Follow the directions and bolt the bracket to the ceiling box. The installation kit for the fan should provide all the necessary hardware.

   Ceiling fans are heavy, so they require support while you attach the wires. Most models provide a way for you to suspend them below the ceiling box while you attach the wires. If yours does not, get a helper to support the fan assembly while you attach the wires.

   Wiring schemes differ slightly from fan to fan, depending on whether they are equipped with a light or speed control. The basic installation of a ceiling fan is no different from that of a standard light fixture. Use wire nuts to attach the fan's black or colored wire and white wire to matching wires in the ceiling box. If a green ground wire is present, attach it to the green or bare wire in the box.

8. **Complete the attachment of the fan assembly to the ceiling box.**

9. **Install the trim and fan blades according to manufacturer's directions.**

10. **Turn on the power and test the installation.**

Installing track lighting

From its theatrical roots onstage, track lighting has today evolved into individual fixtures along a track mounted on a wall or ceiling. Because you can place the light fixtures anywhere on the track and adjust their direction, a track-lighting system is a good choice when you want to direct light to a specific area, like a wall of artwork or down a long hallway, or when you want to accommodate changing lighting needs.

An advantage of track lighting is that the track can be powered by a single source, usually a ceiling box, and the lighting fixtures can be attached anywhere along the track. Because track systems vary, become familiar with the assembly before you begin following the instructions to install it.

One end of the track is designed to accept wiring from the ceiling outlet and connect it to the rest of the track. This end is attached to a plate that screws to the ceiling box. The wiring scheme is exactly the same as for any fixture. You connect like-colored wires together, and the green or bare ground wire attaches to the grounding terminal on the track or cover plate.

Follow these basic steps to install a track lighting system in an existing ceiling box:

1. **Turn off the power from the fuse or circuit panel.**

   You may find several pairs of wires in the ceiling box. Some of these wires may be controlled by different circuits than the fixture you're working on is. Be safe: Use a circuit tester or turn off the power to the whole house to be certain that all wires in the box are dead.

2. **Remove the old fixture as described earlier in this section.**

3. **Pull the existing black or colored wire, white wire, and green or bare wire that were connected to the old fixture through the opening in the new cover plate.**

4. **Attach the plate to the ceiling box with the screws provided.**

5. **Use the lighting track as a template to locate the position of the mounting screws on the ceiling.**

   Have a helper hold the track in place while you use a pencil to transfer the location of the mounting holes in the track to the ceiling.

6. **Drill a hole for the mounting toggle bolts in the ceiling.**

   Depending on the weight of the track, manufactures specify different types of fasteners for holding the track system to the ceiling. Most even supply the fasteners. In some cases, plastic plug-type anchors are sufficient, but to be on the safe side, we recommend installing toggle bolts. This type of anchor holds the most weight and isn't difficult to install. It requires a hole in the ceiling the same diameter as the folded toggle.

7. **Follow the manufacturer's directions for securing the track to the ceiling.**

   If the track is held up by toggle bolts, they must be preassembled on the track and then the whole assembly held in place while the individual toggles are pushed through the predrilled ceiling holes, as shown in

Figure 13-13. Thread the screw through the mounting hole in the track and then reinstall the toggle on the screw. After you push the folded toggle through the hole in the ceiling, it unfolds inside the ceiling and provides a secure grip. Tighten the screw to pull the track tight to the ceiling.

8. Pull the wires through the end of the track and attach them to the screw terminals, as shown in Figure 13-13.

The black or colored wire goes on the brass-colored screw and the white wire on the silver screw. The bare or green grounding wire is attached to the green screw.

9. Install the cover plate on the end of the track to hide the wiring.

10. Follow the manufacturer's directions for mounting the light fixtures.

You attach most track fixtures by slipping a mounting flange into the center channel of the track and then turning the fixture to force the flange under the track so that it contacts the internal wiring.

Track lights, like other electrical devices, have a specific current rating. Before you install more than five or six fixtures, check the amperage rating of the system. Most will carry 15 amps. Overload the circuit, and the breakers will be popping so much you'll think that Orville Redenbacher is living in your basement.

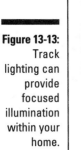

Figure 13-13: Track lighting can provide focused illumination within your home.

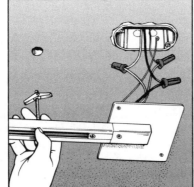

A. A mounting flange fixes the light to the ceiling. (Step 7)

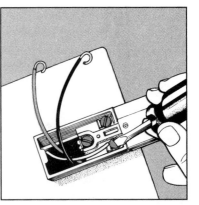

B. Wires are color-coded for coordination with screw terminals. (Step 8)

Adding a receptacle or switch using surface wiring

If you don't mind the industrial look of surface wiring, the easiest solution may be to add an additional outlet or switched ceiling fixture. With surface wiring, you eliminate the hassle of running wires through walls. If you already have an outlet in the room, you can use surface-wiring systems to expand it.

A protective system called a *raceway* contains the wiring like a hard-covered extension cord. Raceway systems vary by manufacturer, but all install in basically the same way.

Check with your local building department before you purchase any surface-wiring components. Electrical codes vary, and some local codes may restrict the use of certain surface-wiring systems.

Here are the basic steps for extending a circuit from an existing wall outlet to an overhead light fixture controlled by a single pole switch:

1. **Turn off the power at the fuse or circuit panel.**

   You may find several pairs of wires in the ceiling or wall box. Some of these wires may be connected to different circuits than is the fixture you're working on. To be safe, use a circuit tester or turn off the power to the whole house so you can be sure that all the wires in the box are dead.

2. **Decide on a source of power.**

   An existing receptacle is your best choice. Otherwise, you'd have to run a new circuit — clearly a job for an electrician.

3. **Sketch out the system.**

   You need an extension frame to fit over the existing outlet box to start the extension and enough raceway and fittings to connect the outlet to the new ceiling fixture. You also need a surface-mounted ceiling-fixture box and a surface-mounted light-fixture box. All these components and the wires are available at most home centers.

4. **Work from the ceiling fixture back to the outlet and install the fixture to the ceiling with the hardware provided.**

   Secure the box base to the ceiling at a joist or use hollow-wall fasteners.

5. **Mount the light switchbox in a convenient location on the wall.**

6. **Install the raceway between the ceiling fixture and the switchbox.**

   The raceway channels that hold the wires running from box to box attach to the walls with special hardware supplied by the manufacturer. Some styles use plastic wall anchors, some use toggle bolts, but all types are easy to install. These systems provide junction fittings for rounding corners, T-fittings for joining two raceways, and connectors for joining the raceways to the switchbox (see Figure 13-14).

7. **Install the raceway between the switchbox and the outlet.**

8. **Run the wires in the raceway.**

To wire the fixture, you need a black wire, a white wire, and a green ground wire. Feed these wires into the raceway between the wall outlet and the switchbox. Leave a loop a foot or so long at each end so that you can wire up the switch and fixture. Similarly, run the wires from the switch to the ceiling fixture, as shown in Figure 13-14.

9. **After the wires are in place inside the raceway, snap on the cover and junction fittings.**

10. **Have lunch (optional).**

11. **Install the ceiling fixture at this point, while there's no power in the circuit.**

Electrical power won't flow to the ceiling fixture until after you connect it to the wall receptacle, so now is the safest time to install the light fixture or new receptacle.

12. **Install the single-pole switch.**

Refer to the instructions for replacing a switch earlier in this chapter, under "Replacing a single-pole switch." Basically, you have three wires running through the wall switchbox to the ceiling box. Tuck the white wire into the back of the box. Cut the black wire in the middle of the loop you made when you installed the wires in Step 8. Strip off about 1 inch of insulation from the end of these wires and then attach the black wires to the screw terminals on the side of the switch.

13. **If the switch has a green screw terminal, attach the ground wire to the switch.**

Cut the green ground wire and strip off the insulation from each end. Then take a 6-inch piece of green wire and strip off the insulation from each end. Twist one end of the pigtail together with the other two ground wires. Complete the splice by twisting a wire nut onto this bundle. Attach the other end of the pigtail to the green screw on the switch. Then push the switch into the box, secure it with the mounting screws, and install the switchplate.

14. **Check that the electrical power is off at the existing wall outlet and then connect the new circuit to the wall receptacle to energize the circuit.**

Connect the black wire to the copper-colored screw and the white wire to the silver screw. The green goes to the bare or green wire in the box.

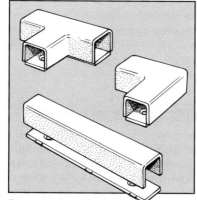

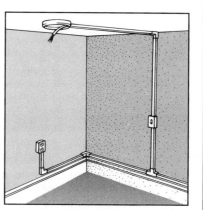

Figure 13-14:
Ideal for
basements
and storage
rooms,
surface
wiring is
more
functional
than
attractive.

Raceway channel parts are designed for easy assembly and installation.

Wires run through the raceway, starting at the wall outlet.

Reach Out and Fix That Phone

The telephone company takes care of the wiring outside your house, but typically you are responsible for the inside wiring. So if a phone stops working, you can either try to fix it yourself or pay the phone company for a service call . . . or you can just sit back and enjoy the peace and quiet.

Telephone troubleshooting

Telephones are low-voltage devices, so they're safe to work on. You have nothing to lose and a few bucks to save if you can figure out the problem yourself. Try these simple tests to track down and fix some common telephone problems:

✔ Check to see whether other phones in your house have a dial tone. If they don't, then the incoming line is the problem. Go to your neighbor's and call for help. If their phone is out too, go home and relax; the phone company is the problem.

✔ If other phones in the house have a dial tone, check that the handset cord is plugged into the phone body, and that the cord leading from the phone to the wall jack is plugged in at both ends. Check to make sure that you're holding a telephone, not a banana.

✔ If all the cords are in their proper places, try swapping one of the phones that has a dial tone with the one that doesn't. If you get a dial tone, it's not hard to figure out that the phone itself is the problem — return it to the manufacturer for servicing. If swapping phones doesn't work, then the problem is in the wires leading from the phone to the wall jack or from the wall jack to a junction box.

✔ If you don't get a dial tone when you swap phones, remove the cover plate of the wall jack and look for a broken or loose wire inside the jack. Check that all the screws holding the wires are tight.

✔ If you can't find a problem in the jack, try tracing the wire leading from the phone jack to the junction box. The wire may be hidden in the wall, stashed under the carpet, or run along the baseboard, depending on whether this extension was wired up before or after the house was constructed. In any case, the wires probably lead to a junction box on the side of your house or in the basement, which the phone company maintains. As you trace the wire, check that all connections are tight and none of the small wires is broken:

- Over time, the screw terminals that secure the wires inside the jack or junction box can loosen. Tightening each screw terminal may fix the problem.

- Wires may break close to the screw terminal. If you see a loose wire in the jack or junction box, strip the insulation off the end of the wire. Then loosen the terminal screw holding the wire of the same color, wind the end of the wire around the screw, and retighten.

Wiring a telephone extension

Adding an additional phone extension to an existing jack has become embarrassingly easy. You have only four wires to deal with, and they're all color-coded. So as long as you aren't color-blind, installing an extension phone is goof-proof. And because phone systems are low-voltage devices, you have little chance of getting shocked.

You can buy everything you need for this project at a home center. Buy a surface-mount modular phone jack and enough round (not flat, modular) four-conductor phone wire to reach from the existing phone jack to the location where you want to install the new wall jack. The wire is usually sold in 50- and 100-foot spools.

Here are the basic steps involved in wiring a phone extension:

1. **Locate the working phone jack most convenient to the new jack you want to install.**

   Remember that the nearest jack may be in an adjacent room. Running the phone wire from an existing jack to the new location is your biggest challenge, so use your imagination. The wire can be left exposed because it carries low voltage. You can hide it along the baseboard, tuck it between the baseboard and carpet, or fish it through walls — it'll be your secret.

2. **Decide where you want the new jack to be and mount the base on the wall or baseboard with the hardware provided.**

3. **Strip 6 inches of the outer insulation off the round telephone wire to expose the red, green, yellow, and black wires inside.**

4. **Strip 1 inch of the colored insulation off each exposed wire.**

5. **Loosen the terminal screws on the new wall jack and wrap the wires clockwise around the matching colored terminals, as shown in Figure 13-15.**

Figure 13-15: Make a telephone extension connection by matching wire colors with terminals, and then wrapping the wires clockwise around the screw terminals.

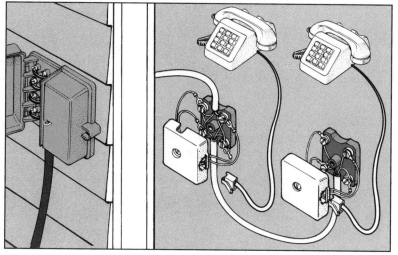

6. **Tighten the screw terminals, making sure that the bare ends of the wires do not touch.**

7. **Replace the cover of the new wall jack.**

8. **Strip the insulation off the end of the phone wire at the existing wall jack.**

9. **Remove the cover from the existing wall jack you're tapping into.**

10. **Loosen the screw terminals and wind each wire around the terminal of the same color.**

11. **Tighten the screws and replace the existing wall-jack cover.**

12. **Plug the phone line back into the existing jack and test for a dial tone; then take the phone to the new jack and test for a dial tone.**

   If you hear a dial tone, sign up for a job at the phone company. If not, keep your day job and recheck your wiring.

Replacing a Porch Light with a Security Light

Outdoor security lights use infrared or microwave sensors to light up whenever someone or something passes within a certain range. Use them to safeguard your house without the expense and inconvenience of leaving a harsh light glaring all night.

Infrared sensors respond to heat and turn on the light whenever a warm object, like a person or car, comes into its field of view. Microwave sensors send out a very high frequency radio wave and sense any movement that causes a disturbance to this wave pattern. Both types of sensors are effective, and the range each sensor covers is marked on the box.

You wire security lights just like an indoor ceiling or wall fixture. Plus, they're great fun for spooking the neighbor's dog when he's out on the prowl. To replace an outdoor light fixture with a security light, follow these steps:

1. **Turn off the power at the fuse or circuit panel.**

   You may find several pairs of wires in the wall box. Some of these wires may be wired to different circuits than is the fixture you're working on. Be safe: Use a circuit tester or turn off the power to the whole house to be certain that all the wires in the box are dead.

2. **Remove the light-bulb cover and bulb from the fixture.**

3. **Unscrew the screws or nuts holding the fixture base to the wall box.**

4. **Lower the fixture base and remove the electrical tape or wire nuts from the black (hot), white (neutral), and, if present, green (ground) wires.**

5. **Use wire nuts to attach the wires from the new fixture to the corresponding wires in the electrical box, as shown in Figure 13-16.**

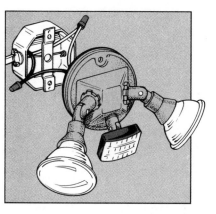

6. **Raise and position the new base plate so you can screw the new bolts through it to attach to the mounting strap.**

   An outdoor fixture has a weather gasket which is inserted between the utility box and the cover plate of the fixture. The gasket helps prevent water from getting into the box. Use the gasket even if you install the light in a weather-protected outdoor area.

7. **Screw in the bulb and replace the bulb cover (if any).**

8. **Turn on the power and try out your toy.**

   Most units have a sensitivity adjustment. You may have to do a bit of experimenting with this setting to prevent the light from turning on when a bird flies by or the neighbor's cat strolls into your yard at 3 a.m. Have a helper walk into the field of view of the sensor. If the unit doesn't light up, increase the sensitivity until it does.

Adding a Low-Voltage Outdoor Light

Low-voltage lighting is an ideal choice for outdoor illumination because it's safe to work with and easy to install. Low-voltage systems, like the one shown in Figure 13-17, are engineered to be modular with easy-to-assemble components. Most systems are powered by a 24-volt transformer attached to a single multiconductor cable, onto which you clamp light modules.

The wiring comes easy. The most time-consuming part is positioning and running the lines, especially if you're digging up the ground to bury the lines and then covering them again. You can also lay the cable directly on the ground or cover it with mulch. If there's any chance that the cable will come in contact with your lawnmower or other garden tools, bury the cable at least 12 inches.

Figure 13-17: Low-voltage outdoor lighting comes in modular systems that you can customize to features of your yard.

Here are the basic steps to installing a low-voltage lighting system:

1. **Install the transformer close to a grounded outlet.**

   The *transformer,* which converts standard 120-line voltage to 24-volt current, should be mounted close to an exterior outlet. Transformers that have a timer can be mounted inside, but those with a photoelectric sensor must be installed outside so that the sensor is exposed to daylight. For obvious reasons, light-sensitive sensors don't work in the shade.

2. **Lay the cable on the ground according to your plan.**

3. **Attach the lighting modules to the cable.**

   Different systems have different connecting schemes, but the general procedure is to position the cable into a slot in the base of the light and then close the clamping mechanism that pierces the low-voltage wire to draw power.

   Extract your finger before closing the clamp, unless you want to be known as Low-Voltage Larry.

4. **When all the lights are in place, plug the wall-mounted transformer into the exterior outlet and test the lights.**

   All permanently plugged-in connections to an exterior outlet must be weather-protected. Special outlet covers are available for this purpose.

5. **Conceal the cable with mulch or bury it in a shallow trench.**

   Even though the voltage is low, it's a good idea not to plug the transformer into the external outlet until the wiring is complete. Low voltage or not, when you're working outside in a moist environment, it's nice to know that absolutely no current is flowing through the system.

Chapter 14

Maintaining and Upgrading Electrical Appliances

In This Chapter

▶ Protecting your home with smoke detectors and carbon monoxide detectors

▶ Safeguarding your appliances and electronic equipment against surges of electricity

▶ Controlling the climate with set-back thermostats, air conditioners, and heating units

▶ Servicing your garage door opener

▶ Keeping your clothes dry, your food cold, and your supper hot

*R*epair and maintenance routines can vary widely from one appliance brand to another, so the information we provide in this chapter is limited to general rules for ordinary maintenance. Your best source of information is in the trusty ol' owner's manual. We have two pieces of advice on this topic:

✔ First, save the owner's operation and maintenance manuals for all your appliances. Stuff them in a box or drawer, or get organized and keep them neat and tidy in a single file for easy reference. Stack them in the freezer, for all we care, but just keep them.

✔ Second, read and refer to these manuals. That's right; we know it goes against all laws of nature, but we're recommending that you actually *read* the owner's manual. You'll be amazed at what you learn.

Most manufacturers these days also have toll-free help service phone numbers that offer answers to simple questions 24 hours a day. Don't be embarrassed to call; that's what the services are there for.

Plug it in!

Professional service people will tell you the *numero uno* reason of unnecessary service calls is — you guessed it — unplugged appliances. Yep, without power, electrical appliances just don't work.

Not only is it costly to call in a repair service person to tell you, "You gotta plug it in!," it's downright embarrassing. We know. So before calling for service or starting a repair, do the following: Make sure that the fuse or circuit breaker is on, the machine is plugged in, and the controls are turned on.

Pay particular attention to the blades on the power cord plug: If they're corroded or slightly bent, they may not be making contact with the blades inside the receptacle. Straighten bent blades and clean them with fine sandpaper or steel wool to remove any corrosion.

Installing a Smoke Detector

Each year, 30,000 people are injured and 5,000 die in fires. Smoke detectors sound an alarm anytime that smoke is present, providing your family with valuable extra minutes to leave the house and move to a safe place.

Every home should be equipped with at least one smoke detector on each level of the house, including the basement, with additional detectors placed in areas of high fire hazard, such as the:

✔ Kitchen

✔ Attached garage

✔ Furnace room

✔ Hallways near all bedrooms

Newer houses may have smoke detectors that are *hard-wired,* meaning that they're incorporated into the electrical system of the house. These detectors offer the advantage of not requiring replacement batteries, and in case of a power failure, most hard-wired units have battery back up.

If your home lacks smoke detectors, small battery-powered, wall-hung units are available at hardware stores and home centers. These units are inexpensive, costing between $10 to $20, and are easy to install.

The detectors come complete with a pair of screws for mounting. Because both heat and smoke rise, you want to install the detectors on the ceiling or on the wall about one foot below the ceiling. Use an electronic stud finder to locate the stud or ceiling joist, and screw the detector securely into the wood framing.

The detectors have a test button. Push the button to test the unit once a month. The detector may also produce an intermittent chirping sound if the batteries are low.

Experts estimate that up to 30 percent of detectors in homes have dead batteries. As a reminder, replace the batteries in spring and fall, when you reset your clocks for daylight savings time.

Installing a Carbon Monoxide Detector

In an effort to conserve energy and reduce drafts and air leaks, people are building new houses to be much tighter, and are sealing older homes to prevent air transfer. Because of this tighter construction, carbon monoxide poisoning has become a major concern. Carbon monoxide is not only deadly, it's also odorless and colorless, making it difficult to detect. This gas is typically produced by a furnace or other heating appliance. Symptoms of carbon monoxide poisoning are similar to flu symptoms, and may include headaches, nausea, and drowsiness. If your family experiences any of these symptoms during the heating season, move the family outdoors and have the house checked for carbon monoxide. If the house checks out clean, perhaps the symptoms are the result of watching too much daytime TV.

Carbon monoxide detectors look like smoke detectors and cost between $50 to $60. They come with screws that you use to mount them on a wall. Consider installing carbon monoxide detectors in your home as well as any location where you use temporary or space heaters: campers, RVs, vacation cabins, or even ice-fishing houses.

Installing Surge Protection

Lightning can cause temporary surges or spikes in the voltage of electrical power lines. In addition to lightning, transient power surges can result from use of motorized appliances or when electric service is restored after a power outage. These power surges can damage expensive home electronic equipment such as TVs, computers, microwave ovens, telephone answering machines, and home security systems.

Power companies install lightning arresters to protect their transformers and other equipment from lightning surges. You can install zap-protection devices, called *lightning surge arresters,* in your home's electrical service panel to protect house wiring and appliances from electrical surges. In-stalled near the electric meter, these devices direct excess power to the ground before it can damage your electrical system or appliances. Your power company can install lightning surge arresters for about $200.

Some appliances now include built-in surge suppressors, but you can also ensure protection of sensitive electrical equipment such as stereos, VCRs, or computers with individual surge suppressors. Simply plug the device into any wall outlet, and then plug your equipment into the surge suppressor. These devices are designed to absorb voltage surges before they can damage your expensive equipment. Plug-in suppressors are available at most electronics or computer stores.

Surge protectors designed for individual appliances typically protect against internal surges only. You get the best protection by using both lightning surge arresters and plug-in supressors.

Installing a Set-Back Thermostat

In cold weather, you keep your house warm to prevent freezing temperatures from damaging the plumbing system and house structure. Of course, a warm and toasty climate makes a happy house for all the folks inside, too. Of course, these are the same folks who want it cool come summertime.

But all that conditioned air costs money. Why pay to heat/cool while no one's there to enjoy it? Enter the *set-back thermostat.* These devices conserve energy by lowering the temperature of your house in the winter and raising the temperature in the summer during times when no one's home. It's a dream come true for keeping the indoor air climate customized to your schedule — and it's all automatic.

You can save up to 20 percent on your heating bills by setting back the temperature while you're sleeping or while the entire family is away at work or school — even more if you set up the temperature in the summer.

Sure, you can set your thermostat back manually, but if your memory is so poor that the family lets you hide your own Easter eggs, install an automatic set-back thermostat. You can program these thermostats to match your own schedule and lifestyle: Program the thermostat to set back the temperature at bedtime and then raise the temperature in the morning, so you awaken to a warm house, then have it set back the temperature again when the family leaves the house and raise it at 4 p.m., so you can return to a warm house in the evening.

Installing a set-back thermostat is a perfect do-it-yourself job, assuming you don't have an electric furnace. If that's the case, let a heating pro install it for you. Otherwise, this easy project will take you only about one hour's work. Here are the basic steps:

1. **Turn off power to the furnace.**

2. **Unpack the thermostat, screws, and the wire ID tags inside.**

3. **Read the directions and notice the wiring diagram.**

   Do this step twice. No kidding; it won't take long.

4. **Remove the cover from the old thermostat to expose the wires.**

5. **Attach the color-coded stick-on wire ID tags on the matching wires coming out of the wall: red to red, white to white, and so on.**

   Heating-only thermostats usually have only two wires; if the thermostat also controls air-conditioning, you may find up to five.

6. **After tagging the wires, remove the old thermostat from the wall.**

   Wrap the wires around a pencil to prevent them from falling through the hole in the wall and into the stud cavity, turning a one hour job into a weekend project.

7. **Use a carpenter's level to establish a level baseline for the new thermostat.**

8. **Use the thermostat base for a template to locate the mounting screw positions on the wall.**

9. **Drill holes in the plaster or wallboard for these screws and insert plastic anchors to hold the screws.**

10. **Use the screws to attach the thermostat base to the wall.**

11. **Attach the wires to the new thermostat using the wiring diagram to guide you in attaching the wires to the correct terminals.**

12. **Match the colored tags on the wires with the same colored terminals on the thermostat base.**

13. **Install the thermostat body on the baseplate, insert the battery, and restore power to the unit.**

14. **Program the thermostat to fit your family's schedule.**

    Jot down a timeline of when the house is occupied and when it's empty. Then follow the instructions that came with the thermostat to input those times in the unit.

Maintaining a Central Air Conditioner

A central air conditioner is a very reliable appliance. If the unit does stop working, there's not much that a homeowner can do; all major service on a central air conditioner should be performed by a pro. However, you can do several simple preventive maintenance tasks to keep the repair person in the shop and not knocking on your door.

✔ **Clean the compressor unit.** Unscrew and remove the cover from the compressor unit (you know, that noisy box outside your house). With the cover off, use the garden hose with the spray nozzle to remove dirt from the interior of the compressor cabinet, as shown in Figure 14-1. Be careful to avoid getting water on the fan motor and other controls. These parts are weatherproof, but they're not designed to take the direct spray from a nozzle. Do clean the air louvers in the sides of the cabinet.

Figure 14-1:
Keep your air conditioner in good shape shape by hosing out the compressor cabinet, oiling the fan motor, and changing the filter.

✔ **Oil the fan motor.** Your air conditioner fan motor, located in the center of the condenser coil, usually has a plastic cap atop the twin oil ports: One oil tube is connected to each end of the motor shaft. Place a few drops of 20-weight motor oil in each tube, as shown in Figure 14-1, and replace the plastic cap.

✔ **Change the furnace filter.** Replace the filter every 30 days. Because the central air conditioning unit uses the furnace blower and ductwork to distribute the cool air, you need to service the furnace filter in the summer, as well as winter. Most filters are located in the return duct at the base of the furnace.

Maintaining Central Heating

Major problems with central heating systems are best left to the professionals. Both gas and oil-fired systems have built-in safety devices designed to protect you and your family. Repairing heating systems may not be suited to do-it-yourselfers, but after the heating system is running properly, you can do many things to ensure that it keeps on running.

Troubleshooting

Imagine that you wake up in the morning, and it's freezing (or so it seems) inside. First, get dressed in some warm clothes (ear muffs are optional) and then check the following:

- ✔ Check that the thermostat hasn't been turned down by mistake. If it has, turn the temperature to the correct setting and huddle by the heating vents until you're toasted up.

- ✔ Turn on a light to check that you have electrical power coming into your house. If you have power, go to the main electrical panel and check for an open breaker or blown fuse. If you find one, either switch on the breaker or replace the fuse (as described in Chapter 13). If the circuit breaker snaps open or the fuse blows again, call a service person for help.

- ✔ Check that the heating unit (boiler or furnace) is turned on. Heaters usually have an On/Off switch. Some units may also have an emergency shutoff switch, which is usually located at the entrance to the utility room or at the head of the basement stairs.

- ✔ Check the oil burner to see whether its red reset button, located on the motor housing (see Figure 14-2), has popped out. If it has, turn off the power to the furnace and then push the button to reset it. On a gas-fired furnace, check to see that the pilot light is lit. If it isn't, follow the directions for relighting the pilot light, which are usually printed on the inside of the door or cover enclosing the burner compartment.

If these tactics don't work, call a maintenance person who has experience with the brand of heater you have. Look in the Yellow Pages under *Heating and Air Conditioning* for companies that advertise that they service all brands, or that include yours in the specific brands they handle. Snoop around your furnace or boiler for a service sticker that may lead you to a local dealer you can call for service.

Figure 14-2: If your furnace or boiler stops working, check to see if the reset button has popped out.

Furnace tune-ups

Hot air furnaces are pretty straightforward devices, but they do require annual maintenance to keep them running efficiently. You can do most of the simple maintenance yourself. There are, however, safety devices on the furnace that you shouldn't mess with. If you've never serviced your furnace, or even seriously looked at it, hang around while a professional service person does the work and ask questions before you try your hand at it.

Before you attempt any furnace maintenance, turn off the furnace switch and, if you have a gas-fired furnace, the gas valve. The furnace switch is usually located alongside the furnace cabinet near the gas valve and controls. Oil-fired furnaces have a red emergency turn-off switch.

Procedures that you, the homeowner, can do include:

- **Clean or replace the furnace filter.** Replacing the furnace filter as shown in Figure 14-3 is an important, but often neglected, task. If the filter is dirty, the blower unit becomes a dust distribution machine, and the furnace does not perform efficiently.

- **Check the belt between the blower and the motor.** The belt should deflect about 1 inch under finger pressure, as shown in Figure 14-3. If it flexes more than that, call a service pro to replace it.

Figure 14-3:
Replacing the filter and checking the belt that connects the motor to the blower are two important maintenance tasks for keeping your furnace running smoothly.

✔ **Clean and oil the blower motor and fan at least once a year.** Check to make sure that the door to the blower cabinet is closed.

✔ **Check to make sure all ducts are connected and seal the joints between the ducts with duct tape.** The ducts are round or rectangular metal pipes sometimes wrapped in insulation running out from the furnace to the various rooms in the house.

✔ **Remove the grille covers from the floor or wall registers in all the rooms.** Usually, a screwdriver is all that's needed to unscrew them. Then vacuum out the dust inside them and clean off the underside of the grille covers so no dustballs are left sticking to them.

Hot-water heating systems

Hot-water heating systems distribute heat throughout a house by pumping water that's been heated in the boiler to radiators or baseboard convectors located in each heated area. Radiators come in many different shapes, but they all function the same way. The hot water from the boiler, not your hot-water heater, heats the radiator, which in turn heats the air around the radiator, which in turn heats you. Sounds complicated, but it's really quite simple.

Despite its name, the boiler doesn't actually boil anything, it just heats up the water. Older steam systems actually had boilers that boiled the water.

Calling on a pro

Have your gas furnace serviced every other year by a professional. Maintenance steps that are best left to a pro include the following:

✔ Perform a draft-hood test to make sure that the chimney is functioning properly.

✔ Perform a carbon monoxide test to check that all the combustion gases go up the chimney.

✔ Inspect and clean the flue, chimney, and connection from the flue to the chimney.

✔ Check the combustion air inlet to be sure that it is not blocked and can provide sufficient combustion air.

✔ Clean, check, and adjust gas or oil burners.

✔ Inspect the heat exchanger for cracks, seam failure, or warpage. This step is important: Faulty heat exchangers allow carbon monoxide to leak into your home.

✔ Perform a flue gas analysis to determine the efficiency of the furnace.

✔ Test and adjust the belt and controls.

Just as a furnace has a blower to move the heated air through the house, a hot-water system (boiler) uses a pump to circulate the water. Maintenance of a hot-water system is basically the same as for a hot-air system. (If you have a steam system, don't mess with it; have it professionally maintained.)

If your boiler is fired by oil, have a professional inspect it yearly; if you have a gas-fired boiler, have it professionally inspected every other year. You can perform basic maintenance procedures yourself, but we recommend having an expert lead you through the basic steps before you attempt them alone.

Hot-water systems vary, but these maintenance steps apply to most boiler systems:

1. **Oil the water-circulating pump (or pumps, if your house has more than one heated zone) at the beginning of each heating season, or as directed by the owner's manual (see Figure 14-4).**

2. **To insure proper heat transfer, remove dirt and grime from all the radiators.**

   Use a stiff bristle brush to loosen the dirt, and pick it up with a vacuum cleaner. Be careful not to bend the delicate fins on baseboard convectors.

3. **Bleed each radiator to remove pockets of air.**

   Use a screwdriver or radiator key to open the bleed valve at each radiator, as shown in Figure 14-4. After all the air has left the valve and water flows out steadily with no bubbles or hissing noise, shut off the bleeder valve.

Figure 14-4:
Regular hot-water system maintenance includes oiling the pumps and bleeding the radiators.

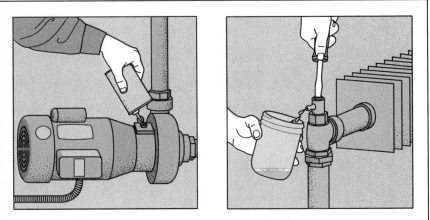

4. **After bleeding all radiators, check the boiler's temperature/pressure valves and add water to the boiler to maintain the proper water level.**

   Use your owner's manual to identify this area.

5. **Check the expansion tank to insure proper air and water levels and to allow room for expansion as the water is heated.**

   Use your manual to find this item, too.

Maintaining Automatic Garage Door Openers

An overhead garage door is heavy and, if not properly maintained, dangerous — especially to small children. Automatic openers that were installed after 1982 have a reversing mechanism that stops them in their tracks and sends them back up if they encounter resistance, like your head, during the closing cycle. Openers installed after 1992 are required to have an automatic back-up system, usually a light beam sensor. Unless these safety mechanisms are maintained, an overhead door can become a lethal weapon.

Get in the habit of performing the following maintenance routines:

✔ At least once a year, lubricate all moving hardware on the opener, including the chain or screw-drive mechanism.

✔ At least once a month, check the safety-reverse feature on the opener.

   • Newer models with a light-beam safety device are easy to test. Place something in the path of the light beam (like a cardboard box or a garbage can; no, don't use the cat) and then press the close button. The door should not operate. Remove the object and press the button again. Replace the object in the path of the light beam, and the door should reverse immediately.

   • With an older opener, test the door by placing a small cardboard box in the path of the door. When you activate the door, it should close until it hits the cardboard box, and then reverse. If the door crushes the box, call a garage door opener repair service to adjust the mechanism. If the door closes with enough force to smash a cardboard box, it can inflict a fatal crushing action on a small child before the reversing mechanism will stop the door.

✔ Daily, *before* backing out of the garage, open the garage door.

Keeping Your Fridge Calm, Cool, and Collected

Basic refrigerator maintenance is often overlooked until the appliance fails. Regularly performing basic maintenance can prevent such diverse problems as an overheated compressor, rapid stops and starts, a refrigerator that runs constantly, a refrigerator that doesn't stay cold enough, and a refrigerator that stops running altogether.

Cleaning the condenser coils

Refrigerators have one of two types of condenser coils: floor-level coils or rear-mounted coils. Figure 14-5 shows how to clean both types of coils:

✔ Floor-level coils are mounted behind the grille at the bottom front of the refrigerator. Use the wand attachment of a vacuum cleaner to clean the coils at least twice per year.

✔ To clean rear-mounted coils, pull the refrigerator away from the wall. The coils are mounted to the back of the appliance via clips and are easily accessible after you wrestle the unit away from the wall. Use a stiff brush or the brush attachment on a vacuum cleaner to clean away the dust buildup from the coils. If the coils are greasy, use a sponge and soapy water to remove the grease. Clean rear-mounted coils at least once a year.

Figure 14-5: Clean floor-level coils with a vacuum cleaner (left), use a stiff brush to clean rear-mounted coils (right).

If you have pets in the house, you need to clean your household appliances more often. Dog or cat dander and hair can clog refrigerator coils, heating ducts, registers, filters, and blower units. Can't part with the pets? Then plan to clean your appliances twice as often.

Putting a lid on refrigerator noise and odor

If your refrigerator is noisy, the cause may be as simple as the unit not being properly leveled. Place a carpenter's level on top of the refrigerator to check whether the unit is level. Use a wrench to adjust the leveling feet at the bottom of the refrigerator.

A rattling noise may also be caused by a vibrating drain pan. The drain pan is positioned behind the grille at the bottom of the refrigerator. Reposition the drain pan so that it doesn't make contact with the sides of the fridge and doesn't rattle.

If you have allergies, or if you smell a musty odor in the kitchen, remove and clean the drain pan. The drain pan catches any water that comes out of your refrigerator, such as that which what comes from the automatic defroster. If water accumulates in the drain pan, bacteria may grow there and cause odors or respiratory irritants.

Another source of noise may be loose or worn compressor mountings. To tighten or replace the mountings, unplug the unit and pull it away from the wall. Remove the access panel if there is one. Then use an adjustable wrench to unscrew the nut that holds one of the mountings, and replace the old mounting with a new one. In the same way, remove and replace all the compressor mountings, doing one at a time.

Maintaining a Clothes Dryer

Common practice for most homeowners is to run appliances until they cough, sputter, and finally grind to a halt. But you can avoid breakdowns and repairs by setting up a regular maintenance schedule. A clothes dryer is a relatively simple machine that combines three factors to dry clothes: heat, moving air, and motion (tumbling the clothes). All dryer breakdowns relate to one of these three functions.

Before starting your maintenance, remember that the number-one problem on service calls is a blown fuse or tripped circuit breaker, or failure to plug in the appliance. Always check to be sure that there is power to the unit before looking for other possible problems.

Always remember to unplug any appliance before starting repairs or maintenance. Electric dryers can be disconnected and moved away from a wall for service. To avoid creating a gas leak in one of the pipe joints, do not attempt to move a gas dryer. Have a service person disconnect the unit, and reconnect the gas pipes when service is done.

Use the following maintenance and repair information to keep your dryer cooking.

Loads of lint

The most common cause of clothes-dryer breakdowns is a buildup of lint. Failure to clean the machine properly can lead to a number of malfunctions, ranging from slow drying to overheating to a jammed idler and premature belt wear.

All dryers have a lint filter that you should clean after every load. These filters are sometimes located on top of the machine, and sometimes in the opening where you insert clothes. Check your manual for specific instructions, but the general idea is to remove the filter, pull any lint buildup off the screen, and return the filter to its original position.

Lint can also build up in the exhaust vent, the exhaust duct, and all moving parts, including the idler pulley that maintains tension on the drum's drive belt. At least once per year, remove the front and back panels and vacuum out lint from the idler, motor, and gas burner or heating element.

On the level

If the dryer is noisy, lay a carpenter's level across the top and check to be sure the machine is level. If it is not level, use an adjustable wrench to adjust the leveling feet at the four corners of the dryer. Tighten any loose parts and check the drive belt to be sure it is not damaged and is properly tensioned.

Dumb and dumber, that's who we felt like when we called a repair service because our clothes dryer wasn't working. Within seconds of his arrival, he noticed that the machine wasn't level. He put a carpenter's level on top of the unit to confirm his suspicions. We all got down on our knees to see the feet on the bottom of the four corners and adjusted them with a wrench. Turns out that the old basement floor where the dryer sat wasn't level. Somehow (probably when we were washing a heavy rug) the unit got out of kilter and threw itself off level. The repairman was out the door within minutes, leaving us several shades redder and several dollars the wiser.

Thar she blowers

If your clothes dryer makes a constant noise when it runs, check the blower.

- ✔ On some dryers, the blower and motor are located at the front of the unit, so you must remove the front panel for access. Move the blower wheel by hand. If it's loose or rubbing against the housing, use a hex-head wrench to loosen the retaining screw on the shaft. Reposition the blower wheel and tighten the retaining screw.

- ✔ On other dryers, the blower is located at the rear, next to the exhaust chute. You must remove the rear panel, then use a nut driver to remove the four screws that hold the chute over the blower. Swing the chute aside and check the blower. Clean away any lint or other debris and inspect the blower. If it's worn or damaged, have a service person replace the blower.

Maintaining Stovetop Burners

Cooking appliances are uncomplicated and, in normal service, may last for 20 years or more. Serious repairs may call for the services of a repair person, but by performing basic maintenance procedures, you can keep your gas or electric stove in good working order.

Gas stoves

To clean the pilot light, use a toothpick or a small wire, such as a paper clip or sewing needle, to gently remove gunk from the hole at the top of the pilot light.

To adjust the pilot light, follow these steps:

1. **Turn off the gas at the shutoff valve behind the appliance.**

2. **Locate the adjustment screw.**

   This screw may be at the side of the pilot light or on the gas line near the manifold at the front of the stove. If you don't see the adjustment screw, pull off the burner knob and look for an access hole alongside the stem.

3. **Turn on the gas and light the pilot.**

4. **Turn the adjustment screw counterclockwise to increase the size of the pilot flame.**

To adjust the flame level on the surface burners, follow these steps:

1. **Loosen the air-sleeve screw on the burner tube at the front of the range.**

2. **Turn the air sleeve to its highest position.**

3. **Turn on the gas and light the burner.**

   Slowly adjust the air sleeve down until the flame shows a correct air adjustment: a steady flame with blue cones about $1/2$-inch to $3/4$-inch high.

Sometimes, a low stovetop flame can be the result of clogged surface burners. To clean the surface burners, follow these steps:

1. **Turn off the gas and inspect the burners.**

   To access the burners on a gas stove, simply turn off all controls and then remove the grates and raise the cook top. (On sealed-top units, just lift off the burner.) Make sure that the portholes in the side of the burner are aligned with the flash tube that runs to the pilot light.

2. **Use a small wire or plastic toothpick to gently clean the porthole orifices, as shown in Figure 14-6.**

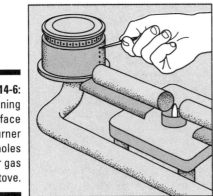

Figure 14-6: Cleaning the surface burner portholes on your gas stove.

3. **Remove the burner by lifting it from its position.**

4. **Wash or soak the burner in hot, soapy water.**

   Clean all the burner orifices with a small wire or toothpick.

5. **Let the burners dry and then replace them.**

   Push the burner tube onto the burner valve and position the burner in its support bracket.

To clean the oven burner, follow these steps:

1. **Turn off all controls.**

2. **Open the oven door to its first stop and pull the door upwards to remove it from its hinges.**

3. **Lift out the oven bottom (most are loose, but some may be held in place with screws) and remove the nut or screws holding the baffle.**

4. **Turn on the oven and check the flames.**

   If the burner flame is not evenly distributed along the length of the burner, the orifices may be clogged. Turn off the oven and use a small wire or toothpick to clean all the burner orifices.

5. **Return the baffle screws, oven bottom, and oven door to their original positions.**

Electric stoves

Most newer electric ranges have plug-in burners with terminals that plug into a receptacle. If a burner on your electric stove won't heat, try this:

1. **Disconnect the power at your circuit breaker or fuse panel and lift the burner.**

2. **Pull outwards on the burner to pull the terminals from the receptacle, as shown in Figure 14-7.**

Burner element

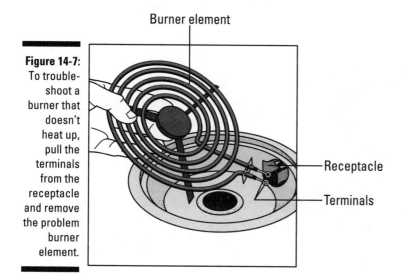

Figure 14-7: To trouble-shoot a burner that doesn't heat up, pull the terminals from the receptacle and remove the problem burner element.

Receptacle

Terminals

3. **Use steel wool to clean the terminal and remove any corrosion.**

   While the burner is out, inspect it for damage. If you see obvious damage, replace the burner with a new one, available at retailers where the brand is sold.

4. **Plug the burner back into the receptacle.**

5. **Turn on the power and check the burner.**

If, after you try the preceding steps, the burner still doesn't heat, disconnect the power again and remove a burner that *is* heating properly. Plug the nonheating burner into this second receptacle, and test to see if it heats up.

- ✔ If it doesn't heat, the fault is in the burner. Replace the burner with a new one.

- ✔ If the burner heats on another receptacle, the problem is in the first receptacle. Remove the drip pan and unscrew the receptacle. To avoid damaging the wiring, don't pull hard. Examine the receptacle. If the metal contacts inside are bent or corroded, replace the receptacle.

Some older electric stoves may have burners that are wired direct, with no plug and receptacle. The connection of wires to the burner is protected by a ceramic block. To remove the burner, disconnect the power and remove the drip pan. Then unscrew the burner and block from the range. Use a screwdriver to remove the spring clip from the ceramic block, as shown in Figure 14-8. With the wires exposed, clean and tighten the wire connections. Replace the two halves of the ceramic block and lock them together with the spring clip. Screw the burner unit in place on the stove. Turn on the power and test the burner to be sure that it's heating. If it isn't, replace the burner.

Figure 14-8:
Remove older burners by unscrewing the spring clip from the ceramic block.

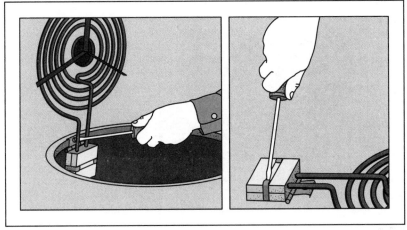

Part V
Improvements Inside and Out

The 5th Wave   By Rich Tennant

"You'd be surprised how much a fresh coat of polish and some new laces increase the resale value."

In this part . . .

Shelving, storage, plus insulation,
Getting it done with fresh inspiration.
Siding, gutters, and a wet basement,
All waiting for paint, repair, or replacement.
Inside and out, from attic to bath,
Read this part to get on the right path.
Find it, fix it, make it all new,
The best way to succeed is by counting on *you!*

Chapter 15

Inside Repairs and Improvements

· ·

In This Chapter

▶ Making the most of your four walls

▶ Molding your home's decorative future

▶ Shelving clutter with storage and display

▶ Getting artistic with ceramic tiles

▶ Surrounding your bathtub the easy way

▶ Staying warm with the right insulation

· ·

*I*f the social analysts who say that we're a nation of stay-at-homers are right, some of us had better spend a little time getting our nests in better shape. Who knows if we're really experiencing a cocooning phenomenon? Who cares? All we know is that these cozy little spaces we call our homes have plenty of room for improvement. This chapter includes our best advice on how to fix up your corner of the cosmos.

Working on Walls

Practically speaking, the walls in your house provide barriers, make compartments of space, and create a floor plan that directs the flow of traffic from one area to another. On an aesthetic level, walls deliver a palette of color and pattern that creates the mood in a room and provides a backdrop for furniture, artwork, and who-knows-what-else. And, of course, they also support the ceiling and roof. But just like every other part of the house, walls are susceptible to damage and the ravages of time. This section includes all you need to know to repair and decorate the walls that keep the roof over your head.

Filling cracks

In wallboard construction, two types of cracks occur in walls or ceilings: hairline and structural cracks. Hairline cracks are caused by faulty workmanship, defective material, or head banging. Structural cracks are caused by movement in the structure or framing of the building. The framing movement is the result of shrinking and swelling of the wooden structural members, such as studs or joists. This movement occurs seasonally, when changes in the temperature and humidity cause fluctuations in the moisture content of the framing lumber. Cracks filled with spackle or other brittle patching compound recur with these movements.

Here's what you need to repair a crack:

- ✔ A hammer
- ✔ A screw gun
- ✔ 1-inch wallboard screws and/or $1^1/_4$-inch wallboard nails
- ✔ A 6-inch-wide taping knife
- ✔ A 10- or 12-inch-wide taping knife or plastering trowel
- ✔ A plastic wallboard mud pan to hold the taping compound
- ✔ Premixed wallboard compound and fiber (or paper) wallboard tape
- ✔ Fine-grain sandpaper

Cracks at the joint of corners may be due to a buildup of taping compound or paint. These hairline cracks are in the excessively thick material; they do not extend through the reinforcing tape itself. To make repairs in these surface cracks, fold a piece of sandpaper over the end of a 6-inch taping knife and carefully sand away the excess material. By folding the sandpaper over the knife blade, you can keep the sanded surface smooth and flat; if you sand a soft, flat surface like drywall with your fingers backing the sandpaper, you may leave an uneven surface. Do not sand through the wallboard tape. After removing the excess material, use a small paintbrush to touch up the corner. Avoid any buildup of paint in the joint; accumulated paint is likely to crack in the future.

Follow these steps, shown in Figure 15-1, to repair a deeper crack with wallboard tape:

1. **Clean out the interior of the crack so no loose material is present.**

2. **Apply a light coating of wallboard compound to the crack.**

Premixed wallboard compound contains about 50 percent water by volume, so it shrinks as it dries. For this reason, several applications are needed to build up a surface and overcome shrinkage.

3. **Embed the paper tape in the wallboard compound and scrape a 6-inch knife along the joint to remove excess wallboard compound.**

   Don't leave wrinkles in the tape: If the crack isn't straight, cut the tape where the crack zigzags and apply the tape so that it is centered over the crack.

4. **Apply a thin coat of wallboard compound over the wallboard tape and smooth it with the wide taping knife to minimize sanding.**

5. **Let the patch dry completely.**

6. **When the wallboard tape and first coat are dry, use a 10- or 12-inch taping knife or trowel to apply a second, smoothing coat.**

   Important: This application is intended to smooth and conceal the tape. Don't pile wallboard compound in a thick coat over the tape; you're not decorating a cake.

7. **Let this application dry completely and repeat with a third coat.**

8. **Use a sanding block to smooth the repair area.**

   To avoid creating sanding dust, use a damp sponge or a special spongy wallboard sander to smooth repair areas. Sponge sanders work best if used after the wallboard compound has hardened, but is not completely dry. Remember that smoothing the wallboard compound with the trowel or knife during the repair process is much easier than sanding the compound after it dries rock-hard.

9. **Apply a coat of wallboard primer and let it dry.**

   The wallboard's now ready for decorating.

Figure 15-1:
Apply a light coat of wallboard compound over the crack and then smooth tape into place with a wide knife (left). When the first coat is dry, apply a thin second coat (right).

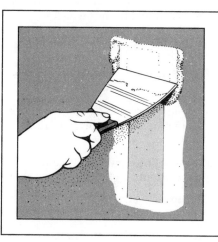

Plaster cracks

The advice in this section for repairing cracks is intended for wallboard construction, but you can follow generally the same patch techniques for plaster cracks.

When patching plaster with wallboard tape, you don't have to cut a V-shape into the crack to retain patching plaster, nor do you need to clean out the inside of the crack. Use a 6-inch taping knife to clean away any broken plaster that is protruding out of the crack and then coat and tape as described for filling in cracks in wallboard.

Repairing nail pops

Often, wallboard nails work themselves loose from the wall framing and appear as small crescent-shaped cracks in the wall. This curious phenomenon, called *nail pop,* usually happens during the first year of the building's life, while the house framing is settling or drying out.

Nailing wallboard became outmoded the day wallboard screws and screwguns were invented. It takes fewer screws than nails to fasten wallboard, and fewer fasteners mean fewer pops. Also, the 1-inch-long wallboard screws provide the same holding power as the $1^1/_4$-inch wallboard nails, but with less penetration of the wood framing. Less wood penetration equals less pop. (We think Einstein said that.)

When you see a popped nailhead or a small crescent-shaped crack, press with the flat of your hand against the wall and notice how the framing has shrunk away from the wallboard. Nail pops are often caused by shrinkage in framing lumber. As lumber dries out, it shrinks away from the wallboard, leaving the nail- or screwheads protruding from the wall.

Follow these steps, illustrated in Figure 15-2, to repair nail pops:

1. **Drive new drywall screws a few inches above and below the popped fastener.**

   The wallboard pulls tight against the framing as the screws are driven into it. The screwhead should dimple, but not penetrate, the paper facing.

2. **Use a hammer and a nail set or large nail to drive the old fastener completely through the drywall and tight against the wall stud.**

3. **With a 6-inch taping knife, apply a coat of premixed taping compound over the dimpled heads of both the old and the new fasteners.**

   Don't pile compound above the surface of the wall; smooth it so that it's flat on the surface.

4. **When the compound is dry, sand it with a fine-grit sandpaper, feathering it to blend in with the surface of the wall.**

5. **Apply a light second coat of compound in the same way and then sand it smooth to match the surface of the wall.**

Figure 15-2: Drive new drywall screws above and below the popped nail to pull the drywall back to the wall stud (left). Before you patch the nail pop, drive the loose nail through the wallboard.

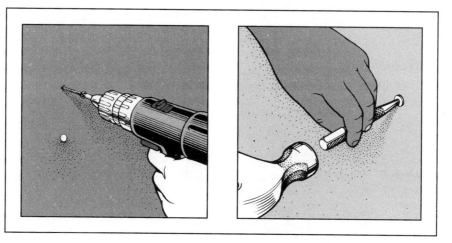

 When you're patching popped nails, shine a strong light across the wall. The beam highlights any defects and reveals even the slightest nail pops. Set a floor lamp about a foot from the wall and use a 100-watt bulb with the lampshade removed. When subjected to strong side-lighting, defects pop out like stars on a dark night.

Patching holes

Nail pops occur all by themselves. A hole in the wall is a whole other matter. You often find holes behind a swinging door, with a nice imprint of the doorknob, or where your dear child ran his tricycle into the wall. Whatever the cause, it's a simple fact of nature: Holes happen.

The challenge of patching holes in wallboard is bridging the gap of a small hole or anchoring a new piece of wallboard in a large hole. In times past, the only way to make those kinds of repairs was to cut away the damaged area to reveal the studs on either side, and then nail the new patch into place on the studs. For years, people used the old cardboard-and-string trick (tying a string to a piece of cardboard and sticking it into the hole so that they could use the cardboard as a base for the patching compound), but that's ancient history. Try some of these new ways for dealing with this age-old problem.

A bridge for small gaps

If the wallboard hole is less than 4 inches in diameter, hang a picture over it. Not good enough? Okay, okay. Use a peel-and-stick patch to cover the hole. These patches consist of a stiff metal backer covered with an adhesive mesh. Here's what to do:

1. **Use a sharp utility knife to trim away any loose or protruding paper facing or loose pieces of the wallboard.**

2. **Peel away the backing paper covering the adhesive and position the patch over the hole, as shown in Figure 15-3.**

   Make sure that the patch is smooth and not wrinkled.

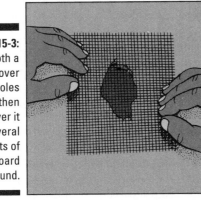

Figure 15-3:
Smooth a patch over small holes and then cover it with several coats of wallboard compound.

3. **Use a 6-inch taping knife to press the adhesive edges into place.**

4. **Apply two thin coats of wallboard compound, letting the compound dry between applications.**

5. **When the second coat is dry, sand the patch smooth so that it blends in with the surface of the wall.**

Wallboard clips for large holes

The key to repairing a large hole is to make a clean cutout of the patch area so that you can insert a same-sized piece of wallboard into the hole. You then screw wallboard clips into the surface of the surrounding wall to hold the repair piece in place. After you screw in the clips, break the tabs off of the clips and apply wallboard compound as you would for other repairs.

Follow these steps, illustrated in Figure 15-4, to install wallboard repair clips:

1. **From a piece of scrap drywall, cut a patch that will completely cover the hole in the wall.**

   Save yourself time and trouble — make the patch a square or rectangle, even though the hole may be a different shape.

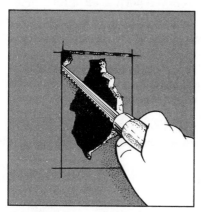

A. Using the replacement patch as a template, cut away the damaged drywall. (Step 3)

B. Push the wallboard clips over the edge of the sound wallboard and secure each clip with a wallboard screw. (Step 5)

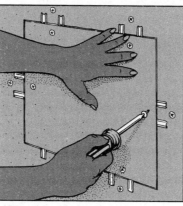

Figure 15-4:
Repairing a large hole in your wall is easy with the help of wallboard clips.

C. Place the wallboard patch in position and secure it by driving a wallboard screw into the wallboard clips. (Step 6)

2. **Place the patch over the hole and trace around it with a pencil.**

3. **Use a straightedge to guide your knife as you cut the wallboard along these layout lines.**

If the patch is large, you can make the project go much faster by using a drywall saw, as shown in Figure 15-4, to cut the wall. Just be careful to avoid wiring and pipes that may be hidden behind the walls.

4. **With the sharp utility knife, cut away any protruding paper facing or crumbled gypsum core from the perimeter of the patch area.**

5. **Install wallboard clips on the sides of the hole and secure them on the edges of the damaged wall by using the screws supplied with the clips.**

Space clips no farther apart than 12 inches.

6. **Insert the wallboard patch into the hole and drive screws through the wallboard patch into each wallboard repair clip.**

7. **Snap off the temporary tabs from the repair clips.**

8. **Apply wallboard tape and wallboard compound to all four sides of the patch.**

9. **When the tape and first coat are dry, apply a second, smoothing coat.**

Important: This application is intended to smooth and conceal the tape. Don't pile taping compound in a thick coat over the tape. Otherwise, the repair will be as obvious as the hole was.

10. **Use a sanding block to smooth the repair area so that it blends with the surface of the surrounding wall.**

11. **Apply a coat of wallboard primer and let it dry.**

Repairing sagging plaster on walls and ceilings

Older houses may have plaster walls and ceilings with wood lath for a base. The wood lath was installed with gaps, called *keys,* between each piece of lath. The plaster was forced between spaced lath, and this keying action held the plaster in place.

As plaster ages, these keys may break away from the lath, and the plaster coating can come loose and sag away from the lath. Sagging is usually visible to the eye. If you have sags in a plaster ceiling, press upward on the area with the flat of your hand. If the plaster feels spongy or gives under your hand pressure, it's a sign that the key strength has been lost. If it's not repaired, the plaster ceiling can collapse, and the heavy plaster can damage furnishings or hurt people.

Whether you patch or replace the sagging plaster depends on the extent of the damage:

- ✔ If the sagging is severe, meaning it's hanging an inch or more away from the lath base, or if it covers a large portion of the ceiling, your best bet is to remove the old plaster and replaster the ceiling, or cover it with wallboard. Not an easy do-it-yourself project.

- ✔ If the sagging is only slight, or covering a small area, you can reattach the plaster to the wood lath by using long drywall screws fitted with plaster washers. The plaster washer is a thin metal disk that increases the size of the head of a drywall screw so that it doesn't pull through the plaster. The drywall screw is threaded through a plaster washer and then driven through the plaster and into the ceiling joists, wall studs, or wood lath. The screw and washer pull the loose plaster tight against the framing, restoring the ceiling. By surrounding the area with plaster washers, as shown in Figure 15-5, you can stabilize the plaster so that it doesn't sag any further.

You may find plaster washers at a hardware store in a neighborhood with very old houses. The only source we know is Charles Street Supply Company in Boston. You can order from the source through a toll-free phone number: 800-382-4360.

To reattach the sagging plaster to the lath, drive the washer with a power screwdriver or drill so that it penetrates either the wood lath, wall studs, or ceiling joists. To avoid cracking the plaster and creating an even bigger repair job, don't pull the plaster tight to the lath in a single motion. Instead, start a few washers around or across the sagged area and drive them snug against the plaster face. Then tighten each of them slowly, moving from one to another, so that the plaster gradually pulls tight against the lath.

Figure 15-5:
Install plaster washers around the edge of the damaged area to pull the plaster tight against the lath.

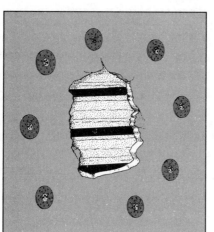

To repair large sags, follow these steps:

1. **Remove the loose plaster.**

2. **Install drywall screws and plaster washers around the perimeter of the loose area, as shown in Figure 15-5.**

3. **Install a drywall patch over the exposed wood lath.**

   See the previous section for instructions on patching wallboard.

4. **Apply primer and a coat of paint by following the directions earlier in this chapter under the section called "Filling a crack."**

   Wallboard compound absorbs a lot of paint, so plan to give the patched area several coats of paint to make it blend in with the rest of the wall.

Decking the walls

When it comes to hanging something on a wall, you have to consider both the surface of the wall and the size and weight of the object you're hanging. For example, a lightweight framed poster doesn't require the holding-power of a heavy architectural plaque or that nifty moose head. And fastening a hanger into hollow wallboard is a whole different process from mounting something to a brick wall.

When you're shopping for hanger hardware, know the following:

✔ **Approximate weight of the object:** Put it on the bathroom scale.

✔ **Dimensions of the object:** Get out the measuring tape.

✔ **The type of wall surface:** Wallboard, plaster, or brick?

As you look at various types of hanger hardware, notice the package instructions. They usually spell out the weight and dimension requirements. Hanging very large or heavy pictures always requires anchoring the picture hanger into wood framing, and you may need two or more hangers for support.

Hollow walls

Most walls have cavities created by the wall studs. Builders use these cavities to run electrical and plumbing lines through your house. Building codes generally require that these lines be protected so that you can nail and drill into most walls and be pretty sure that you will not damage one of these lines.

But remember: Whenever you nail or drill into a wall, be careful. If, while drilling, you encounter unexpected resistance, STOP. Drywall, plaster, and wooden studs are rather soft compared to steel or copper pipes. Don't push harder on the drill; instead, back off and investigate the source of the resistance. You can't even begin to imagine the amount of damage you can cause if you drill into a copper water pipe. "Thar she blows!"

Use the following items to hang lightweight objects on hollow walls:

✔ Small finishing nails and brads driven at a 45-degree angle into drywall or plaster

✔ Hook-type hangers that are held in place with a nail

✔ Adhesive hangers

To hang medium-weight objects, use one of these items (pictured in Figure 15-6):

✔ *Molly anchors,* or hollow-wall anchors, are combination screws surrounded by casing. As the screw is tightened, the casing around the screw collapses against the wall interior. Predrill a hole and insert and turn the screw to collapse and tighten.

✔ *Toggle bolts* are another type of hollow-wall anchor. They have spring-loaded wings that expand inside the wall. Predrill a hole, remove the winged toggle from the screw, and place the screw through whatever you want to hang. Then replace the toggle and insert the assembly into the wall. Tighten the screw to pull the toggle tight against the inside of the wall.

✔ Plastic *expansion plugs* fit snugly into predrilled holes in the wallboard. As you drive a screw into the plastic plug, the slotted base of the plug spreads and locks against the perimeter of the hole.

Find the stud

Where possible, anchor any hardware into the wall studs, not the space between them. To find the stud locations, you can go the high-tech route and use an electronic stud finder — a gadget that locates studs in the wall by measuring the density of various points in the wall. When you pass the stud finder over a wall stud, a light signals the stud location. (Sorry folks; this device won't help you find the stud in a crowded bar.)

For a low-tech way to find the stud, remove the shade from a lamp and set the lamp with bare bulb about a foot away from the wall. The nail locations will be highlighted by this side-lighting. Or, get down on your hands and knees and look at where the baseboard molding has nailheads showing. Wherever you see a nail-head, especially if they appear to be 16 inches apart, it's likely that there is a stud behind it.

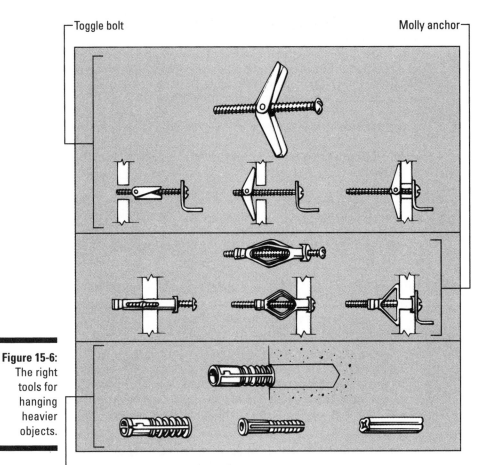

Toggle bolt   Molly anchor

Plastic expansion plug

Figure 15-6:
The right
tools for
hanging
heavier
objects.

Brick and masonry surfaces

Penetrating hard surfaces like brick and concrete is more difficult than getting through ordinary wallboard. For this job, you need an electric drill with a masonry bit to predrill a hole.

To hang lightweight items on brick or masonry surfaces, follow these steps:

1. **Drill a hole in the masonry the same depth and diameter as the anchor.**

2. **Tap the plastic plug or anchor into the hole.**

3. **Drive a screw into the plug to expand it and lock it inside the hole.**

To hang medium-weight items on brick or masonry surfaces, do the following:

1. Drill a hole in the masonry the same depth and diameter as the anchor.

2. Tap an expansion-type anchor into the hole.

3. Drive a screw into the anchor to expand it and lock it inside the hole.

Installing Miter-Cutless Molding

Wood molding adds character to any room, plain and simple. Molding transforms ordinary walls to something special because it adds a sense of detail and architectural interest, and it defines the space. Put wood molding on walls at the ceiling or a top wainscoting, and around doors and windows to make the room more distinctive.

Years ago, you needed a miter saw and the talents of seasoned craftsperson to create complicated 45-degree cuts, called *miter cuts,* in molding. Today, even a first-time do-it-yourselfer can install molding, thanks to modular molding systems that eliminate the trauma of having to make miter cuts. Modern decorative trim blocks require only square cuts. The straight end of the molding butts right against the blocks, so no intricate joinery is necessary. All you need to install modular molding are nails and construction adhesive, making it a completely foolproof system that even a chimp could do; trouble is, you can never find a chimp when you need one.

Modular molding systems like the one shown in Figure 15-7 include the following elements:

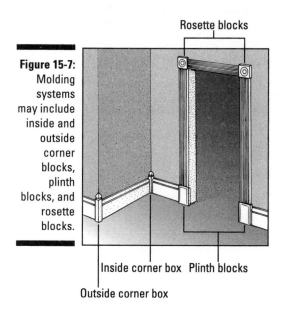

Figure 15-7: Molding systems may include inside and outside corner blocks, plinth blocks, and rosette blocks.

Rosette blocks

Inside corner box   Plinth blocks

Outside corner box

✔ Inside and outside *corner blocks* to join baseboard in different corner configurations

✔ *Plinth blocks* to join the base molding to door casing trim at the floor

✔ *Rosette blocks* to join door and window casing

You can find a variety of these systems at home centers. Some are made of wood, others of rigid polystyrene foam, but all are designed for easy installation.

Planning and shopping advice

Before you begin your adventures in molding, follow these preparation steps:

1. **Make a rough sketch of the room and note each wall dimension, including all the corners and walls that create corners.**

   If you're trimming a window or door, make a sketch with measurements.

2. **Count up the total number of inside and outside corners.**

3. **Calculate the number of molding sections you need, based on your measurements.**

   Molding comes in 8- to 12-foot sections. For each wall, plan to buy a section of molding slightly longer than the wall's length. That's right, you want the molding *longer* than the wall; otherwise, you end up saying something intelligent like, "I cut it twice, and it's *still* too short."

   You don't want to end up with a wall pieced together with cut-up sections of molding; instead, plan to use any leftover molding on the short walls.

4. **Choose the size of blocks based on the width of molding.**

   Most systems have a standard size rosette and plinth block for casings $2^1/_4$ inches wide. Larger blocks are used for moldings up to $3^1/_2$ inches wide. The inside and outside corner blocks are approximately 6 inches and can be trimmed to length.

5. **Gather up your tools and supplies.**

   Purchase or locate the following:

   • A small box of 4d finish nails

   • A tube of construction adhesive

   • A caulk gun

- A miter box
- A backsaw
- Measuring tape
- A hammer
- A nail set

Trimming out a room, step-by-step

After you've measured, shopped, and gathered your tools, follow these steps to trim the room:

1. **Before you think about making any cuts, paint or stain the wood molding and blocks.**

   By finishing the wood before you install it, you don't have to worry about getting paint or stain on the wall. Plus, you're less likely to miss spots when you're not crouched down on the floor or up on a ladder.

   Finish the backside of the molding as well as the front side to prevent an unfinished surface from absorbing moisture and swelling or shrinking.

2. **Set up a work area where you can work on the pieces production-style; the job takes very little time.**

   Use sawhorses set out in a garage or backyard, or clear a workbench for the long pieces of molding. In another area, lay down a large piece of cardboard or a pair of long two-by-fours for the blocks. Spread out the wood strips so that you can reach all sides of each block easily. Don't forget to put down a dropcloth on the floor to catch drips and spills.

Base molding

Begin trimming a room at the floor. Follow these steps to install base molding:

1. **Start at an inside corner behind a door and install an inside corner block.**

2. **Move to the next corner and position another block.**

   When you reach an outside corner, the notch in the back of the block automatically positions the piece correctly on the wall.

3. **Drill three $^3/_{32}$-inch holes in the outside corner block for nails.**

4. **Install the block with 4d finish nails.**

5. **As you work, measure the distance between the blocks, as shown in Figure 15-8, and then cut a piece of base molding to the length it needs to span.**

   To assure a square cut, use a backsaw and miter box to hold the molding securely while you cut it to length.

6. **At door openings, position a plinth block at the base of both sides of the jamb, set approximately $1/8$ inch back from the jamb, as shown in Figure 15-8.**

7. **Mark the wall with a pencil line on the wall side of the plinth.**

8. **Measure the distance between the last corner block and the plinth mark and cut a piece of molding to size.**

9. **Drill holes in the base molding and plinth and push the molding tight against the last corner block.**

10. **Nail the base in place, beginning at the inside corner and moving toward the plinth block.**

11. **Push the plinth tight against the base and nail it in position.**

12. **Continue working your way around the room installing the base molding and then fill in nail holes and gaps with a wood filler.**

Figure 15-8:
Measure between corner blocks and then cut the base molding to length (left). Use a plinth block for an easy transition from the horizontal base molding to the vertical door casing (right).

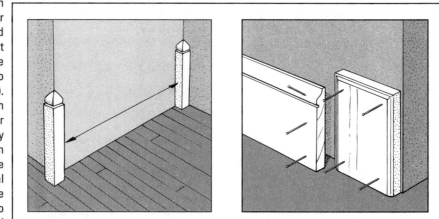

Molding around windows

Plinth and rosette blocks make trimming out doors and windows easy. The process is the same whether you're working on a window or door. To trim a window, start at the sill and follow these steps:

1. **Install a rosette block approximately $^1/_8$ inch back from each side of the top corner of the window jamb.**

2. **Measure and then cut a piece of molding to the length needed to span the distance between the window sill and the corner rosette block.**

   To assure a square cut, use a backsaw and miter box to hold the molding securely while you cut the molding to length,

3. **Measure the distance between the top rosette blocks and cut a piece of molding to size as shown in Figure 15-9.**

4. **Nail down the top strip of molding, centering the casing on the wider block.**

5. **Fill nail holes and gaps with a wood filler and caulk any open joints between the sill and the molding, or the rosette blocks and the molding, with acrylic latex caulk.**

6. **Apply primer and a good quality latex paint to window molding.**

Figure 15-9:
Install
the rosette
blocks at
the upper
corners of
the window
and then
cut pieces
of molding
to fit
between
sill and
rosette and
between
the top
rosettes.

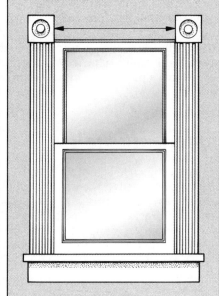

Molding around doors

To trim a door, begin at the plinth block at the floor level and follow these steps:

1. **Install a rosette block approximately ¹/₈ inch back from each side of the top corner of the door jamb.**

2. **Measure the distance between the plinth block on the floor and the corner rosette block and then cut a piece of molding to that length.**

    To assure a square cut, use a backsaw and miter box to hold the molding securely while you cut the molding to length.

3. **Measure the distance between the top rosette blocks and cut a piece of molding to size.**

4. **Nail down the molding, centering the casing on the wider blocks.**

5. **Fill nail holes and gaps with a wood filler.**

Building Shelves

A simple wall shelf adds form and function to a room. Use it to display a treasured collection of Beanie Babies or to store cookbooks in the kitchen. A shelving system that uses brackets and uprights to hold the shelves is a bit more costly and time consuming to install, but it's a project worth tackling. And closet shelving is downright rewarding because it puts you on the road to peace and order, knowing that, when you open your closet door, you're not in danger of getting clobbered with falling objects. Whatever shelving you choose, it's always a treat to have a place for everything and everything in its place.

Putting up a simple wall shelf

A single small wall shelf like the one shown in Figure 15-10 consists of the shelf itself and the brackets that are fastened to the wall. The shelf is either secured to the brackets or, sometimes, just rests on top of them. A wide single shelf typically has at least two brackets fastened to the wall studs; more brackets are needed for longer shelves. Simple brackets are available in hardware stores or home centers, and a wide variety of decorative brackets are sold in all kinds of stores, catalogs, and just about anywhere household furnishings are available.

Figure 15-10:
Secure
shelving
brackets to
wall studs to
assure that
the shelf can
safely
support a
heavy load.

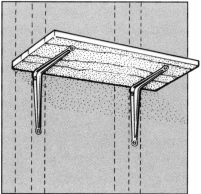

Here's what's involved in installing an out-of-the-box decorative wall shelf with two brackets and one shelf:

1. **Locate a wall stud and mark the location for the first shelf bracket on the wall.**

   Follow the instructions in the sidebar called "Find a stud," earlier in this chapter, to locate a stud in the wall. Then hold a shelf support bracket over the stud and use it as a template to mark the location of the mounting screws on the wall.

2. **Install the bracket with screws that are long enough to penetrate the wall stud at least an inch or so.**

3. **Mark the location of the second stud.**

   Wall studs are usually placed 16 inches apart, so measure 16 inches from the bracket you just installed. Place a carpenter's level on the first bracket to extend a level line to the second stud, and then hold the second bracket in position. Mark the location for the second set of mounting screws on the wall.

4. **Install the second bracket with screws that are long enough to penetrate the wall stud at least an inch or so.**

5. **Install the shelf on the support brackets. Use short screws to secure the shelf to the brackets.**

Installing a shelving system

A shelving system is made up of three basic components: the shelves, the *standards* (the long vertical slotted strips fastened to the wall), and brackets that fit into grooves along the length of the standards. Because the shelf sits on top of these brackets, you can adjust the height of shelving for a variety of configurations, as shown in Figure 15-11.

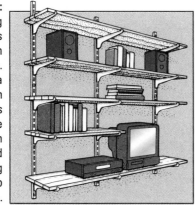

Figure 15-11:
Shelving systems come in many styles. Choose a system that's flexible enough to hold everything you want to store.

Before you invest your hard-earned dollars in a shelving system, consider these shopping tips:

- ✔ Make a preliminary shopping/learning expedition to select a shelving system and pick up a planning brochure with the system's standard and bracket specifications. Pack a lunch; this trip may take a while.

- ✔ Decide how many shelves you want and how you want to arrange them. Make a sketch of the wall, noting the location of wall studs so that you can plan the design.

- ✔ Choose the standard size and shelf depth and style to fit the items you plan to store and display, such as deep shelves for large items, narrower ones for smaller things. Plan to space the standards about 32 inches apart and allow a maximum overhang of a sixth of the shelf length.

- ✔ If you must fasten the shelf to a hollow wall, choose mounting anchors based on their weight-bearing capacity. Don't be embarrassed to ask for help!

- ✔ Read the directions on the package, noting how many uprights and brackets and what width and length of shelves are included. Most systems have brackets for at least two widths of shelving, so make sure that you buy the correct sizes. Some systems include the mounting hardware; some don't. Don't leave the store without everything you need.

Follow these steps for installing a component shelf system with standards and brackets:

1. Use a stud finder to locate the studs on the wall; they're usually placed 16 inches apart (some are 24 inches apart).

Plan to install each standard on the center of the stud. Make light pencil marks on all the wall studs in the vicinity of the spot where you plan to install the shelving unit. (You may have to adjust the exact location slightly so that the standards will be attached to the studs.)

2. **Mark the location for the top screw hole on the first standard and drill a small pilot hole through its top hole.**

3. **Use a carpenter's level to straighten the standard so that it's plumb and then mark the location of another mounting screw.**

   To mark the spot for the next screw, place a pencil on one of the mounting screw holes in the bracket, as shown in Figure 15-12.

4. **Swing the bracket to one side and then drill a pilot hole for the mounting screw.**

5. **Reposition the upright and install the mounting screw with a Phillips-head screwdriver.**

6. **Locate the proper position of the second standard.**

   To position the second standard, place a shelf support bracket in the standard hanging on the wall. Then install another shelf support bracket in the same slot of a second standard. Hold the second standard over the next wall stud and then place a level (alone or on a piece of shelving) on the brackets and move the new standard up or down until the shelf is level, as shown in Figure 15-12.

Figure 15-12:
Use a carpenter's level to ensure that the first standard is plumb (left), and that subsequent uprights are level with the first one (right).

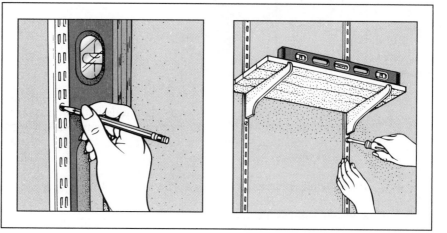

7. **Mark the location on the wall of one of the mounting screws for the second standard and install it as you did the first one.**

8. **Repeat with the remaining standards.**

9. **Install the shelf support brackets into the standards.**

These brackets usually tap into slots that lock them in place.

10. **Install the shelves.**

Adding a wire shelf system to a closet

You can tame closet clutter by installing a closet organizer with ventilated wire shelves, as illustrated in Figure 15-13. You still have to *hang up your clothes,* but opening the closet door is far less intimidating when you don't face a potential avalanche. By reorganizing the inside of your closet, you can almost double your closet space — making the chore of sorting through your stuff to install shelving well worth the effort. The installation is the easy part; the real work is cleaning out the closet and realizing that you used to actually fit into some of those clothes.

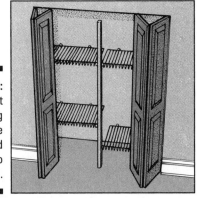

Figure 15-13: Closet shelving systems are flexible and easy to install.

These systems are sold as individual components to fit any size closet and as closet kits designed for various sizes. For example, a kit for an 8-foot closet includes four shelves, one support pole, a shoe rack, and mounting clips and screws.

Here's what you need to install a wire shelf system:

- ✔ Carpenter's level
- ✔ Screwdrivers
- ✔ Measuring tape and pencil
- ✔ Hacksaw for cutting the metal shelving to length
- ✔ A free afternoon

Getting ready — the worst part of the job

Before you can install a closet wire-shelving system in your closet, you have to do the following prep work:

1. **Remove all the stuff inside the closet.**

   Just do it! Think of this as an opportunity to get rid of items you don't wear or use. Donate the booty to charity or to anybody who can use it; just get rid of it.

2. **Remove the existing shelving and the clothes rod.**

   You may need a pry bar to remove the shelving if it's nailed into the walls; otherwise, it's a matter of unscrewing screws or fasteners or pulling out nails that hold the shelf and pole in place.

3. **Patch any nail holes that remain from the old shelving with a wall-board compound.**

   See the "Patching holes" section, under "Working on Walls," earlier in this chapter.

4. **If the walls are dirty and dingy, give them a quick coat of paint.**

   Trust us. The extra effort will pay off every time you open the closet door.

Wire shelving step-by-steps

To install the shelving system, follow these steps:

1. **Read through the instructions that came with the shelving a few times.**

2. **Determine the height for the main shelf, hold a carpenter's level at the approximate height, and mark a level line on the wall with a pencil.**

3. **Mark the locations for the wall clips.**

   Make a mark $2^1/_2$ inches in from either end of the shelf line and $^1/_2$ inch above the shelf line. Then mark 1-foot intervals along a level line connecting the two marks.

4. **At each mark, drill a hole $^1/_4$ inch deep and insert the wall clip, as shown in Figure 15-14.**

5. **Insert a screw into each wall clip and tighten them into the wall.**

6. **Put the end caps on one end of the shelf and measure and cut the shelf to length on the other side.**

7. **Put the other end caps on the cut end.**

8. **Hang the shelf on the wall clips, as shown in Figure 15-14.**

9. **Hold the shelf level, with the lip of the shelf toward you and facing down.**

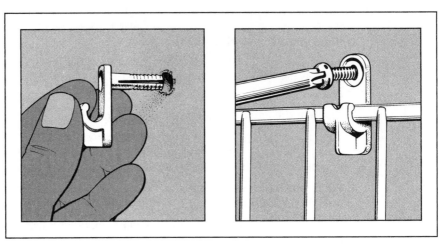

10. **Position the wall brackets on the side walls so that the shelf lip fits into the "U" and mark the holes.**

11. **Lift up the shelf until it's level (perpendicular to the wall) and drill holes for the anchors.**

12. **Insert the anchors.**

13. **Position the wall bracket, insert the screws, and tighten.**

14. **When both ends are installed, tighten the screws of the wall mounting brackets.**

Repairing and Installing Ceramic Tile

Ceramic tile is a beautiful and durable material. Its hard surface makes it an ideal material for just about any room in the house. Ceramic tile has never been more popular, so it's readily available at home centers and tile retailers. The only challenge with tile is choosing from the range of sizes and styles — everything from plain vanilla to custom designs in every imaginable color and decorative pattern.

Because tiling is often installed in the kitchen and bathroom, it's susceptible to water damage. The grout between the tiles gets wet, and water can seep behind it, destroying the seal. The following sections include tips on repairing and installing ceramic tiles.

Repairing ceramic tile

Some of the most common repair projects involve regrouting or refastening loose tile or replacing damaged tile. Because tile is such sturdy stuff and because the repair procedure is straightforward, this task is suitable for even the most timid do-it-yourselfer.

Regrouting ceramic tile

Ceramic tile is available in a variety of sizes, and the joints between the tiles are sealed with grout to prevent water from penetrating between the tiles and damaging the base or substrate. Expansion and contraction of the wall supporting the tile can cause the grout to crack. You can fix random hairline cracks in the grout simply by filling them with premixed grout. If cracks become extensive, it's time to regrout the entire project.

To regrout ceramic tile, you need these tools and supplies

✔ Grout

✔ A rubber float

✔ A grout saw to remove the damaged grout

✔ A squeegee, sponge, bucket, and clean toweling

See Figure 15-15 and follow these steps to regrout tiled surfaces:

1. **Clean the tiled surface to remove soap scum and grime.**

   Washing the tile with chlorine bleach removes any mildew or mold from the tile. Rubbing alcohol takes care of stubborn soap scum. Dynamite works well for removing the tile itself (a thought that's sure to cross your mind when you're in the midst of scrubbing).

2. **Use a grout saw to remove old grout from between the tiles.**

   Wipe the cleaned tile with a damp sponge to remove any dust or grout chips.

3. **Mix new grout according to the manufacturer's directions.**

   Use a latex additive rather than water for better adhesion to the tile and any old grout that may be left in the joints.

4. **Use a rubber float to spread a coat of grout over the entire tile area.**

   This is much quicker than trying to apply grout to each individual tile joint. To remove excess grout, pull a squeegee at a 45-degree angle to the tile to avoid wiping the grout out of the joints. Then use the handle of an old toothbrush to strike the joints and force the grout deep into the seams.

5. After the grout becomes firm, but before it dries, use a damp sponge to wash away excess grout.

Expect a slight haze to remain on the tile. You can use a clean, dry towel to buff away the haze.

Figure 15-15:
Use an inexpensive grout saw (left) to remove the old grout between tiles. Then rub new grout into the tile joints with a float (right) held at a 45-degree angle to tile.

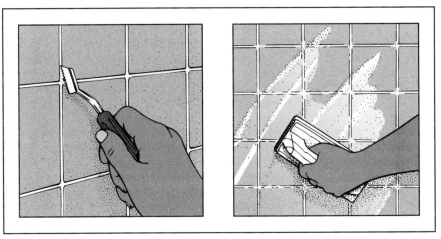

Don't apply grout to the joint connecting the tub to the tile. Movement at this point, due to the weight of people and water in the tub, can cause ordinary grout to crack, allowing water to enter. Instead, apply a tub-tile caulk at the joint with a caulk gun or with a squeeze-tube of caulk. Smooth the caulk with a wet finger and wipe away excess caulk with a damp sponge.

Fixing a loose tile

A loose tile is usually caused by failed grout that permits water to enter between the tiles. Think of grout as a Dutch boy with a fat thumb. To fix the tile, do the following:

1. Carefully remove the loose tile, prying gently with a putty knife or small scraper.

Scrape off as much old tile adhesive as possible from the area where the tile was removed and from the back of the tile. Dry-fit the tile into the hole to be sure that the tile will set level in the repair area.

2. Use a putty knife or notched trowel to apply tile adhesive to the back of the tile.

3. **Press the tile into the hole, using a twisting motion to be sure that the adhesive is in full contact with both the neighboring tiles and the substratum.**

4. **Wipe away any excess adhesive.**

   Most tiles will adhere to the substratum without sagging away. If necessary, use masking tape to hold the tile in place while the adhesive sets.

5. **After the adhesive is set, use premixed grout to seal the joints between the tiles.**

6. **Wipe away excess grout with a damp sponge and then polish the tile with a clean towel.**

Replacing a section of damaged ceramic tiles

Ceramic tiles may become damaged or loose over a large section. To replace a section of tile, follow these steps:

1. **Use a cold chisel (a thick short steel bar with a flat tapered point) to break each damaged tile into several pieces, as shown in Figure 15-16.**

   Wear eye goggles when breaking the tiles.

   Set the chisel at the center of the tile, and strike it sharply with a hammer until the tile cracks. Continue on this rampage until each damaged tile is broken into six or more pieces.

2. **When the tiles are broken into smaller pieces, use a chisel or a small pry bar to pry out the broken pieces of tile, being careful to avoid damaging adjoining intact tiles.**

   When all the damaged tiles are removed, inspect the base or substratum to be sure that it's intact.

Figure 15-16:
Use a cold chisel to strike the tile in the center to break it into small pieces that can be removed without disturbing adjacent tiles.

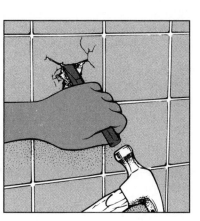

3. **Use a stiff scraper or sharpened chisel to clean away any tile remnants or adhesive residue.**

   After you clean all the tile and adhesive residue out of the hole, test-fit a new tile in the area. Be sure that the tile fits into the hole and that it's flush with the adjoining tiles.

4. **Use a notched trowel to spread tile adhesive on the back of the replacement tile.**

5. **Press the tile into the hole, and twist it to ensure full contact between the tile adhesive and the base or substratum.**

   Place a block of scrap two-by-four over each tile and tap the wood with a hammer to be sure that the tile is completely seated in the hole. Allow enough time for the tile adhesive to set, according to the directions on the label.

6. **When the adhesive has set, use a rubber float to spread tile grout over the joints between the old and new tiles.**

7. **Wipe off excess grout with a squeegee and then use a clean towel to buff away the remaining haze.**

8. **Use a clear spray-on tile/grout sealer to seal the grout against grime and water entry.**

Installing a ceramic-tile backsplash in the kitchen

For easy cleanup and a bright decorative touch, install ceramic tile on the backsplash between the countertop and upper kitchen cabinets. Choose from a wide array of styles and colors, including mosaic tiles (1-inch-square tiles that are attached to a mesh base to form), handpainted decorative tiles, or stock tiles that match almost any decorating scheme.

Measure the height of the area for the backsplash and use this size as a guideline in choosing the right tile. Remember to plan for $1/8$-inch grout lines.

You can install ceramic tile directly over wallboard, plaster, or existing plastic laminates like Formica. Clean the application area to be sure that it's free of loose paint, grease, or wax that may interfere with proper bonding of the tile adhesive. If you're installing the tile over a plastic laminate, use a solvent to remove any wax and sand the surface with coarse paper to help the adhesive bond to the plastic.

Tile installation varies depending on the size and type of tile, but here are some guidelines to use as you lay out your blacksplash:

1. **Mark the location for the first row and column of tiles, as shown in Figure 15-17.**

Figure 15-17: Adjust position of the first row to provide equal-sized tiles at each end. Then hold a vertical row of tiles in position to check the spacing between the top tile and cabinet.

Gauging available space helps you know where to position the first tile and how many full tiles you can install above it.

- Set the first row tiles on the backsplash, if it's flat, or on the back of the counter itself. Slide the row of tiles back and forth until the amount of tile that overhangs each end is equal. Mark these points with a pencil or nonpermanent marker.

- To determine out how many tiles will fit between the counter and cabinets, place a tile on the backsplash, and then place one on top of it. Hold the second tile in place while you move the first from below to above it. Walk these two tiles up the wall, marking the location of each tile, until a full tile will not fit.

2. **To help keep the tiles aligned as you install them, use a carpenter's level and a pencil to draw a level line on the wall.**

Use the top-most full-tile mark that you make on the wall as a starting point for drawing lines. Put the level on the mark, draw a line on the wall, and then move the level down the wall to extend the line. Use this layout line as a guide as you install the tiles. The top of the tiles should stay aligned with this line as you work across the wall.

3. **Use a notched trowel to spread the adhesive on the wall, as shown in Figure 15-18.**

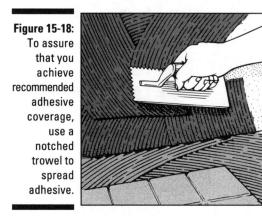

Figure 15-18:
To assure that you achieve recommended adhesive coverage, use a notched trowel to spread adhesive.

4. **Set the tile in place using a twisting motion (the tile, not you) to ensure full contact between the tile and the adhesive.**

   Most tiles have small spacers formed into the tile edges, so the tiles are self-spacing at the joints. For some types of tile, the dealer may recommend using small plastic spacers between the tiles to ensure that the grout joints are uniform in width.

5. **Install all the ceramic tiles, and let them stand until the adhesive is set.**

6. **Grout the cracks between tiles following the directions in the "Regrouting ceramic tile" section, earlier in this chapter.**

Installing a Bathtub Surround

Tired of tile? An alternative to tiling the walls around a tub is to install a plastic or fiberglass tub surround. These surrounds are available in kits with either three or five panels designed to universally fit the standard bathtub alcove. A surround can be installed over plaster, wallboard, or an existing but deteriorating ceramic tile base. Home centers sell surrounds in various sizes, styles, and colors.

The three-panel kit consists of two end panels with formed corners to provide joint-free protection against water entry, plus a back wall panel that spans the length of the tub. Because the surround panels are installed using adhesives, be sure that the surface where you will install the surround is free of loose wallpaper, peeling paint, or extensive areas of loose ceramic tile.

When purchasing a tub surround kit, check the instructions on the carton to find out the type of adhesive it requires. You also need a tube of tub-tile caulk to seal the joint between the bottom edge of the surround panels and the bathtub.

Here's how to install a tub surround:

1. **Remove the tub spout, hot and cold water faucet handles, and showerhead, as well as any attached soap dishes and the shower rod or doors.**

2. **Carefully clean the surrounding wall of any soap scum or dirt and repair any structural damage to the walls.**

3. **On the end panel, mark the hole locations for the plumbing pipes by using a template made from a piece of the surround-kit carton.**

   Test-fit the cardboard template to be sure that you accurately marked the location of all the spigots, knobs, or other controls before transferring these marks to the surround panel.

4. **Use a hole saw to cut the plumbing holes in the panel, like the ones shown in Figure 15-19.**

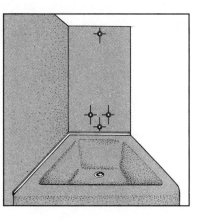

Figure 15-19:
Locate the position of the faucet controls, spigots, or other plumbing pipes and then use a hole saw to cut opening in end panel.

5. **Apply adhesive to the center panel and install it.**

   Apply a $1/4$-inch bead of adhesive in the pattern suggested by the kit instructions. For most adhesives, you push the panel into place so that the adhesive makes full contact with the wall. Then pull the panel away for five minutes to allow the adhesive to cure before pushing the panel into final contact with the wall.

6. **Install the back-end panel in the same way.**

7. **Install the plumbing-end panel in the same way.**

8. **Hold the panels in place overnight with masking tape, as shown in Figure 15-20.**

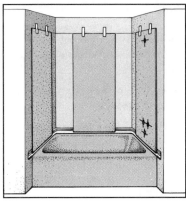

Figure 15-20:
Install the
back side
and end
panels with
adhesive,
and tape
them in
place
overnight
to set.

9. **Install the corner panels, which cover the space between the end and back panels.**

   If the kit has five panels, install the corner panels last, as shown in Figure 15-21. Apply adhesive to the panels and carefully position them so that the ends of the corner panels overlap the other panels, sealing out water.

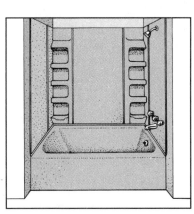

Figure 15-21:
Corner
panels
connect the
back and
end panels.
All joints
between the
panels must
be caulked.

10. **Use tub-tile caulk to seal the crack between the tub and the bottom edges of the surround panels.**

11. **Replace the showerhead, water control handles, and tub spout.**

Insulating Your Home

One of the easiest jobs for a do-it-yourselfer is also one of the most valuable: adding attic insulation to cut down heating bills. Admittedly, there's not much glamour in crawling around in your attic, and visitors won't even be able to tell that you've done anything. But you'll enjoy the payback every month when your utility bill comes.

Upgrading attic insulation

The long-standing popularity of fiberglass insulation is based on several important features: Fiberglass is inert, vermin-resistant, and fireproof, and it has excellent R-value per inch of thickness. (*R-value* is a measurement of the resistance to heat flow. The higher the R-value, the more effective the insulation.)

The problem with fiberglass insulation is that handling the stuff is like petting a porcupine: The glass fibers produce an irritating itch when they contact bare skin. Plus, medical experts suspect that inhaling airborne glass fibers can be hazardous to the lungs. Imagine that!

To eliminate these problems, fiberglass insulation manufacturers developed a product called *polywrapped fiberglass batts*. The batt insulation is encapsulated in a perforated polyethylene covering that prevents airborne fibers and protects the skin from glass fiber contact. The product looks kind of like a fiberglass sausage.

The perforations in the polywrap allow moisture to pass through, so the poly does not form a vapor barrier when applied over existing insulation. This feature makes the polywrapped insulation ideal for upgrading an attic insulation blanket. For areas where a vapor barrier is desired, insulation batts are available with the perforated polywrap on one side of the batt, and a solid polyfilm on the other side. When using the vapor-barrier type of poly, the vapor barrier side is applied with the barrier toward the warm-in-winter side of the wall or ceiling.

If your ceilings lack adequate insulation, choose the polywrapped batts. You can install polywrapped batts on top of any type of existing insulation. The usual practice is to install the new polywrapped batts at right angles to the existing insulation, as shown in Figure 15-22. You can cut the batts with a sharp razor knife or large scissors.

Upgrading crawlspace insulation

If your house is built above a crawlspace, heat may be escaping downward through the floors. Information on required insulation performance, expressed in R-values, is available from your local building department. Whatever the R-value recommendations, it's a good idea to install insulation batts that are as thick as the floor joists are wide.

Figure 15-22:
To add additional insulation to an attic, place fiberglass batts or rolls without a vapor barrier perpendicular to the floor joists.

To upgrade crawlspace insulation, choose polywrapped fiberglass batts with a perforated polyfilm on one side, and a poly vapor barrier on the other. Install the insulation batts with the poly vapor barrier toward the warm-in-winter side, in other words, facing up in all but the warmest climates.

To install the batts, press the batts into the cavities between the floor joists, as shown in Figure 15-23, and staple the insulation to the joists. You can also secure batts in place by stapling hardware cloth or chicken wire to the joists. While installing the batts, avoid wrinkles that can let warm air or moisture pass between the batts and the floor joists. Make sure that the vapor retarder is in full contact with the subfloor.

Figure 15-23:
Install crawlspace insulation between floor joists with the vapor barrier facing up towards the warm area above.

Chapter 16

Outside Repairs and Improvements

∙ ∙

In This Chapter

▶ Patching up the sides of your house

▶ Keeping rainwater in its place

▶ Washing decks and patios

∙ ∙

*M*aintaining the exterior of your house requires a little fundamental knowledge. Proper upkeep basically boils down to water (pun intended) — in particular, preventing water- and weather-related damage that can do such dastardly deeds to the siding, roof, and basement of a home. Sure, you may prefer to be out swinging a golf club or roaming the beach. But before you go, take a walk around the outside of your house and look for telltale signs of wear and damage. Sooner is better than later for exterior maintenance and repairs that can make a long-lasting difference in your home's value and appearance.

Repairing Siding

As exterior defects go, it's hard to find one more unsightly than damaged siding (pink flamingo lawn ornaments are a close second). These blemishes on the face of your house include dinged or dented sections and exposed sheathing where a section of siding is missing.

If you're lucky, you may find some leftover pieces of siding tucked away in the garage or storage shed. If you have to buy replacement siding, check out the oldest building materials supplier in your neighborhood. The store's probably had other requests for similar siding, so you're likely to find what you need there.

Wood siding

Wood siding comes in many forms. Common types are lap siding and board-and-batten siding:

- ✔ *Lap siding* is the most popular style of wood siding. It's installed horizontally, with the thick edge facing down and overlapping the board below it. Lap siding can also be made of interlocking boards that fit together as they're nailed in place.

- ✔ *Board-and-batten siding* is made up of vertical strips of wood. The *batten* is the thinner piece — usually 1-by-2-inch or 1-by-3-inch — and the *board* is wider, usually 4 to 6 inches wide. The boards are installed first, and then the narrower battens trim and conceal the joints.

The procedure for repairing and replacing all the different types of wood siding is basically the same.

Repairing small holes

In general, you leave the siding in place to patch small holes in siding. To replace a section of damaged wood siding, you have to remove or pry out the damaged board and replace it with a new piece and then caulk the joints. When the work is done, sand the surface and paint or stain to match the siding.

For patching small holes in wood siding, you need a scraper, putty knife, and wood filler. If the siding is old and weather-worn, choose a wood filler system with a hardener that stabilizes the wood before you apply the filler.

Here's how to do it:

1. **Use a scraper to clean out the repair area; dig out loose wood fibers and remove any loose material in the hole.**

2. **Use a putty knife to apply an epoxy wood filler.**

   The filler has the consistency of peanut butter. Spread it on to fill the voids. You may have to make more than one application; if so, let the first one dry until it's hard and then apply more. Build up the patched area to match the surface or contour of the wood so that, after you sand the area, no clue remains of where the patch is, except the color.

3. **When the filler's dry, sand it smooth.**

   This is the boring part, but the most important step because it conceals the repair area; like a good tummy tuck, no one can detect that it ever happened.

4. **Touch up the patched area with primer and then paint or stain it to match.**

Replacing a piece of wood-lap siding

When a small section of lap siding is water-damaged, split, or deteriorated, follow these steps (illustrated in Figure 16-1) to replace it:

1. **Raise the siding above or below the repair area, by gently prying under its edges, so that you can work on the damaged piece.**

   Use spacers (small wedges of wood) to separate and raise the piece of siding above the damaged board; you can then remove the nails — concealed under the siding above the damage — that hold the damaged board. Be gentle. Wood can be brittle; if you're not careful, you'll end up having to re-side the entire wall.

2. **Stand back and look at the damaged piece of siding, noticing where the siding is nailed into the framing studs behind it.**

   Plan to reinstall the new piece to the same solid backing. Cut out the section at least a foot on either side of the actual damage.

   Use a handsaw or, if you have a circular saw and know how to use it, set the saw to the thickness of the siding to cut out the damaged area; finish cutting the damaged board with the handsaw under the upper course. Cut the nails holding the surrounding siding by sliding a hacksaw blade under the overlapping board.

3. **Clear out the work area by removing any loose wood chips.**

   Make sure the wall sheathing is intact; if it's damaged or torn, replace it, leaving about a 6-inch overlap to slide under the surrounding siding.

4. **Carefully measure for the size of the replacement piece of siding, allowing for a $^1/_{16}$-inch expansion gap at each end, and cut a new board to fit.**

   Give the end cuts a coating of primer or stain to seal them before installing.

5. **Fit the new board into position and nail it in place with blunt-tipped, thin-shank siding nails.**

   To fit the board, protect the bottom edge with a scrap wood block and then tap until the new piece is aligned with the existing siding. Use the same type of nails used on the rest of the siding to nail the new board in place.

6. **Use paintable silicone or acrylic latex caulk to fill the joints between boards and to cover nailheads.**

7. **Touch up the patched area with primer and then paint it or stain it to match.**

   To replace more than one piece of siding, follow the same procedure and stagger the joints for a better appearance.

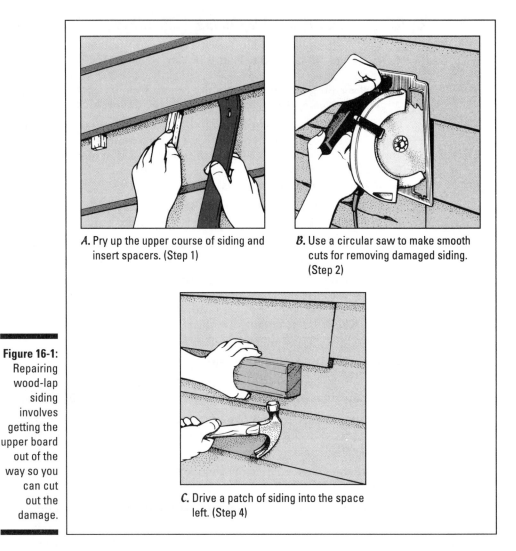

A. Pry up the upper course of siding and insert spacers. (Step 1)

B. Use a circular saw to make smooth cuts for removing damaged siding. (Step 2)

Figure 16-1:
Repairing
wood-lap
siding
involves
getting the
upper board
out of the
way so you
can cut
out the
damage.

C. Drive a patch of siding into the space left. (Step 4)

Replacing a piece of board-and-batten

The overlap of board-and-batten siding is easier to deal with than lap siding. Follow these steps to replace a piece of board-and-batten siding:

1. **Use a pry bar to remove the battens on both sides of the damaged board.**

   Gently pry up the narrow strips. Begin at the top and work your way down both sides of the batten, first with a gentle nudge to lift the board slightly along its entire length. Then go back and pry harder until it's completely loose, and remove the batten. If the nails are straight, you can reinstall them; if they're bent, replace them with new nails of the same type and size.

2. **Use the pry bar to remove the damaged board in the same way that you removed the batten.**

3. **Carefully measure for the size of the replacement piece, allowing for a $^1/_{16}$-inch expansion gap at each end, and cut a new board to fit.**

   Give the end cuts a coating of primer or stain to seal them before installing it.

4. **Nail on the new board with the same type of nails used on the rest of the siding.**

5. **Use a silicone acrylic caulk to fill the joints between boards, the overhead soffit, or cover boards.**

   You can also fill any nailhead holes with this caulk.

6. **Nail on the battens.**

   Drive any exposed nailheads below the surface with a nail set.

7. **Touch up the patched area with primer and then paint it or stain it to match.**

Vinyl siding

Vinyl siding is pretty tough stuff, but it's not indestructible. During the cold weather, vinyl can become as brittle as grandma's hip — if it's struck sharply, it's likely to crack.

Because the color is molded into vinyl siding, you can't cover up the patch with a coat of paint as you can with wood or aluminum siding. Another snafu with vinyl siding is that you may have trouble finding replacement siding. If you live in a subdivision, the builder may have used a brand not sold to consumers. If you live in a house with old vinyl siding, the correct color may be difficult to find. Siding's not like an appliance that you can track down with a model number. You can remove a section to look for a manufacturer's name, but you aren't likely to find one.

Patching over a section of damaged vinyl siding

The following steps are what's involved in repairing a section of vinyl siding:

1. **Stand back and look at the damaged area to decide how much of the siding needs to be covered by a patch.**

   Keep in mind how the joints are spaced. As you look at the wall of siding, remember that you want the joints to be staggered, not one directly above or below another.

2. **Use a sharp utility knife to cut off the nailing flange from a matching (or as-close-as-you-can-find) piece of siding to form your patch, as shown in Figure 16-2.**

   Make the patch at least 6 inches longer at each end than the crack or hole that you want to cover.

Figure 16-2: Cut off the nailing flange from a matching piece of siding. Insert the patch under the course above and then snap the lower lip around the course below.

3. **Apply a liberal bead of silicone caulk around the perimeter of the back of the patch.**

   Place the patch over the defect and push it in place. Slide the patch upwards to push the top of the patch as far under the section of siding above it and to engage the hooked bottom of the patch over the lower edge of the vinyl siding.

Replacing vinyl siding

Replacing a section of vinyl siding isn't difficult, but figuring out how to get at the fasteners that hold the siding in place does take a bit of ingenuity. This type of siding has overlapping joints that lock together with hidden fasteners that complicate the repair task. Luckily, someone (Mr. Zip, perhaps?) invented a *zip tool* for separating the panels of vinyl siding. When you want to replace a piece of dinged vinyl siding, the zip tool is a must-have.

The zip tool is a hooklike apparatus that you insert under and slide along the bottom of a piece of siding, as shown in Figure 16-3, and then twist downward. The zip tool lifts up the siding and releases it, exposing the top of the lap. These tools are sold at home centers, lumberyards, and any place that sells vinyl siding.

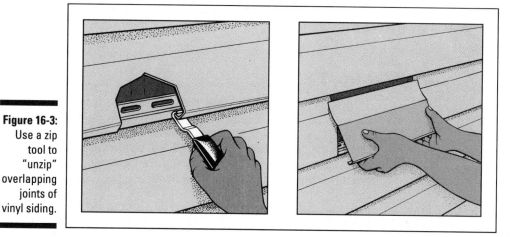

Figure 16-3:
Use a zip
tool to
"unzip"
overlapping
joints of
vinyl siding.

Replacing a section of vinyl siding

Here's what's involved in replacing a section of vinyl siding:

1. **Use the zip tool to pry apart the siding above the repair area.**

   You work this tool up under the lower lip of the piece of siding above the damaged section until it hooks the locking flange. Then pull down on the tool as you move it toward the closest joint. As the lower edge of the siding comes unhooked, you can lift it up to see the nails holding the damaged section in place.

2. **Use tin snips or a sharp utility knife to cut out the damaged section.**

   Then pry out the nail holding the damaged section to the sheathing and remove the piece. Save the nails to use again.

3. **From a new sheet of siding, cut a replacement piece about 2 inches longer than the piece you removed.**

   Install the new section by hooking the lower flange over the siding below and pushing the nailing flange under the piece above. Force the nails in the old slots with a pry bar slipped under the top piece. Don't pound the nails tight against the nailing flange, the siding must be able to move to allow for expansion and contraction.

Repairing Stucco

When stucco repairs are needed, you're typically faced with filling cracks, patching larger areas, and trying to make the new repair match the color and texture of the existing work. Repairing stucco isn't the easiest job in the world, but then again, it's not brain surgery, either.

Don't make stucco repairs when the surfaces will be below 45°F during the curing process.

Stucco mixes

You can use either a dry-mix mortar that you add water to, or make your own mix using one part white mortar cement to two parts sand. Add water cautiously to achieve a pliable mortar that's firm enough not to slump. If you want to tint the mix to match a shade, you can add up to 5 percent dry weight of mineral pigments. Keep in mind that the mix changes color as it dries, so experiment with some sample tests first.

Premixed stucco patching material is available in buckets for larger repairs. For repairing cracks, use stucco caulk, which comes in tubes and remains flexible so that it bridges the gap and won't harden completely — think of it as denture cream for your house.

Keep a spray bottle of water handy because you want to keep the stucco wet. The surface is porous and quickly absorbs moisture. The repair stucco absorbs more readily when you keep the area misted with water.

Filling small holes and cracks

Stucco walls develop cracks in time. Most such cracks can be caulked and painted, but when a crack reaches over 1/4 inch wide, or when chunks of stucco fall off the wall, it's wise to repair the area rather than rely on caulk.

Here's what's involved in fixing a small crack or hole in stucco:

1. **Mix the amount of stucco patching material you need for the size job you're doing.**

   Follow the specific directions on the stucco patching material and pay attention to the climate and humidity conditions.

2. **Use a hammer and cape chisel to make the crack wider on the inside.**

   A *masonry cape* chisel has a flat, small wedge tip that's ideal for creating grooves and cleaning out a joint. A standard cold chisel also works well.

   Use a putty or utility knife to chip away loose stucco down to *sound material;* that is, a surface that's stable beneath the cracked area. Brush away all loose material and dampen the area with a spray bottle of water.

   Always wear safety goggles when chipping and cleaning stucco.

3. **Force the stucco mix into the crack with a trowel or putty knife, slightly overfilling it.**

   After letting the mix stand for about 15 minutes, firmly work it down flush with the surface.

4. **Spray with a fine mist morning and night for three days to slow the curing time of the material.**

Patching larger areas

For larger damaged areas, remove the surrounding stucco until you hit a surface that's stable beneath the cracked area. Gently push on the area to see that it's solid and attached to the surface below it. If it feels loose, you have more than a patch job and you need to call in a contractor who specializes in stucco repair work.

Assuming that the damaged surface is sound, you can patch the stucco by following these steps, illustrated in Figure 16-4. You want to build up the thickness of stucco to the thickness of the surrounding original material, which usually takes three coats:

1. **Wash the area thoroughly and prepare it for the stucco.**

   If the wall is concrete, brick or clay tile, use a wire brush to rake mortar joints and chip concrete out to provide a surface for the patch material to adhere to.

   If the stucco is applied over sheathed wood stud walls, remove all but a border of the old building paper and fasten on overlapping new water-proof building or asphalt paper with a stapler. Cover with self-furring wire mesh lath which acts as a framework for the stucco to grab onto. Fasten this lath to the building using galvanized steel roofing, nails, or rust-resistant fasteners; aluminum is a no-no.

2. **Apply the first coat of stucco with a steel trowel.**

3. **As soon as the first coat becomes firm, scratch it with the edge of your trowel or a *scarifier,* a tool that looks like a wire comb or rake.**

   Keep the repair damp with occasional misting, about every five hours — less, if the outside temperature is cool.

4. **Apply a second ³/₈-inch coat; level and smooth this coat with a wooden float.**

   A *float* may sound like a very technical tool but it's nothing more than a flat rectangular piece of wood with a handle. Floats, sold in the masonry section of hardware stores and home centers, are designed to smooth on substances like wet concrete.

5. **To cure the material, keep the surface moist for two days by spraying with a fine mist morning and night.**

6. **Allow at least five days for drying.**

7. **Apply the finish coat about ¹/₄ inch thick with a stiff brush.**

   For a stippled effect, flick stucco on the patch with the brush and then slightly smooth the texture with a steel trowel.

A. Force a base coat through mesh to completely imbed it. (Step 2)

B. Scratch the first coat to score, but not remove, the stucco. (Step 3)

C. Use float for the second coat (Step 4), a stiff brush and a steel trowel for the top coat. (Step 7)

Figure 16-4:
Resurfacing
damaged
stucco.

Painting the repaired surface

If you haven't tinted the top coat of stucco, or if the pigments didn't quite match, you can paint the repaired surface with either exterior masonry house paint or latex house paint — tinted, if necessary, to better match the wall color.

Cleaning and Repairing Gutters and Downspouts

Gutter work isn't fun, but there's no excuse for not doing it twice a year in the spring and fall. Why then? Because you gotta remove all the fallen leaves, twigs, and other strange droppings that come from the sky and clog up the system. Just do it — if you don't, expect untold water damage that can cost you big bucks.

Inspect and clean

Take a walk around the house (yes, the outside) looking for any of these signs: leaks caused by holes in the gutter or downspout, drooping or bent gutters, dented downspouts, missing or loose brackets and hangers, and rust spots on metal gutters.

Climb a ladder and have someone — preferably, someone heavy and strong — stabilize the ladder from below. (Consider getting a stabilizer attachment extension ladder to avoid resting the ladder on the gutters, which can crush them.) Don't use a metal ladder if there is any risk of electric shock.

To remove leaves from gutters, use a plastic cup, a large kitchen spoon, a garden trowel, or an official plastic gutter scooper. Use a putty knife to remove the hardened and sometimes soggy debris. We prefer the two-person, two-bucket method, which involves one worker on the ladder scraping the gutter crud into a bucket. If that's you — wear rubber gloves! When the bucket's full, exchange it for an empty one with the ground person. This tag-team approach keeps the work flowing (you want to get the job over with as fast as possible). Move the ladder down the length of the house until all the crud's gone.

If the downspout is plugged, use an electrical fish tape or plumbing snake to remove the clog. Then take a garden hose up the ladder and flush the system out so that you're sure that the blockage has opened up.

For about $3 you can buy a *Gutter Getter*, a plastic scoop for removing debris. It flexes to fit inside your gutter and spares you the unpleasant task of handling the messy leaves and dirt in the gutter. We suspect this device would also be great for serving mashed potatoes.

Often a clog gets lodged in the corner pieces or elbow of a downspout. If you can remove the elbow component of the downspout gutter, poke a stick through the debris that's lodged or hardened inside. Flush with water and then reassemble the downspout.

To prevent further clogging, install a gutter device (such as a leaf strainer, mesh grid, or cover), especially at junctions where the gutter joins the downspout. Downspouts are designed to keep the rain water flowing through the system. If you have leafy trees that chronically plug the system, prune the offending trees before you do anything else.

Repairing a metal gutter

Gutters can last a lifetime if they're well maintained. But even with routine maintenance, gutters may eventually develop leaks, ranging from small pinhole leaks caused by minor rusting to major holes, broken joints, and missing downspouts.

Touching up small problems

Thoroughly clean the interior of the gutter by scraping it with a wire brush. Wash it with water and then scrape the surface to roughen it. One of those green (or any other color) scouring pads works well. When the climate's dry, use roofing cement (available in cans or caulking guns) applied with a narrow putty knife for small pin holes. Apply the patching material so that it feathers out thinner at the edges, as shown in Figure 16-5.

Figure 16-5:
Patch small gutter holes with roofing cement. Smooth the patch so water will flow over it.

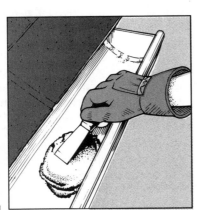

Patching larger problems

For a larger section of damaged gutter, use an asphalt-coated glass fabric embedded in the roofing cement. This material is sold in the roofing repair section of home centers. It comes in a roll anywhere from 4 to 6 inches wide, and you cut it to the length needed:

1. **Cut the glass fabric so that it covers the repair area and extends a few inches beyond at both ends.**

2. **Apply roofing cement to the repair area with a wide putty knife.**

3. **Lay the patch in the cement, smoothing it with a putty knife, and then cover the patch with more cement.**

   See Figure 16-6.

Figure 16-6: Large gutter holes require a patch; aluminum flashing material or asphalt-coated glass fabric are good choices.

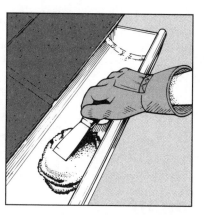

Large sections of steel gutters can rust out. You can cut out these sections of the gutter trough with a fine-toothed hacksaw and then replace them with overlapping sections of new gutter material or aluminum flashing, 2 inches longer than the original. Bend the patch to fit the gutter and then seal the patch in place with gutter repair compound or roofing cement and then support it at both sides of the patch with new hangers.

Downspouts that leak

Many times, the gutter troughs are in good condition but a torrent of water is still coming out of the gutters rather than down the downspouts. The downspouts are connected to the gutters with short drop outlets attached to the gutter. These short spouts can become rusted, inviting leakage, which is a problem that's not hard to fix.

If the rust or corrosion damage to the spout is extensive, you can replace the section of gutter that contains the damaged drop outlet. If the spout has only a few small leaks, a bit of roofing cement is all you need to seal it up. Apply the cement or caulk around the perimeter of the spout as shown in Figure 16-7. You can use a piece of window screen embedded into the caulk or roofing cement to bridge small holes in the joint between the spout and gutter.

Add a downspout diverter, also called a *splash block,* to carry the rainwater away from the house. These gadgets, made of cement, fiberglass, or plastic, protect the near-perimeter of the house.

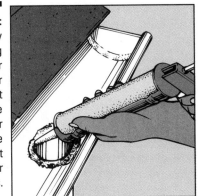

Figure 16-7:
Apply
roofing
cement or
gutter
sealant
around the
perimeter
of the
downspout
to repair
minor leaks.

Avoiding a Wet Basement

The only sure way to avoid a wet basement is to live in a house that does not have one. Because you're reading this section, we assume that you have either a basement or way too much free time. Even if you've never had a moisture problem in your basement, wetness can crop up at almost any time. (We're talking about the basement, not you.)

Keeping a dry basement is mainly an issue of keeping water away from basement walls and floors. Water is a persistent and powerful force, which you may be able to defeat without spending big money hiring a waterproofing contractor. Unless you live in a floodplain, in a perpetual swamp, on top of a flowing spring, or on a houseboat, you can do a number of things yourself to help.

Dampness and condensation

You know that you have a wet basement when a family of beavers moves in. If the issue is simply excessive moisture condensing on cool walls or on cold water pipes, check to be sure that the clothes dryer and basement showers aren't venting inside; if so, vent them outside. Check for humid air entering through open basement windows and, if you discover that's the case, consider buying a dehumidifier.

You may have trouble determining whether basement moisture is coming from inside the basement or from the outside via water seeping through the wall or floor. One easy moisture-detector test that you can perform involves taping a piece of aluminum foil to the floor and walls. Apply duct tape to all sides of the foil to completely seal it to the wall or floor.

Wait a couple of days and then take a look at the foil. If you see condensation on the exposed surface of the foil, then the source of excess moisture is probably coming from inside your house. In this case, increase the ventilation for the basement or install a dehumidifier.

If condensation appears on the underside of the foil (between it and the floor or wall surface), the moisture is probably coming through the wall or floor from outside. In this case, your best remedy is to stop the source of the water outside the foundation.

Downspouts and gutters

Lousy rain systems are the most common cause of wet basements. Tighten up your rain systems by cleaning out debris from the gutters and checking to see that, when it rains, the rainwater flows properly through the downspouts and away from the foundation. Eyeball the gutters for droop, caused by loose or missing brackets; check the slope with a level. (See the "Cleaning and Repairing Gutters and Downspouts," earlier in this chapter.)

Make sure the downspouts are not dumping water right next to the basement wall. Installing splash blocks can help direct the water away. Better yet, consider extending the downspouts 6 to 8 feet away from the house.

Grade and drainage

Over time, fill-dirt near the house settles, as do patio slabs, driveways, sidewalks, and concrete porches abutting the foundation. Plantings too near the basement mature and press against the foundation. (Furthermore, plant materials near the walls are an open invitation for termites.) All these factors direct a lot of water directly down the wall.

If your inspection reveals any low spots or if the ground is flat or slopes toward the basement walls, it's important to raise the grade so that it definitely slopes away from the wall for at least 4 feet, preferably even more. If the lot is such that you can't get adequate drainage away from the house, you may need to dig a shallow trench, or *swale,* 6 feet or more beyond from the wall to direct surface water away. Lining the swale with gravel underneath the topsoil can increase its capacity to carry water. (See Figure 16-8.)

Concrete work that slopes toward the walls may need to be replaced or elevated by a contractor, who can pump mud under pressure beneath the slabs to jack them up.

Any drywells or subsoil piping that you have leading directly to a storm sewer should be checked for blockages or breaks. Tree roots and other blockages can be removed with the same equipment used to clean a sewer.

Plantings spaced away
from foundation

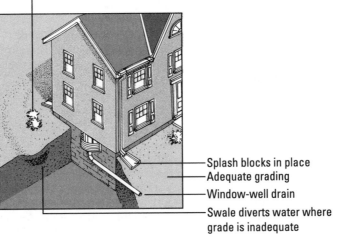

Figure 16-8:
Directing water away from the house with proper site planning is key to a dry basement.

Splash blocks in place
Adequate grading
Window-well drain
Swale diverts water where grade is inadequate

The sump pump

If you have a sump pump, check it periodically to make sure that the pit in which it sits is free of debris and that the pump is adjusted to cycle properly. Also be sure that water is entering the sump during heavy rains. See Chapter 12 for information about repairing a sump pump.

Major, big-ticket problems

Most other basement water problems are probably best left to the pros, who can do things like replacing or installing sump pumps, installing outside perimeter drainpiping, and sealing exterior walls.

Troubleshooting a Leaky Roof

A roof can leak in all kinds of places and for all kinds of reasons. When you consider the great variety of roofing types and materials, you can understand how the subject could fill an entire book.

What we can do here is cover the basic causes of roof leaks, how they occur, how they look, and the logic behind different repairs. Then you can decide whether to attempt the repairs yourself or hire a pro.

Condensation caused by poor ventilation under a soffit looks like a leak, but isn't. You can fix the soffit condensation by installing vents in the underside of the soffit and in the roof itself.

Covering the basics

A roof is usually a three-part system:

- ✔ The top surface, which is often shingles
- ✔ A middle layer of waterproof building paper
- ✔ Flashing

All roof leaks boil down to water somehow getting under or through that top surface. (Of course, the top surface around chimneys, pipes, valleys, and roof edges is the layer of flashing.) Figure 16-9 shows the most common locations of roof leaks. Just remember, every leak has a cause and a cure.

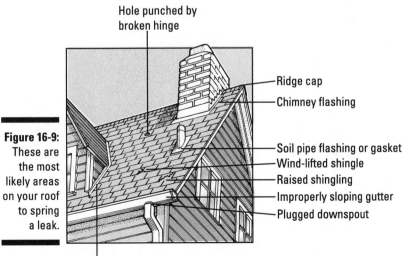

Hole punched by broken hinge

Ridge cap

Chimney flashing

Soil pipe flashing or gasket

Wind-lifted shingle

Raised shingling

Improperly sloping gutter

Plugged downspout

Dormer valley and flashing caulk

Figure 16-9: These are the most likely areas on your roof to spring a leak.

A leak caused by water getting through a broken or missing shingle is easy to understand, but not always easy to fix. But there are many other sources of leaks besides the obvious.

During the winter, a lack of soffit vents can cause the snow on your roof to melt and form an ice dam. The pool of water behind the ice blockage can seep under the shingles and leak into the house. So even a roof in good shape can all of a sudden start to leak. To prevent this problem from recurring, increase the soffit ventilation or install heat tape along the edge of your roof.

Looking for clues: A project for a rainy day

If you have an accessible attic, look for leaks during a heavy rain, as shown in Figure 16-10. Follow water running down the sheathing or rafters upwards to the source. Poke a wire or small nail in the hole so you can find the spot from the outside, and mark the area inside with an indelible marker.

Figure 16-10: The attic is a good place to catch a leak in the act; water flows down a rafter or across a ceiling joist before is stains the ceiling.

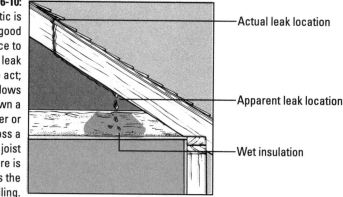

Actual leak location

Apparent leak location

Wet insulation

Examine very carefully around waste pipes, vents, chimneys, and where valleys and dormers are fitted into the roof structure for any signs of water leakage, which likely means the flashing either has holes in it or is not sealed around every edge. Also while it's raining, check for water overflowing from gutters.

Emergency shingle repair

Even a small leak over time can cause major damage. Stopping this leak isn't difficult, but remember that the fix is only temporary. If one shingle is starting to fail, you can bet that more are getting ready to go. Although this fix can stop the water on a short-term basis, plan to have a roofer inspect the roof before you encounter big problems.

First of all, stay off the roof while it's still wet. You won't save any money if you have to call a roofer from your hospital bed to make the patch. Doctors are one of the few professionals who charge more than contractors. We also assume that you've located the leak from inside the attic and have wisely marked the spot from the inside so that you can find it when you venture out on the (dry) roof.

The materials for repair are simple: All you need is a 3-foot-long piece of aluminum flashing, at least 12 inches wide. Then grab your hammer and a small piece of scrap wood and climb up on the roof.

Locate the bad shingles and slip the aluminum flashing under the shingles. Drive the aluminum sheet as far up under the shingles as it will go by placing the scrap of wood against lower edge of the aluminum and tap the wood with the hammer.

Everything in the system must be overlapped with the direction of the water flow to prevent water from getting under the edges.

Sealing it right

Apply roofing cement so that it works with the natural flow of the water. Smooth and taper the portion of your patch that faces uphill. A big blob of roofing cement can trap water behind it and form a little pool which will eventually work its way under the roofing cement and ruin your patch. The goal is to get the water to run right over the patch and not have an excuse to drop in.

Deteriorated sealants must be completely removed before resealing. Cover every exposed nailhead, bracket, or strap and every single inch of every joint between the roofing. After examining for any damage underneath, seal down wind-lifted shingles with a dab of cement placed under the shingle. Replace damaged and broken shingles and check out buckled shingles — often a sign of water leakage underneath. Also replace or seal any lifted roof cap shingles that protect the ridge of the roof.

Power-Washing Siding and Decks

An electric or gas-powered washer has to be among the more useful and labor-saving machines a homeowner can get his or her hands on. Plus, they're just plain fun to use. If Mr. Clean were a Power Ranger, he'd carry a power washer — "Stop or I'll rinse!"

Small electric power washers go for as little as $150; the gutsy gas models are three or more times that. You can spend a fortune on features and pure power. You can also rent a really killer unit for about $65 a day.

Power washers (or *pressure washers,* as they are also called) usually have a control on the machine itself to vary the pressure of the water stream, which is called its psi (pounds per square inch). The nozzle on the hand-held wand is rotated to vary the spray pattern from round to fan shape, and sliding the nozzle in and out varies the size and intensity of the shaped water stream. With an accessory turbo-nozzle, you can create a sort of swirling motion to help scrub a surface.

The jet of water spraying out of any power washer can be lethal. Always exercise good judgment when using a power washer, and most importantly, never use the equipment around other people or pets.

Except for periodic clear-water flushings to maintain cleanliness, use deck wash, house wash, or vinyl-siding wash in concentrated solutions. These chemicals are metered into the water stream either from a bottle attached to the hose or siphoned from a container. Be sure to read the operating instruction of the power washer so that you understand exactly how the unit works.

Preparing the site

High-pressure water finds its way into any unsealed opening in its path, so make sure to protect everything you expect to spray:

- ✔ Tape plastic garbage bags over exterior wall vents. These include vents for a clothes dryer, fireplace, heating system, and attic gable vents. Do the same on exterior receptacles and kill the power to them, just to be safe. Be sure to remove all the tape and plastic immediately after finishing the job.
- ✔ Close all windows and doors.
- ✔ Move all furniture and equipment away from the site.
- ✔ Protect shrubbery and plants by covering them with dropcloths or plastic tarps, as in Figure 16-11. Remember to remove the coverups as soon as the spraying is complete.

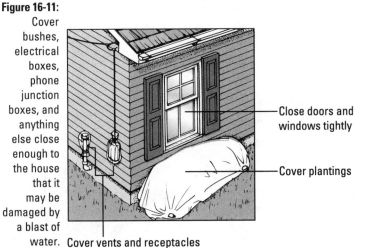

Figure 16-11:
Cover bushes, electrical boxes, phone junction boxes, and anything else close enough to the house that it may be damaged by a blast of water.

Close doors and windows tightly

Cover plantings

Cover vents and receptacles

Doing the job

No matter what you're washing, siding or deck, follow these basic guidelines:

- ✔ Don't do it on a windy day!

- ✔ Wear rain gear, especially boots and safety goggles.

- ✔ Cautiously test pressure adjustments before directing the stream. Span the width and working distance on an obscure area of the house or deck while observing any damage you may be causing to the surfaces. If you notice siding flying off the house, turn down the pressure or back up a couple hundred yards.

- ✔ Practice your spray angle by holding the sprayer to the surface until you get the results you want.

When power-washing siding, be careful not to direct the spray of water under lap siding or directly at glass or door jambs. If you have an old house, be very careful not to damage the siding with a powerful blast of water. Spray one section of siding about 4 feet wide, beginning at the top of a house wall and working across it horizontally.

To power-wash a deck, as shown in Figure 16-12, begin with the decking that adjoins the side of the house and work your way out from the house.

Figure 16-12:
Begin washing a deck close to the house and work your way outwards, covering small areas at a time.

Part VI
The Part of Tens

The 5th Wave — By Rich Tennant

All I said was it'd be nice to have a deck and a privacy fence. But you know Stuart, since his retirement he's been so restless for things to do...

In this part . . .

A tradition in *...For Dummies* books, the Part of Tens is a potpourri of handy-dandy ways to make your life a little easier. From saving energy to hiring a contractor, from safeguarding your residence to filling your toolbox with the basics, this part is home to some "well, of course" ideas that can make a big difference in the kingdom you call "home."

Chapter 17

Ten Ways to Avoid Common Painting Mistakes

So, you have your paint, your brush, and your masking tape — you're ready to go! Right? Wrong. Check the following sections to ensure that you don't fall victim to common painting pitfalls.

Spend Extra Time Preparing for the Job

Most do-it-yourselfers get so anxious to roll the paint on the walls that they don't spend enough time *preparing* to paint. For example, if you're an impatient painter and don't take the time to prepare the surface beforehand, you could wind up not only with dustballs dried in the paint but also paint that peels off because it can't adhere to the dirty surface. Similarly, a few extra minutes spent masking or removing doorknobs and other hardware helps to ensure professional-looking results — and a long-lasting job.

If you skip the preparation, you'll have to live with the imperfections. On the other hand, if you enjoy painting, ignore this step and you'll get to do the job all over again in just a few short months.

Paint into the Wet Edge

Don't paint away from wet paint. Paint *into* wet paint so that the most recent stroke of paint blends in with what you've already applied. Start rolling or brushing a couple of feet away from the last area you painted, and work back toward that area. If you don't, the paint may have dried enough when you eventually do paint over the area that you will, in effect, be giving it a second coat. This may cause noticeable overlap marks and a blotchy finish with different shades of paint. Yuck!

Don't Skimp on Paint

Some folks apply paint like it's fine French Champagne. Paint is the cheapest of commodities, so don't use it too sparingly or you'll end up having to apply two coats when you usually only need one. Whether you're using a brush or a roller, load up with a heaping helping of paint and then spread it on. Make sure you have an evenly distributed amount of paint on the roller so the application is even across the surface.

Don't Use Too Much Paint

The flip side of being a tightwad painter is using so much paint that it drips and sags. Neither creates the result you want. Don't apply paint as if you're slopping dinner to hogs. Load a brush with paint, and then tap the brush against the edge of the paint can to shake off the excess. With a roller, make sure that the paint is on the roller surface and not pooling in the ends of the roller frame. When paint pools, the excess paint is forced out and leaves streak and drip marks on the freshly painted surface — not the look you want!

Be Even-Handed with the Roller

It sounds simple enough, but you may need to practice a bit to get the hang of applying an even coat of paint. The trick to applying an even coat varies, depending on whether you're left-handed or right-handed, whether you're using an extension handle, and how tired you are — no kidding! Early in the job, you're likely to roll with gusto. But by the end of the job, your strength and enthusiasm may lessen, changing the consistency of the application. Just be sure to take note of how (un)evenly the paint is spreading and try to adjust the pressure accordingly.

Always Use a Primer on New Wallboard

New wallboard is like a sponge that soaks up every ounce of moisture you put on it. So new wallboard definitely needs to be primed with a PVA wallboard primer designed for new surfaces. A primer equalizes the surface absorption so that the new paint application is even. If you don't use primer, a new paint application will be blotchy and uneven, especially at the seams along the joints of the wallboard panels.

Combat Stains with a Stain-Blocker

You *can* paint over lipstick, ball-point pen marks, and other stains, but unless you use a stain-blocker, the stains bleed right through the paint. And no matter how many times you repaint over them, the stains will keep recurring, like a bad dream. Pre-treat stained areas with a stain-blocker, such as B-I-N, which is sold as a spray or brush-on primer.

Remove Tape from Window Glass

You've been a good scout and used masking tape on all the windows so that you don't have to scrape paint off the glass. If you leave the tape there too long, however, the sun makes it hard and brittle. Trying to remove it is like trying to break through cement. As soon as the paint is tacky, pull off the tape to avoid a difficult job in the coming days.

Don't Buy Cheap Stuff

You can find all kinds of disposable brushes and inexpensive pans and rollers, but you're better off investing in a few good pieces of equipment. The throwaway element of buying cheaper equipment is tempting, but it's not advisable. If you want a good-looking (and longer-lasting) paint job, you're better off shopping wisely and investing in quality, not quantity.

Clean Up Your Equipment

Cleaning paint tools at the end of a job is probably the last thing you want to do, because you're tired and glad the work is done. But do it anyway. Wet paint is easier to clean off than dry paint, and regular cleaning ensures that your painting gear will last as long as long as you do.

Chapter 18
Ten Important Ways to Burglar-Proof Your House

In This Chapter

▶ Putting crime in the spotlight

▶ Keeping a lived-in appearance

▶ Securing all points of entry

▶ Using good judgment

*W*hat's the use in making the best of your home if it's not secure from the elements? And just as you'd never dream of cutting costs by forgoing a roof, you should take steps to ensure that your home is safe and secure from the *human* elements, too. In this chapter, we dole out some good advice on how to keep the burglars out and your valuables in.

Trim Shrubbery near Doors and Windows

What does landscaping have to do with intruders? Concealing a door or window makes it just that much easier for an intruder to fiddle with the lock or break the glass. If the doors and windows are hidden from passers-by, the broken glass or jimmied lock can go unnoticed. Clear the entrances to your house so that anyone who enters is easily visible from the street.

Don't Make Your Vacations Obvious

When you leave town, don't broadcast your absence to the neighborhood with a lawn strewn with newspapers or a dark house. Call ahead and halt deliveries of newspapers, mail, bottled water, or whatever else arrives automatically on a set schedule. If you have a trusted neighbor willing to take in the deliveries, give him or her a key.

Make your house look as lived-in when you're away as it is when you're home. Buy automatic timers that connect to lamps and use them throughout the house. Use your regular routine as a guideline to schedule their on and off sequences. Ask the neighbors to park their cars in your driveway. Parked cars are signs of life and normal activity. Arrange to have the lawn mowed or the sidewalks shoveled.

Don't leave a chatty message on your answering machine announcing the fact that you're out of town. Leave a message with a generic reply saying, "We'll get back to you." Or leave no message at all. Taking these small steps ensures that no one knows you're not home.

Use Outdoor Light as a Deterrent

If you have a typical exterior light fixture, add a security light control, which is a detector that turns on the light when a person passes near it. Or get an automatic light with a photosensor that turns itself on when the sun goes down.

Secure Your Basement Windows

Basement windows are a no-brainer for an intruder because they're so easy to break open and are often not visible to street traffic. To secure basement windows, install a keyed sash lock made of aluminum. Or install metal grilles or grates, an even stronger deterrent.

Secure Your Sliding Glass Doors

A sliding glass door can give a burglar an opening wide enough to *drive* through. Just lift the movable panel out of its tracks, and you're in. A solution to this problem is using a lock with screws that connect the two door panels together so one can't be removed. You can also buy a slider lock, which mounts on the surface of the upper door frame. It has a key that extends a bolt into the top jamb.

Whichever type of lock you choose, be mindful that if the sliding glass door is a primary entrance to the house, you don't want to have to find a key to unlock it from the inside in an emergency. Installing a security bar that adjusts to fit into the track so it blocks the sliding side is also a good deterrent.

Upgrade Exterior Doors

A flimsy basement or porch door secured by an inside latch can be kicked through without causing most people to break a sweat. Upgrade exterior doors so they're made of solid-core wood or steel, and secure them with a deadbolt lock.

Get a Fantasy Dog

If you don't own a dog, create the illusion that you do by posting a "Beware of Dog" sign at the back door. Get a big dog bowl, paint "KILLER" on it, fill it with water, and leave it by the back door. The appearance of a dog may just be the deciding factor that sends a would-be intruder away from your house.

Of course, you could always get a real dog, as long as you can provide a loving home with plenty of time to care for and nurture the animal and space for it to roam in a fenced yard. But that's another book! (Check out *Dogs For Dummies,* by Gina Spadafori, published by IDG Books Worldwide, Inc., for all you need to know.)

Secure Ground Floor Windows

Secure all first-floor windows with a lock designed specifically for the type of window you have. Home centers and hardware stores have a wide selection of locks — some with motion detectors — designed to be installed on double-hung, casement, and sliding windows.

Secure the Entrance from Your Garage into Your House

An attached garage is a calling card for intruders. After they're inside the garage, it's only a matter of moments until they can be working on the door to the house — completely hidden from view. If the door into your house is a typical hollow-core interior door, replace it with a solid-core wood or steel door fitted with a dead bolt lock.

Don't Keep Keys in Obvious Places

Don't hide house keys in obvious places: the mailbox, under the doormat, tucked under a rock in a planter near the door in a box marked "House Keys." If you must leave a key, be creative and stash the key in an unlikely spot that's not particularly easy to reach.

Chapter 19

Ten Great Ways to Save Energy

In This Chapter

▶ Adjusting your temperature

▶ Sealing out the elements

▶ Conserving light

▶ And more!

*B*eing energy-conscious has become very hip — not to mention politically correct. Even if being considered "hip" and saving the planet don't concern you, wasting your money should. This chapter gives you some energy-saving tips that will help you to be a dutiful Earthling while saving you a few bucks, as well.

Install a Setback Thermostat

Installing a setback thermostat may reduce your heating and cooling bill by 20 to 30 percent in a year. This special thermostat has a programmable clock that allows you to control the temperatures in your house at all times. Why spend money to heat an empty house when your family is at school or work?

New units are easy to install, and the payback in energy consumption — translation: *energy dollars* — makes this a must-do project that you can complete in an hour or less.

Look for Holes in Your House

They're not always obvious, but they *are* there. Fill the cracks and holes in your house with caulk to plug up the leaks that allow heated air out in the winter and cool, conditioned air out in the summer. Walk around the exterior of your house looking for gaps and openings. (Open windows don't count.)

Use caulk to seal gaps, cracks, and splitting in the following places:

- ✔ Around the water spigot, dryer vent, any utility pipes, or cutouts in the siding

- ✔ Where different siding materials (for example, a concrete foundation and wood siding, or a brick fireplace and siding) meet

- ✔ Between window casings and siding and under window sills

- ✔ In the cracked frames of fixed storm windows

- ✔ In splitting wood or gaps under door thresholds

Access points to unheated spaces are another source of air infiltration. Use caulk to seal joints around a fold-away attic door or around the trim of a garage door with entry to the house.

A good quality silicone caulk works in most situations. For odd-shaped gaps and difficult-to-reach openings, stuff in rope caulk or spray in foam caulk, which fills the void as it expands.

Seal Windows and Doors

Tighten up inefficient windows and doors with weather stripping. This is a no-brainer that saves you money. Easy stick-on weather stripping applied around the perimeter of doors and windows does a first-rate job for a few pennies.

A door sweep installed on the bottom of exterior doors will fill a gap often left at the lower part of the door, where it meets the floor. If you have an attached garage, get a garage-door weather-stripping kit to seal a large door opening that's sure to let in cold air.

Do you feel cool air at the electrical receptacles and switches on the outside walls of your house and wonder where it's coming from? The culprit is the opening around the electrical cutout. You can plug up the gap with foam weather-stripping inserts, which act as a gasket to stop the flow of air. They come in sheets of four, and each insert has cutouts for the receptacles or switches.

If you feel a cold or hot draft of air at an attic door, use door weather stripping around its perimeter to seal it. If you feel a cold draft when standing outside, go into the house.

Add Insulation

Upgrading attic insulation has never been easier. Just lay polywrapped batts in place over loose-fill insulation, and your payback is lower energy costs. The encapsulated batts don't cause itching, so they're easy to handle; just cut them to size and roll them out. (See Chapter 15.)

If the existing insulation is lower than the top joist, lay new insulation on top to fill the cavity. Then add another layer perpendicular to the first layer. If the existing insulation fills the cavity, lay the new insulation perpendicular to it.

Open Your Windows

Reduce the need for air conditioning by opening your windows. Rely on good old Mother Nature to send cooling breezes your way, especially during the evening hours. Make sure that no heavy window treatment or furniture is obstructing the flow of air. Open windows throughout the house so the cool air can circulate.

Use Fluorescent Lights

Switch to compact fluorescents. They're easy to install and a long-lasting alternative to incandescents (the typical light bulb). The compacts can last 9 to 13 times longer than comparable incandescents and save a whopping 64 to 82 percent. Yes, they cost more. But they're a long-term investment that can be maximized if they're used where a light stays on for hours at a time. Like their long, skinny cousin, the standard fluorescent, compact fluorescents need a small ballast to modify electrical power. The ballast generally comes built into an adapter base that screws right into a standard incandescent socket. Some have a replaceable tube; others come as an all-in-one unit. New dimmable models are now available.

Lower Your Water Heater Temperature

Lower the water-heater temperature to the "warm" setting, 120 degrees. This setting cuts back on your energy consumption and also eliminates the possibility of someone getting burned by scalding water. If you have an old, non-insulated water heater, pick up an insulating blanket for the unit and wrap it up to contain the heat.

Use Washers and Dryers at Night

Use your clothes washer and clothes dryer at off-peak times, which, in most parts of the country, are after 10 p.m. and before 9 a.m. Regularly clean out the lint filter when using the dryer and, a few times a year, check the vent cover in the wall and remove any lint buildup. Set your washer to a lower temperature, or wash with cold water only.

Filter Watch

If you don't do anything else, be an attentive filter watcher. It's not a very exciting pastime, but it's one that could save you some serious cash. During the heating season, replace the furnace filters every month. In the summer, wash or replace air conditioner filters during high-use periods. Every couple of months, take out the snow brush you use on your car and pull the refrigerator away from the wall. Dust off the compressor coils on the back of the refrigerator. (And while you're at it, clean the floor and get rid of those dust bunnies!)

Use a Low-Flow Restrictor

Replace your showerhead with a low-flow restrictor, which reduces the flow of water, but still gives you a comfortable shower. Water heating is a good 20 percent of the total consumption in a house. So lowering the daily flow of hot water will save you money for a very low investment — the cost of the showerhead restrictor. The only drawback: You'll be 20 percent less clean. (Just kidding!)

Chapter 20

Ten Things to Remember When You're Hiring a Contractor

● ●

In This Chapter

▶ Planning for success

▶ Visualizing the project

▶ Choosing the right person for the job

● ●

*I*f you're planning a big project (or even a small one that you don't want to do yourself), choosing the right contractor is a critical step. This chapter provides you with some guidelines that not only help you choose a good contractor, but also help you give contractors the information they need to complete the job to your liking.

Plan Ahead

Plan remodeling projects months before you want to have the job completed. You need time to find and interview contractors, check their references, fine-tune the requirements of the project so you can ask for bids, and then actually get the job scheduled. Katie has a surefire formula for this planning process: She doubles the amount of money Gene predicts and triples the time he thinks it should take. She's usually right on. Katie also warns: Never hire a contractor who thinks that Tyvek is a famous Swedish explorer, woven valley is a salad dressing, or step-flashing is aerobics without pants.

Use Pictures

Don't *tell* contractors what you want; show them pictures of it. Clip from magazines, make copies out of books, do whatever it takes to create a visual reference as a starting point for discussions. Don't leave any room for confusion or ambiguity.

Compare Bids Fairly

If you get bids from more than one contractor so you can do some comparison shopping, make sure that the bids cover the same work. Sometimes, a project grows and expands in scope. The more you talk to contractors, the more suggestions they have and the more the job description changes. Just remember to compare like bids for like work. If you see a large range in the dollar amounts of bids, it just may be because the bids cover different work.

Be Available During a Project

You must have a decision-maker always available (at least by phone) during a project. The contractor has to be able to talk to a homeowner when something unanticipated comes up — and something unanticipated *always* comes up. For example, a plumber is tearing out the old lines for a new bathtub installation and finds a 12-inch space in a hidden wall cavity. Do you want to incorporate that found space in the new design and add a recessed shelf? Someone should always be available for those kinds of spur-of-the-moment decisions. So plan ahead to decide who that person will be.

Choose an Appropriately Experienced Contractor

Choose a contractor or construction company with experience for the kind of work you want done. Don't hire a rough carpenter who has years of experience framing houses to do a precision job involving multiple miter cuts, such as installing a cornice ceiling molding. A handy jack-of-all-trades who can repair all kinds of appliances is probably not the best craftsman to fabricate a new Corian countertop.

Establish a Payment Schedule

A typical payment schedule for a job is in thirds. For example, you pay one third up front, or when signing a contract; another third when the work is approved by a building inspector; and the last third when the work meets your satisfaction. Make sure that the contract spells out the payment schedule along with the exact specifications, model numbers, and so on for the materials to be used and the time frame for completion. Before signing a contract, ask to see confirmation that the contractor is bonded and has insurance and that you're not liable in case of any accidents to workers on your property, including subcontractors and delivery persons.

Make Room for Materials

Finding a place to store things isn't a big deal if it's just one new toilet. But if new flooring or cabinets or a whirlpool tub is involved, figure out where you will store the new material when it's delivered. If you have a garage that's not filled to capacity, you're in luck. Otherwise, you may have to do some fancy furniture footwork to find a designated resting place that's protected from the weather and burglars.

Expect Dust

Anticipate a lot of dust and clutter, even in rooms and areas of the house where no work is being done. A house is a complex network of rooms, mechanical systems, and materials (in case you hadn't noticed), and when you work on one part, you're affecting the whole thing. You may be working up in the attic, but the dust from your endeavors isn't going to stay there, no matter how hard you try to contain it. And if you're refinishing floors or sanding wallboard, expect a whole house of grit and dust to deal with. (Isn't remodeling fun?)

Be Prepared to Go Elsewhere

Be resigned to contributing to the local economy, and plan to eat out if any of the work is in or near the kitchen. Plan to visit the laundromat if the utility room is involved. And if you're a one-bathroom house, get friendly with your neighbors, because you may be dancing on their doorstep.

Expect Problems

Assume the worst-case scenario. Presume Murphy's Law will be in full force. Expect delays and disappointments. Maybe you'll get lucky, and things will run smoothly. And maybe your waistline will return, your hair will grow back, and Elvis will sing at your daughter's wedding.

Chapter 21

Ten Ways to Make Your Home Safer and More Accessible

*Y*our home is your castle, right? Well, you may find that your modern-day castle is becoming a modern-day hassle. This chapter gives you the lowdown on how to ensure that your house is safer and more convenient for you and your family.

Improve Lighting

Yes, we're getting older (and slower and fatter . . .), and one of the realities is that we need better lighting — up to three times more than when we were in our twenties — for clear vision. Upgrade lamps with glare-free bulbs or halogens for reading, sewing, or other hands-on work. In the kitchen, add fluorescents under cabinets and over work areas where you cut vegetables and prepare foods. Improve bathroom lighting with additional lights on the sides of the vanity for better glare-free illumination. Don't forget to upgrade the lighting at the top and bottom of staircases and add a night light in the hall and bathroom so you're sure-footed in the middle of the night.

Make the Floor Slip- and Trip-Proof

Remove any throw rugs or small areas rugs that you may trip on — they may look nice, but they're dangerous. When choosing carpeting, look for a low-pile style with thin padding for easy footing. For the bathroom floor, where many accidents happen, choose a non-slip or slip-resistant flooring.

Replace Electrical Switches

Replace electrical switches with rocker switches. These switches are easy to operate, even for arthritic hands, because you can use the palm or back of your hand, even an elbow. It's a simple switch replacement, similar to those discussed in Chapter 13, that makes operating a light switch as easy as a simple touch.

Safeguard Your Shower

In the bathroom, install grab bars on shower and tub walls. Having a sturdy bar to hold onto prevents falls on a slippery surface and makes it easier to get in and out of a tub or shower. The grab bar must be fastened to wall studs or blocking bars installed behind drywall. For fault-free footing, you can also buy slip-proof mats to place on the floor of the shower or tub.

Get a Handle on Bathroom Faucets

Choose a lever handle if you're replacing a faucet in the kitchen or bathroom. The lever is easy to operate with a simple nudge up or down from the back of the hand.

Replace Door Knobs with Levers

Replace round door knobs with lever handles. Again, the lever action is simple to operate because it doesn't require strength and muscle coordination. Levers are particularly handy when your hands are full or dirty; you can open the door with your knee or elbow.

Remove the Clutter

Check out hallways and stairways. If you're like us, the stairs are lined with stuff waiting to be carried up or down. Consequently, they're an accident waiting to happen. Remove everything from the stairs so you have a clear passage, and keep it that way. Provide lighting at the top and bottom so you have good visibility.

Add a Bench to the Entryway

Make your entryway inviting. Finding the house key is always a challenge, but more so when you're loaded with packages. Add a bench or chair near the door where you can set down grocery bags and packages. Don't clutter the area with flower pots or plants, which you could easily trip over.

Light Your Outdoor Walkways

Use a low-voltage lighting system to increase lighting along the path or walkway between the garage or driveway and your door (see Chapter 13). Don't get fancy by using different grading material on this walkway. A change in surfaces can trip you up.

Reorganize the Garage

Make sure that the car doors have plenty of room to open without hitting stored objects. Get rid of stuff you don't use; hang things on the wall, and add shelves where they're needed. Prevent accidents by creating a wide open traffic pattern around the car, lawn equipment, bicycles, and other gear stored in the garage.

Chapter 22
Ten Ways to Kid-Proof Your Home

- -

In This Chapter

▶ Devices, floor plans, and habits that create a safe environment for kids

▶ Inexpensive, easy-to-install gadgets that can truly be lifesavers

▶ Common home hazards you may never have thought of

- -

Most people think of home improvements as projects that make their living space more attractive, efficient, and enjoyable. But the most valuable improvements you can make are simple measures that protect your children from dangers lurking in every room in the house. If you have young ones in your home, consider this chapter a checklist of top-priority improvements, and don't put them off another day.

Install Locking Guard Latches on Cabinets

In the kitchen, add locking guard latches to lower cabinets, especially those containing cleaning supplies or harmful solvents and chemicals. These locks, available at hardware stores and home centers, are easy to install and very effective.

Empty out a small lower cabinet just for kids, and keep it stocked with a few old pots and pans of their very own to play with.

Add Oven Locks and Stove-Knob Covers

Make the stove less of a threat by adding oven locks and stove-knob covers.

When you're cooking, remember to turn pot handles away from the range front so they can't be reached by curious toddlers.

Clear Off the Counters

When you arrange your kitchen, remember to keep long cords, glass objects, knife racks, appliances, and anything with sharp edges far from inquisitive hands. Don't tempt kids with interesting items, such as a breakable cookie jar or colorful pottery, on the kitchen countertop.

Safeguard the Bathroom

When you have young ones around, you have to be especially mindful of water temperatures. To prevent the risk of scalding in the bathtub or shower, lower the water heater to 120 degrees. Or replace the tub faucet with an anti-scald protection device for toddlers (which has a restart button to resume the natural temperature range and flow for grown-ups).

The bathroom is also a high-risk area for drowning. Remember, just a couple of inches of water is all it takes to block out oxygen to our bodies. Never leave standing water in a bathtub and keep the toilet lid down, preferably secured with a lid lock.

Also secure cabinets with a lock and remove any old drugs, makeup, scissors, razor blades, and any other potentially harmful items. Move all cleaning items to a safe and inaccessible cabinet.

Cover Electrical Switches and Outlets

Throughout the house, use outlet plug covers on switches and receptacles. These inexpensive devices pop right over electrical outlets and prevent little fingers, forks, and other objects from tapping the deadly current of electricity flowing through your house's wiring.

Decorate from a Little Person's Perspective

Sharp-cornered tables are often just the right bruising height for a toddler's head. Cover these corners and edges with cushioned protectors or foam bumpers so that the inevitable impact isn't harmful.

Don't place a chair or stool next to an open window, a stair railing, a countertop with sharp utensils, or an ironing board. Make sure that all the furniture is stable. Beware of setting heavy objects — like irons, books, and television sets — on top of furniture that could topple over if nudged by kids or bumped by bouncy seats.

Have a fireplace and wood-burning stove? Protect little ones by adding glass doors or a permanent screen or railing.

Kids' furniture can be dangerous, too. Choose a toy chest with a lid that stays open in any position so that it won't unexpectedly fall onto a child searching for what's inside. Look for a toy chest that has ventilation holes for air, just in case a little one decides to climb in, close the lid, and play submarine. If you have a toy chest without ventilation, drill air holes in the sides and bottom.

Arrange kids' furniture — such as a crib or high chair — far from anything with a long cord, such as miniblinds, a telephone, speaker wires, or electrical cables. All these items can be dangerous to little ones who get themselves twisted and entangled. Keep cords coiled and taped together far from the reach of toddlers.

Secure Your Doors

Doors can be very appealing and inviting to inquiring little minds. You can buy special door hardware that secures folding doors and sliding doors, making them trickier to open and less likely to pinch shut on little fingers.

Employ Gadgets Like Smoke Detectors, Flashlights, and Cordless Phones

Install smoke detectors, carbon monoxide testers, and an automatic night light (see Chapter 14). Place these devices outside of all bedrooms and near rooms with smoke-generating appliances like the kitchen, utility room, and garage. Be sure that a night light is always on to prevent a sleepy walker from stumbling in the dark. Keeping a flashlight handy in every room is also a good idea; in case of a power outage, you can light your path no matter where you are.

Use a cordless telephone instead of a traditional telephone so you can keep your kids in your sight while you chat with Cousin Marge.

Safeguard Stairways and Balconies

In a house with stairs, install gates at the top and bottom of all stairways. And don't store things on the stairs like a book or a stack of clothes. The items create an accident waiting to happen for kids of all ages who don't see them and lose their footing.

If you have a balcony, get a balcony guard, which is a piece of fabric netting that ties to the railing so a little one can't squeeze through the openings.

Put Away All the Little Things

Keep bite-sized items out of sight, out of mind, and out of reach. Small children love to put anything in their mouths — jewelry, paper clips, coins, cat food. The list of things toddlers have been known to eat is downright disgusting! Following around a two-year-old for a couple of days waiting to "rediscover" your favorite cuff link is no fun. And although every parent should know how to help a choking child, preventing the object from getting lodged in your child's throat in the first place is the better approach.

Chapter 23

Ten Quick Fixes to Transform Any Room

*W*ant to make an almost instant transformation in your home without using high-level plastic explosives? The following ideas are real no-brainers. These lazy-boy improvements will quickly and effortlessly change the look of a room. Well, you may have to do some physical activity, but it's worth it!

Rearrange the Furniture

Moving your furniture around is good for the soul — if not your back. You get a certain satisfaction of playing house, no matter how old a kid you are. Try some of these ideas, and you may be surprised at how different and appealing a new look and traffic pattern in a room can be:

- ✔ Move the largest piece of furniture to the longest wall that you see as you enter the room. This creates a certain balance to the room and makes a powerful first impression.

- ✔ Pull your furniture away from the walls. Forget about lining the walls with sofa and chairs. That strategy is fine for a doctor's waiting room, but not conducive for comfort and conversation.

- ✔ Find a focal point, like a window with a view, a fireplace, or a large painting on a wall, and center a futon on that wall with a coffee table and chairs across from it.

- Place a sofa or love seat at an angle across a corner, with a table and lamp behind it.

- While you're at it, vacuum all those dust bunnies you find under the furniture. You'll probably find the sock you've been missing for over a year!

Clear the Clutter

There's a place for everything, and everything should be in its place. That's easy for us to say, but we don't always practice what we preach! Yet nothing feels better than sorting through a stack of old catalogs, magazines, or newspapers and taking the discards to the recycling station. As you acquire new reading materials, stash them in baskets next to your favorite reading chair.

Give kids their own place to stow their stuff. A box, a closet, or a corner of a room is all they need, along with a reminder to return their toys to their storage spot.

Wash the Curtains and Windows

Mother knows best. Our mothers used to wash all the windows and curtains every spring. You may not have a clothesline to hang them out to dry so they'll smell oh-so-fresh, but you can throw them in the washer and dryer and get results that are almost as good. While the window treatment is down, give the window and trim a good dusting and washing. Make your mother proud.

Buy a New Rug

Yes, new rugs cost money. But you'll be amazed at the way a new rug can transform a room. If you have ugly wall-to-wall carpeting or less than perfect flooring, a new area rug is a great cover-up. Choose a design and colors to complement your furniture. A rug laid under the seating area in a living room or den does a great job of unifying the furniture because it pulls all the pieces together. In a dining area, a new rug under the table draws attention to the table and chairs. It also prevents chairs from scratching the floor every time someone pulls one to or away from the table. To focus on an entrance foyer, use an area rug to define the space. The rug also absorbs rain and snow from shoes and boots. In a long hallway, a runner makes a cozy path from bed to bathroom, especially in the middle of a cold night.

Tie Back Curtains or Draperies

You can use just about anything to tie back curtains, and it'll look smashing. Tiebacks open up a room to daylight and add a bit of decoration, to boot. Forget about the typical ones made to match the fabric. Make 'em more interesting by using tassels, ribbons, lace, kerchiefs, vine wreaths, napkin rings — the possibilities are endless. However, to avoid the *Beverly Hillbillies* look, don't use rope, garden hose, or the elastic waistband from your old pair of underwear.

Make Your Child's Room Special

Create a mini gallery for your Little Rembrandt's artwork. When the masterpieces are grouped together, they make a delightful wall display. Use those handy foam tape mounting tabs designed for lightweight posters and paper. They're removable and won't mar the surface.

For a fun way to decorate a child's room, add a ceiling full of stars. Get stick-on stars, moons, or the whole galaxy, and put them on the ceiling.

If you want to have fun and get a little messy, let your kids autograph the walls with their hand prints. Just dip their little paws in latex paint, and use their hand prints to make a track up the walls and across the ceiling.

Replace Drawer Pulls or Hardware on Cabinets

For the most dramatic effect, make this change in the kitchen or bathroom where there's lots of hardware to notice. Choose new hardware with the same size and number of holes as the existing hardware. Just unscrew the old and install the new. While you have the hardware off, clean the cabinet fronts. Make a list and count all of the cabinets and drawers so that you buy the right number of replacements.

Fill an Empty Room with Plants

Floor plants are an investment that grows with you, and they're an inexpensive addition to a room without much furniture. If the budget is tight, buy plants one at a time or when they're on sale. Choose different sizes and types of plants and put them in matching containers. They'll add warmth and color to any room. Don't forget to take care of them!

Change the Pictures in a Room

Move the favorite seascape from the bedroom into the living room, bring the botanical print from the dining room into the hallway — you get the idea. You probably have a storehouse of art throughout the house, but you're so used to looking at them in their usual setting that they've become part of the wall. By simply rearranging the artwork you have, you'll bring a new look to a room.

Group Your Collectibles Together

Make a smashing showcase on a shelf, dresser, or wherever you have room to display a collection. Group the items so they're visible, yet protected from day-to-day living. Hang family photos in matching frames in a hallway to make them a dramatic feature. Corral a herd of ceramic elephants on a narrow shelf, or fill a corner with clay pots of herbs. The point is to keep them together and accessible so that everyone can see and enjoy them.

Appendix

Home Improvement Help Online

• •

*T*he *Internet* is a collection of files, networks, and services packed with information (and, okay, more than a little fluff). It's home to several Web sites relating to home construction, repair, and remodeling, including our very own HouseNet. Check out *The Internet For Dummies,* 3rd Edition, by John Levine and Margaret Levine Young or *Netscape and the World Wide Web For Dummies,* 2nd Edition, by Paul Hoffman (both published by IDG Books Worldwide) for basic instructions and information on surfing the Net.

Browsers, Search Engines, and Bookmarks

The World Wide Web is a graphical window to the Internet, and to access it, you need a *Web browser.* The two most popular Web browsers are Netscape Navigator and Microsoft Internet Explorer. Online services such as America Online also come with their own built-in Web browsers.

Special Web sites, called *search engines,* are available to help you seek out topics of interest on the Web. Most browsers now have their own search utility that enables you to find sites of interest. Enter words like *house* or *home improvement,* and a long (really long) list of related sites appears. When you find a site that looks appealing, click on it to be whisked to its home page.

To record the address (or *URL,* for uniform resource locator) of a site you may want to visit again, use your browser's *bookmark* or *favorites* feature. Then, the next time you want to revisit the site, just click on your bookmark or favorites listing, find the site you want to visit, and click on it. Bam! You're there.

Web Sites

There's plenty of information about home repairs and remodeling on the Web. Type in the name of just about any manufacturer, retailer, publication, or television program followed by the tag `.com` (for commercial), and you'll find their Web site. Organizations have Web sites, too; except the tagline at the end of their URLs is either `.org` (organization) or `.gov` (government agency) or `.edu` (education).

Of course, we're a little partial to HouseNet, but we're pleased to see so many other sites with really useful content for do-it-yourselfers. Most of these sites have an "Ask the Expert" area, where you can post a specific question. The following is a rundown of some special-interest sites with really good home improvement stuff.

HouseNet

Our online neighborhood just keeps growing with people and information. Visit our site at `www.housenet.com` for all things relating to home improvements, decorating, and lawn and garden projects. For members of AOL, we're part of the Interests channel, at keyword: **housenet**. Our goal is to provide the most information and the best experts for house and gardening questions. Our pros manage message folders and talk with callers in our chat room. You won't find a welcome mat much wider than ours — friends send friends here.

Ask the Builder

Building a house or in the planning stages of remodeling? Then you're sure to have questions. Try `www.askbuilder.com`, the URL for Tim Carter's Web site. Tim's a syndicated columnist who posts his columns online. Search past columns to find information about the topic you're interested in.

Building Materials and Wood Technology

The University of Massachusetts at Amherst site for students learning about the manufacture, distribution, and use of building materials is a gold mine for interested homeowners, too.

Their Web site at `www.umass.edu/bmatwt/index.html` has feature articles ranging from building codes, to ice dams, to wood underlayment, to controlling termites and carpenter ants. If you're the type of person who has questions and wants definitive answers about building materials such as preservative-treated wood and wood-destroying fungi, you'll find this site fascinating.

NAPS-NET Home Improvement/Decorating

If you like to read the Home section of your local newspaper, you'll enjoy www.napsnet.com/home/home.html, home of a huge collection of articles about home improvements and decorating. This site, sponsored by NAPS (North American Precis Syndicate, Inc.) features articles submitted by associations, public relation firms, and government information offices. Look through lists of hundreds of articles to find the topics of interest to you.

Preparing for and coping with crises — FEMA.gov and FCES Disaster Handbook

Not to be maudlin, but you really should take a look at the Federal Emergency Management Agency Web site. It does a darn good job of preparing you for some pretty scary stuff. Visit www.fema.gov to link to a number of sites about preparing for natural disasters — everything from earthquakes to tornadoes to winter storms.

At http://hammock.ifas.ufl.edu:80/txt/fairs/35353, the Florida Cooperative Extension Service offers a Disaster Handbook full of practical advice about how to prepare for and cope with a crisis, even to the detail of explaining which documents you should keep in a safe-deposit box and which should be in your possession at home in a waterproof, fireproof lockbox. Forewarned is forearmed.

Energy conservation from EREN and the Home Energy Saver

Uncle Sam does it right! If you want to know about saving energy at home (or anywhere else, for that matter) the Energy Efficiency and Renewable Energy Network has a one-stop content spree at www.eren.doe.gov. It lists the links to all home energy and energy technology Web sites. There's even *Kids' Stuff,* which has information on kids' science projects about solar, wind, and other clean technologies.

At http://eande.lbl.gov/CBS/VH is an energy-related site called The Home Energy Saver. This site, developed at the Lawrence Berkeley National Lab with funding from the EPA, includes a Virtual Home Energy Advisor, which lets you analyze your house for energy savings and even build a virtual home to estimate its energy consumption and cost. First, the site asks you some general questions about your house, and then you get the option of estimating your energy bills for heating and cooling, water heating, or appliances. Each option uses a computer model to estimate energy consumption based on home characteristics. Let's hear it for the government!

Homeowners clearinghouse

Homeowners rights, home inspection, working with builders and remodelers, financing and refinancing, buying and selling a house — find all this and more at www.uha.org, the Web site for the United Homeowners Association.

Don Vandervort's HomeTips

HomeTips, at www.hometips.com, is a helpful site hosted by home and workshop writer, Don Vandervort. Search this site for articles on a number of building and repair topics, such as electronics, plumbing, heating and air conditioning, roofing, doors, windows, and floors. Don's site features tips, guides, product information, questions and answers, helpful links, and some plain old "Dang Good Ideas."

Wood care

Furniture, flooring, cabinets, even molding and millwork. If it's made of hardwood and it's in your house, the Hardwood Information Center at www.hardwood.org has the definitive word. The Hardwood Manufacturers Association offers a library of articles about decorating with, selecting, and caring for hardwood in your house. Find simple solutions for stubborn floor stains, ways to make your kitchen child-friendly and accessible, tips for decorating with molding, and insider information about buying upholstered furniture.

Newsgroups

The Net has thousands of *newsgroups,* a sort of virtual bulletin board where you can post new messages about a specific topic or respond to existing messages. How you access Internet newsgroups depends on the browser or online service provider you use. Consult the online help for your particular system. Two current newsgroups focusing on home improvement information are misc.consumers.hous and alt.home.repair.

Index

●●

(continued)

(continued)

(continued)

• Z •

IDG BOOKS WORLDWIDE
BOOK REGISTRATION

Register This Book and Win!

We want to hear from you!

Visit **http://my2cents.dummies.com** to register this book and tell us how you liked it!

- ✔ Get entered in our monthly prize giveaway.

- ✔ Give us feedback about this book — tell us what you like best, what you like least, or maybe what you'd like to ask the author and us to change!

- ✔ Let us know any other *...For Dummies*® topics that interest you.

Your feedback helps us determine what books to publish, tells us what coverage to add as we revise our books, and lets us know whether we're meeting your needs as a *...For Dummies* reader. You're our most valuable resource, and what you have to say is important to us!

Not on the Web yet? It's easy to get started with *Dummies 101*®: *The Internet For Windows*® *95* or *The Internet For Dummies*®, 4th Edition, at local retailers everywhere.

Or let us know what you think by sending us a letter at the following address:

...For Dummies Book Registration
Dummies Press
7260 Shadeland Station, Suite 100
Indianapolis, IN 46256-3945
Fax 317-596-5498

BUSINESS AND **GENERAL REFERENCE BOOK SERIES FROM IDG**

COMPUTER BOOK SERIES FROM IDG